The
Pantomime Life
of
Joseph Grimaldi

The
Pantomime Life
of
Joseph Grimaldi

LAUGHTER, MADNESS AND THE STORY
OF BRITAIN'S GREATEST COMEDIAN

Andrew McConnell Stott

CANONGATE
Edinburgh · London · New York · Melbourne

Published by Canongate Books in 2009

1

Copyright © Andrew McConnell Stott, 2009

The moral right of the author has been asserted

First published in Great Britain in 2009 by Canongate Books Ltd,
14 High Street, Edinburgh EH1 1TE

www.meetatthegate.com

British Library Cataloguing-in-Publication Data
A catalogue record for this book is available on
request from the British Library

ISBN 978 1 84767 295 7

Typeset in Filosofia by Cluny Sheeler, Edinburgh

Printed and bound in the UK by CPI Mackays, Chatham ME5 8TD

FSC
Mixed Sources
Product group from well-managed
forests, controlled sources and
recycled wood or fibre
Cert no. TT-COC-002341
www.fsc.org
© 1996 Forest Stewardship Council

Josie, Cissie and Floyd

CONTENTS

PART THREE 1811–37

LIST OF ILLUSTRATIONS

12. Charles Farley as Cloten in *Cymbeline* by Thomas Charles Wageman, 1821 (University of Illinois Theatrical Print Collection, University of Illinois at Urbana-Champaign)

13. Mr Grimaldi as Orson (Robert Gould Shaw Collection, TS 937.8 F v.1, The Harvard Theatre Collection, Houghton Library)

14. 'The Favourite Comic Dance of Messers Bologna Jun. and Grimaldi' by Rudolph Ackermann, 1807 (V&A Images/ Victoria and Albert Museum)

15. Grimaldi as Clown in *Mother Goose*, c.1807 (Garrick Club/ Art Archive)

16. Joseph Grimaldi by John Cawse, 1807 (© National Portrait Gallery, London)

17. 'A View of the Confusion at Sadler's Wells', 1807 (The British Library)

18. Covent Garden Theatre by Pugin and Rowlandson, 1809 (Lebrecht Music and Arts)

19. 'Killing No Murder, as Performed at the Grand National Theatre' by George and Isaac Cruikshank, 1809 (© The Trustees of the British Museum. All rights reserved.)

20. Drury Lane Fire by Abraham Pether, 1809 (Guildhall Art Gallery, City of London)

21. 'Mr. Grimaldi and Mr. Norman in the Epping Hunt', 1813 (Lewis Walpole Library, Yale University)

22. 'Grim Joey Dashing Little Boney into the Jaws of a Russian Bear', 1813 (Harry Elkins Widener Collection, Harvard University, HEW 2.7.4)

23. 'Mr. Grimaldi as Clown' by Rudolph Ackermann, 1811 (Lewis Walpole Library, Yale University)

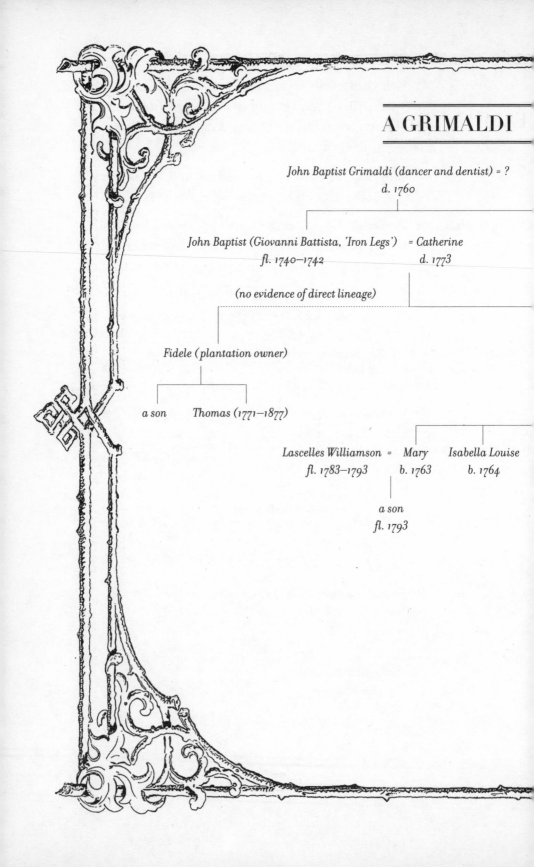

A GRIMALDI

John Baptist Grimaldi (dancer and dentist) = ?
d. 1760

John Baptist (Giovanni Battista, 'Iron Legs') = Catherine
fl. 1740–1742   d. 1773

(no evidence of direct lineage)

Fidele (plantation owner)

a son   Thomas (1771–1877)

Lascelles Williamson = Mary   *Isabella Louise*
fl. 1783–1793   b. 1763   b. 1764

a son
fl. 1793

FAMILY TREE

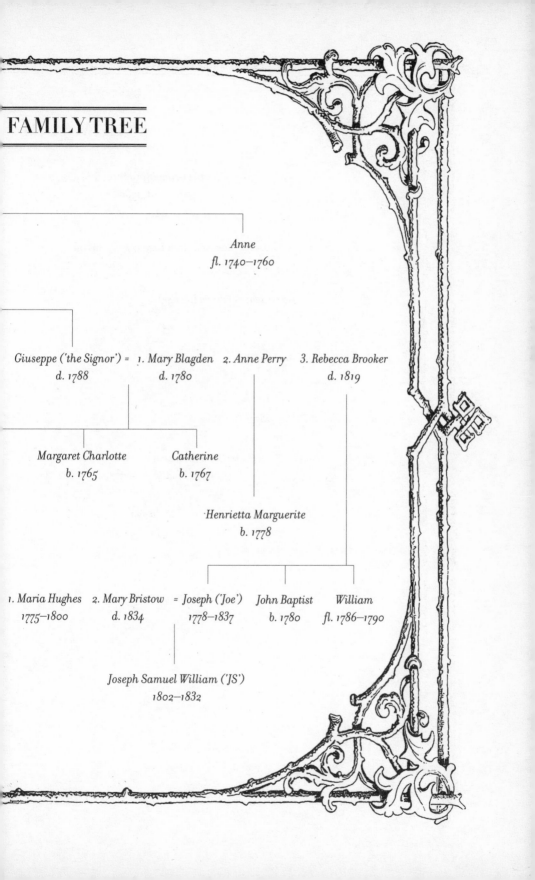

Anne
fl. 1740–1760

Giuseppe ('the Signor') = 1. Mary Blagden   2. Anne Perry   3. Rebecca Brooker
d. 1788   d. 1780   d. 1819

Margaret Charlotte   Catherine
b. 1765   b. 1767

Henrietta Marguerite
b. 1778

1. Maria Hughes   2. Mary Bristow   = Joseph ('Joe')   John Baptist   William
1775–1800   d. 1834   1778–1837   b. 1780   fl. 1786–1790

Joseph Samuel William ('JS')
1802–1832

PROLOGUE

THERE'S NOTHING PARTICULARLY FUNNY about Hackney, especially when you're sweaty and cold. Dragging a heavy suitcase down the Kingsland Road on a damp day in early February had left me feeling both. A delayed flight meant that I'd arrived in London twenty-four hours late, and now, struggling past the pound stores, Turkish sports clubs and electronic bazaars offering to unlock my mobile phone, I was seriously worried that I was going to be late for church. I didn't want to miss the clowns.

I was heading for Holy Trinity, a small but handsome tabernacle settled inconspicuously on a back-street in Dalston. It's here that a memorial service has been held every year since 1959 for Joseph Grimaldi, Regency superstar and father of modern clowning, a service that enjoys some notoriety, thanks to its congregation of working clowns who attend in full slap and motley. As I bumped through the door and finally dumped my bag, I was relieved to find that they hadn't started. Instead, they stood around drinking tea and being disarmingly normal, a friendly and excited group of children's entertainers and retired circus acts clearly at home with the level of glamour implied by the scuffed-up Scout hall they used as a dressing room. Augustes and Pierrots swapped news with American hobos, while a Coco with a pin head and a tiny bowler hat seemingly reassured his colleague about his prosthetic forehead and mechanical eyebrows. Were it not for the extravagant dress, they could have been any other group of people with a shared enthusiasm. Indeed, I suspected many of membership of the Caravan Club.

The service itself was more disconcerting. I had been a stand-up comic myself and, having twice sought help for depression, was inclined towards the lugubrious in comedy, yet even this left me unprepared for the level of shabby melancholy in which I was about to be immersed. Maybe it was because I was a jet-lagged atheist who was deeply ambivalent about clowns, but I found the experience about as pleasant as a night in a derelict fun park. Presided over by the Vicar of All Saints, and the Clowns' Chaplain, the service began with a clown procession that was followed by prayers, hymns, a sermon, a skit with balloon animals, and Clown Rainbow reading nervously from the Gospel of St Luke: 'Blessed is he, whosoever shall not be offended in me.' There was something intractably laconic about it, especially the sincerity with which they offered worship, like a displaced people pleading to come home.

In a sense, that was what they were, because for decades clowns have occupied an ever-diminishing niche in popular culture, their flapping shoes, hoop-waisted trousers, and streams of multi-coloured handkerchiefs more evocative of forced laughter and jaded memories than genuine fun. Commensurate with their decline is a rise in 'coulrophobia' – the fear of clowns – fuelled by horror flicks and comic-book villains whose particular psychosis troubles the line between laughter and terror. Feeling like an ungrateful guest, I realised it was a prejudice I shared, especially as I caught myself calculating how many diseased minds were lurking behind those blood-red smirks.

Apparently, I was not the only one. The attraction of the abominable draws a big crowd and every year the service is packed with curious onlookers and camera crews who greatly outnumber the dedicated few. By the time I arrived, a busful of Swedish teenagers had already filled the unreserved seats, leaving the aisles to groups of hip young Londoners in futuristic shoes. They were there to enjoy the eccentricity, soaking it up as they would their regular weekend dose of performance art. It might have been scripted, then, when the man who plays Grimaldi at these events received a nasty poke in the eye just minutes before he was due to go on. Bravely, he went through with his act – a rendition of 'Hot Codlins', Grimaldi's most popular song, rendered gruesomely fascinating by the contrast of his angry crimson eyeball against the alabaster greasepaint – and ran to a waiting ambulance the moment he had finished. I was later told that he sat dejectedly in his costume at Accident and Emergency for several hours.

It's hard to imagine a more perfect tribute.

INTRODUCTION

Poor Joe! It was like the boys and frogs;
it was sport to us, but it was death to you.

William Robson, *The Old Play-goer* (1854)

MIDNIGHT ON BOXING DAY 1810 saw frosts so severe that the Thames froze over. The chill coincided with the news that the old, blind king, George III, had descended into his final fit of madness. This and the weather meant that the streets around Covent Garden were unusually deserted. Even the pickpockets, dressed in stolen dinner jackets to blend in with the theatre crowds, had taken the night off from their foists.

On Bow Street, the remains of the Theatre Royal, Drury Lane, stood forlorn in the moonlight like a ruined abbey. Destroyed by fire a year ago, and still to be rebuilt, it looked crippled and pitiful opposite the huge white stockade of its rival, Covent Garden, just yards away. Rich sepia light streamed through those windows, accompanied by booming laughter that tumbled across the walls and cobbles, erupting into stinging peaks before rolling back and exploding again, followed by bursts of showering applause.

The three thousand souls packed into Covent Garden had no thought for the cold, immersed as they were in the climax of the year's new pantomime, *Harlequin Asmodeus; or, Cupid on Crutches*. In an auditorium that smelt of orange peel and candle-wax, and sitting beneath chandeliers the size of galleons, they'd already endured a bill that included Shakespeare's

As You Like It and a dire tragedy called *George Barnwell* – six hours of drama – though they showed little sign of fatigue. All eyes were fixed on the grinning face that emerged from the curtain, entirely white save for the gaping cavern of its mouth, and a pink and green plume wobbling suggestively on its head. Limb after rantipole limb climbed out from the wings, followed by a quarrelsome body seemingly trying to outrun itself, the whole barely having time to settle before leaping off, hands on hips, covering the enormous width of the stage in only four bounds.

This was Joseph Grimaldi, known to everyone just as 'Joe', a clown in the ascendant. Wearing a pink shirt and appliquéd breeches that gave way to blue spotted tights, he skipped casually sideways, his ballet slippers depositing him nimbly outside a grocer's shop, where his rolling eyes suddenly narrowed to meet an incoming thought. Casting sly glances in every direction, his busy hands dipped among the vegetables, pulling out two extremely large mushrooms, which he placed carefully beside him on the floor, before returning to rummage with unbreakable concentration. Two oversize rhubarb stalks followed, a foot and a half long and nine inches across, which he stood upright on the mushroom caps. Next, he rolled out a cabbage the size of a beach ball, heaved it into place atop the rhubarb, added a long carrot to either side, placed a melon on top, and stepped back to admire his creation.

His self-congratulation was short-lived. A window opened in the shop and a masked figure leant out, his glittering patchwork arm bearing a sword, with which he fetched the vegetable man a thwack. Suddenly, the creature seemed different. A carrot arm appeared to twitch. Grimaldi looked puzzled. The arm moved again. Grimaldi blinked. Then the melon rotated, revealing a face to the audience that turned to its creator. Grimaldi screamed. The vegetables are alive! A mushroom foot moves forward, then the other, and, with a shambling gait and carrot arms outstretched, it began to bear in. Terrified, Grimaldi retreated, fishing out two large turnips, which he grabbed by the stalks to use as boxing gloves. The vegetable man stopped to observe his opponent's odd pose, his knees bent in a manner that recalled the fashionable art of pugilism, then squared up. A bell was rung in the orchestra pit and the bout began, the adversaries exchanging cautious exploratory jabs until the monster made its move, coming at its master with unexpected speed, its carrot arms relentlessly batting at Grimaldi's head until he is forced to throw up his turnips and flee the stage.

The audience was in hysterics. Grimaldi had been their idol since he first came to prominence in 1806, having been thrust into the highest sphere of celebrity with a virtuoso comic performance in the original production of *Mother Goose*, a show that took record profits and ran for longer than any other pantomime in history. Its success brought him national recognition, enormous fees, and a social circle that included Lord Byron, Sarah Siddons, Edmund Kean, Matthew 'Monk' Lewis and the entire Kemble family. The critics Leigh Hunt and William Hazlitt sang his praises, the young Charles Dickens edited his *Memoirs*. The press even credited his routine in *Harlequin Asmodeus* with inspiring Mary Shelley's *Frankenstein*.

But though Grimaldi was a clown, he was neither a children's entertainer nor a circus act. Instead, he graced the royal stages of Covent Garden and Drury Lane and was a shareholder in the famous summer theatre of Sadler's Wells. In all these venues, his speciality was pantomime, the Regency's most popular and consistently lucrative form, and a mirror of the age with its ridiculous extravagance, liberal, self-regarding wit and obsession with being bang up to date. Grimaldi's pantomime had little in common with its modern counterpart, whose principal boys, pantomime dames and oh-no-it-isn'ts wouldn't come into being until almost a century later. For a start, its bawdy, energetic humour, as explicit and visceral as a Gillray or Rowlandson cartoon, was primarily aimed at adults. Neither was it solely reserved for Christmas: the royal theatres traditionally unveiled their new pantomimes on Boxing Day, but their old ones played throughout the year. Summer pantomime was also common, with smaller theatres like Sadler's Wells introducing as many as four new shows in the course of a season, which ran from April to October.

Pantomime had first appeared in Britain in the early eighteenth century. An anglicisation of Italian *commedia dell'arte* blended with opera and ballet, it was initially thought to be a revival of an ancient Roman entertainment. Despite the inaccuracy, it soon became popular in its own right, especially under its first great exponent, John Rich (*c.* 1692–1761), who based much of his work on classic mythology, merging comic and serious scenes in equal measure. Towards the end of the eighteenth century, the serious scenes were purged, and by the time Grimaldi emerged, pantomime had become purely a vehicle for vigorous slapstick and satirical gags. Consisting of two loosely connected parts, a lavish opening that mobilised all the tinsel and pageantry available to the theatre, and a core sequence of ten to fifteen scenes known as the 'harlequinade', Regency pantomimes took their cues from fairytales, current affairs or, in deference to the Prince of Wales's love of the Oriental arts, Eastern stories like *The Thousand and One Nights*.

Dialogue was conspicuously light, save for sung recitative and doggerel verse. This was partly due to convention, and partly to arcane licensing laws that refused to acknowledge pantomimists as legitimate actors and so disqualified them from speaking on the public stage. Various attempts had been made to introduce speech throughout the period, but were generally rebuffed by audiences who, like William Hazlitt, thought 'a speaking pantomime is not unlike a flying wagon'. The action was mimed by actors wearing 'big heads', huge papier-mâché masks that gave the appearance of carnival mascots or life-size Russian dolls, yet this still left little chance that the audience would fail to grasp the plot, as half of the enjoyment of pantomime sprang from its repetitious and ritualistic form.

Stories invariably revolved around a pair of devoted young lovers kept cruelly apart by a tyrannical parent or malicious rival, until hope appeared in the guise of a beneficent intermediary who promised the young lovers happiness upon the successful completion of a quest. For reasons never sufficiently explained, the quest also required the principal characters to be magically transformed into the protagonists of the harlequinade, four figures that were instantly recognisable to every man, woman and child in Britain: the fleet-footed and shimmering Harlequin and his gauzy, dove-like lover, Columbine, and their enemies, the elderly 'libidinous, miserly Dotard', Pantaloon, and his titular manservant, Clown.

Once the transformation was complete, the big heads were discarded, the harlequinade began, and the newly altered characters embarked upon a frenetic chase. With the gift of a magic sword, the original 'slapstick' primed with gunpowder to lend it a satisfying crack, Harlequin stayed one step ahead of Clown and Pantaloon by using it to transform anything it touched, transformations that were enabled by 'tricks', ingenious bits of scenery that turned one thing into another. As the quality of the tricks frequently determined the reception of the pantomime, they were some of the most closely guarded secrets in the theatre, and even today we are not entirely sure how many of them worked. Harlequin used them to effect his escapes and torment his pursuers, turning their sedan chairs into prison cells, their postboxes into lions' mouths, and piles of vegetables into belligerent monsters.

Unlike the fairy-tale settings of the opening, much of the harlequinade took place against a background of the sights and sounds of contemporary London. Smoky with sea-coal and jam-packed with fast-moving pedestrians and even faster traffic, the Regency metropolis was well on its way to modernity, its population having more than doubled during Grimaldi's lifetime from one to more than two and a half million. Teeming and prosperous, in spite of two decades of intermittent war with France, Londoners were avid for entertainment. Indeed, Bonaparte may be credited with inspiring the birth of the modern entertainment industry in all its sumptuous, glamorous, vapid and commercial glory, as theatre was never so profitable or popular as it had been during the Napoleonic wars. Bills and posters papered every fence and pillar, advertising plays, oratorios, scientific demonstrations, exotic menageries, fireworks, mechanical puppets, sermons, galleries, freak shows, tomahawk displays by American Indians, and what the *English Illustrated Magazine* described as 'the man who performed the disgusting feat of eating a fowl alive'.

At the height of the Regency, more than twenty thousand Londoners attended the theatre every night, a figure that climbed considerably once the numbers visiting the capital's various concert halls, pleasure gardens and exhibition rooms were taken into account. Theatre was a shared experience, a place of national communion that addressed a surprisingly democratic cross-section of society, which, in its eating, drinking, smoking, fighting and heckling through long nights of drama, was as diverse and lively as any public square or marketplace.

Drama itself was in the midst of a revolution. Following the death of Britain's premier actor-manager, David Garrick, in 1779, the theatrical world engaged in rapid change, dismantling the strictly policed divisions between comedy and tragedy that had governed drama for almost a century and experimenting with new forms, new attractions and new types of shows. Plays increasingly made way for show-stopping

spectacles enabled by technological advances that allowed battles to be enacted, sieges to be staged and palaces set on fire.
They were experiments encouraged by indulgent audiences
incredibly open to novelty, at least until they felt some invisible
line had been crossed, at which point they were liable to
riot. Until that point was reached, however, they sat happily
through plays starring dogs, elephants, prepubescent children
and lifelike men-o'-war floating on tanks of real water. The
proscenium was a window through which Londoners enjoyed
the pleasures of dominion, a world perceived through imperial
eyes – abundant, exotic, various and yielding.

London was central to both Grimaldi's personal and professional identity, for despite his Italian heritage, he had been
born and bred in the city, a one-time resident of the slums that
multiplied in the shadow of Drury Lane, and the airy
suburbs of Islington and Pentonville, semi-rural hamlets set
apart from the smog by the green acreage of Spa Fields.
Grimaldi's clown was a Londoner in hyperbole: channelling
its voracious consumerism and infusing his clowning with its
manic energy, flamboyant theatricality and love of show.
Described by one pantomime arranger as a 'half-idiotic,
crafty, shameless, incorrigible, emblem of gross sensuality',
Grimaldi's clown was cunning, covetous and childlike in his
wants, an uncensored mass of appetites and an embodied
accumulation of unconscious desires. Everything tempted him,
calling him forward and enticing him to touch, tinker and
meddle, with an impetus that overrode all considerations,
especially the law.

Pressed against each other in the bulging metropolis and
closely monitored by their political masters, who feared the
growing rise of Radicalism and dissent, Londoners revelled
in Grimaldi's lawlessness, watching him commit a litany of
crimes that outside the theatre would have been rewarded with
transportation or death. 'Robbery became a science in his

hands,' wrote one commentator, recalling with relish the way he would pilfer a leg of mutton and, with 'bewitching eagerness', extract handkerchiefs and pocket watches with 'such a devotion to the task' that he 'seemed imbued with the spirit of peculation'.

Though abundantly gifted and publicly adored, Grimaldi's private life was marked by tragedy and depression. A profound melancholic who suffered from hereditary madness, he had survived a traumatic childhood at the hands of a deranged father, only to see his successes marred by incapacitating bouts of paranoia and insecurity. A naturally self-deprecating man, he was naïve in business and careless with money, and when an economic downturn left him struggling, he found himself incapable of earning a living, having been crippled by the leaps and falls that had so delighted his audience. Being forced to retire in the prime of life was doubly cruel, as the stage was the only place in which he was spared his anxieties. He was 'petulant, and suffered under nervous irritation and morbid sensibility', wrote Henry Downes Miles, a sportswriter who followed the clown's performances religiously. 'We never met with a performer so nervous: he had no self-reliance until he was in the heart of his mystery, and then he had no fear.'

Grimaldi's hopes devolved to his only child, a boy also called Joseph, whom he personally tutored in the art of clowning. But the second Joseph Grimaldi rejected both his parents and his calling, and as his own signs of psychological instability began to develop, he ran wild, heaping shame upon his family and linking his famous name to insanity and dissipation. A mythology quickly attached itself to these unhappy circumstances, an effect of the new celebrity culture and the brooding fancies of Romanticism that constantly speculated on the source of their subjects' talents. Grimaldi's comic brilliance became indivisible from his troubles, a necessary burden that lent his clowning substance and credence to the idea that comedy was somehow the by-product of misery, and that clowning somehow concealed an ineffable sadness. It has been an abiding myth. Comedy demands sacrifice, and Joseph Grimaldi was about to become its first martyr.

PART ONE

[1778–1800]

THE WONDERS OF DERBYSHIRE

Shou'd Harlequin be banish'd hence,
Quit the place to wit and sense,
What wou'd be the consequence?
Empty houses, empty houses.

David Garrick, *The Theatrical Candidates* (1775)

WHEN THE ENGLISH NATURALIST Martin Lister visited the fashionable Paris fair of Saint-Germain, he was surprised to find 'a very Pit or hole' sunk eight feet into the middle of the street. Stepping down twelve perilous steps, he was sucked into a press of people, all trying to squeeze through the same narrow doorway and into the fairground while hoofs and cartwheels clattered dangerously close to their heads. Spat out the other side, he emerged into a cacophonous market, covered with a huge timber roof and criss-crossed by claustrophobic alleyways, so uneven that he was sure he would have fallen, were it not for the 'vast croud of people which keep you up'.

Travelling at the dawn of the eighteenth century, Lister had come to experience for himself an event that Parisians had been celebrating since the Middle Ages, a boisterous island of pleasure and intemperance that appeared in their city for six weeks every year between February and Palm Sunday. Stuffing themselves in by the thousands, 'helter-skelter, masters with valets and lackeys, thieves with honest people. The most refined courtesans, the prettiest girls, the subtlest pickpockets', fairgoers browsed through an infinite array of merchandise, stocked up on pills, spices and exotic preserves, shopped for wigs, and bought locks for their houses, barrels for their cellars, linens for the boudoir and mirrors for their toilette. Braced by Armenian coffee and curious philtres, they splashed out on luxury goods, jewellery and Moroccan leather, lace, perfume, porcelain, full-size sculptures and oil paintings, and gorged themselves on an assortment of sweetmeats and pastries. When not shopping or eating, they enjoyed an illegal flutter at dice, cards or skittles, or sojourned to one of the many 'cabarets' that sold wine at the front and girls at the back. Suitably refreshed, they perused the many curious diversions that filled one end of the yard like a clearing-house for entertainments. Bearded ladies battled for attention next to sword-swallowers and ingenious automata; gladiators fought combats alongside mountebanks and balladeers; and theatre troupes hoped to lure an audience into their ramshackle booths with a free farce before they could be distracted by a rhinoceros or a firework display.

To the merchants who manned the stalls, the attraction of the fair was commercial, as within its walls they were able to offer their goods free from the monopolies and restrictions that ordinarily governed city trade. The same went for the many performers, known as *forains*, who came from all corners of the kingdom and beyond to take advantage of the lack of jurisdiction of 'official' theatre companies like the Comédie-Française, whose royal patents gave them the right to suppress unlicensed theatrics. Yet even when they could make themselves heard above the blare of music and drunken yells, 'serious' drama was rarely on the agenda. *Forains* specialised in novelty and spectacle, all that was brash and never-before-seen, performed by a versatile troupe of dancers, pantomimists, acrobats and funambulists – tightrope walkers who dealt in death-defying tricks, such as spinning in mid-air while hanging from one foot, or standing on one leg and playing the violin.

The closest approximation to drama they offered were farces in the style of the Italian *Commedia*, a traditional form of improvised comedy where stock characters chased, cursed and cozened each other all the way to predictable ends. Dismissed by one Parisian critic as 'little more than a type of deformed concert', their plots were thin excuses for rude jokes and physical horseplay. An example was Gueulette's *Le Marchand de Merde*, a play that tells the story of the oafish valet Gilles who each morning defecates on the doorstep of a young gentleman called Léandre. Dismayed by his ripe dawn deliveries, Léandre enlists the help of canny Arlequin, who, posing as a wealthy *marchand de merde*, convinces Gilles that he is literally sitting on a gold mine. Duped, Gilles sets himself up in business, enthusiastically filling a barrel with his merchandise, which he offers around town with the cry, 'Buy my shit, it's fresh,' until an outraged apothecary attacks him with a stick.

The broad comedy of *Le Marchand de Merde* pleased the raucous and easily distracted crowd, though a subtler vein of humour could also be detected running through its satire of unscrupulous Parisian commodity-culture and its desire to get rich quick. This was typical of a continual game of cat-and-mouse the *forains* played with the paranoid agents of the Bourbon police, exploiting the licence of the fairground to voice grievances that otherwise went unspoken in the repressive atmosphere of the *ancien régime*. Italian performers in particular had a reputation for sailing close to the wind, and the fairs were full of them as a consequence of their expulsion in 1697 from legitimate Parisian theatre business for scurrility.

All of Europe agreed that Italy produced the most talented and sought-after comedians, a fact Lord Shaftesbury, writing in 1700, attributed to the 'Spiritual Tyranny' of that country, where the repressive activities of the state led its people to express themselves in comic fashion: ''Tis the only manner in which the poor cramped Wretches can discharge a free Thought,' wrote Shaftesbury, as 'the greater the Weight is, the bitterer will be the Satire. The higher the Slavery, the more exquisite the Buffoonery.'

If it was exquisite buffoons you wanted, then Grimaldi's family had them by the cartload. A group of travelling *forains*, they had connections to Malta and Genoa and even claimed distant kinship to the royal house of Monaco, although their true origins had long been lost in the trail of dust that followed them from town to town. Their patriarch was Joe's great-grandfather, John Baptist Grimaldi, who was both dancer and dentist, pursuits that were far from incompatible in an age when renowned surgeons performed their operations in theatres to paying audiences.* His daughter, Anne, another dancer, travelled with him, as did his son, also called John Baptist, though better known by his Italianised name, Giovanni Battista. Completing the family were Giovanni's partner, Catherine, and their son, Giuseppe, the boy who would one day father Britain's legendary clown.†

---

* A popular turn on the Pont-Neuf was 'Big Thomas', a tooth-puller who accompanied his operations with jokes, impressions and a performing monkey.

† Some accounts of Joseph Grimaldi's ancestry claim his great-grandfather was the Neapolitan opera singer Cavaliero Nicolini Grimaldi. Nicolini, whose several triumphs included creating the title role of Handel's *Rinaldo*, enjoyed five years of unprecedented popularity in London, thanks to the frenzy for Italian opera that swept through the capital at the beginning of the eighteenth century. 'Every limb, and every finger, contributes to the part he acts, insomuch that a deaf man might go along with him in the sense of it,' wrote Joseph Addison in 1710, having found himself utterly enraptured one winter evening by his graceful physique and the 'greatness of air and mien [that] seemed to fill the stage, and at the same time commanded the attention of the audience with the majesty of his appearance'. While there is a strong temptation to find a hint of Joe in the singer's command of mime and striking voice, until now biographers have failed to notice that Nicolini was a castrato, who, like all of his kind, had been unmanned by the Church as a boy. He retired to a luxurious Venetian villa in 1730, childless and rich.

The Grimaldis were typical of their kind: eccentric, fearless, superstitious and crude, they took their chances where they found them, and professed a pragmatic morality of the road. In a trade that was characterised by crabbed and filthy playing spaces, official harassment and a peasant audience, they at least toiled at its upper end. Giovanni was even something of a star. A comedian, pantomimist and *sauteur* (a kind of gymnast specialising in incredibly high leaps that were achieved by bending one leg at an oblique angle and coiling it low to the ground before jumping explosively into the air), he eventually grew tired of the family business and sought to make it on his own. Naturally, this meant the Paris fairs.

He and Catherine are recorded appearing in 1740 at Saint-Germain as members of the Grande Troupe Étrangère, performing in the pantomimes *Dupres, or Nothing is Difficult in Love*, and *Harlequin and Columbine Captive*. The visit was a success, for in 1742 he was back, having been invited to perform at the largest and most prestigious theatre at Saint-Germain, the semi-permanent and almost-respectable Opéra-Comique.

It was here during a performance of *Le Prix de Cythère* that the Grimaldi family first leapt to national prominence. According to legend, the show was visited by the grand figure of Mehemet Effendi, ambassador of the Ottoman Sublime Porte. The ambassador, a vain and preening man, announced his presence by taking the box nearest the stage and, excited at the prospect of performing before such an eminence, Giovanni bet his colleagues that he could jump as high as the chandelier that flanked the box. He won his bet with his first leap but, in doing so, kicked the chandelier with enough force to smash it. One shard found its way down the throat of the laughing Mehemet, while a second hit him in the eye. Blind, choking and humiliated, he was quick to complain of the indignity he had suffered at the feet of a mere jester, and demanded that Grimaldi be punished before the full Court. A public act of

contrition was accordingly arranged, only for Giovanni to seize
it as a further opportunity for self-promotion by lacing his apology with such a dash of fairground double-talk that he reduced
the courtiers to hysterics, heaping further dishonour upon the
injured man. When news of the affair reached the people of
Paris, they delighted in the audacity of this son of the marketplace who had ridiculed the loathed Turk, and adopted him as
their new hero, conferring on him the heroic nickname 'Jambe
de Fer', or 'Iron Legs', and singing his praises in a
popular squib:

> Hail, Iron Legs! immortal pair,
> Agile, firm knit, and peerless,
> That skim the earth, or vault in air,
> Aspiring high and fearless.
> Glory of Paris! outdoing compeers,
> Brave pair! may nothing hurt ye;
> Scatter at will our chandeliers,
> And tweak the nose of Turkey.
> And should a too presumptuous foe
> But dare these shores to land on,
> His well-kicked men shall quickly know
> We've Iron Legs to stand on.

But Iron Legs's new-found celebrity was short-lived.
Over-confident in his popularity with Court and *canaille*,
he misjudged their temper and performed something so scandalous at his next appearance that he was immediately arrested
and thrown into the Bastille. What he did, exactly, is
unrecorded but, given the infamous licence of the French
aristocracy, it must have been particularly bad.

It was a mercifully short stint in prison, and after his
release, Iron Legs made himself scarce, leaving France and
arriving in London in July 1742. London was a popular destination for Continental performers, whom it attracted with high

fees and the promise of celebrity. But Iron Legs had a further incentive, as his father had settled there in the mid-1730s. Now semi-retired, John Baptist ran a successful business as 'Surgeon Operator for the Teeth' in Martlett Court, Covent Garden, while also making occasional appearances as Pantaloon to the Harlequin of the celebrated John Rich. Reunited with the old man, Iron Legs begged to be introduced to Rich, who in turn offered him work at Covent Garden theatre, first as Scaramouch in *L'Antiquaire* and later in a number of dances. Yet the comparatively staid air of an English royal theatre disagreed with him: only four months after his arrival, Iron Legs was already planning to leave, though not before first devising a scheme to fund his passage back to Europe. Henry Angelo, the proprietor of a famous London fencing school that doubled as a clearing-house for gossip, remembered being told the story of Iron Legs's sudden departure:

> Rich, the manager of Covent Garden Theatre, who was ever ready to catch at anything that was novel, or of pantomimic tendency, listened with rapture to Grimaldi, who proposed an extraordinary new dance: such a singular dance that would astonish and fill the house every night, but it could not be got up without some previous expense, as it was an invention entirely of his own contrivance. There must be no rehearsal, all must be secret before the grand display in, and the exhibition on, the first night. Rich directly advanced a sum to Grimaldi and waited the result with impatience. The *maître de ballet* took care to keep up his expectations, so far letting him into the secret that it was to be a dance on horse shoes, that it would surpass anything before seen, and was much superior to all the dancing that was ever seen in pumps. The newspapers were all puffed for a wonderful performance that was to take place on a certain evening. The house was crowded, all noise and impatience – no Grimaldi – no excuse; at last an apology was made. The grand promoter of this wonderful, unprecedented dance had been absent over six hours, having danced away on four horse-shoes to Dover.

Having successfully defrauded Rich, Iron Legs's career entered a serious decline. Nothing was heard of him for several years, until he eventually turned up in Flanders in the company of a stage-struck bookseller he had duped into funding a troupe. Although he had added conjuring to his various skills, the venture met with constant ill fortune that culminated in an attack by bandits on the road to Brussels. Having been stripped and robbed, Iron Legs, the bookseller and Iron Legs's mistress, 'a Parisian lady of questionable character', would have been murdered on the spot had not the lady thrown herself upon the brigands' mercy and promised to become their collective wife in return for her lover's salvation. They agreed, and departed with their prize, leaving the dejected comedian to tramp into Brussels alone, wearing the only thing he had left, a tattered Harlequin's costume. By 1760 he was either dead or disowned: his father's will, dated 11 March that year, neither mentions him by name, nor leaves anything to a son.

~

With Iron Legs slipping into the Belgian sunset, his son Giuseppe had already emerged as a formidable talent. Giuseppe had been born on the road in either France or Genoa some time between 1710 and 1716, and entered a long theatrical apprenticeship almost as soon as he could walk. Iron Legs was a demanding master, expecting long hours and high standards of his son, and inflicting brutal punishments when he failed to meet them. Neither was the despotism of his methods offset by the comforts of warm maternal love, as what little glimpse we have of Giuseppe's mother, Catherine Grimaldi, reveals a woman with a face like a millstone, a 'squat, thick, strong figure . . . endowed with so much agility and strength, that she could break chandeliers' as well as Iron Legs himself.

This intimidating bruiser, who went everywhere with a brace of loaded pistols, was so similar in appearance to her husband that many believed her to be his mother, sister or daughter. 'So equivocal was the lady's character', wrote Thomas Dibdin, the author of *Mother Goose*, 'that no one has been able to ascertain the precise degree of relationship.'

Parental incest would certainly explain Giuseppe's many peculiarities. Like his parents, he was short, stocky and strong, described as having 'more the agility of a roebuck than a man', with a face built for gurning and licentiousness. His deep voice rolled with a thick accent, churning French, Italian and English into a curious pidgin that many listeners found hilarious. They also had cause to fear him: he had a fierce temper and was prone to dark moods and unpredictable bursts of violence.

Like his father, Giuseppe served his time at the Paris fairs before making his way to England. The date of his arrival is not exactly clear. Joe's *Memoirs* put it at 1760, when it is said he arrived as part of the retinue of George III's bride, Princess Charlotte of Mecklenburg-Strelitz, in whose household he was employed, like his grandfather John Baptist, as a dentist. In later life Giuseppe would often refer to this period, announcing his exalted patronage in advertisements placed in provincial newspapers prior to his appearance on regional tours. In actuality, his royal service seems to have been short-lived and less than auspicious. A popular story (refuted by Joe) tells how he found the Queen's constant toothaches annoying, until one day, having received yet another summons to St James's Palace, he marched angrily into her bedroom, prised open the royal mouth and, ignoring her protests, pulled out the offending tooth with a single, unceremonious yank. He was lucky to be merely dismissed.

Whatever the truth of his royal service, Giuseppe couldn't have come to England in Charlotte's bridal entourage, as by

January 1758 he was already performing at the King's Theatre, Haymarket, accompanied by his formidable dancing mother, who had emigrated with him and remained a part of his household until her death in 1773. Giuseppe only danced at King's twice before being wooed by David Garrick, the legendary actor-manager of Drury Lane, who kept an eye on foreign theatricals and had heard of Grimaldi via contacts in Paris, who assured him he was *'sublime et divin'*. Garrick employed Giuseppe as Drury Lane's *maître de ballet*, training the dancers and choreographing comic dances, whose names — 'The Cow Keepers', 'The Italian Gardener', 'The Millers' and 'The Swiss' (in which he injured himself) — invoked the spirit of Iron Legs and the clamour of the fairs. The tone was perfect for the sort of afterpieces that ended a long night of tragedy and farce, and Giuseppe found himself amply praised in the London press, one critic going so far as to proclaim him 'a man of genius'. Like his father, he was capable of extraordinary leaps, reaching such heights that it only seemed to be a matter of time before he did himself a serious injury. As the *London Chronicle*'s review of 'The Millers' put it:

> Grimaldi is a man of great strength and agility: he indeed treads the air. If he has any fault, he is too comical; and from some feats of his performing, which I have been a witness to . . . those spectators will see him, it is my opinion, with most pleasure, who are least solicitous whether he breaks his neck or not.

Keen to exploit his popularity, Garrick conscripted him into the pantomime in the role of the venal old codger, Pantaloon, for which he received even higher praise, the press describing him as 'the best Clown we ever saw'.

With success came rewards: a handsome salary of six pounds a week that put him among the chief earners of the day, and lucrative engagements teaching the children of wealthy families to dance, his most exalted pupils including the young Duke of York and his princess sisters. Then in 1763, he was given the position of *maître de ballet* at the summer theatre at Sadler's Wells, Islington.

As Giuseppe's public reputation grew, so he began to find himself increasingly at odds with the close-knit theatre community who didn't know what to make of the strong and savage comedian they nicknamed 'Grim', 'Old Grim', 'Grim-All-Day', or, most often, simply 'the Signor'. With a manner that seemed constantly to provoke, his relationship with Garrick, in particular, began to sour. It was inevitable, for the great Shakespearean maintained a barely concealed contempt for pantomime, which, while not as extreme as that of *The Times* correspondent who saw it as 'an alarming symptom of a nation's degeneracy', echoed the opinion of the journalist John Corry, who held its popularity to be proof of the increased imbecility of contemporary audiences, who favoured their 'glittering pageants' to literature, 'which by filling the imagination . . . prevented the toil of thinking'.

There was some substance to his argument, as the all-powerful *ton*, those addicts of pleasure and intrigue who presided over the world of fashion, had set clear limits on how much of Garrick's art they were willing to endure. They needed something frivolous to help them digest their nightly helping of edification, and were led in their tastes by no less a person than the monarch, George III, who never enjoyed a night at the theatre as much as when moved to tears of laughter by a clown who swallowed carrots whole.

Garrick remained resolutely allergic, reacting furiously to a mischievous rumour that claimed he'd once appeared as Harlequin at Covent Garden. Accordingly, it was common knowledge that the best way to annoy him was to accuse his acting of being 'pantomimical'. Professional jealousy was partly to blame – he hated anyone even daring to impinge on his fame, and had once had to leave a puppet show as the applause for Mr Punch was making him sick – but there was also a fair dash of xenophobia in his view. Fondness for panto-mime, this miscegenetic Franco-Italian cuckoo, threatened to smother his beloved Shakespeare, an anxiety he had frequently verbalised in entertainments such as *Harlequin's Invasion* (1759) and *The Theatrical Candidates* (1775), which presented it as an immigrant force silencing native genius. Yet, as manager, there were profits to consider, and it was necessary to be pragmatic. Pantomime, as Garrick was reluctantly forced to agree, was good for business. 'If you won't come to *Lear* or *Hamlet*,' he wearily conceded, 'I must give you Harlequin.'

Such concessions only made it harder to deal with the Signor's increasingly obnoxious behaviour, and if Garrick had ever borne any respect for Giuseppe Grimaldi, by 1769 it had gone for good. It was the year of Garrick's Jubilee, the three-day festival in Stratford-upon-Avon he had planned as a devotional hymn to Shakespeare but which had ended as a muddy and expensive fiasco. The Signor had been cast as Fal-staff in a pageant of Shakespearean characters that never happened due to torrential rain, though he still insisted on being paid. The dispute dragged on for almost two years, with the Signor persistently pressing his claims, and Garrick fending him off, until he finally snapped, berating the Italian as a 'Tartar' and an 'impudent fellow', and writing to his brother that he was 'ye worst behav'd Man in ye Whole Company and Shd have had a horse whip'. His opinion was confirmed when Giuseppe Grimaldi marched into Garrick's office, dropped his breeches and saluted him with a face that had been freshly painted on his arse.

Sowing backstage rancour was Giuseppe Grimaldi's speciality. A dispute with the scenic artist Philippe-Jacques de Loutherbourg ended in an impromptu duel, the Signor wielding his violin bow and the painter his brush, leaving

Grimaldi with a daub on his face that 'looked as if he had cut his head into two parts'. De Loutherbourg, an amateur faith healer and acolyte of the shadowy magician and con-artist Count Cagliostro, seethed with an intensity that prophesied doom: 'As they are both sprung from great families,' wrote a witness, 'it is expected this affair will not end so comically.' But backstage spats were nothing compared to his behaviour during his brief tenure at a new venue, the grandly styled Royal Circus and Equestrian Philharmonic Academy, which opened its doors on Great Surrey Street (now Blackfriars Road) in 1782.

The manager of the Royal Circus was Charles Dibdin, one of the eighteenth century's most prolific writers and composers, who was hoping to cash in on the vogue for equestrian entertainments, exhibitions of trick riding and daring horsemanship, which, remarked one Continental visitor snottily, 'a certain class of Londoner cannot see too often'. The star was the dashing Charles Hughes, who, accompanied by his beautiful and quixotically named daughter, Sobieska Clementina, thrilled audiences by flipping backwards and forwards from the backs of three galloping horses and vaulting over them forty times in succession. The equestrian shows were to be followed by lavishly staged spectacles performed by a company of all-singing, all-dancing children that included such future stars as Maria de Camp and Maria Romanzini – fifty of them, 'of both sexes, from six years old to 14,' wrote the *London Chronicle*, 'intended to act speaking pantomimes, operas, medleys, drolls, and interludes'.

Dibdin hired the Signor to train the children, but it was a disastrous choice. Grimaldi started scheming almost immediately, weaselling his way in with the backers and driving a wedge between them and the manager, despite earnest protestations to Dibdin's face that he 'conceived himself under the highest obligations' and 'would rather die' than do anything against his interest. This was nothing compared to his treatment of the children, whom he subjected to regular beatings and sadistic punishments, which included locking them into a specially built cage that was pulled forty feet into the fly-tower and left to dangle for hours above the stage. When it was full, he put others into a set of stocks he'd brought to the theatre, although they were too big for most of the children, who simply slipped out their legs and wrists and started 'playing at top or marbles' until the Signor came to set them free.

Even in an age that believed strongly in the improving qualities of corporal punishment, Grimaldi's methods were extreme. Dibdin was constantly called away from business to deal with complaints from angry parents until eventually the local magistrates intervened and ordered 'a compleat investigation into the morals of the place'. Dibdin appeased them, only to have them return almost immediately after Grimaldi choreographed a comic dance for the children called 'The Quakers', which was so libellous and potentially obscene that the usually docile Society of Friends got a court injunction to have it stopped. Legal action proved unnecessary, as the wrangling and disarray that had plagued the Circus from its first day meant that they failed to secure the requisite licence and were forced to shut down only six weeks after opening. The order came in the middle of a performance, and so upset the rough and ready Lambeth crowd that a riot was averted only when the magistrate ran away. Hughes and Dibdin were immediately dispatched to Bridewell prison and the Royal Circus fell apart.

On his release, Hughes turned his back on the affair, working in England only briefly before taking his family to St Petersburg, where he found favour with Catherine the Great. Giuseppe Grimaldi, meanwhile, threatened to sue the proprietors for four hundred pounds he believed he was owed 'for teaching the children'. But the threatened lawsuit never came to pass, possibly because he was forced to lie low in order to avoid the attentions of the Reverend Rowland Hill, a vicar who accused him of sending the Circus children out to steal the lead from the roof of his new chapel across the road.

Dibdin never forgave Grimaldi, and blamed him for everything, convinced that he had been on a demonically inspired mission to destroy him. Even twenty years later, he retained an untempered spleen for this 'practised Italian', recording in his memoirs that his 'nauseous history would sully the foulest paper' and insisting that,

> he knows, in himself, exactly, the degree of merit he actually possesses; and, in the same proportion that you give him credit for any thing beyond it . . . you become his dupe . . . the milk of human kindness which you afford him, mixing in him with the malignant qualities of his mind, turns to slow poison; which, unseen, he spits upon you as it may, occasionally, serve his purpose.

∾

Reports of the Signor's erratic behaviour from 1769 onwards might be explained by the onset of syphilis, a disease he had contracted two or three years earlier. There were ample opportunities for sex in his profession, though the Signor indulged to extreme lengths. His particular taste was for gamine dancers, especially those who had barely passed puberty. As *maître de ballet*, he was surrounded by attractive young women, and in the feudal world of eighteenth-century theatre, where maestros ran their departments like personal fiefdoms, sleeping with the dancers was an ancient right.

One of these mistresses, Mary Blagden, was a girl he had met in his initial season at Drury Lane when he was in his mid-forties and she just thirteen. Shortly thereafter, she became the Signor's wife. They married in 1762 at St Paul's, Covent Garden, after the Signor had sought and received consent from her father because she was still a minor. The marriage flourished at first, and over the next five years they had four daughters: Mary, baptised at St Paul's, Covent Garden, on 19 January 1763, Isabella Louise, baptised at St Paul's on 14 October 1764, Margaret Charlotte (b. 1765) and Catherine (b. 1767). But though she was young and fruitful, Mary Blagden's own testimony reveals the Signor to have been a cruel and neglectful spouse.

Many years later, Mary Blagden would take the unheard-of step of initiating divorce proceedings against him, citing systematic abuse that had gone on for more than sixteen years. According to the petition, he 'began to behave cruelly towards her' almost immediately after their wedding. Just days after the birth of their first child, as she lay nursing, he attacked her without provocation, beating her badly and pulling her around the floor by her hair. The attacks became habitual and, having beaten her up, he would lock her in the bedroom for hours at a time, attacking his daughters should they dare to intercede. At mealtimes, he threw knives, forks and plates at her, inflicting injuries so bad she was unable to dance at the theatre. To physical cruelty, he added psychological torture. At night, he consorted with prostitutes, hanging around in brothels until four or five in the morning, at which time he would go home and wake his wife and tell her 'of the several acts of debauchery he had on the preceding nights been guilty of and would then without the slightest provocation very much abuse and ill-treat her'. There were also some long-standing affairs with the young dancers and acrobats at Sadler's Wells, including Isabella Wilkinson, a handsome tightrope dancer and virtuoso of the 'musical glasses', who turned his head with her fur-lined shorts and ability to play the cymbals, violin, pipe and tabor while standing in mid-air. Having dallied with her, he moved on to her sister Caroline, from whom he most likely contracted syphilis.

Despite falling to the disease, the Signor still insisted on having sex with his wife, then pregnant with their fourth child, and, inevitably, she became infected. In 1770, he abandoned them all, setting up house on his own in Chelsea and returning only twice a week to order dinner for himself and his servant before sending the scraps to Mary, 'who chiefly lived in the kitchen of the said house, by reason he . . . constantly locked up and took with him the keys of the several other rooms'. During one of these visits, he beat her so badly she was blind for ten days, while on another, he imprisoned her in her bedroom for six weeks, commanding his mother to stand guard at the door with her ever-present pistols.

Somehow, Mary Blagden managed to escape, taking refuge with her own mother while living in constant fear of her husband's return. Yet by this time the Signor had lost interest in his family and was living with a woman named Anne Perry, who had taken to calling herself 'Mrs Grimaldi'. In spite of her airs, Anne Perry had no claim to exclusivity, for the Signor was having another affair with a 'short, stout, very dark' dancer named Rebecca Brooker. Rebecca had been dancing at Drury Lane since the age of three, encouraged by her father Zachariah, a tough Cockney butcher who kept the Bloomsbury slaughterhouse, and made money on the side by renting her out to Garrick as an 'occasional fairy'. In October 1773, with a view to setting her up in a career, Zachariah bought his daughter an apprenticeship with the Signor, placing her on the roster of apprentices known as 'Grimaldi's scholars' and handing over a substantial fee in return for 'exercises in music, dancing, oratory, etc.'.

When the Signor came across Rebecca he added an additional clause to her contract that went far beyond the usual demands for cash and obedience. Henceforth, she was to renounce the company of men and be prohibited from 'contracting herself in matrimony or committing any other acts whereby the said . . . Grimaldi shall lose the benefit of the said Indentures'. Having legally ensured her chastity and marked her off as his personal property, Giuseppe Grimaldi set about seducing her. Rebecca was less than fourteen, the Signor at least fifty-five.

From now on, the Signor divided his time between the house he shared with Anne Perry at 125 High Holborn, and Rebecca Brooker's tiny room in Stanhope Street in the parish of St Clement Danes. In 1778, both women fell pregnant and gave birth within days of each other. Anne Perry had a daughter on 16 December they named Henrietta Marguerite, and two days later, as Drury Lane held a benefit performance for the City of London Lying-in Hospital, Rebecca Brooker gave birth to a son they called Joseph Grimaldi.

Though largely ambivalent about the birth of a fifth daughter, the Signor was overjoyed at the arrival of his first son, and when his own pantomime, *The Wonders of Derbyshire*, was cancelled due to the indisposition of one of its principal performers, he hit the town hard, boasting to anyone who would listen what a good omen it was to have a child born so close to the new pantomime season and how he would have him on stage as soon as he could walk.

~

In theatrical terms at least, Joe was born at the dawn of a new era. On 18 January, when the child was exactly one month old, David Garrick slipped into a coma and died two days later with the parting words 'Oh dear'. It was an inauspicious end for one who had spent his life at the heart of the Shakespearean maelstrom, though the funeral more than made up for any lingering sense of anticlimax: its long cortège snaked its way from his home at the Adelphi to its final resting place at Poets' Corner, attended by aristocratic pallbearers and a host of distinguished mourners that included Samuel Johnson and Edmund Burke. The Signor was not invited.

For the first few years, Rebecca and her child lived alone in the warren of slums parcelled between Clare Market and the royal theatres, an area peopled by the dancers and supernumeraries who toiled in the vast theatrical mills. It was a particularly noxious part of town, with a perpetual smog, 'like a great round cloud attached to the earth', and was notorious for prostitution and the rows of sagging houses that crowded in on one another so closely that the puddles in the street rarely dried.

The Signor remained elusive, maintaining a number of addresses and probably women too. In Lambeth, he kept a house with a garden that he decorated in winter with artificial flowers, as well as another lodging on the Islington Road, opposite the gates of Sadler's Wells. His principal residence, though, remained the house on High Holborn with Anne Perry. He was certainly there during the Gordon Riots in the summer of 1780, eight days of anti-Catholic violence that caused more destruction to London than that suffered by Paris during the entire French Revolution. With a sectarian mob descending on Holborn, smashing and looting any property that did not prominently display the words 'No Popery', the Signor was in trouble: he'd failed to hang a sign and the rioters were certain to know he was a foreigner and, most likely, a Catholic. With the kind of nerve only a true comedian can possess, he waited until they were almost at his door, before sticking his head from the second-floor window and, 'making comical grimaces', called out, 'Gentlemen, in dis hose dere be no religion at all.' There was a tense moment before the crowd burst out laughing, gave him three cheers, and moved on to set fire to the Bank of England.

It was to be one of Anne Perry's last memories of her 'husband', for on 13 September that year, Rebecca delivered another of the Signor's children, a second boy they called John Baptist in memory of Iron Legs. With thoughts of a profitable theatrical dynasty dancing around his head, the Signor unsentimentally dropped Anne and Henrietta to move in with Rebecca and his sons.

It was an equivocal promotion for Rebecca, but with it came a marked improvement in her standard of living and the chance to depart the verminous rooms in Clare Market for a well-appointed apartment in Little Russell Street with 'three or four female servants', and that once-essential symbol of eighteenth-century urbanity, now become rather gauche, an African footman named Sam. Joe's *Memoirs* seek to portray it as a largely happy household, while remaining silent on the topic of his father's polygamy and his own illegitimacy. Neither do they make any mention of any siblings save John, which is particularly intriguing as the Signor's will suggests that Rebecca had a third son called William, born around 1786. William remains a mystery, as absent from all other records as he is from the *Memoirs*, even though he, Joe and Mary Blagden's daughter, Catherine, all performed together on Boxing Day 1789, billed as 'the three young Grimaldis'.

Many of these omissions were required by the standards of decency expected of nineteenth-century memoirs, and wherever Joe finds himself unable to recount the truth, he offers homely platitudes, such as the assertion that the Signor 'had the reputation of being a very honest man, and a very charitable one . . . never known to be inebriated'. But even the veil of Victorian decency could not completely silence the Signor's fury, and Joe confesses that he was as violent, neglectful and overbearing with them as he had been with Mary Blagden and the children of the Royal Circus, being especially fond of lifting them by their hair, throwing them into corners, and promising beatings, which he would then defer for weeks and sometimes months. 'This was ingenious,' recall the *Memoirs*, 'inasmuch as it doubled, or trebled, or quadrupled the punishment, giving the unhappy little victim all the additional pain of anticipating it for a long time, with the certainty of enduring it in the end.'

Joe found it hard to extricate himself from his father's madness, which inevitably set him so far apart from his peers that he became a target for the taunts of local children, especially when he was forced to walk every Sunday to his grandfather's house in Bloomsbury in the Signor's bizarre idea of Sunday best – an emerald green jacket and satin waistcoat embroidered with large flowers, matching green breeches, and a laced shirt and cravat, with ruffles at his wrists and buckles on his knees and shoes, the ensemble completed with a jew-elled cane and a cocked hat that gave him the appearance of a particularly prosperous leprechaun. Invariably he'd attract a barracking pack of children 'a street or two long', and though he claimed to enjoy the attention, it was an early introduction to an alienating dynamic that would persist throughout his life: a figure of ridicule apart from the crowd.

By far the Signor's most oppressive attribute was the long shadow of morbidity he cast over his family, thanks to an acute obsession with death and, in particular, being buried alive. Every idle moment would find him poring over a smeared and grubby copy of *The Uncertainty of the Signs of Death*, a book by the French physician Jacques-Bénigne Winslow that purported to be a medical manual for ascertaining the difference between real death and mere death-like trances, but was little more than a series of horrific anecdotes. Pale and trembling, the Signor would let out long, heartsick moans as he read of the young lady of Auxbourg who, believed dead, was interred in the family vault, until, some years later, 'one of the same Fam-ily happening to die, the vault was open'd and the Body of the Young Lady found on the Stairs at its entry without any fingers on the right hand', gnawed down for food; or the unfortunate woman of Basingstoke, discovered by boys who heard screams emanating from the vault beneath their school and came across her having clawed her face into ribbons, 'to that Degree, that notwithstanding all the Care that was taken of her, she died in a few hours in inexpressible torment'.

Though many of his superstitions had taken root in the fairgrounds of his youth, where *forains* relied on a polytheistic array of talismans and saintly intercessions to preserve them from breaking their necks, the Signor's fear of being buried alive was not entirely irrational. In 1785, the *Morning Post* reported that Giuseppe Grimaldi had been found dead in Brighton, sitting upright in his chair at breakfast. In fact, he had simply slipped into unconsciousness, something he did 'three or four times a year [when] he eats himself into a second sleep, and he appears as dead', possibly as the result of a diabetic condition. More irrational was his conviction that he would die on the first Friday of the month. The comedian Jacob de Castro recalled being told of a recurring dream in which the devil appeared to the Signor to inform him he was coming to collect him on that day, though, infernally, omitted to specify which month. As the first Friday of each month came, the Signor kept an anxious vigil in a room he had filled with clocks, blanched with terror until daybreak, whereupon he let out a relieved sigh and said, 'Now I am safe for anoder month.' It was a fear he immortalised in a piece of pantomime business known as the 'skeleton scene', a skit that remained popular for more than a century after his death, in which 'the clown depicts in a most woefully comic manner all the horror and alarm which may be supposed to seize upon a nervous person when alarmed by the vagaries of a visitant from the world of spirits'.

The boys were not preserved from these horrible fantasies, for, haunted by phantoms and sunk deep in ghoulish accounts of last-minute resurrections and scratched coffin lids, the

Signor frequented the neighbourhood graveyards, speculating aloud on the causes of death as his reluctant children scuffed along in his wake. The church of St Clement Danes, a mere spit from their lodgings, was the favourite destination for these morbid peregrinations, and in particular, the grave of the actor Josias Miller. 'Honest Joe Miller', read the headstone, 'was a tender Husband, a sincere Friend, a facetious Companion, and an excellent Comedian.' Looking down at Miller's grave, the Signor must have wondered how much of this epitaph, if any, could be truthfully applied to himself.

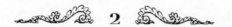

2

THE WIZARD OF THE
SILVER ROCKS

... here more than once
Taking my seat, I saw (nor blush to add,
With ample recompense) giants and dwarfs,
Clowns, conjurers, posture-masters, harlequins,
Amid the uproar of the rabblement,
Perform their feats. Nor was it mean delight
To watch crude Nature work in untaught minds;
To note the laws and progress of belief;
Though obstinate on this way, yet on that
How willingly we travel, and how far!

William Wordsworth, *The Prelude* (1805)

SADLER'S WELLS OPENED ITS DOORS at five o'clock on Easter
Monday 1781 for the first night of the new season. By the time
the curtain went up at six, the house was packed with noise
and expectation. The bill included 'the inimitable Mr. Saunders', standing on his head on top of a drinking glass balanced
on a swinging rope; tumbling by Placido Bussart, a gymnast
who had once amazed Marie Antoinette by somersaulting
over a file of eighteen grenadiers with upright bayonets; and
a tightrope act by Paulo Redigé, the 'Little Devil', who was
conducting a torrid affair with another of the evening's main
attractions, 'La Belle Espagnole', a busty Spaniard who danced
the fandango on a tightrope while accompanying herself on the
castanets. Acrobatics were followed by a 'serio-comic,
prophetic, political, musical piece' entitled *The Medley; or, a*

Masque in a Masquerade, and a pantomime called *The Wizard of the Silver Rocks; or, Harlequin's Release*. Somewhere in the midst of this mish-mash of variety that was the speciality of the Wells, Joseph Grimaldi made his full theatrical début at the age of two and a half years old.

It was not the first time Joe had been before an audience: six months before, the Signor had made good on his promise to have his son on stage as soon as he could walk, bringing him out at Drury Lane for his 'first bow and first tumble'. Tonight was a different proposition, dancing with one of his half-sisters in a fully rehearsed and choreographed routine. His performance was flawless. It had to be: any nerves he felt were entirely subsumed by the thought of his father's wrath should he set a foot wrong.

As the eldest son, Joe had the dubious honour of being the most closely tutored of his father's protégés. Like most theatrical parents, the Signor saw little point in allowing his son to go idle when he could be learning a trade and earning a wage. By the age of two, Joe was already used to long days being drilled in the skills necessary for a career in harlequinade: lessons in mime, dancing, gymnastics and buffoonery, to which he brought his abundant gifts, an expressive face and 'eloquent legs'. Eight months after his Sadler's Wells début, he had already progressed enough for the Signor to try him in his very first pantomime, and on Boxing Day 1782, Joe made his début as Little Clown in Drury Lane's *The Triumph of Mirth; or, Harlequin's Wedding*. It was a double début for the Grimaldis as, with the exception of one solitary performance in 1778, it was the first time the Signor had taken the role of Clown – all the more remarkable given that it was one of the most physically demanding roles in the theatre and he was in his seventies. Thus, Drury Lane saw both its youngest and oldest ever Clowns take the stage on the same night, father and son dressed as exact replicas of each other, Joe mimicking the

Signor's actions like an impish familiar, a routine he managed so well it produced a rare flush of parental pride in the old man, who boasted of such 'great doings for a mere baby ting'.

Also in the cast was Carlo Delpini, a legend of pantomime who had arranged all the tricks for the piece. Delpini was king of the transformation scene, the instantaneous conversion of one object into another at the hand of its hero, Harlequin, the prince of mutability and cipher for the age of revolutions that saw the potential for change in everything. Harlequin achieved his effects through the expert timing of the stage-hands, who released catches on hinged flats, letting them drop to reveal new objects painted on the reverse side. Alternatively, canvas flaps or holes might be cut into trick backcloths, allowing Harlequin to leap into a fireplace or through a mirror, while semi-transparent sheets could be painted to change entire scenes, depending on whether they were lit from the back or the front.

Delpini was well known to the Grimaldis, having been an apprentice of Iron Legs back in the 1740s and, for years, a regular fixture of the London theatres. His influence on Joe would prove enormous, as the young Grimaldi would soon begin his own experiments in tricks and transformations, although for now Delpini just seemed like a younger version of his father, strong and athletic, outspoken in his heavily accented English, and more than a little insane. Most uncannily, Delpini cherished superstitious fears about death and was particularly sensitive about the number eight, being convinced that he would die in 1788. Inculcating a fertile sense of doom had clearly been an important part of Iron Legs's tutelage.

In fact, Delpini wouldn't die for another thirty years, although it wasn't for want of trying. He was just as reckless as the Signor and constantly running risks. 'Delpini fears nothing; he runs all hazards,' wrote *The Times*, as if to say, 'Catch him while you can.' Several weeks later he was gravely injured in *The Death of Captain Cook*, a serious pantomime performed at the Haymarket. At a royal fête in Frogmore, he was nearly killed when a Pierrot levelled a musket at him and accidentally let it off in his eye. The Prince of Wales was horrified, and declared the accident had entirely 'dampened the remainder of the day's entertainment'. He had been inordinately fond of bald little Delpini ever since he had commissioned him to supply entertainments for his coming-of-age ball at the Pantheon. He had also failed to pay the bill, thereby granting the pantomimist the great honour of being bankrupted by a prince.

Together, the luminous cast saw to it that *The Triumph of Mirth* was successful enough to survive until almost the end of March 1783, a respectable run for the day, which meant that young Joe was often in the theatre until well past midnight. When he wasn't needed, the Signor placed him in a corner of the green room, commanding him to be still and silent on pain of death, although his compliance rarely lasted longer than the time it took his father to leave. This was especially the case when there were actors around to tempt him with a toy or a guinea in exchange for a trick – gifts his father would later lock away with the characteristically morbid warning, 'Mind, Joe, ven I die, dat is your vortune.'

At these times, the all-too-familiar threat of a beating was no match for the new and intoxicating lure of laughter, to which Joe was becoming increasingly alive. Given his background, it was hardly surprising that these comedic instincts should emerge as, besides the relentless training, he'd spent his young life immersed in the Signor's madness, where arbitrary justice and irrationality had led him to understand the world as a shifting plane of ambiguities, void of the anchors of reason and authority a parent conventionally provides. The result was an acute sense of the ludicrous that acted as a sanctuary. When Joe performed, it wasn't merely the attention he was seeking, or the beaming delight he felt at making adults burst into loud guffaws, it was that feeling of being taken away by laughter, laughter that was both a giddy lightness and tumbling mudslide, an invisible hand leading him to absurdity and smothering him in its inimitable suchness. It was, wrote Henry Downes Miles, one of Joe's first biographers, in a typically Victorian phrase, 'what opium is to the Turk . . . the "life of life"', and Joe was instantly hooked.

Coaxed by a coin, he would jump up and run through a full repertoire of faces and tumbles that could only be stopped by warning of the Signor's return, whereupon he'd dart back to his corner and look cowed and obedient. Soon, the extravagant contrast between these exuberant pranks and feigned servility became the best part of the joke, and the green room kept itself amused by shouting 'Joe, your father's coming,' just to enjoy the transformation. This often backfired, as it did one night when the Earl of Derby, frequently backstage as he conducted his affair with the actress Elizabeth Farren, offered Joe half a crown if he'd throw his own wig on the fire. Joe did it without thinking and the room went up in a blaze of laughter that lasted as long as it took the company to notice the Signor standing in the doorway. Incandescent, he fell on his son, delivering several sound thwacks before the Earl could intercede by proffering the smouldering wig on the end of a poker.

By the time *The Triumph of Mirth* was finished, Joe had become an established juvenile performer at Drury Lane, and that summer, he was taken on fully at Sadler's Wells, dancing, marching in processions, and playing monkeys, imps, fairies and demons to order. It was the beginning of a long and demanding apprenticeship that would last for many years.

~

The London theatre scene at the end of the eighteenth century was as hierarchical and partisan as anything in British
society, dominated as it was by the two imposing theatres
royal, Covent Garden and Drury Lane. These venues had been
granted a monopoly on spoken drama under Charles II, which
they guarded jealously by systematically suppressing any
theatre that dared to utter dialogue on stage. With only the
corner of Bow Street and Russell Street to separate them, they
were close neighbours, although culturally they could not
have been further apart. Covent Garden was a bastion of
establishment respectability, a loyal and monarchical institution patronised by the King and his Tory ministers, while
Drury Lane was home to the Whig opposition, radical repub-
lican sympathisers and the exclusive cliques of the Prince of
Wales, Charles James Fox and the members of the Duchess
of Devonshire's Devonshire House salon.

Such extreme factionalism underscored the theatre's
political role. Since the Restoration, it had been an extension
of public life, forming, in the words of the *Constitutional
Review*, 'an absolutely constituent part of our political system'.
Far from being centres for the passive consumption of entertainment, theatres were popularly thought of as representative
assemblies or national debating chambers, where the division
of the auditorium into ranks of boxes, galleries and pit seats
provided a perfect vision of society in miniature from the most
exalted citizens to the many prostitutes 'openly selling and
delivering the articles they trade in'. Audiences took their
places with a sense of collective ownership, never allowing
actors to forget that they appeared at their pleasure. They came
and went as they pleased with scant regard for what was
happening on stage, punctuating the evening with a series of
interruptions, first from the fashionable set who caused a stir
by taking their boxes in the middle of the play after their
dinner parties had broken up, and then again by the bargain

hunters who took up the unsold seats for half price at the end of the third act. No wonder, then, that the author Matthew Lewis should advise budding playwrights that, if they wanted their work to be understood, they had to open act four with a summary of the entire plot.

Heckling was commonplace – Dr Johnson's biographer, James Boswell, was extremely proud of himself for entertaining the audience 'by imitating the lowing of a cow' – and respectful silence, though not unheard of, was more than likely the result of the natural ebb and flow of chatter than attentive consideration. Actors retaliated as best they could. When playing Lear, Garrick placed 'hush men' throughout the house to keep the noise down during his important scenes. John Philip Kemble preferred irony: interrupted mid-sentence by a crying baby in the audience, he stepped forward and gravely intoned, 'Ladies and gentlemen, unless the play is stopped, the child cannot possibly go on.'

A further 'exuberance of liberty', as one foreign visitor called it, was the audience's right to throw things, especially from the gods, or the upper galleries. The pit was bombarded with a constant hail of nutshells, apple cores and orange peel or, the ultimate prize, a direct hit on one of the liveried servants keeping his master's place in the boxes. An apple to the head was getting off lightly. Bottles, glass and bits of wood were often pitched into the orchestra, and one lady's shoulder was dislocated by a piece of brass that weighed at least a pound. Even she was comparatively lucky next to the actor Thomas Hollingsworth, who was almost killed when he was hit in the eye by an apple skewered on a knife.

But the ultimate demonstration of the audience's authority was a riot, and while there hadn't been a serious one at Drury Lane for almost thirty years, a row of spikes still lay across the orchestra pit to deter stage invasions. Recent disorder at the opera house had resulted in a three-hour brawl that was noteworthy only for featuring so many combatants there was hardly room for them to grapple one another, let alone swing a punch. The rest of the audience stayed on to watch, 'more pleased than ever they were at a regular entertainment', according to the *Morning Herald*.

Like the royal houses that sustained them, the fortunes of the royal theatres sank and rose, although, by virtue of its strong company and talented manager, the Irishman Richard Brinsley Sheridan, Drury Lane was currently in the ascendant. Sheridan was a young and ambitious adventurer with boundless energy and a brilliant mind who, through a series of complicated and ultimately unsound financial manoeuvres, had managed to raise enough money to buy a controlling share in the theatre after Garrick had retired. At twenty-eight, he was already famous as the author of four enormously successful plays, one of which, his masterpiece, *The School for Scandal*, had been greeted with such thunderous laughter on its opening night that the writer Frederick Reynolds was convinced the building was about to collapse on him as he walked by.

Sheridan was quick-witted and enormously charismatic, and owed his rapid ascent in society to an inherent understanding of the basic theatricality of aristocratic life. He presented his emotions for public consumption with some frequency, fainting lifeless into the arms of Edmund Burke after a marathon oration at the Warren Hastings trial, or appearing at Garrick's funeral with a train of black velvet carried by six pages, refusing to utter a word for grief. To his civic persona, he added a rakish mystique that had won him an army of admirers, despite his unusual features and bright red face. It was a visage Lord Byron admired greatly, describing it as half 'god', with 'an eye of peculiar brilliancy and fire' that also 'shewed the satyr'.

Sheridan's decision to move into management was not motivated by a desire to succeed Garrick as Britain's foremost theatrical man so much as to gain access to Garrick's connections. Determined to be an intriguer, Sheridan had set his sights on penetrating the heart of the Whig élite, using his role as manager to ease himself effortlessly into their circles and sit with them in their boxes. Fawning over glamorous friends did not sit well with the responsibilities of running one of Europe's largest theatres, however, and its day-to-day business was constantly overshadowed, first by his long and chaotic pursuit of a seat in Parliament, and then, having been returned as MP for Stafford in 1780, by an equally disordered retention of it. The neglect would not have been so bad had Sheridan been capable of delegating responsibility, but his erratic habits and long absences kept the theatre in a permanent state of disarray, best embodied in the state of his office, which was littered with unpaid bills and a 'funeral pile' of manuscripts he had promised to consider but never read.

Putting off artistic decisions was one thing, but it was his chronic malfeasance and extravagant expenditure that had the biggest impact on Drury Lane. Payday, recalled the actress Maria de Camp, meant a backstage crew of 'carpenters, painters, scene-shifters, understrappers of all sorts and plebs in general' mobbing the staircase and narrow passageways that led to his office, crying, 'For God's sake, Mr Sheridan, pay us our salaries!'

'Certainly, certainly, my good people,' he would answer, 'you shall be attended to directly,' whereupon he would enter the treasury, sweep the week's receipts into his pockets and escape from the building by an alternative route. Another trick was to promise to pay everything he owed just as long as he could first borrow fifty pounds. If that didn't work, he simply charmed people into submission, descending from his office like a blessed saint. 'So cordial were his manners,' remembered James Boaden, a hungry author who had camped for hours in the stairwells and anterooms of the theatre, 'his glance so masterly and his address so captivating, that the people, for the most part, seemed to forget what they actually wanted, and went away as if they had only come to look at him.'

Even the Signor was defeated by his unnatural charisma. He had once forced his way into Sheridan's house in Hertford Street, pushing past the servants and threatening to beat him in front of his guests, who included the Mayor of Stafford, unless he was immediately paid what he was owed. Sheridan protested in the haughtiest terms but, unable to dent the Italian's resolve, he finally wrote a banker's draft that he delivered in a conciliatory handshake. Delighted with his fearsome reputation, the Signor went straight to the bank where, instead of the forty pounds he was expecting, he received just four – Sheridan had deliberately omitted the zero. But rather than going back and making good on his threats, the Signor was impressed by the audacity with which he'd been fleeced, stopping Frederick Reynolds in the street to exclaim admiringly, 'O vat a *clevare* fellow dat Sheridan is!'

As for the company, Drury Lane boasted two of the country's biggest stars, the siblings Sarah Siddons and John Philip Kemble, a pair of grave and statuesque tragedians who dominated the theatre in the years after Garrick. Mrs Siddons in particular was an incomparable talent, the finest actress the stage had ever seen. She was distant, imperious, possessed of 'a somewhat masculine beauty' and described by Hester Piozzi as one of 'the noblest specimens of the human race I ever saw'. To Sheridan, she was a 'magnificent and appalling creature', whom, he couldn't help remarking, he found about as sexy as the Archbishop of Canterbury. He was in the minority, for at the height of her powers she attracted an enormous band of devotees. Drawn by her strong voice, imposing figure and majestic features, they came nightly to indulge their fix of 'Siddonean idolatry'. Particularly enthralling was her delivery, which at its most effective could be employed on a single line, intensifying sentences as slight as 'Was it a miserable day?' with such an electric charge that the audience could be heard to catch its collective breath. This was exactly what they paid for. Guided by the spirit of Romantic sensibility, they surrendered themselves to the swells of emotion in which she specialised. As James Boaden wrote,

> I well remember (how is it possible I should ever forget) the sobs, the shrieks, among the tender part of her audiences; or those tears, which manhood, at first, struggled to suppress, but at length grew proud of indulging. We then, indeed, knew all the luxury of grief; but the nerves of many a gentle being gave way before the intensity of such appeals; and fainting fits long and frequently alarmed the decorum of the house, filled almost to suffocation.

Her brother, too, sought to ascend the highest peaks of human emotion, although he was hampered by a natural reserve that meant he often came across more like the Roman Catholic priest he had originally planned to be than the high-Romantic artist he became. Like his sister, John Philip Kemble cut a stately figure, tall and thin, with the classical features particularly suited to Roman patricians. His performances were noteworthy for displaying a total immersion in the reality of the play-world, a level of concentration that was almost unique among his colleagues, who were often accused of being too aware of the audience and wasting their energies in trying to provoke them into applause with nods and winks and all kinds of attention-seeking tricks.

Wishing to pursue a psychological element in his acting, Kemble was the first *Macbeth* to have the ghost of Banquo played by an empty chair rather than the conventional man in a sheet, and one of his greatest innovations, it was said, was never allowing himself to look bored while waiting for his turn to speak. His delivery was also notorious: he spoke as though he literally held a plum in his mouth and peppered his speeches with tortuous pauses that sent the prompter into fits. He was also at the vanguard of a one-man mission to return 'proper' pronunciation to an English language he considered to have slipped into derelict habits, wilfully transposing vowels and collapsing consonants until he pronounced 'beard' as 'bird', 'conscience' as 'conshince' and 'virtue' as 'varchue'. As the stage historian Charles Beecher Hogan once pointed out, if Kemble had ever cause to say, 'It is odious that the merchant has no mercy for my hideous aches,' the audience would have heard, 'It is ojus that theh marchant has no maircy for meh hijjus aitches.'

Not that he was the only one at Drury Lane to speak strangely. In his devotion to the Whig oligarchs, Sheridan had adopted their famous 'Devonshire House Drawl', a cliquey patois that was 'part baby-talk, part refined affectation', whose most notable aspects were the elongation of vowels, unexpected stresses and the syrupy pronunciation of 'you' as 'oo' (as in 'I *looove* oo').

~

With such powerful stars and matters of state to attend to, pantomimists remained second-class citizens at Drury Lane, regardless of their popularity. It was a different story at Sadler's Wells, the oldest and the best known of London's many minor theatres, a group of eccentric venues, including the Royal Circus and Astley's Amphitheatre, that operated on both the edges of town and the margins of respectability. While the Drury Lane season was organised to convenience the families of rank and fashion who descended upon the capital for the beginning of the new parliamentary session in September and departed for the country in late spring, the Wells's season began on Easter Monday and ran throughout the summer.

In this way it could make the most of its fine pastoral setting on the banks of the New River, at the end of a neat avenue of poplars in the middle of three square miles of meadows that bordered Clerkenwell at the south and the new Pentonville estate in the north.

The first playhouse to occupy the site had been a simple wooden music room, erected in 1685 to entertain the five or six hundred people who came daily to take the medicinal waters that Thomas Sadler had uncovered in his garden, land that had once been part of the monastery of St John, Clerkenwell. A number of enterprises followed, with mixed results, until in 1746 the property was taken over by a local builder named Thomas Rosoman, who established a permanent company for the theatre and housed it in a new stone building. Rosoman prided himself on offering quality entertainment by profes-sional performers, but to make sure he didn't run foul of the royal 'patent' theatres, he offered it free, charging patrons only for the compulsory pint of port, Lisbon or punch that was necessary to gain admission. Unsurprisingly, Sadler's Wells gained a reputation for drunkenness and providing performances 'only to persons who had rendered themselves in some degree incapable of judging their merit', prompting the inevitable accusations of immorality and vice. 'Most of the unhappy wretches who pay their lives as forfeit to the law', warned one respectable ladies' journal, 'are such as frequent these ill-conducted places of recreation, where their imagina-tions are enflamed to a degree of madness that makes them run on any crime and danger for the gratification.'

Though such horrors were clearly overstated, early audiences were, if not exactly criminal, certainly of a lower order than those found at Drury Lane: maids and footmen – mop-squeezers and fart-catchers, as they were prosaically known – tradesmen, apprentices and boisterous sailors wrapped around their 'red-ribboned Mollies'. Similarly, its isolated spot a mile beyond Clerkenwell made it an attractive haunt for thieves and brigands who waylaid playgoers as they stumbled through the fields, knocking their shins against the network of leaky wooden pipes that carried the waters of the New River, or getting tangled in the washing lines that serviced the city's laundry industry. Though actors venturing out of the theatre after dark were able to protect themselves with pistols or a blunderbuss they rented from the stage door, picking off the audience was easy. If they had no money, they were mugged for their wigs and hats.

By the time the Signor arrived as *maître de ballet* in 1763, the management had made a concerted effort to promote the Wells as a respectable and credible place of entertainment, refitting the auditorium and raising the ceiling for greater ventilation, although the fact that they had to install an orna- mental iron railing along the water's edge to stop people 'throwing in their dogs, etc.' suggests that there was still some way to go. In time, its reputation grew steadily, although it wasn't until the management mounted horse patrols and posted linkboys to light the way between Islington and the City to ensure their clients' safety that a more affluent crowd at last ventured northward. This, combined with the engagement of a rope-dancer called Jack Richer, 'one of the handsomest and best made men in England', as beautiful as he was grace- ful, meant that by the time Joe made his début in *The Wizard of the Silver Rocks*, the Wells was at last beginning to emerge as a summer resort of the fashionable and well-to-do.

As the patent theatres held a monopoly on speech – so strictly enforced Carlo Delpini once found himself in prison after he'd dared to utter the words 'roast beef' on a minor stage – Sadler's Wells was forced to approach its business with unflagging ingenuity, filling the bills with a stream of novelties and entertainments that didn't require any dialogue. Aside from innumerable variations on dancing, tumbling and rope-walking, the Wells specialised in serious and comic pantomimes, the former denoting mimed melodramas, and 'burlettas', a bastard, quasi-operatic genre that dodged the limitations of the law by restricting speech to rhymed recitatives accompanied by 'orchestral twinklings'. On the occasions when only words would do, the audience were apprised of a character's thoughts by means of cartoonish banners, dialogue painted on flags, and labels pinned to actors – a practice William Wordsworth alluded to in *The Prelude*, when he recalled a youthful visit to the Wells to see a performance of *Jack the Giant Killer*: 'The garb he wears is black as death, the word 'Invisible' flames forth upon his chest.'

Non-dramatic acts, like the 'Fantoccini' – ingenious mechanical puppets – or the Catawba Indian chiefs newly arrived from America, were little more than staged versions of the many curiosities and raree-shows that could be found about London on any given day of the week. Others were more lavish, in particular what Wordsworth referred to as 'recent things yet warm with life', the dramatisations of current affairs on which Sadler's Wells was starting to build a reputation. This could mean something as simple and hasty as songs mocking modern follies, like James Graham's 'Celestial Bed', a mattress on which infertile couples were 'guaranteed' to conceive (the Duchess of Devonshire had been a customer), or an acrobatic display in which Paulo Redigé leapt through 'an Air Balloon all on Fire' a mere two days after Vicenzo Lunardi had mounted London's first-ever manned balloon flight from the artillery fields in City Road.

At its most ambitious, Sadler's Wells staged full military re-enactments like *The Battle of Fockschau*, which replayed Hungary's recent defeat of the Turks using every device at the theatre's disposal to give the audience a window on to world affairs. Recasting the conflict in suitably melodramatic shades of good and evil, the whole company did battle among gun-smoke and cannon-blasts to the accompaniment of a thundering score. A variation on this theme had the soldiers played by dogs, 'dog dramas' having become popular following the 1784 phenomenon of Moustache, a dog whose performance in a play called *The Deserter* required him and his platoon of hounds to mount an attack on an enemy position. Frederick Reynolds fondly recalled seeing the dog 'in his little uniform, military boots, with smart musket and helmet, cheering and inspiring his fellow soldiers to follow him up the scaling ladders, and storm the fort'. It was such a hit with the fashionable set, he said, that the Wells 'resembled the Opera House on a Saturday night'.

Not unsurprisingly, the season following Moustache's triumph was a veritable menagerie: a hare beating a drum, bulldogs lifted twenty feet into the air on a balloon by their teeth (to demonstrate British tenacity), a singing duck, two horses dancing a minuet, and a pig, much admired by Samuel Johnson, that could read and tell the time.

~

With engagements at both theatres, Joe was working non-stop from the start of the Drury Lane pantomime on Boxing Day through to the end of the Wells season in late summer. Compared to most of the working-class children living around Clare Market, he was well-off, with opportunities and good pay. Yet even by eighteenth-century standards, the theatre was a poor environment for a child, peopled by a dissolute crowd who, according to Sir Walter Scott, prosecuted 'their debaucheries so openly that it would degrade a bagnio'. Actors could be charming, brilliant and philanthropic, but they were also fickle, vexatious and capable of taking vanity and dissipation to extremes. The air backstage was as thick with feuds and adultery as it was with mould and patchouli, encouraged by a prurient public who loved theatrical gossip and the *frisson* it added to performances. The green room was a constantly shifting terrain of jealous factions plotting to have their enemies disgraced or paying footmen to have their rivals jeered. Endemic alcoholism and the temptations of a celebrity lifestyle inspired habits that led frequently to an early grave. In this hard-drinking age, in which the Prime Minister regularly downed a bottle of port before attending Parliament, and the Prince of Wales drank six bottles of claret after dinner, which 'scarce made a perceptible change in his countenance', actors habitually outdid civilians from the moment they were dressed, reeling through rehearsals and delivering slurred performances before going on extended sprees that ended in run-ins with the Watch.

Sheridan led by example, along with his good friend, Drury Lane's star singer, Michael Kelly, who, looking back on his time at the theatre, admitted, 'My wine bills were very large; the purple tide flowed by day and night; and I never stopped it, for then "I took the DRUNKARD for a GOD".' (Kelly's nickname was 'Composer of Wines and Importer of Music'.) Even the ascetic Kemble had problems controlling the opium and alcohol he took for asthma brought on by the stress of constant performing, and which sometimes caused major lapses in judgement, such as when he appeared in Maria de Camp's dressing room and attempted to molest her (she went on to marry his brother, Charles).

Many had been horrified by the very public decline of the beautiful Sophia Baddeley, a singer and actress captured in her prime by Zoffany. Revelling in her popularity, she took a succession of rich and aristocratic lovers, squandered her money and damaged her health with extravagant living. Debts forced her out of London, and she died in Edinburgh an emaciated wreck on the verge of starvation and driven insane by an addiction to laudanum. Ironically, Baddeley lived in fear of her five-year-old son being corrupted by the theatre and begged Sheridan to petition his powerful friends for charity so that she might send him away to school. She was wary, no doubt, of the many sexual predators that lurked both before and behind the curtain.

Joe would also have been familiar with this type, as his father was one of them, although the exploitation of children in the theatre ran far deeper than individual cases of sexual abuse. Implicit in the very idea of eighteenth-century theatre, and central to its mission to entertain, was the display of children for the sexual titillation of older men. This was the real motivation behind Charles Dibdin's attempts to found a company at the Royal Circus in which no performer was older than fourteen. It was not just the Signor whose morals were being investigated by the Surrey magistrates, for, as the *London Chronicle* observed darkly, 'horsemanship . . . was only intended to be served up as a dessert'.

The trend lasted far enough into the nineteenth century to be condemned by Dickens in the character of *Nicholas Nickleby*'s Ninetta Crummles, a fifteen-year-old 'infant phenomenon', fed an 'unlimited allowance of gin-and-water' to keep her looking ten. It was not without reason that Sheridan called his theatre 'the greatest Nursery of Misery and Vice on the Face of the Earth'.

Irrespective of the hazards, children were everywhere – as performers, in the *corps de ballet*, as house servants and assistants to the prompters, stage-hands, call-boys and seamstresses, or being nursed during rehearsals by actresses who refused to let pregnancy slow their careers.* All the Grimaldi children were made to perform, though none of them relished

---

* Dora Jordan had played a fifteen-year-old boy while heavily pregnant, and Madame Mercerot, one of the Signor's apprentices, continued her sword fights until a month before she was due. Both were outdone by Sarah Siddons, who went into labour while performing in *As You Like It*.

it like Joe.* Not only was Joe a natural, but life at the theatre was far preferable to life outside it, and provided him with a ready-made gang of like-minded children as friends. The best of these were Richard Lawrence and Robert Fairbrother, two talented boys who had also been performing since infancy. Richard was the son of a Sadler's Wells tumbler and swordsman, Joseph Lawrence, who was sometimes billed as 'the Great Devil' and sometimes as 'Le Grand Saut du Trampolin'. Richard had initially followed in his father's footsteps but eventually chose music over acrobatics to become a good composer and band leader, a decision that was probably influenced by a near-death experience at Astley's Amphitheatre when a flying chariot he was riding in fell from the fly-tower and plummeted to the stage. Fairbrother, 'friend Bob', as he was known, was another slum child employed for a pittance in supernumerary roles. He was friendly, industrious and quick, and while he would soon outgrow the ranks of extras to become a decent pantomimist, he had keen entrepreneurial instincts that led him first to become a fur wholesaler and then an undertaker, before eventually becoming Sheridan's confidential secretary at Drury Lane.

With so many of them and so little supervision, the children frequently ran wild, even while performances were taking place. 'There was no keeping the little boys in order . . . they made such a terrible noise behind the scenes,' complained Michael Kelly, of a flock of sprites summoned to appear in *Macbeth*. Intended as a whimsical atmospheric interlude, they had burst on to the scene like a riotous mob, breaking the set and scaring the actors, egged on by their mischievous ringleader, a boy called Edmund Carey, who would later become

---

* A possible exception was Mary, the Signor's eldest daughter with Mary Blagden, who had married one of his apprentices, the gangling underdog Lascelles Williamson, whose best turn was the 'Elizabethan egg dance', a sort of blindfold Highland fling in which he bobbed in and out of a circle of eggs without breaking them.

the most famous tragic actor in Britain under the name of Edmund Kean.

But their exuberance was more than outweighed by the hardship they were forced to endure. As an adult, Kean would claim that he had had to wear callipers at the age of four due to the severity of the acrobatic training he'd received at Drury Lane. True or not, child performers were certainly expected to risk illness and injury, working sixteen-hour days in buildings that were cold, dark and leaky, hazardous concatenations of dingy workshops, greasy corners, trapdoors and lethal machinery that gave one observer the impression 'of being in an unfinished house before the floors are laid'. Most of their time was spent in the Stygian gloom of communal dressing rooms heated by one small wood-burning stove, or in the enormous, dripping cellars where they rehearsed among long-forgotten props and fraying scenery.

Under the stern eye of the Signor, the children would start the day lined up facing the wall with their soles pressed flat against the skirting and their heels together to 'set' their feet. The very youngest would then be given lessons in posturing – holding dramatic poses representing historical or classical subjects – while around them the older ones progressed through a series of exercises in balancing, gymnastics, walking on stilts, slack-wire and tightrope walking, singing, dancing, fencing, and performing on musical instruments (Joe, like his father, was a competent violinist).

The Signor was not the only martinet. If anything, the equestrian prodigy Andrew Ducrow's father was even worse. John Ducrow, the 'Flemish Hercules', known for balancing coach wheels on his chin, made his son sit under his chair like a dog while he drank himself senseless, horsewhipped him if he fell or made mistakes while training, and was once so enraged when the boy dislocated a wrist and an ankle that he set fire to their house, forcing Andrew to douse the flames while hobbling around on his crutches. Another time, he beat him for breaking a leg during a performance. Joe, older than Andrew, couldn't bear to see it, and once intervened to stop one of the beatings becoming something far worse. Such random interventions were the only form of appeal the children had. Occasionally a dissenting voice might be heard, such as that of Robert Paulet, a visitor to the Wells, who asked, 'Whence can arise the pleasure of seeing children suspended in the air, or tossed about, at the utmost hazard of their lives, to gratify the avarice of unnatural parents?' To the vast majority of theatregoers, this was the view of a crank minority.

By six years old, Joe was already established as a professional, catching the eye of a critic from the *Gazetteer* at a benefit for Covent Garden's recently arrived Continental dancer Augustin Bithmere, who wrote that 'the infant son of Grimaldi performs in an astonishing manner'. By seven, he confirmed his status through the accumulation of regular injuries, the first acquired at Sadler's Wells playing the Signor's monkey, led by a chain attached to his waist that the Signor would use to swing him around his head 'with the utmost velocity'. One night it broke, hurling Joe into the lap of a gentleman seated way back in the pit. Another time, playing a cat in *Hurly Burly*, the Drury Lane pantomime for Boxing Day 1785, Joe ran onstage in costume only to fall thirty feet through an open trap because someone had forgotten to cut eye-holes in his suit. He was lucky to break only his collarbone, but was unable to perform again until the Sadler's Wells season opened the following Easter. On these occasions, the Signor would mix a soothing embrocation to a recipe he had inherited from the Paris fairs. Made from 'two new-laid eggs, half a pint of verjuice, two ounces each of camphorated oil and spirits of turpentine', it was to be rubbed into the muscles two or three times a day and accompanied by an edifying cocktail of vinegar and gin.

Though the theatre took up almost all of Joe's time in these early years, there was a period between the end of the Sadler's Wells season and the beginning of the Drury Lane pantomime when he was unemployed. During these three- or four-month breaks, the Signor enrolled him in Mr Ford's Academy, a boarding-school in Putney, where he learnt to read and write alongside a number of other theatrical children who included Henry Harris, son of the manager of Covent Garden and Joe's future boss. Joe liked school well enough, though he had no great talent as a scholar, admitting as an adult that he had always been a poor reader who found it especially difficult to learn his lines. The *Monthly Magazine* recalled that, even in his prime, Joe was 'like Bottom the Weaver, "slow of study"', taking five or six weeks to mellow himself into one of his songs. Until he had done so, he used to bring in a large sheet, on which the words were inscribed, and, to use his own phrase, 'ax their leave to sing it to paper'.

Neither did he speak well, particularly conscious of his unusual voice, an Italian–Cockney hybrid described as 'laugh, scream, and speech' all at once. It was ideal for buffoonery, but it made him uncomfortable when called upon to read aloud in class. His struggles with literacy were unsurprising given the patchy nature of his schooling, but there is also a strong possibility when we consider the disproportionate instance of dyslexia among performers in general, and comedians in particular, that his difficulties with reading were more signifi-cant, in turn reinforcing his commitment to humour as a means of masking social embarrassment.

Joe much preferred sketching and drawing to reading and writing, and the quality of his drawings preserved in the Harvard Theatre Collection show him to have been an able draughtsman. He also began to develop his life-long passion for making scale models of scenery, a hobby he'd learnt from Delpini. Possessed of an amazing memory for detail, he would rebuild entire sets in miniature and make improvements to misfiring tricks and unwieldy changes. His collection of models eventually grew so large that he ended up giving most of them away.

Mr Ford's also gave him the opportunity to experience at first hand the most notable privation of any eighteenth-century education – school dinners. Gruesome meals of milk porridge, stewed shins of beef and 'scanty mutton scrags' were served up daily, indigestible treats washed down with each boy's weekly allowance of two and a half gallons of small beer. These horrors made such a lasting impression on Joe that even fifteen years later he was still playing through the miseries of the table, animating his clown with a scouring hunger that caused him to raid butchers' shops in search of a paradisaical pie or the perfect string of sausages with which to stuff his capacious clown pockets.

Thus the pattern of Joe's childhood became fixed around the twin orbits of school and the theatre. When not spending long days backstage and performing at night, he struggled over grammar, played with his brother John and their friends outside Drury Lane or swam in the New River before tracking home, tired, to their house in Little Russell Street and the love and serenity of his mother. It was a demanding life, physically challenging and subject to strict discipline, but full of excitement and the thrill of laughter. All that, however, was about to change.

3

HARLEQUIN'S FROLICS

We ought not therefore be surpriz'd at the seemingly whimsical Precaution of some Persons, who have in their Wills ordered, that they should not be put in their Coffins till at least forty-eight Hours after their apparent Death, and till all the different Methods of Incision, Puncture, and Burning have been tried upon them, in order to acquire a greater Certainty of their Deaths.

Jacques-Bénigne Winslow, *The Uncertainty of the Signs of Death* (1746)

JOE'S FATHER FIRST SHOWED signs of failing health on 13 January 1784, midway through a performance of *Fortunatus*, in which he was appearing as Clown. The exertion of clowning in his early seventies had finally caught up with him, and reports from the theatre claimed that he was 'extremely ill'. Within three weeks, however, he had rallied, his legendary strength allowing him to reprise the role eighteen times in a new pantomime called *Harlequin Junior* before the close of the Drury Lane season and the resumption of duties at Sadler's Wells. When Drury Lane reopened for the 1784–5 season, the Signor was there again, playing Clown in a 'pantomime olio', a compilation of favourite scenes, 'partly new and partly selected from old and approved pantomimes', called *The Caldron*, that ran through the end of one season and the beginning of the next, right up until the début of *Hurly Burly*, the new Christmas show, in which he played Clodpate, one of Clown's many guises.

That Boxing Day was a bad one for both father and son, as the performance in which Joe broke his collarbone also proved to be the Signor's final appearance at Drury Lane. At some stage during the performance he was unable to continue, and the management had to pull the entire production and replace it with an old favourite called *The Romp*, a substitution that the *Morning Chronicle*, even as it noted Grimaldi's absence, found much better than the original fare. The change was good for two nights, but the managers couldn't wait. Eager to unveil their new production with its expensive new scenery and tricks, they replaced the Signor with his son-in-law, Lascelles Williamson. Laid up and sensing a mortal shift, on 25 February he made a will, yet by the summer the whole family, if not the entire theatrical world, must have wondered if the old bastard was ever going to die. July saw him back and in fine form, recording his first ever appearance at the Haymarket in a pantomime produced by Carlo Delpini called *Here, There, and Everywhere*.

The Signor's ubiquity was confirmed the following year when he was featured prominently in a poisonous little volume called *The Children of Thespis*, a survey of London celebrities by the verse satirist Anthony Pasquin. Pasquin was the pseudonym of John Williams, a dissolute and disaffected outsider who was not above using the threat of his pen as a means of coercing painters and performers into buying gifts and dinners for him and his friends, although his portrait of the Signor clearly demonstrates that he received no bribes from that quarter.* It was a toxic little ditty:

---

* Though some found Pasquin raffish and witty, most people thought him highly undesirable, a fact that was spectacularly proven when he tried to sue his rival, William Gifford, for libel. The judge not only threw out Pasquin's case, he publicly congratulated Gifford for defaming him, saying, 'I do most earnestly wish and hope that some method will ere long be fallen upon to prevent all such unprincipled and mercenary wretches from going about unbridled in society to the great annoyance and disquietude of the public.' He was also very smelly. Having once asked his best friend, Lord Barrymore, what he should wear to a masquerade, he was told, 'Go in a clean shirt, Anthony, and no one will know you.'

What monster is this, who alarms the beholders,
With Folly and Infamy perch'd on his shoulders;
Whom hallow'd Religion is lab'ring to save,
Ere Sin and Disease goad the wretch to his grave,
'Tis Grimaldi! Alas, Nature starts at the name;
And trembles with horror, and reddens with shame!

The poem goes on to imagine the Signor's soul called to account in a cod-Miltonic hell filled with pasteboard allegories rearing up to denounce a man so mired in wickedness that angels weep, Justice begs to see him hanged, and Mercy, having heard his confession, involuntarily vomits.

While devoid of literary merit, Pasquin's fantasy of Grimaldi in Hades was exceptionally well timed, as shortly after its publication the Signor paid for his crimes in full, dying on 14 March 1788, in a room off a court in Stangate Street, Lambeth. The poet was happy to take the credit, adding a note to the second edition of *The Children of Thespis* that read, 'the detested caitiff personified in this description, read his portrait, reflected and expired'. The actual cause was dropsy, a swelling of the organs and tissues brought about by frequent compression and inflammation of the joints. Giuseppe Grimaldi had survived Pasquin's squib just as he'd survived decades of dissipation, and if anything in particular could have been said to bring on the condition, it was the handstands and pratfalls that marked his sudden adventures in clowning.

Joe and John must have wondered if he was really gone. It wasn't the first time they had seen their father lying dead, then suddenly springing back to life – there were his food-induced comas, and once, about a year ago, he'd decided to fake his own death. The Signor had been keen to discover if his boys really loved him or simply endured him in the hope of receiving an inheritance, and with the help of Sam the footman, he decided to put their feelings to the test, darkening the drawing-room of Little Russell Street, laying himself out on a table and covering himself with a sheet as Sam went off to break the news to the children. Whatever nauseous unease or perverse exhilaration the Signor felt at mimicking death, it was quickly forgotten the moment Joe and John came in to view the corpse. Joe, who immediately sensed that something was up, let out a long, theatrical wail. John, who saw nothing but 'relief from flogging and books', couldn't hide his delight, and started singing and skipping around the table, clapping his hands. 'You cruel boy,' Joe reprimanded him, loudly and tearfully, 'hadn't you any love for your dear father?'

'Don't be such a fool,' said John. 'Now we can have his cuckoo-clock all to ourselves.' The *Memoirs* record:

> This was more than the deceased could bear. He jumped from the bier, threw off the sheet and attacked his younger son most unmercifully; while Joe, not knowing what might be his own fate, ran and hid himself in the coal cellar, where he was discovered fast asleep some four hours afterwards by Black Sam, who carried him to his father, who had been anxiously in search of him, and by whom he was received with every demonstration of affection, as the son who truly and sincerely loved him.

Another version of this story was passed down by the reviewer Thomas Goodwin, whose father had been the music librarian at Covent Garden. In this account, the Signor had gone missing 'and the report quickly became current that he had fallen from the cliff at Margate'. Three or four days later, he appeared at home, but instead of finding his family in deep mourning, he found them perfectly happy and stoically resigned to their loss. Goodwin's version also concludes with a rampage.

This time there would be no vengeful resurrection. Giuseppe Grimaldi was quite dead, having prepared for his long-anticipated foray into the afterlife with a distinctive combination of meticulousness and malice. His will was particularly divisive, despite its desire to 'avoid all disputes' by forming the estate from the proceeds of a public auction of everything he possessed, including the collection of all outstanding debts for benefit tickets and monies owed 'for the teeth'. This last point supports the insistence of the *Gentleman's Magazine* that the Signor maintained his dentistry throughout his career and not just as a complement to his provincial tours. 'His temper led him into a variety of disagreements with managers,' it claimed, 'on which occasions he returned to tooth-drawing as a matter of course,' and with some success: 'As his manners were remarkable, and his dialect ridiculous, many visited him, rather to notice his peculiarities than test his skill.' Another obituary noted that his skills included 'Dancing Master, Dentist, Conjurer, Clown at Sadler's Wells, and Practitioner in Physic', this final talent presumably acknowledging the modest celebrity of his embrocation, which was in time bottled and marketed by a Dr Chamberlain, who had a practice near the Wells.

The sum of these various sales and collections was to be 'put out to the best advantage in behalf' of Mary and the boys, Joe, John and the mysterious third son, addressed with particular affection as 'my dearly beloved William'. There was no reference whatsoever to Mary Blagden's daughter Isabella, or to Anne Perry's Henrietta Marguerite, or to Joe's mother, Rebecca Brooker. Two other daughters by Mary Blagden, Margaret (now Margaret Farmer) and Catherine, were bequeathed merely 'one shilling each for their bad behaviour'. What they had done to deserve such a rebuke is uncertain, although Pasquin had already intimated a family rift: 'In their hate of his principles, all are agreeing,/And the *fruit* of his *loins* curse the *cause* of their being.' Most probably, they had sided with their mother. (Mary Blagden herself had died when Joe was almost two. She never received her divorce, and was buried as Mrs Grimaldi.)

The instructions for the Signor's burial did not suffer from any kind of oversight; in fact, they omitted nothing. First, he made sure his family followed the advice of *The Uncertainty of the Signs of Death*, which counsels that bodies should be sent to their graves only after forty-eight hours, having had candles applied to their feet and needles inserted under their nails to guarantee death. In the end they waited seven days, just to make sure. After that, the Signor desired that Mary, as eldest daughter and most trusted child, 'see me put into my coffin and the day that I am buried to sever my head from my body'. Mary had not the slightest inclination to decapitate her own father's corpse, though the terms of the will were clear and even provided her with an additional five pounds to compensate her for her 'mourning'.

A surgeon was summoned and, turning her head away, she placed a finger gingerly on the cleaver's handle as he bore down, making heavy going of the bone and gristle. Her father's wishes fulfilled, Mary was to retrace the steps of one of his graveyard walks by following the body to Northampton Chapel, Exmouth Street, a stone's throw from the Wells, and, remaining vigilant against any miracle resurrection, complete the interment by placing 'a headstone . . . at the top of my grave, [at] the place where I wish to lay . . . as I have often showed it to her'. In fact, she was not able to have him placed exactly where he had wished, at the Pantheon between the windows, probably due to the express stipulation that the cost of the entire funeral, including his headstone, should not exceed ten pounds. Two months later, a fitting public memorial was published in the form of a souvenir print sold by J. Barry of Oxford Street. Entitled 'Grim-All-Day-at-Breakfast', it showed an oleaginous gargoyle toasting a crumpet and cackling over a bosomy dancer a fraction of his age.

According to the *Memoirs*, the Signor's estate came to fifteen thousand pounds, an enormous sum, given that a half-share in a patent theatre, the sole province of high financiers, cost around thirty thousand. Such riches seem unlikely in light of the Signor's many sudden and violent demands for money, combined with the fact that when he died his salary was only 16s. 8d. a day. In addition, he was frequently changing address, moving from one rented accommodation to another, more like a man trying to avoid his creditors than one who was comfortably off. The point is moot, as whatever the Signor was actually worth, Joe saw none of it, due to the actions of the executors – Tom King, a one-time manager of the Wells, who was now up to his neck in Sheridan's mess, running the day-to-day business at Drury Lane, and Joseph Hopwood, a lace manufacturer who lived in Long Acre behind Covent Garden. King thought the world of Joe but his present responsibilities vexed him beyond all reason and he was far too harried to pay any attention to the matter of the Signor's will. The administration of the whole thus fell on Hopwood, who was facing financial difficulties of his own and used the money to float his business. He quickly went bankrupt and fled the country, leaving Joe with nothing but 'a broadsword and a guinea'.

~

With no father to support them and their inheritance gone, the young Grimaldis were suddenly vulnerable, and their straitened circumstances immediately forced them to move into cheaper accommodation as the lodgers of Mr and Mrs Bailey, furriers, who lived in Great Wild Street at the north end of Drury Lane. As an act of charity, Mr Ford, the schoolmaster, offered to legally adopt Joe and let him continue his education. It was a generous thought, but Rebecca had to decline as her nine-year-old son was suddenly the family's principal breadwinner. Sheridan, himself a father and partial to random acts of charity, altruistically raised Joe's salary to twenty-five shillings a week when he heard of the Signor's death, and also allowed Rebecca to take a dancing engagement at Sadler's Wells, thus effectively doubling her salary in the four months the seasons overlapped.

But for Joe it was a very different story at the Wells. His summer salary was abruptly cut from fifteen shillings a week to three, and his duties expanded to include helping the carpenters and scenemen, and other menial work. Rebecca complained, but it was that or nothing: what use was the son of a dead clown when he didn't even have his own act, let alone the talents of the current juvenile darling of the stage, the three-year-old singer Allan Ramsay, 'the fairy of the Wells'? It was a predicament best summarised in a disheartening press notice that confirmed Joe's obscurity even as it fawned over Ramsay, saying, 'We remember two or three years back a young son of Grimaldi's who frequently entertained us in the likeness of a Monkey; but the fairy of the Wells can do more, and gives us a Song and Recitative in such correctness and execution, that . . . every other specimen of infantile acting is left far behind.'

As poverty pressed in, Joe's younger brother decided to leave home. John had always hated the theatre, and though he could be prevailed upon to earn a shilling whenever extras were required, he despised the drills that seemed always to end in a beating. John saw the Signor's death as a longed-for manumission and a chance to fulfil his dream of going to sea. Richard Wroughton, a comedian who had taken active charge of Sadler's Wells in 1782, had witnessed John's dissatisfaction and kindly used his contacts (Sadler's Wells being a perennial favourite with sailors) to secure him a place on an East Indiaman departing for the Cape. When Rebecca pointed out that they couldn't pay for all the kit and provisions necessary for John to take up such a position, Wroughton gave him fifty pounds, saying only, 'Mind, John, when you come to be a captain you

must pay it me back again.' Preparations were quickly concluded, but as John made his farewells and found his berth, he
was dismayed to learn that his ship wouldn't be sailing for
another ten days. Impatient to get going and to put as many
miles between himself and the memory of the Signor as possible, he noticed that the frigate alongside them was preparing to
drop down to Gravesend with the next tide. Abandoning the kit
that had been bought with Wroughton's money, as well as most
of the clothes off his back, he stripped down to his breeches
and swam to the King's vessel where he entered himself
as a cabin boy under a false name. It was an ungrateful and
impetuous thing to do, but John was only eight. They wouldn't
hear from him again for nearly sixteen years.

$\sim$

Though the Signor's death had enabled John to imagine a
future, it left his brother at a loss. Even for all his neglect and
ire, Joe still considered the Signor a 'severe but excellent parent'. He had been his patron and tutor, the mentor who had
introduced him to the thing he loved most. What was more, he
was a concrete presence on which he could fix his thoughts, the
living embodiment of life's threats and promises, which, when
taken away, had left him susceptible to formless fears and
loathed introspection.

Though still very young, Joe already knew what it was to
feel uncomfortable in his own skin. The easy confidence he
had shown in the green room came less naturally now, and he
became shyer offstage, with a tendency to melancholy. This
was one inheritance that couldn't be taken from him, the
spectre of depression that would only strengthen as he
matured. Fortunately, he was resourceful enough to try to
fend it off, and in the weeks and months that followed the
Signor's death, he busied himself, walking to his grandfather's

butcher's shop in Parker's Lane to cut carcasses with his cousins, or investing time in his nascent hobbies, establishing a coop of racing pigeons and beginning a collection of butterflies that would eventually grow to more than four thousand specimens. The quiet respite of these solitary activities served as its own embrocation in this season of uncertainty, and he spent long, calming hours stalking his prizes through the cornfields of Dartford and Camberwell, or searching the sky for the sight of a familiar wing.

It was a necessary defence. Europe was on the verge of a war that would continue unabated until he was almost forty years old, and even the comfortingly institutional surroundings of the theatre were becoming increasingly unstable. Just a few months after the Signor's death, George III suffered a bilious attack that would culminate in his first full episode of insanity. As it seemed increasingly likely that the King would be declared unfit to rule, the Whigs began an aggressive campaign to have the Prince of Wales declared Regent with a full range of monarchical powers. Realising that this would signal the death of Tory influence, the Prime Minister, William Pitt, sought to limit the terms of a Regency as strictly as possible, thus opening up a partisan battle that plunged the country into agonies of strife. With a scarcity of accurate information in the capital, London was awash with rumours and disgust at the apparent delight the Prince of Wales was taking in his father's illness.

These were problems that Joe could have easily avoided had not Sheridan insisted on bringing the trouble back to the theatre. Deploying his legendary opportunism, he had presented himself as the official liaison between the Whigs and the Prince of Wales, assuming the mantle of master-negotiator and gatekeeper to the Prince's wishes, thus attaining what he'd always wanted: everyone's attention, and a monopoly on intrigue. From that moment on, he proceeded to behave as if he were the sole person capable of delivering the nation, which naturally produced more rancour within the party than it spared. Even his dear friend and ally the Duchess of Devonshire couldn't help, remarking that he played 'a sly game' and 'cannot resist the pleasure of acting alone', while the independent MP Sir Gilbert Eliot thought him an incorrigible old ham, writing to his wife that 'He employs a great deal of art, with a great deal of pain to gratify, not the proper passion in such affairs, but vanity; and he deals in the most intricate plotting and under plotting, like a Spanish play.'

As Sheridan abandoned Drury Lane in favour of hectic politicking and the avid pursuit of his own importance, November passed into a bitterly cold winter. In a frost-bitten foreshadowing of the King's final illness twenty years later, the Thames froze from Putney to Rotherhithe, a bear was baited on the ice at Wapping, and booths were set up offering roast ox and Punch and Judy shows. Joe made his first appearance since the death of his father, playing a demon in Drury Lane's *Harlequin Junior*, but it was not a happy return to the stage. Sheridan, 'uncertainty personified', as the actress Sarah Siddons had dubbed him, allowed his negligence to run on unchecked, terminally shattering the patience of his long-suffering acting manager, Tom King. Though all too familiar with his proprietor's prolonged absences, King could no longer abide his inability to delegate the slightest responsibility and, unable to persevere, he resigned on the eve of the new season. He explained his decision in a long letter to the press, composed from the solitude of a country retreat, in which he complained of the 'something undefined, if not undefinable' nature of his status, along with his powerlessness 'to approve or reject any dramatick work; the liberty of engaging, encouraging, or discharging any one performer; nor sufficient authority to command the cleaning a coat, or adding, by way of decoration, a yard of copper lace, both of which, it must be allowed, were often much wanted'.

King's sudden departure threw the company into disarray, and a successor was not named until two weeks into the new season when Sheridan managed to pay attention long enough to cajole his principal actor, John Philip Kemble, into overseeing daily affairs. Though generally well-organised and utterly devoted to the theatre, Kemble was pathologically unsuited to management, which favoured penny-pinching book-keepers and populists like Garrick, who had been known to say, 'I dare not innovate for my life.' Kemble, by contrast, thought of himself first and foremost as an artist and scholar. He studied a text 'with metaphysical exactness', rarely embarking upon a part unless he had first legitimised it with historical research. 'To be critically exact', wrote James Boaden, 'was the greatest ambition of his life.' Though he had been brought up in his father's provincial troupe of travelling players, showmanship and hucksterism remained alien to him, and it pained him greatly to have to deal with petulant actresses and irascible alcoholics and their unreasonable requests. To compound matters, the harsh winter, the King's madness and the unrest that preceded his appointment conspired to make it a particularly dreadful time to take it up: attendances were down and the company at large had taken the managerial uncertainty as an excuse for widespread truancy. Worst of all, they were singing 'God Save the King' up to eight times a night. At least the King's longed-for recovery in February 1789 put paid to that, but even the heartfelt rejoicing and the sight of Sarah Siddons dressed as Britannia was not enough to defuse the feelings of disquiet that had wormed their way into the marrow of Drury Lane. Revolution had exploded in France, polarising British opinion. At the theatre, that giant screen of the cultural imagination, audiences became sensitive to the slightest political insinuation. Paranoia was all the rage, reflected in the dark anachronisms of Gothic drama and its recurring themes of haunting, tyranny and surveillance.

There was little time for pantomime. Like Garrick before him, Kemble conceded its place in the repertoire while considering it insufferably low, permissible only so long as it conformed to his written decree that it should always be 'very *short*, very LAUGHABLE, and VERY CHEAP'. In 1789, the high point of Joe's season was playing Young Marcius opposite Kemble's Coriolanus: 'I'll run away till I am bigger,' he said prophetically, 'but then I'll fight.' Things were little better at Sadler's Wells, where he emerged from the workshops only to be lost again in processions and prison scenes inspired by the vogue for all things Bastille. The bloody insurrection across the English Channel meant only one thing to managers, 'the *Bastille* must bring money', and the minor theatres fell over themselves to be the first to offer it.

Although he was before an audience only rarely, Joe was nonetheless subject to a gruelling schedule that was especially tough when the seasons overlapped. A typical day began with the walk from the rooms he shared with his mother and the Baileys in Great Wild Street a mile and a half out to Islington to attend rehearsals from ten in the morning until two in the afternoon. As eighteenth-century crowd scenes were notoriously chaotic and unrehearsed, most of his time was spent in the carpenter's shop before walking back to Great Wild Street for a meal and a short rest, then returning to Sadler's Wells in time for the curtain at six. The remainder of the evening was spent charging in and out of the theatre's steamy fug in a variety of mêlées and processions that required him to change costume up to twenty times a night, while moving scenery in between.

When the curtain finally fell at eleven, Joe left immediately for Drury Lane to appear in the afterpiece. If the show at Sadler's Wells ever ran over, as it frequently did, especially on those nights when new pieces were introduced to the bill, he had no choice but to run. Even after a long day and night of work he somehow found the energy to cover the ground – across the fields to St John's Street, through Clerkenwell, scattering the sheep at Gray's Inn and Lincoln's Inn Fields, before turning at last down Drury Lane – in less than eight minutes.

Walking home on the night of 17 June, he would have seen the sky above Haymarket glow orange as flames engulfed the King's Theatre. It was initially thought to be an accident – unsteady footlights and untrimmed candles were constant hazards – but two years later, the deathbed confession of Pietro Carnevale, the acting deputy manager, revealed arson: he had preferred to raze the opera house than allow a rival to succeed him.

~

For a child born into pantomimical aristocracy, Joe's rise in the profession had almost completely stalled, his role as heir to his father's celebrity seemingly forgotten. But the Signor's death had not just robbed him of a teacher and patron, it also threatened London with a clown vacuum. Delpini had fallen out of favour. Sacked from Covent Garden, rejected by Drury Lane, and asked not to come back to the Haymarket after causing an affront, 'he thought that when Grimaldi died he would inherit that clown's fame,' sneered *The Times*, 'but forgot that it was first requisite to possess his abilities'. Drury Lane had been making do with the services of the auxiliary actor, Tom Hollingsworth. Hollingsworth, described as 'remarkable short in person, but rather lusty', played upwards of thirty different parts a season, in a long career he'd had the misfortune to see summed up in print with the words, 'of acting I have seen enough . . . but none as bad as thine, I vow to God!' Davison, one of the Signor's apprentices who performed at the Royal Circus and Royalty Theatre, struggled through unfavourable comparisons with his master, 'that excellent performer . . .

which admitted no competition', while, judging by the absence of reviews, the Signor's son-in-law, Lascelles Williamson, had also failed to impress.*

Covent Garden, meanwhile, oscillated between two unsuitable candidates: William Stevens, obscure save for a brief glimmer of popularity after ousting Delpini; and John Follet the younger, who had inherited the role from his father, a much better clown, and notable both for being the man who set George III laughing 'almost to suffocation' by swallowing whole carrots, and the one who had shot Delpini in the eye.

The situation would have been dire, were it not for the meteoric rise of a six-foot Frenchman named Jean-Baptiste Dubois, the 'Goliath of clowns', which coincided precisely with the passing of the Signor. The sole existing portrait of the Frenchman shows him to be primped and powdered, a porcelain-featured libertine in the style of Moreau's aristocratic lovers, although the image could not be more deceptive. Dubois was one of the most courageous, athletic and physically gifted performers of the eighteenth century, first arriving in Britain sometime in the 1770s as a trick-riding clown both at Astley's Amphitheatre and Jones's Equestrian Amphitheatre, Whitechapel. Even in his earliest performances, he demonstrated the enormous versatility that would make him a star, vaulting over seven horses and their riders ('which is one more than any person ever vaulted over in England'), acting in mimes, dancing a hornpipe, and descending from horseback to imitate birdsong 'in a manner far superior to anything of the kind ever performed in this kingdom'. This particular skill was known as 'julking' and was often performed to full orchestral accompaniment.

---

* It might be that Williamson had forgone clowning in favour of a double-act he had been working up with Joe's half-sister Mary, which they eventually developed into a family concern with the arrival of a baby. The infant's first appearance was the mirror of Joe's, in a musical extravaganza at Astley's Amphitheatre entitled *The Caledonian Lover's Village Festival*.

When Jones's closed down in 1787, Dubois moved seamlessly into non-equestrian theatre at the Wells, proving both his dexterity and his versatility as a rope-dancer, tumbler, trampoline artist, strong man and singer, listed in *Doane's Musical Directory* as a tenor who could also play a variety of musical instruments and was skilled enough at archery to play William Tell, shooting apples from children's heads. He clowned in pantomimes, performed 'macaronis' – medley entertainments of jokes and songs – and was a master of chironomia, the art of mime and gesture. Inevitably, he came to the attention of Drury Lane, who not only hired him as Clown to replace the much-missed Signor but, having uncovered his considerable talent for acting, used him as Scaramouch in Carlo Delpini's popular afterpiece, *Don Juan; or, the Libertine Destroyed*, and fitted him with straight roles in *Richard Cœur de Lion*, *The Siege of Belgrade* and even Sheridan's *The Critic*.

Dubois's appeal stemmed from the disconcerting energy he exuded whenever he walked on stage. According to James Peller Malcolm, an antiquary who bought a season ticket to the Wells every year and attended every performance sitting in the same seat, he had a natural affinity with the sinister that made him particularly suited to traitors, murderers, savages and any 'dark, malicious and ambitious part'. 'The transitions in his countenance,' wrote Malcolm, 'from smiles to threats, from approbation to abhorrence, are masterly performances. I have seen him, when (pursued by a person whom he had injured, and whose parent he had murdered) disguised as a ghost, betray such dreadful emotions of terror, horror, guilt, confusion and revenge, that I could almost suppose the fiction a reality.'

Dubois imbued everything he did with this same unnerving strangeness, an atavistic monstrosity he covered with only the thinnest veneer of civility. For this reason his signature role was the Wild Man in *Valentine and Orson*, a mimed romance based on a medieval Flemish legend of twin brothers separated at birth. As the feral brother raised by a bear, Dubois mixed 'the tricks and sagacity of the monkey with the gleams of matured reason' to deliver a performance so forceful that Malcolm declared it 'a thorough insight into human nature, debased'. He brought the same intensity to his depictions of exotic enemies, Arab and African bogeymen that pandered to imperial fantasies of Oriental barbarity. Malcolm records his performance in 'a recent character of a Moor' where 'his motions are no longer European, they are those of the savage: grimaces, glaring search for the most vulnerable part of his antagonist's body, and endeavours to fix a firm footing, to dart like a tiger of his prey, characterise every muscle'. Versatility, however, remained the key to the success of this 'true son of Proteus' as, after he had terrorised his audience with baleful histrionics, a quick change saw him back on for a 'most wonderful and unexpected performance on the Cymbals'.

Success did not change Dubois, who remained shrewd and entrepreneurial, and in many ways the archetypal *forain*. There was more than a hint of the gangster in the way he presided over his court at the Sir Hugh Myddleton, the pub across the way from Sadler's Wells that acted as a clubhouse and labour exchange for performers and scenemen, cashed promissory notes and loaned advances. He and his associates had their fingers in more than a few pies: even when he was taken on by Drury Lane, he managed to persuade them to pay him an additional six guineas a week to oversee the theatre's stables, where he bought and sold horses for himself as well as the stage, and also appeared to have traded in wood.

But Dubois didn't merely play the man of action, he actively engaged in real-life heroics, once saving the entire Astley's company from drowning after a storm blew up on the voyage back from Dublin. Astley had hired the cheapest ship available, a packet incongruously named *Venus* that had a clutch of emaciated paupers and two wanted Irish rebels in its hold, holes in the sails, compasses that gave different readings, and only two lifeboats, one bottomless, the other with a broken side. The voyage was supposed to take seven hours but took forty-eight, and when the weather turned nasty and the ship began to flounder, the scared and beleaguered captain was forced to admit that he'd never sailed across the Irish Sea and had no idea what he was doing. Relieved by Dubois and a retired navy man named Fitzgerald, they managed to keep *Venus* afloat, and steer her safely back to Holyhead.

Joe did not like Dubois. Not only had his unexpected demotion left him in the Frenchman's shadow, he was also in his line of fire: it was Joe's head he used to practise shooting apples for his role in *William Tell*. Like the Signor, Dubois kept a number of pupils and, as an anonymous manuscript reveals, after his father's death, Joe learnt 'all his pantomimical amusements under Dubois'. This, however, was a claim that Joe would vehemently deny his entire life. He resented the arrogant ruffian and the feeling was mutual. Dubois saw Joe as a relic, an annoying little boy who needed to submit to this brave new age regardless of a surname that conferred status in the pantomime world. Besides, he already had a favourite apprentice in Frank Hartland, the son of an Islington hairdresser, and would shortly introduce his own son, Charles, into the profession. Such animosity made for a bad-tempered first performance together, as Joe and 'dearly beloved' William watched Dubois climb into their father's shoes at Drury Lane, since he had accepted the invitation to play the part of Clown in *Harlequin's Frolics; or, the Power of Witchcraft* on 7 February 1789.

A hint of competition can perhaps be detected in the reviews, which, while praising individual performances, declared the piece 'stale and flat': 'The pantomimic trash brought forward under the title of HARLEQUIN'S FROLICS,' said one, 'not even the matchless grimace and activity of DUBOIS, the new Clown from Sadler's Wells, could save from indignation [although] the tricks of the MONKEY, though stolen from HARLEQUIN'S CHAPLET were admirably played off by that little Marmozet Grimaldi.'

~

For all the ill feeling that existed between Joe and Dubois, the end of the 1791 season saw them working in closer proximity than ever before. Sheridan had taken a long-overdue decision to rebuild Drury Lane. Its company had outgrown the faded auditorium and subterranean world of peeling dressing rooms and reeking cellars more than a decade before, but renovation had proved a constant headache due to the theatre's location in an oblong stableyard in the middle of a dense block of properties that were owned by multiple lessees. Expansion had been chaotic and irregular, resulting in a hotchpotch of accommodations that were connected to the main building by boxy extensions, sloping staircases and mazy passageways, and subject to a patchwork of tenancy agreements that caused ludicrous problems of jurisdiction – more than once the company were evicted from their scene room for failure to pay the rent. Calls for a third patent theatre to meet audience demand had been steadily growing, and the double threat of competition and lost revenues forced Sheridan's hand. Borrowing heavily, he persuaded the Duke of Bedford to buy up all the necessary plots and sell him the leases, then engaged the Prince of Wales's pet architect, Henry Holland, to remodel the entire building.

Drury Lane shut down for three years, and the displacement of its company, first to the soulless and grandiose King's Theatre and then to the Haymarket, served to draw Joe much closer into the community at Sadler's Wells, suddenly the oldest continuously running theatre in London. The Wells retained its comforting smell of lamp oil, and though Joe's lot had hardly improved, a number of factors lent it an appeal that couldn't be replicated under Kemble. The first was the quality of its clowning. Regardless of personal animosity, Dubois was a superlative clown, and Joe couldn't help but absorb his lessons night after night.

There was another significant addition in the engagement of Pietro Bologna, an old-school *forain* described as 'a handsome Italian, who swung on the slack wire with amazing grace and ease, and was the most whimsical and laugh-compelling clown we ever saw'. He arrived at the Wells with his wife and three children, Jack, Louis and Barbara, all of whom performed. Like the Grimaldis, the 'Blognas', as they were known in London, had ties to Genoa but were more properly citizens of the clown diaspora, nomads who had perfected their acts at the Paris fairs before finding their way across the Channel. Unlike the Grimaldis, they were known as a happy, friendly, loving family, 'well behaved honest people', in the words of the respected manager of the York circuit, Tate Wilkinson.

Joe, who craved stable family life, was immediately drawn to them, becoming especially close to Jack, then studying his father's speciality of balancing on a slack-rope while playing a flute through each nostril and accompanying himself on a drum. Jack was three years older than Joe and immediately enrolled him as his sidekick, treating him with rambunctious brotherly affection. They had much in common, for not only was Jack an excellent acrobat with a gift for 'trick and expression', he was fascinated by models and mechanics. In the late eighteenth century, with the line between scientific demonstration and popular entertainment indistinct, Jack and Joe found much to engage their imaginations in London's many attractions. The most famous of these was the brainchild of Drury Lane's former scenic artist Philippe de Loutherbourg, a series of animated dioramas grandly titled the 'Eidophusikon'. Visitors to a small, but splendidly appointed private theatre in de Loutherbourg's house in Lisle Street, off Leicester Square, were treated to a sequence of marvellous moving scenes, rendered in intricate detail and three dimensions that included the sun setting over Dover, the cataract at Niagara Falls, and 'Satan arraying his Troops' on the shores of a lake of fire.

As it is highly unlikely that two grubby theatre waifs would have been allowed into de Loutherbourg's exclusive salon, they would naturally have gravitated to the west end of the Strand, the noisy, traffic-jammed junction between Westminster and the City that was one of London's busiest shopping areas. Here, spread throughout the pokey arterial back-streets, an abundance of shows and curiosities was to be found, shows like Haddock's Androides, ingenious automata that could draw pictures and answer questions, or Madame Tussaud's 'Cabinet of Wax', exhibiting the likenesses of the leading figures of the French Revolution. This was also the site of Cox's Museum, the rare and ornately decorated home of richly bejewelled clockwork figurines that moved and played music to visitors who almost universally declared the experience to be acutely unnerving.

Nearby, at Exeter Change, Jack and Joe could have enjoyed all manner of 'rational' entertainments – hydraulic demonstrations of the power of water, lectures on ballooning, and a 'philosophical fireworks display' – or entered Pidcock's Royal Menagerie, a scanty collection of beasts, where for an extra penny you could watch the keeper put his head in the lion's mouth. Less expensive entertainments included marvelling at the working guillotine outside Fore's print shop or, in the summer, lying on the grass at Bermondsey Spa and watching the fireworks explode above a view of the Tower, and walking to the fairs that sprang up each year in the suburbs of Peckham, Greenwich and Tothill. Bartholomew Fair, the British equivalent of the Parisian fairs that had given succour to the original Grimaldis, was the biggest and brashest of them all, and an event to which Joe looked forward every year of his life. Taking in the freak shows and down-at-heel tumblers, the boys would chatter incessantly, dreaming up their own implausible devices, and imagining triumphant routines full of exciting machines and mechanical wonders.

All Joe needed now were opportunities to develop his skills on stage, and his chances greatly improved with the arrival of a new proprietor in Richard Hughes. In partnership with his close friend William Siddons, the disloyal and pain-fully envious husband of the famous Sarah, Hughes had bought a half-share in Sadler's Wells after a long and lucrative period of management in the provinces. Both men had been strolling players under John Philip Kemble's father, Roger, eking out a living around Worcester and the Welsh borders in a company that was run, according to the playwright Thomas Holcroft, like 'a small kingdom, of which the manager is the monarch'. Though maintaining the operation on a shoestring, Kemble senior refused to relent on artistic standards, which he imbued in his children, demanding professional excellence from his troupe in addition to thrift and obedience. Kemble's authori-tarianism was an anathema to many of the free spirits and lost souls who made up a travelling theatre, among them Siddons, who was banished for romancing Kemble's fourteen-year-old daughter, although for Hughes, the patriarch's Spartan commitment was an inspiration.

Hughes had joined the company after running away from an apprenticeship to a Birmingham button-painter, and though unremarkable in his dual roles as scene painter and utility actor (his acting, it was said, was 'not of the first rate'), he absorbed Kemble's managerial lessons well, implementing them when he was offered his first managerial position at Plymouth's Dock Theatre. As theatres went, it was not good, described as 'one of the most inconvenient in England', but he still managed to squeeze a profit from it by enticing trade from the nearby barracks and shipyards and economising wherever he could. Success led to the acquisition of a number of provincial playhouses, in Exeter, Weymouth, Truro, Penzance, Dartmouth and on the island of Guernsey. London, and Sadler's Wells, was to be the jewel in his crown.

As an administrator, Hughes was the polar opposite of Richard Brinsley Sheridan. Both were full of energy and innovation, but there the comparison stopped. Hughes was considered 'industrious to an extreme', skilfully balancing the affairs of his various companies while continuing to perform small parts and painting the scenery himself to keep down costs. Yet his commitment to upholding the hierarchy he'd worked so hard to ascend didn't immediately win him friends in Islington. His insistence on status was reflected in his first important decision as proprietor, a move to consolidate the Wells's gradual gentrification by separating the private boxes even further from the regular stalls in the hope of enticing aristocrats previously deterred by the abhorrently democratic seating. To this, he added an emphasis on decorum, insisting that the ladies be properly dressed at all times and on the 'punctuality, propriety and attentiveness' of his company, something the Bohemian London cast felt smacked of prudery and provincialism. He had an abrupt, disciplinarian manner that to some was refreshingly 'prompt, explicit, and decisive', though others thought he demanded 'the most abject servility' and maintained a mania for efficiency that kept him constantly on the lookout for signs of waste that would result in an angry scolding whenever they were found.

This 'Master Manager' and 'perfect Man of Business' devoted himself so tirelessly to his theatre that by the summer of 1792 he was introducing a new novelty every week. High turnover did not necessarily signal low quality in this age of industry and empire, that saw profusion as virtue and an endless stream of variety as evidence of its supremacy. Having such a well-stocked theatrical bazaar was the central pillar of Hughes's campaign to improve the overall standing of the Wells by attracting members of the nobility. Not only would their presence confirm it as the most respectable of the minor theatres, but it would act as a further induce-ment to his core audience, ordinary Londoners who liked their pleasures vindicated by the presence of their betters. Moreover, it was working. 'To those who have not visited Sadler's Wells in the last five or six years,' wrote *The Times* in 1793, 'the concourse of Nobility and Fashion now to be found at that elegant little Theatre must prove a matter of astonishment,' a fact that was confirmed by the number of sumptuous carriages that stood outside on midsummer nights, 'a train of coronets . . . altogether as familiar to the eye in the Wells Yard as at St. James's Square'.

While the name Grimaldi was still infrequently on the bills, Hughes thought Joe a 'clever lad' and was happy to put him back before the crowd on a more regular footing. With his dark curly hair and Mediterranean skin, Hughes decided he might best be deployed as a moustachioed villain, and saw to it that he received instruction from the Wells's resident swordsmen, Messieurs Durenci and Bois-Maison, master men-of-arms who tutored him in a full armoury of fearsome weapons. Some nasty cuts and fairly decent roles followed – as an evil Sans Culottes in *The Sans Culottes and the Grand Culottes*, as Hatred in *Pandora's Box* and Jacky Suds in *Mars's Holiday; or, a Trip to the Camp* – all of which was enough to bring sufficient recognition in the company to merit a part-share in a benefit night, an evening that would earn him his very first grown-up review, an encouraging paragraph that somewhat deflated Hughes's hopes of casting him in action roles: 'The comic abilities of this youth are very great,' it read. 'We wish him his deserved success.'

~

When Drury Lane finally reopened in March 1794, it was the largest theatre in Europe, with a seating capacity of almost four thousand that brought to an end the mad rush and dangerous overcrowding that had often required the doors of the old auditorium to be screwed shut to prevent patrons spilling out into the halls. That London's theatres were desperately in need of modernisation had been proved just one month before when fifteen people had been crushed to death at the foot of a stairwell at the Haymarket. The enlarged auditorium guaranteed a seat, but it also meant an end to the anticipation and intimacy that James Boswell had enjoyed on those nights when he struggled to find a place a full two and a half hours before the curtain rose. It also meant that the actors were dwarfed. 'The nice discrimination of the actor's face, and of the actor's feeling, are now lost in the vast void of the new theatre,' wrote Lord Torrington, while Mrs Siddons warned William Dowton, an actor débuting that season, 'You are come to act in a wilderness of a place.'

Henry Holland's building not only made an impact on acting styles, it also influenced the repertoire by demanding spectacles of an entirely different register. Kemble obliged with the first hit of the new house, an anglicised French romance called *Lodoiska*, that told the story of two imprisoned lovers (played by Michael Kelly and his real-life mistress, Maria Crouch), and their rescue from Lovinski Castle by an accommodating horde of Tartars.

The scenario was entirely secondary to the effects, especially those of the third act, an extravaganza of fire and combat intended to be literally explosive. The spectacle began with the Tartars storming the castle to the accompaniment of 'shouts, drums, trumpets, and cannons', after which real flames rose at the back of the stage, followed by a series of deafening booms as 'the battlements and towers fall in the midst of loud explosions'. Behind the scenes, an army of carpenters fanned braziers with enormous bellows to produce flames eighteen feet high, while a heavy reflective backdrop engulfed the stage in an intense red glow. As extras scurried through the mêlée throwing handfuls of saltpetre into the flames, Mrs Crouch appeared, trapped in the highest tower. With the battle raging below and the orchestra shrieking away at full volume, Kelly dashed to her rescue, sprinting across a bridge high above the stage to save his lover just as a carpenter knocked out the supports and both bridge and tower collapsed in a blaze.

It was a triumph of choreography that called for perfect timing both on stage and off. Even the draughts in the corridors had to be carefully managed lest they cause Mrs Crouch to be consumed by flames, as they had threatened to do one night in the opening week. Kelly had noticed the danger and ran to her, but the carpenter knocked the bridge down too soon and he fell to the stage just as her tower began to collapse. Hitting the ground only seconds before she did, he somehow managed to recover himself and catch her in his arms, carrying her out of the smoke to the front of the stage, where they received a standing ovation. The audience, oblivious to the danger, was in raptures, and from that moment on, Kelly and Crouch were obliged to repeat the impromptu stunt nightly.

Bodies were needed to feed this grandiosity and the company was subsequently enlarged. Joe was now constantly on stage, albeit in crowds and country dances, or as a page or red-cheeked stable-boy in polite comedies like *The Belle's Stratagem*. By 1796, at the age of seventeen, he at last graduated from the juvenile ranks and became an adult member of both companies, but he was still earning less than he had been when the Signor died. It was time to reinvent himself.

4

THE FLYING WORLD

While the hour of pleasure flies,
Unimprov'd ne'er let it pass,
In our Masque a Moral lies,
Truth exposes here her glass;
Like the Bee of its honey the blossoms beguile,
And our efforts reward in return for a smile,
Those efforts still destin'd your Joys to maintain,
By your sanction thus cherish'd, new vigor shall gain.

Charles Isaac Mungo Dibdin Junior,
Peter Wilkins; or, Harlequin in the Flying World (1800)

JOE GRIMALDI GREW IN CONFIDENCE with every new performance, thanks largely to the encouragement he was receiving at Sadler's Wells and the consistent improvement of his roles. For this he could thank a man called Thomas Pitt. Like Joe, Pitt was a young man in the midst of forging himself. He had come to London in 1794 after reading in a Scottish newspaper that Sadler's Wells had staged one of his burlettas, *The Rival Loyalists*, without asking his permission. Having met the proprietor, Richard Hughes, he was taken into the company, and as it was Hughes's policy to delegate artistic matters, Pitt was given the job of stage manager, a catch-all position that required him to be author, director, producer, set designer and whatever else the situation called for.

Though Pitt had been born into a theatrical family, his actress mother Harriet had wanted to spare him the iniquities of theatrical life, farming him out as apprentice to his uncle, a furniture-maker, with the long-term hope that he would one day come to be the Lord Mayor of London. Her aversion to the theatre was the result of her appalling treatment at the hands of Pitt's father, Charles Dibdin, the hapless manager of the Royal Circus, and devoted enemy of the Signor. Dibdin senior was a self-important poetaster with a persecution complex whose career had been steadily deteriorating ever since his writing partner, Isaac Bickerstaffe, had been forced to flee to France to escape prosecution for sodomy. Charles had fathered two illegitimate sons with Harriet Pitt before renouncing the entire family so thoroughly that Thomas later claimed 'he had seen his father so seldom, that, having weak eyes, he should not know him if he met him in the street'. But given his parentage, not to mention that his godfather was David Garrick and his onstage début had been playing Cupid to Sarah Siddons's Venus, it is unsurprising that Pitt saw his future in the theatre. As soon as he was ensconced at the Wells, he signalled his intention of remaining a theatrical man by asking everybody to call him Thomas Dibdin, a move that greatly angered his father.

Thomas had inherited his father's ability to write prolifically and at great speed, and quickly earned a reputation for being able to begin a play on Monday morning and have it finished by the following Saturday. This pleased Hughes immensely, and soon the joke around town was 'Write to Tom Dibdin, and you'll get it by return of post.' Though his ambition was to write legitimate drama at one of the patent houses, his keen eye for absurdity overrode everything. One story has it that, aboard ship, Pitt had once seen a sailor catch fire. His shipmates quickly threw a rope around him and chucked him overboard, but as they heaved him back up, the rope slipped from his waist to his neck and strangled him. Instead of being horrified by the man's ordeal, Thomas found it funny, remarking drily that 'The poor fellow had actually undergone the triplicate horrors of burning, drowning and hanging.' It was exactly this sort of comic atrocity he brought to Islington, and within months of his arrival, Sadler's Wells had the reputation for staging the very best pantomimes in town.

One of these was *The Talisman of Orosmanes; or, Harlequin Made Happy*, taken from the *Tales of the Genii* and promising 'the Orgies of the Persian Enchanters'. It opened on Easter Monday 1796, and although Dubois was in the initial cast, the recent death of his wife (for which Kemble cancelled the Drury Lane pantomime as a mark of respect) prompted him to leave London for America and a series of engagements at the John Street Theatre in New York, then the city's only playhouse. Free of his oppressor's yoke, Joe gave himself licence to dig into his role as Morad, a globe-trotting witch who lived in a magic box, singing, 'Every ill my thoughts employ/And man's disaster be my joy.' The performance was roundly praised by both Dibdin and Hughes, but it was the praise of another member of the Sadler's Wells community that had the deepest effect on Joe.

Like Samuel Johnson before him, Joe was finding himself increasingly disconcerted by the preponderance of pale bosoms and silk stockings that surrounded him at the theatre. Most of his friends felt the same. Jack Bologna had been romancing a girl called Harriet Barnewell, while Bob Fairbrother had been seeing the daughter of the Grimaldis' old landlady, Mrs Bailey, and had picked up some bankable skills as a furrier into the bargain. Joe was much shyer than Bologna, whose tall, athletic figure and captivating accent gave him seemingly boundless confidence, and far less pragmatic than the industrious 'friend Bob'. Instead, he nursed an impractical flame for Dora Jordan, Drury Lane's principal comic actress. She was seventeen years his senior and at the height of her fame, though still very much a credible object of affection with her bouncing figure, 'delicious voice' and splendid legs, which had won her legions of admirers – mostly men who liked to see her cross-dressed and in breeches. Dora Jordan was also the mother of three children, and for the past four years had been living a contented life of semi-rural domesticity with the Duke of Clarence, the future William IV.

In Joe's eyes, these facts only made her more appealing for, as he had shown through his attachments to the Bolognas and the Redigés, he was drawn to people who seemed capable of leading stable family lives. The real attraction of Mrs Jordan, though, was her easy, natural humour and a laugh that the critic Leigh Hunt found 'social and genuine', like 'sparkles of bubbling water'. 'When the whole stream comes out,' he wrote, 'nothing can be fuller of heart and soul.' To the boy for whom laughter was the transcendental palliative, Dora Jordan was a goddess, and when the opportunity arose, he was quick to confirm his devotion with an offering.

One morning following rehearsal at Drury Lane, Dora Jordan had noticed Joe carrying a case of his favourite butterflies, Dartford Blues. He stood mute and blushing as she leant over him to admire the great care with which each specimen had been displayed. It was all the encouragement he needed, and following the evening performance at Sadler's Wells, he ran home to fetch his net and set out on foot for Dartford shortly after midnight, reaching his hunting grounds at five in the morning. There he stayed until one in the afternoon before walking the fifteen miles back to London to perform, only to turn around again as soon as the curtain dropped to return to Dartford and chase more butterflies. So it continued for three consecutive days, at the end of which, having covered almost ninety miles on foot and virtually renounced sleep, he had finally caught enough butterflies to present a surprised but pleased Mrs Jordan with two frames of lovingly set Blues.

Joe's affection wasn't to last, however, as Dora Jordan was soon to be usurped by a new and younger idol recently arrived from Plymouth, Maria, one of Richard Hughes's nine children.

The Hughes family lived in the big house at the corner of the Wells's coachyard, and Maria was constantly in and out of the theatre, running errands during the day and taking her place in the proprietor's box at night, sitting demurely beside her mother, Lucy, and older siblings, Julia and Richard junior. Maria had made friends with Joe's mother, Rebecca, who had flourished since the Signor's death, emerging as a lively and contented woman and something of a mother-hen to the entire company.

As Rebecca was still dancing at the Wells, she made it her habit to spend the afternoons sewing and chatting in the ladies' dressing room between morning rehearsals and the evening performance. Occasionally Joe would join her there, although as Maria started to become a regular, he found a reason to attend almost every day. Glancing timidly over his teacup and trying not to catch her eye, he found her pretty and vivacious, more than able to hold her own in this fast-talking group, and blushed alarmingly when she happened to praise his performance as Morad.

Deep infatuation followed, but with it came a debilitating sense of defeat. Maria had the advantage over Dora Jordan of being both unattached and more or less his own age, but as the manager's daughter she was no more attainable than the consort of the king-to-be. Worst of all, Joe had no idea what, if anything, Maria thought of him, and the dual miseries of self-doubt and unrequited love conspired to ruin his success in the pantomime. The feelings worked themselves deeper, to a point where he was dumbstruck and mortified in her presence, and once even fled the room in tears. Displaying all the classic symptoms of teenage love, he 'ate little, drank little, slept less' and moped around the workshops in despair.

These were symptoms Joe's mother's friend Charlotte Lewis, wardrobe mistress at the Wells, recognised immediately. Having witnessed countless backstage romances and met her own husband in the same way, she was well attuned to Maria's subtle enquiries into Joe's health, and the way in which she tried to uncover, with all apparent artlessness, if his absences were due to a romantic attachment elsewhere. Offering her services as an intermediary, Mrs Lewis persuaded Joe to convey his feelings in a letter. He set reluctantly to it, taking a whole day to compose a note that filled less than half a sheet of paper. Thankfully, her instincts were spot on, for the moment she passed the note into Maria's trembling hands and watched her devour its crabbed and crooked contents, it was clear that the manager's daughter had been a hostage to emotion herself. Sobbing with relief, Maria ran immediately to her father's box to see Joe on stage and give him a signal that she shared his feelings. Her simple smile released Joe from an agony of anticipation, and he was suddenly so disoriented by elation that he lost his place in the performance and only returned to his senses when he was flattened by a falling table and badly injured. The table was carrying sixteen men, suspended from the teeth of the Sicilian strongman, Concetto Coco.

Maria went to see the patient the next morning and found him lying on the sofa with his arm in a sling, in high spirits even though he had passed the night in intense pain. Confirmed in their mutual affection, he pressed her on the question of marriage, although she refused to consider it on the entirely reasonable grounds that he was only seventeen. Moreover, she insisted there could be no correspondence between them without the full knowledge of her parents, which Joe didn't relish as Hughes had the power to halt his career in an instant and was formidable when he felt betrayed. After lengthy pleading from Joe, Maria agreed to tell just her mother, who, as a member of the afternoon tea set, was fond of him and sufficiently indulgent to keep the secret, thus allowing Joe to court her while buying time to secure his place in the proprietor's favour.

The problem of backstage gossips remained: although Dubois was in New York, his cronies still packed the theatre. Under the protection of the maternal triumvirate of Mrs Brooker, Mrs Lewis and Mrs Hughes, Joe and Maria were forced to embark upon a long and secret courtship that was a model of discretion. Clandestine meetings and stolen walks took place in the meadows behind the theatre and along the New River. Sometimes they met in the neat little tea garden across from the Wells, with its chalybeate spring and the zigzag borders that sheltered them from prying eyes. Maria admired his solid figure, his tenderness and touching vulnerability. While not exactly handsome according to the mutton-chopped, Light Dragoon standards of the day, his face was kind, expressive and without guile. He was also very funny – deliberately so, but also with a disarming tendency to mix up his words when he was nervous. To Joe, Maria was the perfect Columbine, beautiful, swift and spirited. She was considerate and nurturing, enjoyed the quiet of his pastimes, while the strong sense of self-possession she had inherited from her father made her confident and apt to take control. Joe and Maria were falling deeply in love.

~

If Sadler's Wells was the bower of bliss, then Drury Lane was the castle of doom. Having embraced Gothic drama in the wake of the French Revolution, Kemble's theatre remained firmly in its terrible thrall, casting aside the mannered dramas of Garrick's day for the dark anachronisms of plays like George Coleman's *Blue-Beard*, and Matthew 'Monk' Lewis's *The Castle Spectre*. The haunted and hysterical tone on stage permeated the green room, where, fuelled by the culture of wine and opium, it poisoned relationships and set nerves on edge. There was little appetite for pantomimical absurdities in such a palpitating atmosphere but, keen to maintain the momentum of his recent success at Sadler's Wells, Joe pressed on, using a benefit night in October to lay out his ambitions before the public of Drury Lane. The bills announced 'an humble attempt at the Clown by Master Grimaldi', wording that said it all: it was a tentative experiment, a dry run he hoped his audience would indulge.

Whether it was pure coincidence or a calculated ploy, Joe's performance as Clown coincided with Dubois's return from America. Piqued by the boy's presumption, Dubois immediately restated his authority by stepping into the Clown shoes in *Harlequin Captive*, which demoted Joe to the role of a servant. It was particularly irksome, then, when only two days later a small injury forced Dubois temporarily to withdraw, leaving Grimaldi as the natural choice to succeed. Even though he had played Clown in *Harlequin Captive* only once, Kemble asked him to cover for Dubois twice more in a dance called *The Scotch Ghost*. These small, incremental advances culminated on Boxing Day 1796, when Kemble cast Joe as Pero, the clown *manqué*, in *Robinson Crusoe*, the pantomime his father had helped to make famous almost a decade before. Once more, Joe made a good impression, undoubtedly helped by playing alongside the poor, tired and diminutive Hollingsworth, who took Clown. But if Joe was hoping he had taken an irreversible step on the road to recognition at Drury Lane, he was sorely mistaken, as following the close of *Robinson Crusoe*, Kemble decided to discontinue pantomimes altogether to make room for yet more blood and thunder.

Though his progress at Drury Lane was blocked, Thomas Dibdin's tenure at Sadler's Wells continued to provide Joe with a stream of good roles. Dibdin, however, was unsatisfied, becoming increasingly frustrated by his inability to break into the patent theatres. At the close of the 1796 season, after only two years at the Wells, he left Islington for a place on the Kent circuit, preferring to write legitimate drama in the provinces than remain a pantomime author in a London minor. The gamble paid off: within eighteen months, he had had a major hit in Maidstone and was offered a job at Covent Garden.

Dibdin's departure was followed by a bad season for the company, resulting in considerable losses for the Wells. A short-term solution was found by William Siddons, who asked his famous wife Sarah to hand over two thousand pounds, which she did, although there were those who hinted she'd done it only to quell the rumour that she had ostracised him for passing on a venereal disease from his mistress in Chelsea. Richard Hughes, meanwhile, was forced to economise. He cut salaries and dismissed a number of performers, including La Belle Espagnole, without hiring replacements. The one new face he took on was a foul-mouthed comic singer called William Davis, known as 'Jew' Davis for his purported excellence in playing Jewish caricatures. Hughes knew his core audience, and he wasn't taking any risks.

Ultimately, the Wells's financial troubles worked in Joe's favour, as Hughes was compelled to make use of what he had, thus pushing him to the fore in a steady procession of bigger and better roles and forcing him to try his hand in untested areas, like singing in burlettas. The increased exposure brought him to the attention of a number of rival managers, the most eager of whom was John Cartwright Cross, an energetic impresario who had made a success of the Royal Circus in the wake of the original Dibdin–Grimaldi débâcle. Cross had successfully lured the Bolognas to the Circus the year before, where Jack was walking the tightrope as his father, Pietro, clowned below. Pietro remained popular but, as the *Monthly Mirror* noted, he was getting older and starting to look fat, and it may have been that Cross was already imagining a pantomime troupe centred around Jack and Joe. He courted Joe persistently, appearing at his shows and sending him letters that invited him to name his terms, but with Maria as his anchor, Joe remained loyal to the Wells.

To underline his attachment to Islington, Joe and Rebecca decided to leave the rooms they shared with the Baileys in Great Wild Street and rent a six-roomed house on the Pentonville estate with Charlotte Lewis and her actor husband. When first pegged out twenty years before, Pentonville had been imagined as a garden suburb for 'gentlemen and affluent tradesmen', and though it was not as fashionable as its developers had hoped, it was quiet and offered airy gardens that backed on to miles of villa-dotted common and a pleasant prospect of Somers Town. Though idyllic, these same fields gave safe harbour to thieves, in particular a gang of housebreakers who had worked the area for several years. At least sixteen had been hanged or transported during the past few months, which served to make the remaining few more desperate.

The Grimaldis and the Lewises had been blissfully unaware of the danger until one night the entire household returned from the Wells to discover a burglary in progress. As the thieves fled, Joe went after them, grabbing his father's broadsword and chasing them into the pitch-black fields, wounding one before he almost cut himself in half by running into the side of a cow. Inside, the house was chaos, with everything overturned or missing. The worst had been saved for his butterfly cases, which, too cumbersome to carry, had been mindlessly smashed save for one solitary box, an act of vandalism Joe found so traumatic that he never had the heart to go butterfly hunting again. A dawn search recovered a parcel of their belongings wrapped in a bloody sheet, abandoned by the wounded thief.

The shaken household tried to return to normal, but within three nights the thieves were back for their swag, forcing the garden door while the occupants were again at the theatre, and fleeing only after the servant's screams roused a group of neighbours who summoned the Watch. The next morning, Joe went down to Hatton Garden to solicit the aid of a shrewd officer named Constable Trott. The constable ordered them all out of doors for the evening, left the garden door ajar and set a trap, taking the villains as they were preparing themselves to murder the inhabitants in their sleep.

∾

Three years of steady progress and surreptitious courtship went by before Maria would finally agree to marriage, and after keeping their affair secret for so long, the circumstances of the proposal were suddenly very hurried. Rumours had been in circulation for some time, but as Joe became increasingly prominent in the company, his rivals, led by Dubois, were even more determined to uncover the truth. The lover's hand was forced, and when Grimaldi wrote to Hughes, away on business in Exeter, to ask for his daughter in marriage, he had no idea what kind of answer to expect.

In the meantime, the ill-wishers gathered momentum. Maria and her brother Richard had gone to Gravesend to visit friends, and when Joe was invited to join them five days later, word of the visit got round the theatre, exciting the curiosity of Hughes's treasurer, Vincent de Cleve. Nicknamed 'Polly' for his tendency to prattle on about other people's business, de Cleve was an oddity. Believed to be of independent means, he kept the theatre's books as a hobby, along with composing music and collecting so many curious objects that his room looked like 'a conjuror's study'.

Polly was an inveterate 'croaker', a backstage doom-merchant who took pleasure in others' bad luck and who 'hated Grimaldi most cordially', being a confirmed ally of Dubois and Frank Hartland, Dubois's favoured apprentice whom Joe had been putting in the shade for the past four years. His suspicions aroused, Polly took himself down to Gravesend to see what he might uncover. He missed Maria, but found Joe in the cabin of the ferry on the way home, and with his letter to Hughes still unanswered, the snide insinuations of de Cleve made for an uncomfortable trip back to town.

Five anxious days passed before an answer arrived, but even then it did little to soothe. 'Dear Joe,' it read baldly, 'Expect to see me in a few days. Yours truly, R. Hughes.' Hughes returned the following week, and by the time Joe finally stepped into his office the accumulated worry of the previous days had left him haggard and drawn. Hughes treated him civilly enough, but when the pleasantries were over, he surprised him by sternly enquiring if he had forgotten the terms of his contract. Confused, Joe replied that he had not, at which point Hughes launched into an angry harangue, demanding to know the meaning of his correspondence with John Cross. Joe stared at the carpet-rods as Hughes recounted the many rumours that had reached him in Exeter, though of the morsels that had come his way none had incensed him so much as the thought of contractual infidelity.

The charge was easily refuted. Along with the original letters from Cross, which Joe had in his pocketbook, there were also copies of his many polite refusals of a place at the Royal Circus. Satisfied, Hughes surprised the boy again by proposing to extend his contract at the Wells for three more years at six pounds a week for the first season, seven for the second and eight for the third. The papers were already on his desk, and he could sign them on the spot. It was shrewd business by Hughes, who had used Joe's anxiety to secure an increasingly key performer on terms that were greatly favourable to the house. The deal concluded, he made to leave, absent-mindedly adding, in his flat Midlands accent, 'Have you anything else to say to me?'

Joe came to his senses and, newly conscious of his original errand, fumbled through a prepared speech, to which Hughes listened impassively. If he'd examined himself sincerely, he would have found scant grounds to object, as the tactic of personal advancement through strategic marriage was something both he and his friend William Siddons had employed with considerable success. At the same time as Roger Kemble had banished William for romancing his fourteen-year-old daughter (thereby guaranteeing her devotion to a dashing chancer who might otherwise have been forgotten), Hughes got his first foothold in management by courting, then marrying the daughter of the proprietor of the Plymouth Dock. At least the boy seemed sincere and he was certainly likeable, if somewhat too earnest.

After a short dictum against the youth of both parties, Hughes gave his consent before throwing open the door to reveal Maria sitting in the next room. 'Joe is here,' he said. 'You had better come and welcome him.' The timing was perfect, for the very next day an unnamed detractor came to the manager's office to denounce Grimaldi for 'winning the affections of a young lady infinitely above him, and, at the same time, the daughter of one to whom he is so greatly indebted'.

Now that they were to be married, Maria insisted that they find a new house, and they took a pleasant one at 37 Penton Street along the same stretch of road as the White Conduit House tavern, famous for its fishpond and cricket pitch. On 11 May 1799, the last night of the Drury Lane season, Joe and Maria were married at St George's, Hanover Square. It was a small ceremony, in keeping with eighteenth-century practice, witnessed by Charlotte Lewis and celebrated five days later with a supper for the entire company at Sadler's Wells and one for the carpenters the following day.

That summer they settled into a quiet suburban existence, exactly the kind of uneventful domesticity Joe had craved since childhood. They spent every day together at the Wells, and when Drury Lane reopened in the autumn Sheridan added Maria to the free list, telling Joe that it was a 'very bad thing . . . to let a pretty young wife be alone of a night'. Sheridan should know. In February, Maria announced that she was expecting a child. Life was finally getting into its stride and, as the *Memoirs* had it, 'all went merry as a marriage bell'.

~

To blissful contentment was shortly added professional advancement. In the three years since Thomas Dibdin's departure, Richard Hughes had failed to find a satisfactory replacement. The job of management had temporarily fallen to Mark Lonsdale, a hardworking but unfortunate writer, but when he also left to join Covent Garden a year later, Hughes was left with no one. It was then that a letter arrived from Thomas Dibdin's brother, Charles junior, asking for the job.

Charles Dibdin junior was thirty-two, another Pitt-turned-Dibdin whose middle names, 'Isaac Mungo', were a doleful reminder of his father's better days. He was a cheerful, tireless and frequently preposterous man with a love of patriotic ballads and convivial dinners. Though a less experienced dramatist than his brother, his ambitions were more in step with his talents, with the result that his temperament was ideally suited to Sadler's Wells. He had been destined for the minors ever since he'd first presented himself to the public as a singer and raconteur, modelling himself on his father's one-man shows, yet stage fright and an inability to remember the words of songs he'd written made a career as a performer untenable.

After running up debts and marrying a querulous dancer named Mary Bates (whom Hughes had sacked four years earlier for demanding a pay rise), he set on the family line of authorship, getting his first job at Astley's Amphitheatre, where he'd been told that the owner, a fearsome, barrel-chested, Northumbrian war-hero called Philip Astley, would 'buy *anything*'. Dibdin offered him a pantomime based on *Don Quixote*, hoping to increase his chances of a sale by providing a mock-up of every single one of the show's twenty-four scenes, which he lugged with fourteen tricks and eighteen bits of scenery all the way to Hercules Hall in Lambeth. This was Astley's curious, gated mansion, stuffed with steaming horses and snarling dogs, which he'd named after a human pyramid trick called the *Force d'Hercule*. The poet William Blake was a neighbour.

Though perfectly aware that many of his tricks wouldn't actually work if they were built, Charles relied on Astley's love of the gaudy by painting everything in gilt and bold colours for, as Dibdin recalled in his own *Memoirs*, 'the Astleyian fancy was apt to be fascinated by such an Exhibition'. It worked. The pantomime was purchased and a three-year contract followed, although working for Astley was more akin to servitude than employment. A man who held that the way to get the best from his performers was to 'never let 'm have anything to eat till they've done acting', Astley required Dibdin to write twelve burlettas, twelve serious pantomimes and twelve harlequinades a year, as well as to compose the eight or nine daily puffs required by the newspapers and provide the comedian, Richard Johannot, with a constant stream of comic songs. Thankfully, Charles was as prolix as his fellow Dibdins, and his reward for this enormous volume of work was a weekly salary of a guinea and a half, though only for those weeks the theatre was open. In vain he tried to negotiate this up, but Astley was immovable and Charles had to content himself with a clause in his contract stipulating that his wife would never have to appear on stage in breeches.

Dibdin endured two years of this 'slavery', following it with a year in Davis and Parker's travelling circus, during which he survived a bayonet charge in Dublin, a collapsing theatre in Bristol and a coach wreck near Macclesfield. Through the intervention of Jean-Baptiste Dubois, he was also saved from drowning in the Irish Sea. A steady job like the Wells was a dream come true, and after Hughes offered him a pay rise of half a guinea a week for the same three dozen new pieces a season, Dibdin, whose aim was always to please his masters, came to London and stayed for the next nineteen and a half years.

~

The first night of Charles Dibdin's regime was to be Easter Monday 1800, although the pressures of management manifested themselves in earnest long before a single thigh had been slapped when Hughes, mindful of the pregnant Maria, pulled him aside and bade him cultivate his son-in-law's talents as best he could. Dibdin's heart sank at the thought of pandering to a favourite, especially the son of the toxic Italian his own father had so vehemently denounced, but after watching Joe at rehearsals and making a note of 'any peculiar whimsicality I saw in him', he was impressed enough to consider using him as Clown. But while persuaded that Joe could hold the role on his own merits, Dibdin still had to avoid the appearance of favouritism if he wasn't to be compromised with the rest of the company, particularly Dubois.

Things had not been going well for the Frenchman and he was in an especially touchy mood. The newspapers still carried regular praise for his talents and 'majestic strength', but he had been beset with problems since the death of his wife. Money eluded him, even though he had taken on extra work arranging pantomimes for the Royalty Theatre in the East End, and plans to set up a performing academy for children had failed to materialise due to the constant harassment he received at the hands of the creditors who greeted him on his return from America. There were also nagging doubts about Charles, his son, now around eleven or twelve, who had yet to demonstrate any great aptitude for the theatre and hadn't featured on a Sadler's Wells bill since infancy.

Dibdin understood the need for diplomacy and lighted on a plan that he hoped would please everybody. Taking the scenario of Robert Patlock's 1751 novel, *Peter Wilkins*, the story of a shipwrecked mariner who discovers an island of flying people, he devised a pantomime that was part *Gulliver's Travels* and part *Robinson Crusoe* in which all the major characters would be doubled: two Harlequins, two Pantaloons and, of course, two Clowns. The solution was ideal: Hughes would be pleased to see Joe take centre stage, while Dubois would retain his rightful place. Best of all, he would raise the curtain on his tenure at the Wells with an innovation that would place his name squarely before the London public.

Further to mark its departure from the regular harlequinade (and, no doubt, to cajole Dubois into going along with it on account of its novelty), Dibdin decided to deck the clowns in costumes that were totally new, 'Dresses', he said, that were 'more extravagant than it had been the custom for such characters to wear', that took the form of garishly colourful doublets and breeches, symmetrically patterned with large diamonds and circles and fringed with tassels and ruffs. This was a particularly significant change, as audiences were used to seeing Clown in the tatty livery of a shiftless servant or a peasant's long smock (*à la* Pierrot), a costume that had served to pin the character, albeit to an ever-fading degree, to an identifiable social origin by essentially replicating the raiment of an Elizabethan dogsbody. By contrast, Dibdin's costume lifted the clown out of any specific context, transforming him into a stylised and inimitable archetype, a firebrand as visually striking as he was reckless and energetic. Rehearsals ran through February and March, with Dibdin hurrying to finish the scripts even as the daffodils were blooming.

~

Easter was an important date in the Georgian calendar, as keenly anticipated as Christmas, and the opening of the summer theatres on Easter Monday saw holiday crowds descending on the Wells in great numbers. Easter 1800 was especially wet and muddy, and the scores of lanterns hanging along the avenue looked particularly forlorn. Inside, the patrons indulged themselves with cold cuts and reached greedily for the bottles they had perched on shelves that ran across the back of the seats. Bruised and spattered riders from the annual Epping Hunt applauded each other for surviving the morning's stag chase, a rather ridiculous jaunt for grocers and aldermen, who puffed away on old nags and carthorses before saluting their heroics with gallons of beer. Up in the gallery, a fat man named Wren sold refreshments with the booming cry, 'Come, ladies, give your minds to drinking,' while a group of laughing sailors tried to pull apart a couple of brawling women who had taken his advice too freely.

If Joe had peeped nervously from behind the curtain as he stretched his hamstrings and chalked his feet, he would have noticed something very different in the fashions of that year's crowd. Trousers and wide-brims were replacing breeches and tricorn hats, and men were more likely to be carrying umbrellas at their sides than swords. Most significantly of all, their cheerful faces were almost entirely unadorned by wigs. Pitt's tax on wig powder had set them out of fashion, and for the first time in many of their lives, men and women showed their real hair in public, like French *citoyens*.

The overture brought some semblance of hush to the house, and as the actors took a deep breath and swallowed their nerves, the curtain rose on Dibdin's first season as stage manager of Sadler's Wells. The first piece was a 'musical bagatelle', called *Old Fools, or Love's Stratagem*, that went down well enough, but Richer's rope-dance was more in keeping with the holiday mood. As clown-to-the-rope, Dubois amply demonstrated why he had been London's premier clown for twelve years by dancing a reel while balancing three spinning caps on his head. Next came a pantomime ballet called *Filial Love, or the Double Marriage*, by which time Joe was already in his first costume of the evening, the tattered kilt of an ancient Briton for his role in a 'splendid historical ballet of action' based on the battles of Boadicea. Swordplay and acrobatics kept his mind off the impending pantomime, and all went smoothly until Boadicea delivered a rousing speech: 'If your breasts conceal one coward care,' she told her troops, 'I'll go alone!' A fracas broke out in the gallery, and as the assembled Iceni turned their heads to squint through the cigar smoke, they saw a sailor leap over the balcony and scurry down the boxes. 'I'll be damned if you do!' he shouted. 'Here, Jack! Let's go, and we'll show 'em as tight work as we did under his honour Admiral Nelson!' Peals of cheering and shouts of 'God Save the King' held up the show for several minutes as the enthusiast was helped back to his seat.

Boadicea finished and a 'grand allegorical transition' was displayed, a rousing pageant portraying the history of Britain from Roman times to the present, followed by comic songs by Mrs Mather and the new singer, Jew Davis, who quickly established himself as a maverick scene-stealer, with the suggestive looks and insinuating faces he used to underscore the lyrics of 'The King's Picture'. When the songs finished, the curtain fell. Wren hawked more drinks and the boozy hubbub swelled as the carpenters put the scenery in place for the final piece, the one they were all here to see, the new pantomime.

At last, it was time for Joe and Dubois to make their entrance. At first the audience weren't sure what to make of these oddly attired figures, but once they'd announced themselves as Guzzle the drinking Clown, and Gobble the eating Clown, and taken their corners in a gluttonous duel to see who could consume the most beer and sausages, they started to roar. Dubois grew fatter and more flatulent, Joe drunker and more incoherent as the contest wore on until, fully victorious over abstemious Lent, the Clowns sang a mock Italian aria, Joe accompanying Dubois on a salt shaker, and Dubois accompanying himself with belches.

After this, the clowns momentarily retired, allowing Mary Dibdin (née Bates) to sing a ballad dressed as a female volunteer. As the moral equivalent of an intermission, she received a lukewarm reception (the only kind she ever got at the Wells), before the harlequinade resumed in earnest and Joe and Dubois joined with the twin Pantaloons in frenetic pursuit of the elusive lovers, Harlequin and Columbine.

Dibdin had been sure to stock *Peter Wilkins* with the three essential ingredients of the genre, 'magic, quickness and variety', packing the harlequinade with inventive transformations. A number of these tricks, constructed by the scene painter, 'Little Bob' Andrews ('a giant in the Art'), were helpfully catalogued by the reviewer of *The Times*, who noted, 'a Taylor's box changing to a basket of cabbages, and a cabbage changing again to a basket of rags, a drum to a Temple of Harmony, a box of Quack pills to a basket of ducks, and one of the pills to a single duck', which, it added, 'is a most extraordinary piece of mechanism'. The duck, apparently a clockwork automaton built to 'the full size of life, with all its motions, &c.', was so impressive that it became the centrepiece of a second *Times* review that came out four days later. 'Had such a thing been projected in the old days of superstition,' concluded the reviewer, 'the inventor would have been publicly burnt for dealing with the Devil.'

Not all the changes were quite so flawless. During the performance, Dibdin noticed that one of the shutters on the Grave
Trap – the long, rectangular trapdoor in the middle of the stage
– was not properly closed. Rushing from the wings to set it right,
he fell through it and was only saved from breaking his back
when his elbows jammed in the narrow space.

The opening night of *Peter Wilkins* was a triumph, and by
the end of the first week the show had become so popular that
the boxes at Sadler's Wells were filled with 'Nobility of the first
rank', including the Lord Chancellor, Baron Loughborough,
who 'applauded unanimously'. News of the new costumes had
also spread among the clown fraternity, who were eager to
weigh the changes for themselves. From the stage, Joe and
Dubois might have spotted John Follet, in from Covent Garden
and trying to look inconspicuous, or perhaps John Porter and
Montgomery, clowns to the horse, whom Dubois knew from
the Royal Circus. From Astley's came Joe's brother-in-law,
Lascelles Williamson, along with Madame Mercerot, William
West and Jean-Baptiste Laurent, all of whom had been apprentices of the Signor. If they were in any doubt, the laughter and
applause spoke for themselves.

It was the first time Joe had played Clown without being
either understudy or stand-in, and he'd proved himself
Dubois's equal, if not his better. The difference in their styles
was striking. While Dubois 'clowned', digging into a seemingly
endless bag of tricks and showing off a vast array of skills, the
effect was studied and artificial, his fabled versatility evidence
that this was just another type of performance among many.
Joe, on the other hand, seemed to draw the audience into
believing in the essential comedic qualities of the man. No
doubt the new costumes worked in his favour, as while Dubois
seemed a little uncomfortable in the unfamiliar attire, Joe
was present at the birth of a new and hilarious creation. The
audience leapt on the association. Eager in their pursuit of

unmediated and sincere experiences, Romantic audiences rejected the studied histrionics of previous generations, and were hungry to acclaim raw and unaffected talents, people who seemed not to act their roles but to live them. In Joseph Grimaldi they had found a natural. This was certainly Charles Dibdin's perception:

> For as Clown and singer of Clown's Songs, exclusive of his excellence in serious pantomime – I despair of 'Looking on his like again' – I never saw anyone equal to him – there was so much mind in everything he did. It was said of Garrick, that, when he played a Drunken man, he was 'All over drunk' – Grimaldi was 'all over clown'.

~

Joe was twenty-one years old, happily married, and had just realised his dearest wish, something he had prepared for since infancy, and surely the most significant moment of his life. Curious, then, that the *Memoirs* should contain absolutely no mention of *Peter Wilkins* or his Sadler's Wells début as Clown. Perhaps the many thrills and challenges he encountered during the season of 1800 were eclipsed by the tragedy that shortly followed.

Maria's pregnancy had been difficult. It had been a hot summer and she had done herself no favours by dancing in a ballet for the benefit of Signora Bossi del Caro at Drury Lane in early June and celebrating the marriage of Jack Bologna and Harriet Barnewell in the same week. Yet by autumn she had reached full term and the couple were filled with nerves and anticipation at the prospect of their baby's arrival. Then on 18 October, the feast of St Luke, patron saint of physicians, Joe was called home from a rehearsal at Drury Lane with the news that Maria had gone into labour. He covered the ground as quickly as he always did, but when he arrived at Penton Place and bounded up the stairs, instead of finding Maria and the midwife he expected, he found his brother-in-law Richard weeping over her lifeless body. Childbirth had claimed another victim: of all the young marriages that ended at this period, seventy-five per cent were caused by the death of the wife.

Maria had known her life was in danger, and though she insulated her husband from her fears, her pocketbook was found to contain instructions for her burial, and a self-penned verse she wished to have inscribed upon her headstone, a naïve, though sincerely felt, meditation on the brevity of life. Conscious of her husband's delicate sensibility, she had made Richard pledge to care for him. Her last words had been 'poor Joe'. She was buried in the Hughes family vault in St James's, Clerkenwell, aged twenty-five, the third daughter her father had lost.

Grief sent Joe temporarily insane. He wept bitterly for the cruel fortune that had destroyed his family in one stroke while sparing him to feel the full brunt of the pain. Convinced he would make an attempt on his own life, Richard kept a constant vigil as Joe closed himself off to everything but his mourning, barely talking to a soul.

Somehow, Joe managed to report to Drury Lane, possibly hoping to find solace in his work. Kemble, inattentive to the private life of a junior performer, cast him as the Second Gravedigger in *Hamlet*. 'Make her grave/straight,' said Joe, staring blankly across rows of candlelit faces, 'The crowner hath sat on her, and finds it/Christian burial.' Maria had been dead for only two days. The absurdity of life had been fully revealed.

PART TWO

[1800–1810]

5

THE MAGIC OF MONA

Ay, in the very temple of Delight
Veil'd Melancholy has her Sovran shrine,
Though seen of none save him whose strenuous tongue
Can burst Joy's grape against his palate fine;
His soul shall taste the sadness of her might,
And be among her cloudy trophies hung.

John Keats, 'Ode to Melancholy' (1819)

JOE MOVED GINGERLY TO the edge of the roof and, carefully lifting his hands, released a bird into the reddening sky, watching it bank and complete a full circle before losing it against the rooftops. Though the bird was gone, his eyes remained fixed. Care had lined his face, drawing dark circles around his eyes, etching his open features into an expression of sad passivity. Snatches of song wafted in and out of windows as the dutiful girls of Clerkenwell practised at their spinets, their notes mixing with the squeak of the water engine being cranked by the prisoners of Coldbath gaol directly across the road. From downstairs came the clatter of busy plates. Any moment, Rebecca would call him down and patiently shepherd him back into the daily bustle with food and the chatter she kept deliberately light. These days, he left the roof only reluctantly.

It was almost twelve months since Maria had died. There had been an intense period of grieving in which he felt he was losing his mind, after which he'd been unable to spend another night at Penton Place. Rebecca had moved them both across Spa Fields to Clerkenwell and a house at 4 Baynes Row, where his first coherent thought had been for his pigeons; he had built a dormer to house sixty of them.

Stepping back, he winced. His foot was wrapped in a thick bandage, and where it stopped at the ankle, an angry streak of burnt skin leapt up his shin. Slowly, he limped down the stairs to find the table set and his things straightened. As Rebecca embarked on another harmless disquisition, a young woman appeared from the kitchen, flushed from the heat. She smiled but didn't speak. Her name was Mary Bristow, a member of the Drury Lane chorus descended from a large theatrical family of unremarkable talents. She had been introduced to Joe the previous December when he was apt to go missing for days at a time, sending his friends frantically searching until they found him wandering by the New River or in the meadows behind Pentonville. Moved by the depth of his anguish, Mary Bristow had offered her friendship, encouraged by Rebecca, who was powerless to help her son. But Joe, barely present in a room full of people, had been too weak and distracted to notice her regular acts of kindness until almost a month ago when she had presented herself as his nurse.

It had been a stupid accident. Appearing in *The Great Devil*, one of Charles Dibdin's 'serio-comic spectacles', based on the current news of a gang of *banditti* terrorising Genoa, Joe had changed costume nineteen times before emerging as Rufo the Robber, holding up a group of travellers. Intending to pull a gun from his boot and fire a blank, he had discharged it prematurely, firing the wad into his foot and setting fire to his stockings. His leg had smouldered while he finished the scene, and by the time he came off, his foot was so badly injured he had been unable to work for a month. Mary volunteered herself to his care, arriving every morning to clean and dress his wound, keep him entertained when he was in the mood to talk, and sit in respectful silence when he was not. Her patient diligence belied a growing devotion, which, for now at least, went unreciprocated. Joe was a miserable patient, his mind either on Maria, or deploring the 'tedious' and 'interminable confinement', whose enforced idleness threatened a blanket of depression even as his body craved rest.

~

By the autumn of 1800, the public's appetite for Gothic spectacle had finally reached a peak, and John Philip Kemble took the decision to reintroduce pantomime to Drury Lane after a gap of three years. Searching for someone to take charge of pantomimical affairs, he hit upon James Byrne, a walnut-faced forty-five-year-old, who had served his apprenticeship at Drury Lane when the Signor was still *maître de ballet*. Byrne was an unusual choice. Jaded and weary, and not at all certain he wanted to be in the theatre, he had recently returned from three years in America with his wife and son, where he had performed lengthy stints in Philadelphia, Baltimore and New York. He had found the experience so disagreeable that he had decided to leave show business altogether and make a go of it working on a plantation in Jamaica.

Having reached the Caribbean, however, tales of hardship and fatal diseases sent the family packing before they had had time to settle in. Ungratifying work at the Royal Circus followed, and a chance to join the company at Covent Garden was squandered when the audience booed him for his 'silly' dance.

Kemble's offer of employment was odd, given Byrne's recent form, but then pantomime was low priority and he had a familiar face. Byrne, too, had his misgivings. Like everyone else, he found the new theatre unwieldy, too big for the intimate visual jokes of pantomime, and making transformations so laboured that one critic compared them to 'the putting about of a large vessel heavily laden'. His cast were similarly uninspiring, makeshift and inexperienced compared with the formidable troupe being assembled at Covent Garden, where Thomas Dibdin, still not being taken seriously enough for his liking, had formed a fertile partnership with an actor and arranger called Charles Farley. Together they had mounted some of the most original pantomimes ever seen, supported by Jack and Pietro Bologna, recently hired as Harlequin and Clown, and the old but still brilliant Carlo Delpini as Pantaloon.

With little to lose, Byrne set about making changes and, in the process, became Joe's unlikely saviour. His success in *Peter Wilkins* duly noted, Byrne promoted Joe to Clown over Dubois, who was dropped completely. Next, he declared that if the pantomime was going to catch the public's attention, it was necessary to innovate. A dancer by both training and inclination, Byrne disliked the stiff athleticism that had characterised the role of Harlequin since the days of John Rich. Rich's Harlequin had been first and foremost a thief and an acrobat, who, when not leaping, would stand in one of five conventional postures, or 'attitudes', representing Admiration, Defiance, Determination, Flirtation or Thought, which, over the years, had become rigidly formalised and inelegant. Byrne favoured a freer and more balletic approach that would retain Harlequin's trademark gymnastics but incorporate them within a liquid and unbroken sequence of movements.

To achieve the full effect, it was necessary also to change his costume, and in a move that mirrored Dibdin's innovations in *Peter Wilkins*, he replaced the full-faced vizard with a small Venetian eye mask, and swapped the loose shirt and trousers for skin-tight fleshings that he decorated with more than fifty thousand spangles. The new Harlequin cut an ethereal figure, a sleek and shimmering silhouette, whose phallic bat and power to transform the world presented an idealised and erotic vision of the trim and dandified masculinity currently being celebrated in men's fashions. The changes would prove as important for Joe as they did for Byrne: during rehearsals, the players noticed that Harlequin's new form incontrovertibly altered the comic balance of power. With Harlequin romantic and mercurial, instead of mischievous and beggarly, the undisputed agent of misrule was indubitably Clown.

Byrne unveiled his changes on 22 December 1800, in a Welsh-themed pantomime called *Harlequin Amulet; or, the Magic of Mona*, and won enough praise to see the show run well into the following April. Joe appeared in almost every scene, first as a 'big head' Punch, concealed beneath a heavy wooden disguise, and then as Clown. The part required immense physical exertion, but when the ludic mist descended Joe did not shirk, and the oblivion it provided was exactly what he sought. The momentum was successfully maintained over at Sadler's Wells, where the 1801 season provided him with further opportunities to assert his ascendancy over Dubois. Dibdin had again decided to double the clowns for his opening pantomime, *Harlequin Alchemist*, although this time he aimed to exploit their rivalry rather than maintain the peace, providing them with a bit of business that asked the audience to decide who should stay and who should go. The setting was a mock duel – a perfect piece of symbolism – and, with challenges issued and seconds appointed, the clowns of Sadler's Wells took to the field to prepare their chosen weapons, the victor being hailed as he who could pull the most hideous face. After rounds and rounds of epic gurning, the audience's cheers delivered Joe as their champion, and consistently returned the same result for the following eight weeks.

When the second pantomime of the Sadler's Wells season débuted in June, Dubois had been relegated to Pero. As Clown, Joe gave no quarter, basking in his new-found favour and relishing every chance to upstage his old tormentor.

Dubois retaliated with everything he had, but his tricks lacked the impact of former years, and sensing he was losing ground, he began to lose his temper. His humiliation was made all the more acute because his son and three of his apprentices were in the cast, nightly witnesses to his defeat at Joe's hand. With 'the latter intrenching so much on the popularity of the former', as Dibdin recalled it, Dubois 'grew discontented', raving at the management and demanding top billing and an immediate increase in his salary, which Dibdin refused. Though he had forty years' experience, and had transformed the art of clowning by harnessing the danger of the equestrian ring and bringing it into the intimate setting of the Wells, Dubois was yesterday's man, and for once the cabal at the Sir Hugh Myddleton failed to rally round him. Dubois left the Wells under a cloud, and though he continued to perform right up until he died a pauper's death in 1814, 'he shone with diminished rays'.

Dibdin certainly had no time for regrets. Urbane and buffoonish though he frequently seemed, he was made of more calculating stuff, and no doubt pitted Dubois against Grimaldi as a means of cutting out dead wood and further pleasing his master, Hughes. Whatever machinations were at work, Joe had realised his life-long dream of being Clown at both Sadler's Wells and Drury Lane, a unique accomplishment he had marked by shooting himself in the foot.

～

Without clowning, Joe might never have made it through those difficult months but, laid up in Baynes Row away from the consolation of work, the consequences of taking refuge in a fictional identity began to catch up with him. Though his onstage persona insulated him from the pain of Maria's death, it simultaneously walled him off from his private life, and now, in the long days of enforced rest, it was obvious that he was dwelling on shrunken ground. The clearest evidence lay right before him in the pretty girl who so assiduously observed her daily rituals, bathing his foot and tying his bandages with vocational patience. She had come to him every day for a month, and continued to come even after his foot had healed. Though Joe came to rely on her, and probably took advantage of her, she mostly left him perplexed.

As soon as he was sufficiently healed, he leapt at the opportunity to return to work. An invitation had arrived to perform for the benefit of a comic singer called Lund, a sometime member of the Sadler's Wells company who spent his winters on the same Kent circuit Thomas Dibdin had worked on. Excursions into provincial theatre were essential for ambitious performers who wanted to push their names out into the country and open up the possibility of lucrative tours. Touring was often the only way for actors to make real money, and while they grumbled about prostituting themselves before Philistine provincial audiences, the ample rewards sent them out on the road year after year. Sarah Siddons did it to fund her profligate family and underwrite her husband's theatrical speculations; Dora Jordan did it to pay her taxes and support the Duke of Clarence and his numerous children; John Philip Kemble, owed thirteen hundred pounds in back pay by Sheridan, simply needed to live.

Given that he was only offered two nights in Rochester, Joe's expectations were far humbler, but it was a positive step nonetheless. The theatre was one of several under the management of an indefatigable widow named Sarah Baker, the daughter of fairground performers who had worked at Sadler's Wells in Rosoman's day. Tough, profane and barely literate, hard work and ruthless economising had made her one of the most formidable figures on the theatrical scene. At sixty-five, she undertook almost every aspect of the business herself, hiring the performers, balancing the books, taking the money and drafting advertisements by cutting the words out of old bills and sewing the bits back together like a blackmail note. Her efficiency even stretched to building her six theatres to exactly the same specifications to enable props, scenery and company to move from one to another with the minimum of fuss. Even the sitting rooms at the back were the same, and without the hour's ride between venues, it was impossible to tell them apart. With her staff, which consisted of her sister, who doubled as actress, dancer, wardrobe-keeper and cook, and a prompter and general factotum who went by the name of 'Bonny Long' on account of being extremely tall and inordinately fat, she amassed a fortune that she banked in six large punch bowls that sat on top of her various bureaux.

Mrs Baker did not fail Joe, who made £160 for one night in an olio, and another as Scaramouch in Delpini's *Don Juan*. Bonny Long paid him entirely in three-shilling pieces, a transaction made all the more bizarre by the prompter's deformity: according to Thomas Dibdin, he had 'ten fingers and no thumbs'. Joe brought the cash back to London, where Mary Bristow was waiting for him. At more than forty times his weekly salary, it was the most he had ever earned in his life, and the accompanying notion that he was suddenly a man of substance undoubtedly influenced his decision to propose to her.

They were married the following month, a fact recorded in the *Memoirs* in astonishingly neutral terms. 'In gratitude for her kindness,' they report, 'Grimaldi married her on the following Christmas Eve, and it may be as well to state in this place that with her he lived for more than thirty years.' That sentence constitutes the most substantial comment on the second Mrs Grimaldi until her death was recorded in 1834. The contrast with the fastidiously detailed recollections of anticipation and obstruction that marked his courtship of

Maria Hughes could not be more striking, and its blank utility, along with its implication that marriage was Joe's way of rewarding her for her loyalty, is a telling sign of his diminished emotional capacity. Yet, arguably, Mary's elected role as nurse and self-effacing protectress of the wounded clown suggests that she shared his view of a relationship built on mutual charity or even communal pity, although ultimately there is no telling. For the rest of their lives, Mary Bristow remained an oblique and only partially rendered figure beside her husband, a shadow in the chorus, companion to a cumulatively sad love.

There was nothing like a honeymoon. Three days after the wedding, on 27 December 1801, Grimaldi was back at Drury Lane where, instead of commissioning a new pantomime, Kemble was happy for *Harlequin Amulet* to be revived with its existing cast. The show was graced with a visit from George III, resplendent in his general's uniform and accompanied by four of his daughters. This was a special honour. The King did not visit Drury Lane often due to its strong affiliation with his obdurate eldest son, and he had been even less inclined since his last visit nineteen months ago when a suicidal madman had risen from the pit and fired a gun at him. The shot missed, and as members of the audience and orchestra had launched themselves at the would-be assassin, the King came to the front of his box to show his subjects he was unharmed. It was the second bullet to have missed him that day. The first had whizzed past him just after breakfast as he reviewed the 1st Foot Guards in Hyde Park, passing straight through the thigh of a clerk of the Allotment Department of the Royal Navy Office, who screamed and bled profusely, even after Lord Cathcart had valiantly asked him if he'd like to borrow his handkerchief to bind up the wound.

The second run of *Harlequin Amulet* closed in March 1802, when the prospect of making more money sent Joe back to

Kent, playing two nights at Mrs Baker's theatre in Maidstone and two in Canterbury. His professional successes were accumulating, though in the eyes of John Philip Kemble he was still very much a servant. During his stint with Mrs Baker, Kemble had announced Joe to appear early on the Easter Monday bill in clear contravention of his articles, which stipulated that he only performed in Drury Lane's afterpieces once the season had begun at Sadler's Wells.

On his return to London, Joe waited for the manager to explain the problem, but the lofty tragedian refused to entertain him, only asserting that he '*must*' come. It was typical of the *froideur* Kemble mistook for dignity, a fatal flaw that in time would make him the greatest enemy of the British theatre-going public. But Kemble was beyond caring: the thankless round of daily aggravations that passed for management had left him a miserable, gouty, drug-abusing wreck. Not another word was said until 26 June, when Joe received an icy little note informing him that his contract had been terminated for the following season. Kemble underlined his distaste for the quarrel by having it signed by the prompter, William Powell, a petty snub deliberately belittling Joe's two decades of service.

This was by no means the last time that Joe would be slighted by a Kemble, but for now it was one of the tragedian's final acts as the manager of Drury Lane. In July he resigned, travelling to the Continent with his friend Robert Heathcoate for a nine-month tour, before returning to take up the management of Covent Garden.

If it had been the Signor who'd been so ignominiously dismissed, Kemble would have been in the infirmary and Grimaldi up before the beak (the Signor had kicked a man in the face for ill-treating him thus). Joe, though, was naturally timid and, instead of lashing out, turned his anger inward, feeding the paranoia that had eaten at him since early adolescence. With his particular talent for torment, he read dark motives into Kemble's actions that became increasingly elaborate each time he raked them over. When he weighed them against the whispering campaign he'd endured at the Wells, they amounted to compelling evidence of a sustained conspiracy against him. His first response was to sue Sheridan, who as proprietor was accountable for the terms of his contract, but was urged against taking such a suicidal course by Richard Hughes, who counselled him to burn the spiteful missive and spend the winter season with him at the Exeter playhouse. The thought of provincial exile made Joe feel even worse, but he had little choice other than to agree. At least Hughes would guarantee him four pounds a week and a full benefit. It was more than he was getting from Kemble.

~

Before the term of his banishment could begin, Joe had another season to get through at the Wells. The theatre had been losing money since 1796, and as revenues declined, repairs had been repeatedly put off until it had gained a reputation as 'the dirtiest and most antique theatre in London'. Musty boxes, a leaky roof and the 'penurious manner in which it was appointed' were the most obvious signs of decay, though in actuality the entire building was troublingly unsafe. As a last-ditch effort to reverse the downward slide, Hughes and Siddons freed up funds through a renegotiation of the lease and hired the architect and machinist Rudolph Cabanel (the brother of the company's principal dancer, Eliza) to remodel the auditorium. The cost of changing the floor plan from a square to a much more contemporary horseshoe, with an enlarged pit and gallery and private boxes based on those at Drury Lane, was seventeen hundred pounds, an enormous expense that put additional pressure on the company to produce a good season. Dibdin rose to the challenge, churning out a dozen new entertainments while simultaneously puffing the elegance of the new house and stressing its fitness to 'accommodate Parties of the Nobility, Gentry, etc.'.

Through a coincidence of public taste, rather than an unconscious expression of their embattled status, combat was the prominent theme of the year. Dibdin had been fortunate to lure Jack Bologna back to the Wells from the Royal Circus. Jack played Harlequin to Joe's Clown, a line of work in which, said the *Morning Chronicle*, they already 'stood unrivalled'. Jack's first job, however, was not pantomime but war, fighting Joe with a battleaxe in *St George, the Champion of England*, and again in a six-handed 'Indian combat' along with Hartland, Banks, Wells and Miller, in *Ko and Zoa; or, the Belle Savage*, *The Times* reporting that the 'dying scene' between the two friends was 'truly affecting'.

Alongside pantomimes and burlettas, there were also some untested novelties, including pony races, an idea Dibdin had come across during his time in Dublin. Hughes did a deal with a local stable-master to provide animals and riders, while the understrappers threw open the large doors at the back of the stage, normally used for installing oversized scenery, to create an unobstructed view that went from the back of the theatre across the stage, through the large doors and over the courtyard to a racecourse laid from the entrance gates on Islington Road to a start/finish line just above the orchestra pit. Three laps was one mile. At first, the races went well, drawing large crowds eager for a punt, but the accompanying rowdiness annoyed the neighbours, who were especially angry at having their fences broken by boys climbing up to peer over the screens Dibdin had erected to prevent people watching without tickets. A summons duly arrived from the magistrate, and the races were commanded to stop.

Still smarting from Kemble's slight, Joe, too, was under pressure, which doubled when Mary announced she was pregnant. He received the news with a mixture of joy and trepidation, given the indelible fact of Maria's death. At least he could control his work and, as undisputed Clown at the Wells, he moved quickly to erase all trace of Dubois and stamp his own identity on the role. The first thing he changed was his look. As Dubois's reputation had rested on his enormous range, he'd cared little for his appearance, dressing himself, as Dibdin recalled, in the traditional character of 'a rustic booby, with red hair', a costume that was at least thirty years out of date. With the season fast approaching, Joe retreated beneath the stage to experiment with costume and makeup, commissioning Mrs Lewis to provide a series of prototype outfits. He canvassed Bologna, Hartland and Davis for their opinions, each waiting patiently behind a screen for him to emerge in yet another ensemble. Tatty country liveries were ousted in favour of bold patterns, vivid colours and a kaleidoscopic medley of circles, stripes and hoops, the dilapidated old servant's clothes discarded in favour of the costume of a 'great lubberly loutish boy', a stylised version of the shirt, ruff and pantaloons Joe had worn at Mr Ford's Academy.

Then there was the face. Where Dubois had merely rouged circles on his cheeks 'in imitation of florid nature', Joe wanted to make a canvas of his entire visage, painting a picture that was sufficiently bold to be seen at the back of a barn like Drury Lane, yet expressive enough to convey the subtleties of character in the intimacy of the Wells. Day after day he sat before the mirror, brush in hand, marking his features, wiping them clean, and starting again, until finally a face emerged from the candlelight that bore a grin so incendiary it refused to be erased. It began with a thick foundation of greasepaint, applied to every exposed inch of face, neck and chest and invading even the nostrils, the ears and inside the lips. He fixed it with a cloud of powder, then painted a blood-red wound, a mile-wide smear of jam, to form the gaping, gluttonous cavern of a mouth. The eyes, wide and rolling, were arched by thick brows whose incredulous curve belied their owner's mendacity, while each cheek received a red chevron that conveyed insolently rude health while being simultaneously suggestive of some exotic beast of Hindu demonology. The whole was topped with a wig, or rather a series of wigs, beneath which he hid his own thick brown curls: red Mohicans, blue three-tufted plumes, an orange and green thistle that was half plumber's plunger, half fox's brush.

With his hands in gloves and his feet in slippers, no part of Joe Grimaldi was left uncovered by this supreme comic being, part-child, part-nightmare. It was one of the most significant theatrical developments of the nineteenth century, and he dubbed it simply 'Joey'.

When the season opened and he went to work, the newness of his Clown was immediately evident. As Dibdin had noted during the run of *Peter Wilkins*, what came through clearest was the degree of mind he brought to clown-ing. Though still a gifted physical performer, Joe had never performed in a circus, on horseback or played clown-to-the-rope, and as such, he gave acrobatics far less emphasis than past performers had. Shifting the attention from tumbling to a fuller sense of character, his Clown had a keener intelligence and a broader palette of emotions than that of Dubois, who had been content to play the halfwit. It was a range he achieved with his incredible face, the single most remarkable face in the history of British comedy, a 'countenance', wrote the *London Magazine*, that 'is a whole pantomime in itself'. Those who saw it uniformly declared it 'indescribable', but when they could be persuaded to hazard a description called it an 'encyclopae-dia of wit' perpetually animated with 'a thousand odd twitches and unaccountable absurdities oozing out at every pore', so flexible that each feature seemed infinitely elastic and could be independently controlled. His eyes, 'large, globular, and sparkling', carried on 'without the aid of each other; one eye was quietly silent and serious, whilst the other would be engaged in the most elaborate and mischievous wink'. With one look, he could accomplish 'more . . . than his rivals could effect by the most injurious and elaborate transformations'. His 'oven-mouth' had a 'never-ending power of extension', his chin touching the buttons of his waistcoat. Even his nose could assume character. It was, in the words of one witness, 'a vivacious excrescence capable of exhibiting disdain, fear, anger, and even joy'.

Joey made an instant impression. The audience loved his explosive insanity and dedication to the pursuit of what Henry Downes Miles called 'clown atrocity', moving Dibdin to declare that nothing short of a 'New School for Clowns' had been founded at Sadler's Wells. It was an inspired comic creation, the definitive articulation of Joe's unrivalled gifts, his professional commitment and long-standing ambitions. There were influences, of course: Delpini's recklessness, Dubois's malice (recast as a playful fondness for torture), and the Signor's irresistible tendency to meddle and remake, along with a liberal dash of all the gypsies, bandits, hermits and revolutionaries he had ever played in the course of his long apprenticeship.

Joey was also an emotional homunculus, a patchwork fabricated from the emotional tatters and psychological compartmentalisation that had reshaped him since Maria's death, that provided access to a universe uncontaminated by adult disappointments and the consequences of mortality. Key to this was the retreat into childhood, as every aspect of his Clown, from his manic energy and schoolboy clothes, to his insatiable appetite for sausages and larcenous will, was suggestive of pre-adolescent desire: 'He always appeared to us to represent a grown child,' wrote the periodical *Oxberry's Dramatic Biography*, 'waking to perception, but wondering at every object he beholds.'

For Grimaldi, though, the return to childhood was categorically not a return to innocence – there was little comfort to be had in revisiting a period of his life that had been unrelentingly complex and traumatic. Rather, being an overgrown child confirmed him as an outsider, incapable of conforming to adult laws, and perpetually excluded from Harlequin and Columbine's marital embrace. This feeling of alienation reflected a puerile, under-developed sexuality, for even though Joey was a form of drag, an experiment in costume and cosmetics that allowed him to explore the boundaries of his identity, it was a transvestism of arrested, rather than embellished, sexuality. Disrupting Harlequin's hymnal dance was the sole reason for his existence, although his motivation was not jealousy or a desire to possess Columbine, but rather the opportunity to mock infatuation through 'mincing affectation', grotesque leers and parodies of ardent love. It was adult desire mimicked by a ten-year-old boy, or the queasy prurience of one who uses obscenity to mask a deeper aversion to intimacy. Abandoned, isolated and incapable of passion, Joey was not an escape from the self, he was a confrontation with it.

~

For all Grimaldi's advances in clowning and his audiences' ecstatic responses, as the season drew to a close it looked increasingly as if the Wells would record another loss. In a last-ditch attempt to claw back some profit, Dibdin arranged a boxing match between the champion of England, Jem Belcher, and the 'Father of the Art', Daniel Mendoza. It was not entirely untried – Covent Garden had tacked a match between Mendoza and his rival Richard Humphries to the end of

Aladdin some years before — and the crowds returned in riotous full voice. Encouraged, Dibdin engaged a stable of boxers to fight nightly bouts, but again the magistrates closed him down. It was a dismal end to the season and rumours began to circulate that the proprietors were going to sell. It was the last thing Joe wanted to hear as he and the heavily pregnant Mary prepared to move to Exeter. Convinced that his sole chance at being a patent Clown had passed, he was in a bleak mood.

Fortunately, a reconciliation with Drury Lane came about, although how is not entirely clear. The *Memoirs* tell the story of a dramatic awakening at midnight by a porter carrying a message from Sheridan: Grimaldi was to report at rehearsals the following day. There had been a commotion during *Blue-Beard*, a piece in which Joe used to fight a combat before the final scene, thus giving the carpenters time to prepare the complicated scenery. (Scene changes in afterpieces could be painfully slow. The King, having once commanded a performance of *The Castle Spectre* and *Blue-Beard* together, was politely told that if it was to end by midnight, it would be necessary to commence the show straight after lunch.) Having failed to arrange a replacement, Kemble left the bored audience with nothing to look at but the curtain, and they began to shout and boo, threatening to make Kemble fight the combat himself. Things rapidly deteriorated and the entire play had to be abandoned. Sheridan was supposedly furious, appearing backstage and demanding an explanation, with the result that Kemble was dressed down and Grimaldi reinstated with an additional pound a week. Satisfying though this would have undoubtedly been, it was impossible, as Kemble was travelling and *Blue-Beard* had not been in the repertoire for at least ten months. Was it an honest mistake, or a fantasy of triumph intended to confirm the reality of his persecution by serving justice on the man who had done him wrong?

However it happened, by the autumn of 1802, Joe was back at Drury Lane and Mary was spared the long and potentially hazardous journey to Exeter. Two months later, on 21 November, she was safely delivered of a son, Joseph Samuel William Grimaldi. Joe was overjoyed, and made earnest, if not difficult, promises to be a better father than the Signor had been. Ostensibly, at least, Joseph Samuel was born into a much more settled environment than his father, with the love and attention of two doting parents. In spite of the recent uncertainty, the family was also enjoying a period of relative prosperity.

Mary returned to the Drury Lane chorus two weeks after giving birth, and though she only earned a pound a week, when it was counted alongside Joe's fees from both theatres they could reckon on a household income of around £180 a year. On top of this came the trips to Mrs Baker's: those four nights in March had been worth £311 alone, making their total income for 1802 equivalent to that of an affluent tradesman. In addition, Mary had persuaded Joe to apply for membership of the Drury Lane Theatrical Fund, an actor's charity that provided a small pension in return for weekly contributions. Though pantomimists were generally ineligible for the Fund as they weren't actors, over the years Joe had accumulated enough small speaking parts to qualify. It was an excellent move. Young and coming from perpetually impoverished theatrical families, Joe and Mary were unused to money and spent freely.

Such profligacy did not go unnoticed and, coupled with Joe's rising visibility, attracted some unwanted attention, most notably from a City gentleman named Charles Newland, who approached the Grimaldis a few weeks after their first lavish Christmas with the baby. His connection to the family is uncertain, though the *Memoirs* suggest that he was known to Joe as a wealthy and respectable businessman, possibly one of the many new acquaintances he had made after the success of *Love and Magic*, the 1802 pantomime that had seen injurious crushes at the Drury Lane box office and casual labourers booking expensive boxes just to guarantee a seat. Newland asked to borrow some money for a business venture, claiming that his own capital was all profitably tied up. He must have been particularly persuasive, for Joe gave him £599, a sum that the *Memoirs* implausibly claim he'd found on the street outside the Tower of London some three years before.

Whatever the actual provenance of this golden egg, Joe happily handed it over, and in a virtual repeat of the fraud perpetrated on his father's estate by Joseph Hopwood, it immediately became clear he'd been cheated. Word came that Newland's businesses had failed, followed rapidly by the news that he'd died trying to flee his creditors by crossing to America. It was a hard blow to endure, especially as the totemic Tower Hill treasure had been found on the same day he'd asked for Maria's hand in marriage. A fool and his money are easily parted, and it would set the pattern for the rest of his life.

$\sim$

Joe's personal financial problems mirrored those of the Wells, where the rumours proved to be true. The disappointment of the previous season, following hard on the heels of an expensive refurbishment, had persuaded the proprietors to rid themselves of their unprofitable theatre, and shares were being offered at a quarter of their original price. The plummeting values were the result of troubling news from abroad – the Peace of Amiens had come undone and it was universally believed that Napoleon's next move would be the conquest of Britain.

William Siddons was particularly affected by the threat. Constantly on the verge of bankruptcy and locked in a perpetual struggle for authority with his wife, he was convinced that the days of theatricals were numbered and was trying to persuade his partners to get out before they were all overrun. One day, while he was casually stealing a look at the contents of Siddons's desk, Charles Dibdin uncovered a plan to sell the Wells to the dramatist Frederick Reynolds and the actor John Fawcett. Alarmed at the prospect of losing his job, he confronted Siddons with his discovery, refusing to leave his office until he had extracted a promise that he would have first refusal if the theatre was put up for sale. The only problem was money. Dibdin had none, but he busily set about building a syndicate with sufficient capital to meet Siddons's asking price that consisted of himself, Richard Hughes, who retained his share, the scene painter Robert Andrews, the composer William Reeve, and two businessmen, Thomas Barfoot, a bankrupt grocer with a roving eye who had had the good fortune to marry the daughter of Penton, the rich north London builder, and his friend William Yarnold. The final share went to Dibdin's brother, Thomas, happy to resume his acquaintance with the Wells as a sleeping partner.

Having successfully purchased William Siddons's share of the theatre, the owners decreed that they would begin their first season by doing 'everything upon a liberal and magnificent scale; and to give such Salaries as would tempt performers of Merit to engage with us'. The resolution was celebrated with a sumptuous dinner at the Hugheses' house in the Wells's yard, at which Charles Dibdin got incredibly drunk.

The following day he awoke with a sore head and a flash of inspiration. They would attract business by restoring the old custom of selling cheap wine with the price of admission. Accordingly, the advertisements for 1803 heralded 'New Proprietors, New Management, New Performers, New Pieces,

New Music, New Scenery, New Dresses, New Decorations, and Old Wine at 1s. 3d. per pint!!!' It was populism on a grand scale but, as usual, Dibdin's feel for the public's fancy was spot on. Then came the expected news: on 18 May 1803, just one month into the new ownership, Britain declared war on France and suddenly a country that always thought of itself as an exporter of wars was under siege. Invasion was said to be imminent, sending the population into a frenzy of fearful speculation, stoked by rumours of tunnels dug under the Channel, fleets of giant balloons that could carry three hundred French marines each, and a slough of propaganda cataloguing the 'cruelty of the Corsican usurper' while simultaneously berating the effeminacy that had allowed Britain to become so weak. Chains of Martello towers appeared along the coasts of Suffolk, Essex, Sussex and Kent, from which soldiers scanned the horizon for signs of an advancing armada as the people readied themselves to repel the horde. 'From being a nation of shopkeepers,' wrote Henry Angelo, as citizen militias up and down the country organised for war, 'we became a nation of arms.'

By the autumn of 1803, more than 342,000 men across Britain had joined volunteer corps. One of the first was Jack Bologna, who enlisted with the regiment of John Barber Beaumont, an insurance magnate and Royal Academician whose troops spent their Sundays fencing and shooting at targets at the Montpelier Tea Gardens in Kennington, south of the Thames.

Contrary to William Siddons's expectations, however, instead of becoming marginalised as an unnecessary frivolity, theatre became more popular than ever. Sadler's Wells had always incorporated warfare into its entertainment through its re-creations of battles, hospitality to sailors and long-standing tradition of announcing victories from the stage, but now, with the constant threat of the French inducing Londoners to eat, drink and be merry, its happy atmosphere of booze and pugnacity perfectly complemented the national mood.

Dibdin couldn't believe his luck. 'As far as my experience goes,' he wrote many years later, 'theatres (in London at least) prosper most during War.' Crisis brought a relevancy to the repertoire and an unexpected depth and piquancy to performances that both reflected and produced the fervent loyalty and turtle-fed John Bullism of its audience. Through their embodiment on stage, many popular images and stereotypes of the struggle against France were given a symbolic patina that they wouldn't otherwise have possessed, galvanised into patriotic ideals by the proscenium frame. It was a spirit to which pantomime became indivisibly fused, using magic and ridicule to repel the enemy, such as when Bologna's Harlequin destroyed French balloons at the Wells, thwarting an aerial invasion in *Goody Two Shoes; or, Harlequin Alabaster*.

If Harlequin was a silent commando, Joey the Clown was an artillery barrage. Grimaldi's innovations had already cut Clown's ties to his Continental forebears, but it was during the isolation of the Napoleonic Wars that he emerged as a uniquely British figure who represented the epitome of national defiance. This was partly a product of Sadler's Wells's repertory system, and the permeability between an actor's various roles. For example, Dibdin had cast Joe as John Bull the previous year in a pantomime called *The Wizard's Wake*, which required him to beat up a character called 'Citoyen François' (played by Frank Hartland) at the Gates of Calais; as the war came closer still, he had opened the season with a prelude in which the characters of Clown and John Bull were virtually fused in Joe:

> John Bull is my name,
> None my spirit can tame,
> I'm upright and downright with all.

I laugh and grow fat,
Crack my joke and all that,
And live at old Liberty Hall.

How ironic that this half-Italian actor, a child of the Babel-tongued theatrical slums, should become synonymous with national pride. But as Clown, displaying his battling obstinacy and contempt for authority, he absorbed and reflected all the stereotypes of Britishness that were championed in opposition to what was perceived as humourless French despotism.

~

The fortunes of war were about to come much closer to the Grimaldi home when, on a quiet night in November, Joe received an unexpected visitor. He was appearing at Drury Lane, playing the servant Aminadab in Susanna Centlivre's *A Bold Stroke for a Wife*, when the old doorkeeper came to his dressing room with news that two men 'of gentlemanly appearance' wished to speak with him downstairs. He ran down between scenes and found two young strangers waiting at the stage door. It was dark, and they greeted him with laughter and familiarity. Certain he was being mocked, Grimaldi turned to leave, but before he could go, the man who had been first to speak spoke again. According to the *Memoirs*, he stood with his shirt open, pointing to a scar on his chest, and said, 'Don't you know me now?', at which point Joe immediately understood that the stranger was his brother, John. Having neither seen nor heard from him for almost sixteen years, and assumed he was dead, Joe naturally clung to his brother and burst into tears.

At that moment, the call-boy brought word that Joe was needed on stage, so he invited both men up to wait. Only John agreed, his companion excusing himself after first soliciting a firm arrangement to meet his friend at ten the following morning. Excitedly leading his brother up the narrow back stairs, Joe sought out Richard Wroughton, the patron whose generosity had first allowed John to go to sea. He found him in the green room, and the amazed Wroughton was delighted to see that John had fulfilled his promise with interest. In return, John was keen to show off. Tanned, fit and wearing fashionable evening dress he accessorised with a gold-topped cane, he looked the model of a prosperous colonist, proudly slapping his breast pocket and announcing that he was carrying six hundred pounds in cash. He was anxious to see his mother, and Joe promised to take him to her as soon as he'd finished his scenes and had time to change. He left John chatting with Wroughton, the comedian John Bannister and William Powell, the prompter, saw to his business and went straight to his dressing room to get ready to take John to Baynes Row.

When he emerged, however, his brother was already gone. No one in the green room was sure when he'd left, though Powell said he'd seen him walking about on the stage a short while previously. There was no sign of him there either, and while the carpenters couldn't help, the doorman was certain he'd left through the stage door just a minute before. Perhaps Drury Lane held too many bad memories, but Joe was certain he'd catch up with him in Russell Street, but after he had run its length several times, there was still no sign. Perhaps he'd gone to call on his boyhood friend Bowley, who lived nearby. Indeed he had – Bowley had received the shock of his life – but he'd already gone off in the direction of Great Wild Street, where the family had lodged with Mrs Bailey before John had left for sea. Joe knocked and rang the bell, but was shooed off by a housemaid who didn't like people calling after dark, and returned to the theatre, assuming John had found his way back there. He hadn't.

Starting to worry now, Joe knocked up old neighbours at random to ask if they'd seen John Grimaldi, but those he called out of their beds at midnight and questioned about a boy everyone knew to have long disappeared assumed that Joe had finally gone mad. At last he ran back to Baynes Row, but John was not there either. When Joe told his mother what had happened, she fainted.

John didn't arrive that night, or the next day or, indeed, ever again. In the weeks that followed, numberless enquiries and searches were made around the vicinity of the theatre and their old family homes. Newspapers and ship lists were scoured for information on passengers and crew. The Hatton Garden police were paid for a special search and, through connections at Drury Lane, an investigation was put into motion at the Admiralty. Still no information was forthcoming.

After a month of fruitless labour, it was time for Joe to face his fears. The Admiralty suggested that he might have fallen victim to a press-gang, perhaps even a gang to whom John was known, but as he had admitted to entering the service under a false name, there was no telling which of the hundreds of thousands of conscripted sailors he was. The police, on the other hand, suspected he had been lured into 'some low infamous den' and been murdered somewhere in St Giles, the eight-acre slum behind the theatres known as 'the Holy Land'. Their principal suspect was the man who had accompanied John to the stage door, and who had so punctiliously arranged to meet him the following day. This was the solution to which the family themselves inclined, although no body was ever found — not in itself particularly mysterious or unusual, as most of the many bodies pulled from the Thames were unidentifiable.

The mystery remained unsolved for the rest of Joe's life, and if not for Bowley and the witnesses in the green room, it might be explained as an apparition caused by stress or dementia. As it was, the family tried hard to console themselves with the fact that although John had left as a boy, he had never forgotten them.*

---

* It was not the end of John Grimaldi's story. In 1877, half a century after Joe had died, the *Louisville Courier Journal* reported the death in Knoxville, Tennessee, of an 'old English sailor' called Thomas Grimaldi, who, despite being a prodigious consumer of tobacco, had attained the grand age of 106. Intrigued by a name that was so famous and so unlikely in the American south, the story was taken up by Joseph Pulitzer's paper, the *World*. Believing they had found the long-lost brother of the famous English clown, reporters were dispatched to Tennessee to discover that, like John Grimaldi, Thomas had entered the Royal Navy as a child, holding the rank of warrant carpenter through the Napoleonic wars and the American conflict of 1812, in which he was wounded during an engagement with a privateer. After leaving the navy, he spent time in the West Indies before returning to Britain, where he married and settled in Cornwall, working as a greengrocer until he emigrated to Lynchburg, Virginia, as a widower in 1856. It was a tantalising find, for the parallels with John's life were undeniable, though there were several details that refused to add up. Chief among these were Thomas Grimaldi's age and parentage. Claiming to have been born in Falmouth in 1771, Thomas would have been John's senior by ten years. Given that ages were often recorded inaccurately at this time, this needn't have proved too much of an obstacle, yet more importantly, he claimed his father was not the Signor, but a wealthy Genoan named Fidele who owned two large plantations in Grenada and several hundred slaves. When Fidele passed away, Thomas had travelled to the West Indies to claim his inheritance, but finding himself beaten to it by an older brother, he retreated to Cornwall with a small patrimony. With little evidence to suggest a relation, the story would have surely ended there, were it not for the contribution of Sir Charles Stewart, MP for Penryn, one of the founders of the Carlton Club and a frequent visitor to London theatres. It was Stewart who suggested to Thomas Grimaldi that he bore a remarkable similarity to the famous clown, and following his suggestion, Thomas supposedly began a correspondence with Joe, although this is unrecorded anywhere, including the *Memoirs*, in which the two apparently agreed that the Signor and Fidele were both the sons of Iron Legs. If this indeed happened, as the *World* reported, then Joe had lost a brother but discovered a cousin.

6

THE SPIRIT OF THE WATERS

IN 1803 THE MOST FAMOUS man in Britain was a sailor. Admiral Lord Nelson couldn't set foot on land without attracting huge crowds and lengthy ovations. It wasn't just that he had achieved magnificent victories at Cape St Vincent, Copenhagen and the Nile, battering the French and easing the threat of invasion, it was that he'd done it with such tremendous éclat. That the quarterdeck of a 104-gun ship was not unlike a stage was a fact not lost on the Admiral, who led with a flamboyant theatricality that married unrivalled courage and improvisational genius to a sincere regard for the welfare of his men and a popular disdain for the upper command. Nelson's dash knitted the public to the war effort with a passion that had been left unmoved by the vapid exhortations of William Pitt or the mentally unstable King. Even his body was an image of heroic sacrifice, his missing arm and blind eye visual mnemonics reminding every man of his duty.

The people's love of Nelson represented the fullest realisation of an infatuation with the navy that the Dibdins had been fuelling for years. The elder Charles Dibdin in particular had a great fondness for seamen, and his vast catalogue of seafaring songs had been one of the principal conduits through which the image of the jolly Jack Tar had been introduced to the popular imagination. Presenting the sailor's life as a lonely voyage of pathos and peril, his ballads were so popular that Napoleon supposedly credited them with more influence on British naval victories than the tactical supremacy of its fleet. Dibdin's children happily took up the theme. It was the success of *Naval Pillars*, Thomas Dibdin's piece based on Nelson's exploits at the Nile, that had landed him a job at Covent Garden, and his brother Charles was producing so many maritime pieces at the Wells that one reviewer suggested the Admiralty should have him decorated for patriotism. Sensing that Nelson's popularity was about to explode, Dibdin kept them coming, yet found himself increasingly frustrated by the intractable difficulties of replicating the foam and swell of the sea on stage. In order to maximise the opportunity before him, he sought to transcend those limitations by introducing the boldest novelty at Sadler's Wells to date: a lake of real water.

One of the many rumours surrounding Siddons's sale of the Wells the previous year had suggested that if Frederick Reynolds and John Fawcett were successful in their bid to buy the theatre, they would exploit its proximity to the New River by making use of its waters on stage. The idea was inspired by the success of Carlo the Wonder Dog, the canine star of Reynolds's Drury Lane play, *The Caravan*, who leapt nightly into a vat of seawater to save a child from drowning – a little trick that netted him a neat profit of £350. If so much could be made from just one scene, reasoned Dibdin, imagine the rewards if the entire stage was replaced with water. However, there was a huge difference between wheeling a tank out at Drury Lane and actually diverting a river.

Joseph Grimaldi painted by J.E.T. Robinson at the height of his fame in 1819.

A bird's-eye view of the St Germain fair, Paris, seen here minus the huge timber roof that covered the entire fairground. It was at St Germain that Joe's grandfather, Giovanni 'Iron Legs' Grimaldi, first sprang to prominence as a great *sauteur*.

'Grim-All-Day at Breakfast': This unflattering commemorative print, published only weeks after his death, is the only known image of Joe Grimaldi's father, the despotic 'Signor'.

Jean-Baptiste Dubois: The archetypal *forain* and dominant clown on the London stage, one journalist wrote that Joe learnt 'all of his pantomimical amusement under Dubois' – a claim Grimaldi denied vehemently throughout his life.

Mr. DUBOIS.

Publish'd as the Act directs, March 1.1794

Dora Jordan: While no images exist of either Joe's first wife, Maria Hughes, or his second, Mary Bristow, the countenance of his first love, the comic actress Dora Jordan, could not have been better known. 'What generous confidence, what a flush of mirth and tenderness, what a breath suspended and then blurting kind of pleasantry, relieved from coarseness by a delicious voice', wrote Leigh Hunt.

John Philip Kemble: The finest actor of his day, known for his austere and noble roles, Kemble is seen here as the Inca champion, Rolla, saving a child from the grips of evil conquistadores in Richard Brinsley Sheridan's Peruvian tragedy *Pizarro*. Though not a particular friend to pantomime, Kemble had many opportunities to admire Grimaldi's talent.

Drury Lane Theatre seen from the stage following its enlargement in 1797. 'You are come to act in a wilderness of a place,' said Mrs Siddons.

'The Manager and His Dog': A satirical print showing the manager of Drury Lane, Richard Brinsley Sheridan, being saved from drowning by Carlo the Wonder Dog, the star of Frederick Reynold's play *The Caravan*. That the artist considered performing animals to be the ruin of the patent theatres is evinced by the pair of bemused camels that look on and the figure of Thalia, the muse of comedy, covering her face for shame.

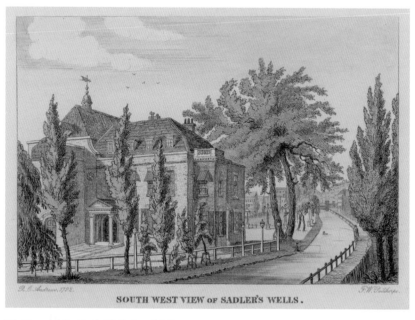

SOUTH WEST VIEW OF SADLER'S WELLS.

'Half-rural Sadler's Wells', as William Wordsworth called it. The theatre stood on the banks of the New River, built in 1613 to provide London with drinking water, and the source for the vast tanks that would become the glory of the Royal Aquatic Theatre.

Thomas John Dibdin, long-time collaborator with Grimaldi and author of *Mother Goose*.

Charles Isaac Mungo Dibdin, junior, the unstinting and clubbable mastermind of Sadler's Wells, with whom Joe had a long and frequently tetchy relationship.

Charles Farley: A funny-looking bachelor with a curiously bubbling voice, this unacknowledged genius of Romantic drama possessed a keener instinct for theatricality, entertainment and spectacle than any dramaturge of his generation.

'Mr Grimaldi as Orson': Though one of Dubois' most successful roles, Joe performed the role of Wild Man in *Valentine and Orson* for his debut at Covent Garden, making it his own with the help of expert tutelage from Charles Farley.

'The Favourite Comic Dance of Messers Bologna Jun. and Grimaldi': Joe and Jack Bologna in their *pas de deux* from *Mother Goose*.

'Sir, I'll just trouble you with a line': Joe as Clown delivering one of the most famous jokes in *Mother Goose*.

Fortunately, Dibdin had the backing of the ever-practical Richard Hughes, who saw immediately how the Wells's cellars might be converted into an enormous reservoir. Work began in the utmost secrecy at the end of the 1803 season. The workmen were locked into the theatre during the day, and at night the gates were guarded by an eccentric watchman called Richard Wheeler, who, according to Dibdin, 'walked more like an automaton than a living being, something in the manner one would imagine that a pair of Tongs would walk'. As stiff-legged Wheeler paraded outside, the stage was ripped up to expose the cellar and make way for the enormous vat that would replace the playing space, essentially a huge wooden bathtub that rested on a grid of dwarf walls erected on the basement floor. At ninety feet from the back of the stage to the front, and twenty-four feet across from wing to wing, the tank was built with tributary channels either side that would allow performers to float gracefully on and off and, when filled, held almost sixty-five thousand gallons of water. A second tank, fifteen feet square and five feet deep, was placed in the flies to provide real waterfalls.

The cost was enormous – close to a thousand pounds – but the proprietors were bullish. Dibdin justified the outlay by claiming it was not merely 'throwing a sprat to catch a herring' but 'baiting with a whale to catch a Leviathan'. Officially renamed the Royal Aquatic Theatre, the opening performance was to be a re-creation of the 1782 Franco-Spanish siege of Gibraltar. Convinced that the endeavour's success rested on its veracity, Dibdin took a trip to the Woolwich dockyards, commissioning shipwrights and riggers to build replica navy vessels on a scale of one inch to one foot. A fleet of ships was created, exact in every detail, down to the working miniature cannons that were cast in brass and complete with sails and rigging. To complete the illusion of perspective, Dibdin turned recruiting sergeant, going into the streets of Islington in search of children and small men to man his flotilla, 'water-boys' to whom he paid 2s. 6d. on top of the usual supernumerary fee to compensate them for their nightly dunking, also providing them with thick duffel trousers, a large fire in the dressing room, burly men to towel them down and a glass of brandy before and after they went in. In spite of these provisions, two still died of consumption brought on by submersion in the water, although, as Dibdin made clear, they had only themselves to blame, as after their performances the boys would 'run to the Public houses, half dry, and sit so for an hour or two, drinking and smoking (for they were generally of the *lower orders*) and hence catch cold'.

A carpenter's strike two days before opening almost sank the entire venture, but on Easter Monday 1804, the proprietors advertised a 'Grand Naval Spectacle on Real Water', banking on the public's curiosity to generate a full house. It did, and the audience were rewarded with one of the most extraordinary sights in all Georgian theatre. Greeted first by a magnificent painted curtain that depicted the English fleet drawn up in battle line against the combined fleets of France and Spain, they spontaneously burst into applause, yet when it was lifted, the sheet of water before them and the model of Gibraltar behind 'acted like electricity; a pause of breathless wonder was succeeded by stunning peals of continued acclamation'.

From downstage, the miniature fleet floated to the front, its sails and pennants shifting in the wind, processed before the orchestra and fired a salute to the audience that put them 'in an extacy'. Having thus presented themselves, the ships readied for battle. Deafening volleys were fired on both sides, as custom-built fireworks (dubbed by Dibdin '*red hot balls*') rained down from the fortress, puncturing sails, dismasting the ships and punching holes in enemy hulls. Shipwrecked children struggled in the waves, mimicking drowning with their feet planted firmly on the bottom of the tank (the water was only three feet deep), until the merciful boats of Sir Roger Curtis, the British officer who had saved many shipwrecked Spanish sailors, bobbed into view. Smoke then rolled out into the auditorium, partly to obscure the disparity of scale between Curtis's men-o'-war and the floundering boys in the water, which when it cleared revealed Dibdin's *coup de théâtre*: the calm sea bobbing with flotsam and the Franco-Spanish fleet smashed and beaten. It was an extraordinary night at the theatre. 'There are no persons who witnessed in 1804, *The Siege of Gibraltar*,' wrote Dibdin many years later, 'will assert other than that it was one of the most novel, imposing and nationally interesting Exhibitions they ever saw.'

Of course, working with a large tank of water was not without its problems. Getting the water into the theatre was a major task, and the tank took twelve men twelve hours to fill, using a specially-built Archimedes' pump. Once inside, it had the benefit of nicely cooling the auditorium, which in July and August approached 'the heat of Bengal', but it also required constant attention to keep it fresh. At its cleanest, the company would use it as a communal bath, floating on their backs after strenuous rehearsals, soothing their muscles and practising songs. It didn't take long to turn brackish, the scum of repeated performances turning it an inauspicious shade of black. Dibdin claimed to refresh the tank every couple of weeks, although Wheeler, the doorman, who years later wrote a bitchy commentary on the internal politics of Sadler's Wells from the Clerkenwell workhouse, insisted that it was allowed to stand for upwards of two months.

There was also the problem of what to do with it when it wasn't in use. Generally, the water was reserved for grand finales, final combats and ultimate tableaux, while for the rest of the show it was covered with fitted planks that served as a conventional stage. Not only did the conversion from one to the other take much longer than the management would have liked, it also robbed the pantomime of the traps and cellarwork it relied on, and wasn't always safe. Dibdin assured the company that the planks were capable of bearing any weight, but was proven wrong by Signor Belzoni, the six-foot-six 'Patagonian Sampson', who crashed right through them having attached an iron girdle to his body and invited eleven men to climb on board. He wasn't the only one to take a dip. The first week of the display was plagued by the antics of sailors who refused to believe the water was real and kept diving in, until Dibdin threatened to have the next one who did so arrested by the Watch. He himself fell in frequently during the first season, usually after rushing on stage to adjust a bit of scenery and forgetting there were no longer any boards.

~

Teething troubles aside, the water was such a draw that Sadler's Wells's first aquatic season saw profits increase five-fold over previous years. Yet if Dibdin thought he had delivered the most extravagant spectacle of the season, he was wrong. That honour went to a thirteen-year-old boy named William Betty, whose brief but phosphorescent fame compromised one of the most surreal episodes in the history of British drama.

Betty's infatuation with theatre had begun several years before in Belfast, where he had seen Sarah Siddons on one of her regional tours. Struck by her magnificence, he supposedly told his father that if he wasn't allowed to become a player he would die. Henry Betty, an adventurer alleged to have squandered his wife's inheritance along with his own, saw reason to believe his small, willowy son and apprenticed him to the prompter of the Belfast playhouse, William Hough, who shaped the boy's enthusiasm and coached him in a series of popular tragic roles. Within two years Betty was being lauded as an infant wonder, appearing on the same stage where Mrs Siddons had made her powerful impression to astonishment and acclaim, publicity his shrewd father used to secure a series of appearances in the English provinces.

The subsequent press resulted in a mad scramble to see the phenomenon. Coaches came up from London, and hotels were booked out by theatregoers curious to catch a glimpse of the boy they were calling the 'Child of Nature' and the 'Young Roscius'. Interest and enthusiasm snowballed until, during a stint at Birmingham, Master Betty was invited to play at Covent Garden for the incredible fee of fifty guineas a night. His father used the invitation as leverage with Drury Lane, where Sheridan also wanted to sign the boy, eventually negotiating an unprecedented deal to appear at both venues on alternate nights.

Within sixteen months of his first performance, and only thirteen, William Henry Betty appeared before the London public at Covent Garden on 1 December 1804, playing Achmet in John Brown's long-forgotten tragedy *Barbarossa*. Easily the most anticipated dramatic performance since Garrick's farewell, by three o'clock the corridors and vestibules of Covent Garden were stuffed with eager fans, and by four the piazza was crowded as far as Russell Street. When the doors finally opened at five, the tickets sold out in seven minutes.

The noise inside the auditorium had reached a deafening pitch long before the play began and continued unabated even after the bell had been rung for the overture. 'Even the power of the orchestra was drowned by the shrieks, screams, and vociferation from all parts of the Theatre,' wrote one witness. The temperature was stifling, despite the stage curtain being raised to encourage a draught, and fights broke out in the dangerously overcrowded pit between patrons and the constables trying to keep order. People fainted, and were pulled from the crush by a detachment of Guards and passed up to the boxes, which had themselves been overrun, much to the fury of those who had bought tickets in advance. Both the prologue and the entire first act went completely unheard in the din, and only in the moment immediately before Betty's first entrance did the clamour in the least subside, temporarily compressing itself into an agitated buzz until the long-anticipated entrance of the boy unleashed it again as a thunderous ovation.

'His admirers', wrote James Boaden, 'made him their *divinity*.' Similar scenes were played out at Drury Lane when the boy made his début there, packed houses that helped both theatres record their highest ever receipts. Betty's fee was accordingly raised to a hundred pounds a night at a time when John Philip Kemble earned thirty-seven pounds a week. At first he played only youthful roles – Romeo and Young Norval in John Home's *Douglas* – but when his repertoire expanded, he revealed a taste for tyrants like Richard III and Zanga in Matthew Lewis's *The Castle Spectre*. Each new role was greeted with the same intoxicated rapture, and when the boy was announced to play *Hamlet*, Pitt supposedly adjourned Parliament so that the Members could be guaranteed a seat. There was even talk of erecting statues in his honour. The boy was the toast of the *ton*, bundled up after each performance and escorted into a carriage to tour an itinerary of lustrous fêtes – Carlton House and Charles James Fox's St Anne's Hill among them – where the prodigy would be fussed over and plied with punch and trifle until well past his bedtime. On rare nights off he would steal the show by going to see other performers, or even unite the wonders of the season by taking in the water at Sadler's Wells, which he enjoyed immensely.

Whatever he did, the money kept rolling in: eleven nights in *Douglas* earned Drury Lane seven thousand pounds – enough for Sheridan to pay the Duke of Bedford several years' back rent and six months' in advance. So consumed was

London by Bettymania, it was as if the world had dissolved around him. 'As for politicks,' wrote Lady Elizabeth Foster, second Duchess of Devonshire, 'though every day an account of Buonaparte's coronation and Russia's decision is expected, nothing is hardly seen or talked of but this young Roscius . . . In short, he has changed the life of London. People dine at f our, go to the play, and think of nothing but the play.'

Why was this boy so enormously popular, and what talents did he possess to fuel passions of such magnitude? In part, it was the simple effect of sharp publicity meeting natural curiosity, the same good showmanship that brought crowds to counting pigs and dancing hares. At its most idealised, though, Betty's appeal drew on a Romantic belief in the proximity of childhood to unadorned nature. If the boy was its representative then, through his gifts, audiences might be granted a pure aesthetic experience stripped of all artifice.

But alongside the promise of communion there sat a more titillating appeal. Women didn't much care for this ornate youth, and Thomas Dibdin, in the audience for his début, couldn't help noticing that the people swooning over him were 'principally men'. *The Times*, similarly noting that men had outnumbered women twenty to one, drew its own conclusions, snarkily writing that, 'Master Betty's success is very naturally the cause of much envy and heart-breaking amongst the Master Polly's and Master Jenny's of Bondstreet and Cheapside, who in all their attempts to distinguish their pretty persons and effeminate airs, have only Mis-carried.'

Betty was beautiful, his admirers praising his 'youthful figure . . . graceful in the extreme', a face that bore 'all the smoothness of boyhood' and his 'full, bright and shining blue' eyes. The blond tresses that fell in ringlets about his shoulders gave him a look of 'extreme juvenility', though he was tall for his age and lissom (the *Morning Chronicle* gushingly informed its readers that he was four feet ten inches high, and weighed six stone three). Men wanted to be near him. His dressing room, wrote John Northcote, one of several artists commissioned to paint him, 'was crowded as full as it could contain of all the court of England and happy were those who could get in at the time his father was rubbing his naked body from the perspiration after the exertion in performing his part on the stage'.

Master Betty was a celebrated object of homoerotic desire, but though the exhibition of children for sexual titillation was a theatrical commonplace, his enormous popularity cannot be explained simply as an outbreak of mass pederasty. His sexuality was as nostalgic as it was provocative, a pristine youth who appealed to the golden days of dormitory and cloister before the introduction of women and the fallen world − in a sense not so dissimilar from the appeal of Joe Grimaldi's Clown. It is also possible that his maleness and juvenility were incidental to his appeal, as dressed in frilly costumes and made up with rouge to accentuate his 'young and girlish beauty', Betty possessed a sexual ambiguity that enabled him to transcend dull, quotidian categories, an unreal, superlunary androgyne, perfectly shaped to fit the erotic ideals of Romanticism. It was, after all, only natural that they should find their expression in a boy, for, at a time in which women were of secondary importance and sexual segregation was practised at almost every level of society, the beautiful male body was an acceptable object of fantasy, less restricted and more accessible than the female form could ever be.

Finally, there was simple escapism. Across the Channel, the armies of Europe were squaring up, moved by new theories of battle that cast off eighteenth-century notions of conflict as discrete strategic encounters between men of honour to embrace the idea of absolute war. Sixteen thousand men were slaughtered on the field at Austerlitz while Master Betty cast his mesmeric spell, and for those unable to articulate their fears, what better expression of the dread that accompanies the responsibilities of adulthood than devotion to a child who plays at being a man?

Betty's bizarre reign upstaged everyone and upset everything, especially those actors who were forced to appear with him night after night, grown men he dispatched in combat and mature women he woodenly wooed. Sarah Siddons had been judiciously ill throughout the entire craze, leaving the boy to act with her understudy, Mrs Litchfield. John Philip Kemble had been similarly indisposed, taking 'frightful' doses of opium for his asthma, and declining to legitimise the public's foolishness by appearing on stage. This didn't keep him from the theatre, though, for whenever Betty performed at Covent Garden, he would sit in his box, grey-faced and sclerotic, loudly expectorating 'as if purposely for the chance of coughing down his paramount opponent'.

Without the luxury of withdrawing from the stage, pantomimists were inevitably roped in. At Drury Lane, *Old Harlequin's Fireside* saw Joe and Byrne performing in a cast that was doubled by children, including Byrne's son, Oscar, and Louisa and Charlotte Bristow, two of Mary Grimaldi's little sisters. As the phenomenon continued into the new year and showed no signs of abating, every theatre was promoting its own child genius, 'some twenty or thirty *young wonders*, or *infant prodigies*', wrote the actor George Cooke, covering every branch of the profession right down to the 'Infant Candlesnuffer'. The papers jokingly consulted a 'correspondent just arrived from Lilliput', who proudly announced that 'a second Jordan, only 18 inches high' would shortly appear, and that 'according to the calculations in different nurseries, seven Garricks, fifteen Kembles, twelve Siddonses, nine-and-forty Cookes, three Brahams, and six Incledons, will be ready to start before the next winter'. Somewhat predictably, Charles Dibdin declared himself 'rather partial to the race', and over the coming seasons brought an army of talented children to the Royal Aquatic Theatre until his ardour was finally cooled when a ten-year-old singer made off with the band-leader's silver plate. Master Sloman, the first of his prodigies, however, ended up staying with the Wells into adulthood. Initially billed as the 'Comic Roscius', he débuted in what turned out to be a decidedly diminutive season that included Katerina Staberin, the 'celebrated German Dwarf', and a rowing match between six small boys in miniature boats.

Like all fads, it was ultimately unsustainable. 'The town could not be kept at *fever* heat long,' wrote James Boaden, as the dual miseries of exhaustion and puberty took their toll on Betty, forcing him to cancel performances as his health began to fail and his voice to break in the spring of 1805. Blame was levelled at his father, accused of mercilessly exploiting his son for profit, and explicitly demonstrating his greed and ingratitude by later dismissing the boy's mentor, Hough. Public sympathy fell firmly on the side of the Belfast prompter, who hit back with the promise of a tell-all memoir featuring 'curious and truly original Correspondence' that would supposedly reveal the extent of Betty's exploitation. Yet these allegations never came to light, as an annuity of fifty guineas was enough to silence Hough for life. That such a small bribe was sufficient in an enterprise awash with money raised its own suspicions. Perhaps Hough himself may have had something to hide. Charges were tacitly aired in the form of a mock application for the job of Betty's new tutor in which a candidate called 'Peter Pangloss' presented his credentials – 'L.L.D and A.S.S' – along with 'a wondrous rod in pickle/Your pretty little Bum to tickle'.

～

Between Betty and the water, Joe was feeling submerged. The positive steps he'd taken had been seriously overshadowed, added to which were the money worries that had plagued him since the peculation of Charles Newland. The fact that Jack Bologna was doing exceptionally well didn't help. At twenty years old, Jack was flourishing. His abilities were fast approaching those of his father, and his passion for tinkering with tricks and machines was beginning to bear fruit, first in the form of his very own 'Hydraulical Performance', in which he choreographed jets of water and coloured smoke to music, and next with a residency at the Lyceum, the Strand theatre they had haunted as boys, where he produced a supernatural magic-lantern show he called the 'Phantoscopia', conjuring apparitions of wailing ghosts and dancing skeletons by projecting images on to smoke and gauze and magnifying them until the audience shrieked in distress. By contrast, Joe's career seemed to have lost momentum, leaving him susceptible to feelings of helplessness, which eventually led to his departure from Drury Lane.

James Byrne had left the Lane in the summer of 1805 to join Thomas Dibdin's troupe at Covent Garden, but finding Byrne's replacement was proving problematic. It was usual practice to recruit dancers from France, and with the wars cutting off access to all but the few willing to make the arduous journey to London via Lisbon, they were at a premium. Having choreographed many occasional dances and *entr'actes* for the Sadler's Wells ensemble, Joe was volunteered to tide them over. Byrne, though, had been earning ten pounds a week when he left, and Joe, taking home a measly four, thought it fair to ask for two additional pounds, a rise, he argued, that should be honoured for the rest of the season and not just until the new *maître de ballet* was found. It was a request to which the new stage manager, his old ally Richard Wroughton, was happy to accede, and when Joe went to collect his salary at the end of the week, he was pleased to see the commitment reiterated by the under-treasurer Richard Peake, who showed him a letter of confirmation from no less a person than Aaron Graham, the chairman of the Drury Lane Board of Management.

Joe worked through the extra hours perfectly happily until three or four weeks later when the Lane hired the squat and muscular James d'Egville as *maître de ballet*. D'Egville's name might have looked appropriately French on the bills, but he was in fact a Cockney, whose real name was Jamie Harvey. His first production was a ballet called *Terpsichore's Return*, intended to introduce to Drury Lane the 'astonishing attitudinarian' Celine Parisot, described by Leigh Hunt as 'very thin and always smiling'. Joe was to play Pan in the piece, though with only a week of rehearsals left, he found his additional salary rescinded by order of the chairman of the board, a move that was doubly unjust as he danced many of his scenes with Parisot, who was on a salary of a thousand guineas for the season. Rightfully furious, he went to see Peake, who showed him an order from Graham stopping the stipend. His old fantasies of persecution rapidly re-formed, to which was added further humiliation in the form of the *Monthly Mirror*'s review that found his 'grimace and gestures . . . offensively coarse', before concluding that 'such exhibitions, reflect disgrace on the stage'. It was the second time they had singled him out for criticism, calling his appearance in last year's otherwise acclaimed ballet, *Cinderella*, a 'blemish . . . of *too base a metal* to mix with a piece of such sterling value'.

Anyone could see that Joe was being misused at Drury Lane, and Mary tried to persuade him to find a place at Covent Garden. But Joe had grown up in Sheridan's plush and oily kingdom and, though he liked to complain, acquiring the nerve to leave was a different matter. Eventually, though, he agreed to petition Thomas Harris, the Covent Garden manager nick-named Jupiter for the omnipotent influence he had acquired through forty years in the business. Harris was known as a friend of pantomime in defiance of those critics who still held afterpieces to be an affront to the dignity of a Royal patent, and understood that by nurturing the talents of men like Thomas Dibdin and Charles Farley he could bring his theatre to an enviable profitability.

The day Joe chose to visit Covent Garden saw the thickest fog to descend on London in more than twenty years. Coaches moved at walking pace, their drivers hallooing to avoid colliding with each other or driving into shop windows, which even with their lamps blazing couldn't be seen from the other side of the street. It was taking Thomas Dibdin for ever to find his way to Covent Garden too. Inching along with a hand out before him, unsettled by the muffled cries and sudden screams that seemed to come from all directions, he almost jumped out of his skin when Joe Grimaldi reared out of the mist. Joe had been lurking by the stage door in the viscous tunnel that was Hart Street, having given his name to James Brandon, the tough old doorman, in the hope of an interview.

Dibdin took him straight upstairs, delighted to hear what he was considering, having himself often pressed Harris to offer him a job. His last four pantomimes, he said, had suffered only for want of a good Clown. Delpini, Dubois and Bologna senior had all been given a run out, but all were irreversibly 'on the decline', suffering from cramp, bile and corpulence respectively. Things had grown so bad that even Farley had chanced his arm, though not with much success. Buoyed by Dibdin's enthusiasm, Grimaldi cheerfully approached the manager's door, but instead of being greeted by the kind and open face of Harris, he met the sacerdotal countenance of John Philip Kemble, and his mood instantly darkened.

'Well, Joe, I see you are determined to follow me,' said the grave tragedian.

'Yes, sir,' said Joe, with uncertainty. Harris was behind his desk, keen to hear his answer. 'You are a living magnet of attraction, Mr Kemble.'

This made Harris laugh, but Joe's eyes remained fixed on Kemble. Luckily, the actor was feeling magnanimous, and instead of the sour purse of the lips and slow shake of the head he was expecting, Kemble acted as intermediary between his former employee and Harris, launching into a fulsome recommendation of his ability, praising the comic skill of the Signor, and declaring Joe a 'true chip off the old block' and 'the first low comedian in the country'. This was unexpected flattery, especially as Kemble had disliked the Signor so much that he had not even bothered to publish an official company notice of his death until several weeks after the event. In the midst of all the Bettymania, Kemble no doubt appreciated the opportunity to hail a genuine performer, and this was sufficient recommendation for Harris, who signed Joe on the spot.

Shaking hands with Jupiter was a curious experience. Thomas Dibdin called it the 'theatrical thermometer', as on first meeting he shook hands only with his little finger, and then, on parting, gave 'one, two or three fingers in proportion to the approbation he meant to bestow'. Joe doesn't mention how much of Harris's hand he got to shake, but he was content enough with five seasons starting at six pounds a week and incremental rises that would soon have him earning double his current salary.

It took about as long for the news of the deal to reach Drury Lane as it did for Joe to feel his way across Bow Street and start dressing for that evening's performance of *Terpsichore's Return*. The green room was already full by the time Joe walked in to discover Aaron Graham furiously pacing before the company. On seeing Joe, Graham launched into a loud harangue, accusing him of treachery and ingratitude. As well as being a member of the Drury Lane board, Graham was the chief police magistrate, and so full of his own authority that he flew into fits and rages at the merest hint of contradiction.

Forced on to the back foot and naturally intimidated, Joe still managed to mount a defence, recounting in detail how Graham had gone back on a deal, and how Peake had shown him the letter containing his explicit instruction to withhold the money. Joe's reply lit a fuse. The merest mention of salaries and managerial abuse had the company rapt, and now that Graham was required to account for himself, he exploded. 'If Mr Peake showed you that letter,' he shouted, 'Mr Peake is a fool for his pains.'

'Mr Peake,' rejoined Grimaldi (who was at this point painted silver, with horns, a thick beard and a pair of furry legs for his part as Pan), 'is a gentleman, sir, and a man of honour, and, I am quite certain, disdains being made a party towards any unworthy conduct as you have pursued towards me.'

'A rather stormy scene followed,' the *Memoirs* recall, during which many voices were heard, until at last 'Grimaldi came off victorious'. Nevertheless, Joe was determined to be out by the end of the week, even when Graham threatened to sue – no empty threat, as he had coerced performers into contracts before – supported by Richard Hughes, who advised him to keep his course.

It was an ugly conclusion to a long relationship. Joe worked unhappily through the final days of his association with the theatre he had been part of for a quarter of a century, though whatever emotions he felt were soon overshadowed by events at sea, and a battle that was both triumph and catastrophe in equal measure. Even as Joe turned on his heels and stormed out of the green room, the schooner *Pickle* was speeding up the Thames with news of victory at Trafalgar and the death of Admiral Nelson. It was difficult to overstate the importance of victory. With the destruction of the most dangerous fleets of

Spain and France, the threat of invasion had almost certainly been lifted, although it rang hollow when weighed against the sacrifice given to achieve it.

A new fog descended as the news spread, one of emotional blankness. Nelson's death, wrote Robert Southey, 'was felt in England as something more than a public calamity: men started at the intelligence, and turned pale, as if they had heard of the loss of a dear friend'. Houses emptied and people came into the streets, but there was rejoicing without joy. The theatres worked up hurried panegyrics, afterpieces that did little to defray the strange pall of sadness that had fallen across public assemblies. One of these was Joe's last night at Drury Lane, dedicated to the memory of the Admiral, his monogram mounted on an anchor and borne on palms and laurels, and saluted as the entire company came on stage to sing a specially rewritten version of 'Rule Britannia'. Having dressed, and left the theatre for the last time, Joe walked through streets that were eerily quiet and beautifully luminous, every window lit with lamp or candle to commemorate their saviour, the 'darling hero of England'.

≈

In later years, Joe would always claim that his departure from Drury Lane was due to ill-treatment, poor casting and 'constant discomfort', yet there was a more practical reason for leaving when he did. It appears that he had already arranged to accompany Charles Dibdin to Dublin, where he and his brother Thomas had leased a theatre for the entire winter season, beginning on 18 November. Given that they had planned their trip around their Clown, offering him twelve guineas a week, plus two more for Mary, it seems likely that he had agreed to go many weeks before his spat with Aaron Graham. Joe was committed to Covent Garden for the following year anyway, so Graham had merely provided him with a convenient excuse to leave early.

The idea for the Dublin trip had come from Quintin Kennedy, an Irish lawyer and friend of Charles Dibdin's father-in-law, who suggested that they take over Astley's Equestrian Theatre Royal in Peter Street. Astley had recently sold it, and the place was lying empty. What was more, extensive renovations to Dublin's major venue, the Crow Street Theatre, meant that it would be closed until February or March, leaving Dibdin to enjoy the city free from competition. They were sure to clean up, said Kennedy, for 'the Public there are actually *mad* for Entertainment'.

Dibdin was all ears. The first summer of the Royal Aquatic Theatre at Sadler's Wells had been an unprecedented success, and the second was even better, even if *The Siege of Gibraltar* had not been so wildly received the second time around. In response, Dibdin added narrative tension to his aquatic pieces, and in so doing devised an entirely new form of theatre he termed 'aquadrama' – melodrama played on water. The format was perfected at practically his first attempt, a fantasy romance set in the Outer Hebrides called *An Bratach; or, the Fairy Flag*. It was also a breakout piece for the jobbing Frank Hartland, who at long last won some recognition at the Wells and had his salary doubled on account of how good he was. But there was no doubting that the scenery was the main attraction, especially the final scene set in Fingal's Cave in which the gorgeous Madame St Louis was flung violently from a precipice by the evil tyrant who had abducted her. London audiences had never witnessed a beautiful maiden being hurled into water before, but they liked it. The Wells was packed to capacity for the remainder of its run, doubling the profits of the year before. Of course, Dibdin was far too gallant to subject a real lady to such an ordeal, especially one as rare as Madame, whose husband had been guillotined in the French Revolution.

At the crucial moment, she was substituted by a 'slim boy', and they chucked him in instead.

With the aquatic windfall 'fast repaying its own purchase money', all the proprietors had the opportunity to live a little more according to their characters. Hughes became even more parsimonious, Barfoot pursued ever more expensive women, and Dibdin threw increasingly lavish dinners, indulged his rapidly growing family (which, already large, would eventually include eleven children) and had enough left to pay off his share of the Wells.

A trip to Dublin, especially under such favourable circumstances, could only consolidate his prosperity, and so, signing the contracts for a fourteen-week lease, he set about putting together 'as great a combination of burletta and pantomimic talent as ever met in a minor theatre'. But plans began to unravel before the Holyhead ferry had even spread canvas. For a start, Kennedy requested £450 up front to arrange the lease, and an additional £100 as a charitable donation to the Lying-in Hospital, which, he said, was a condition of the patent. More expensive still was the cost of transporting all the things that could not be easily (or cheaply) procured in Dublin, items like velvet, lace, satin, silk, foil and spangles, ribbons, epaulettes, swords, armour, and specialist costumes like the 'Court Dresses of the Jews'. Even more costly was the necessity of sending bulky pantomime tricks separately by coach. But the biggest problem of all, entirely contrary to Kennedy's promise of exclusivity, was the discovery that a rival company was already plying its trade in Dublin.

The news had arrived before they had even left, sent in a letter from Dibdin's old employer, William Parker, whose troupe had been in Ireland for several months. Parker proposed that the two companies join forces, but Dibdin refused flat out. There was no love lost between him and the wiry old circus manager with whom he had argued furiously in the past,

and as manager and impresario of the most modern and celebrated minor theatre in Britain, he saw no reason to join
forces with anyone.

The crossing itself was happily uneventful, and even
though the weather was poor and the drizzle relentless, Dibdin
was pleased to find that the advance party had made good
progress in preparing the theatre. The manure had been
cleared from the ring, and although the ripe smell of ferment-
ing hay and horses still clung to the matting, the benches that
had been fitted at least made it look like a London pit. There
was even some good news – a band had been hired at five
pounds a week less than he had expected to pay. He couldn't
ask for much more than that, and Dibdin spent the first night
in Dublin 'as socially as friendship, good humour, and good
cheer, could make us'. The next morning, Parker arrived and,
with a supercilious smile, said he was sorry his offer had been
turned down, and did Dibdin know that the Crow Street
Theatre was to reopen in days? This intelligence made Dibdin
balk – the renovations to Crow Street were not supposed to
be finished until the spring. Apparently, its manager, having
got wind of Dibdin's interlopers, had tripled the number
of men on the job and engaged the strongest company his
theatre had seen for years in order to repel what he saw as an
outrageous assault on his territory. 'You're sure to lose at least
two thousand pounds,' concluded Parker, tipping his hat and
walking away.

Thrown into a theatre war he hadn't anticipated, Dibdin
panicked and inexplicably bought a pair of incredibly expensive chandeliers ornamented with faux gems to hang above the
wings. Next he went to work promoting his company, hand-
delivering the forty or fifty letters of introduction the brothers
had procured from Irish émigrés in London, although this
proved a wasted effort as only one of the addressees actually
showed up during the run. He also left complimentary tickets

with a host of dignitaries, including the Mayor of Dublin, who then attempted to extort him for a licence he didn't need. Dibdin drank heavily that afternoon and resorted to 'papering' the house, handing out free tickets to give the impression of popularity. By the time the curtain rose, he delivered a slurred and barely audible prologue of welcome to a half-empty pit. The fashionable boxes were especially deserted, an effect of the Act of Union that had come into force at the beginning of the year, dissolving the Irish parliament, transferring its MPs to Westminster and, in the process, uprooting so many aristocratic families that the city felt more like Paris during the Terror than the beamish Irish metropolis. Those who remained opted to rally around their indigenous playhouse, shunning Dibdin for his presumption in assuming that the city would rush to him merely because he came from London.

The first acts were barely applauded. *Philip Quarll*, a romance about a shipwrecked hermit who lived with a monkey, came to a premature close because the ladies 'thought the Monkey's Tails indecorous and disgusting', and Dibdin realised he was truly sunk when Joe Grimaldi went on to sing his best comic songs to silence. No one could fathom it, until a member of the audience told them that the songs were already well known in Dublin, pirated by Parker's comedian, who had been singing them for weeks.

The abysmal first night over, Dibdin turned to pantomime to save his theatre, hurriedly preparing *Harlequin Aesop*, a parody of female fashions, and replacing its British travelogue scenes with hastily painted Irish backgrounds of the Lover's Leap at Dargle, the waterfall at Powerscourt and the Giant's Causeway. The entire company worked through the night to get it ready in time, but even this novelty made only twenty-four pounds. Shaking his head, Dibdin sent back to his brother in London for money to pay the salaries and the tricks for another pantomime called *The Talking Bird*, while in the interim he dealt with the catalogue of assorted nuisances that attached themselves limpet-like to failure. These included Miss Helme setting fire to her Columbine dress moments before the show, and the band having a violent backstage punch-up that could be heard clearly throughout the entire auditorium.

Even the atrocious weather refused to abate. Water had been the making of Dibdin in Islington, but here it finished him off. Like all of Astley's jerry-built hippodromes, the theatre was essentially an enormous lean-to built against the back of a crumbling old mansion. Instead of slate or tiling, the roof was covered with large plates of sheet iron, with joints so eaten by rust that when it rained, as it did almost every night of the season, water came through in torrents that drenched the seats and refreshed the ammoniacal tang of horse piss that clung deep inside them. Rain fell directly on to the pit and dripped in the boxes, defying the bundles of rags and rigged-up tarpaulins that were supposed to keep it out. Even the minefield of tubs and saucepans laid out backstage to catch the leaks could not prevent the appearance of puddles, some of which were so large that the ladies had to be carried to the edge of the stage to avoid soaking the hems of their dresses. Most of the patrons would leave to take shelter elsewhere, though some of the more resourceful ones brought umbrellas and sat the storms out. A particularly heavy downpour in December saw the seats empty in seconds, leaving the actors performing mid-scene to a deserted house.

Despite the continual run of disasters that befell the company, Joe and Mary had a wonderful time. Baby Joseph, known as JS, was too ill to travel. He had been sickly from birth and had been left in the care of Rebecca and the extended Bristow clan. Relieved of parental concerns, they were free to enjoy themselves. In the company of Jack Bologna and his wife Harriet, they found Dublin to be the most hospitable of cities as, armed with only a single letter of introduction to a man called

Captain Trench, a relative of the Earls of Clancarty, within a week they had received more invitations than they could possibly accept; coaches were laid at their disposal and they were treated to bounteous dinners of mutton and cream. To return the favour, they threw a party to celebrate Twelfth Night, for which Joe mixed a rum punch so potent that half the guests had to be carried out.

The contrast with Dibdin's misfortune couldn't have been greater, as with the generous backing of his new Irish friends, Joe even managed to do well financially. Dibdin had planned to end the season early, cancelling the benefit he was due to share with Joe. Joe, however, offered to buy out Dibdin's half for twenty pounds if he would let it go ahead, to which the cash-strapped Dibdin readily agreed, unable to imagine for a moment that Joe would sell £197 worth of tickets, including a hundred each to his landlord and Trench. There were also some expensive gifts. Trench gave him a snuff box worth more than thirty pounds, and an ebony walking-stick with an ivory clutch handle inscribed '*Joey Grimaldi, 1805*'. Dibdin, understandably sour, was somewhat mollified when Joe gave him a much-needed loan of a hundred pounds.

The Wells company in Dublin stumbled on until shortly after Christmas, when Dibdin was approached by Jones, the Crow Street manager, whose season was also suffering from rain and polite society's exodus for London. Jones invited the Sadler's Wells company to merge with his, an offer Dibdin gratefully accepted, playing out the dregs of a miserable January before moving in with Jones to perform afterpieces to thin houses until late March. The end couldn't come soon enough, and when they finally came to count their losses Parker's prediction proved to be perfectly correct – the Dibdins were in for more than two thousand pounds.

Dublin was an unprecedented disaster for the brothers, effectively destroying any chance of financial security for either man for the rest of their lives. This, however, may have been exactly the point. Unknown to Charles, Quintin Kennedy, the man who had put him on to the Peter Street venture, also served as Philip Astley's agent. Relations between Astley and Dibdin had been strained for a while, and had only recently survived a fracas after Dibdin had hired an impressionist whose routine included an impression of the Lambeth manager. It seems remarkable that Dibdin hadn't anticipated that the hot-tempered military man wouldn't take such mockery in good sport and, sure enough, his son turned up at the Wells ready to defend the family honour. As a youth, John Astley had been an elegant and graceful dancer, who had once performed at Versailles and been honoured with a diamond-set medal and the title of 'English Rose' by Marie Antoinette. In his prime, he had been proud and quick to aggression, 'not a man to be intimidated', said Dibdin.

Astley junior took a box and waited until the impressionist had taken the stage before standing up to brandish a horse-whip and announce to the audience that if the act was allowed to continue he would beat the man in full view of the public. Dibdin dropped the curtain immediately, which disappointed the audience so much that the uproar took a full half-hour to die down. Astley senior thanked him for his actions in an open letter to *The Times*, while the impressionist, fearing for his safety, had his son bound over to keep the peace.

But this was nothing compared to the bigger problems that faced the Astley empire. Just a year before the Dublin débâcle, his Lambeth Amphitheatre had been consumed by flames, destroying forty houses and claiming the life of John Astley's mother-in-law. Old Astley had been in France where, during the short-lived Peace of Amiens, he had success-fully petitioned Napoleon for ten thousand pounds' worth of property and fourteen years of back rent he had lost on his Parisian theatre during the Revolution. When war resumed he was interned, yet managed to break free by feigning illness and being granted leave to visit the spa at Piedmont, whence he fled down the Maine, hijacked a postilion at the German border, drove to the banks of the Rhine and escaped via the coast of Schleswig-Holstein. On arrival in London, he learnt that his wife had died the week before, his double loss compounded by chronic under-insurance that forced him into a number of expediencies, of which selling his Dublin theatre was one.*

Even in adversity, Astley remained a dogged and fierce competitor, outlasting almost every other manager in London over a career that spanned thirty years, including Charles and Thomas Dibdin's father, whose Royal Circus he had especially despised. Jealously noting the success of Sadler's Wells's aquatic enterprise as he embarked upon the long process of rebuilding his flagship theatre in Lambeth, and fully cognizant of their chances of failure, Astley may well have contrived to send the young Dibdins on a wild-goose chase. It is an intri-guing possibility as, after all, what better way to teach an up-and-coming manager about the risks inherent in management?

---

* Astley might well have accomplished his escape by swimming much of the way: despite being enormously fat, he was an expert swimmer, who once floated on his back all the way from Westminster Bridge to Blackfriars holding a flag erect in each hand for a bet. He also owned a very large bathing-machine for the use of the general public, which he stationed on the Vauxhall side of Westminster Bridge. After his death, the Sadler's Wells treasurer, Polly de Cleve, as executor of his will, claimed to have taken possession of all the verse Astley had written on the subject of his wife and son, both of whom, it revealed, he hated prodigiously.

7

MOTHER GOOSE

Well, wonders, for certain, they never will stop,
The stage is transform'd to a poulterer's shop:
These fashions of Lunnun seem queer to a clown;
Once the town pluck'd the geese, now a goose plucks
  the town.

'John Grouse and Mother Goose', sung with unbounded applause
by Mr Emery, of the Theatre Royal, Covent Garden (1807)

IT TOOK SIX DAYS for the company to get back from Dublin. The crossing, never pleasant, was worsened by foul weather, though the discomforts of travel only really made themselves felt after they landed at Holyhead. The booking agent had forgotten to reserve Joe a seat on the coach, and as Mary took her place inside, he was forced to sit outside with the luggage. None of the passengers was exempt from being bumped and jolted along the abysmal roads, rutted, muddy and often impassable outside summer, but Joe had to endure the added privations of rain and cold that no combination of greatcoats and blankets could repel.

At Red Landford, they encountered a frost so intense it rendered him insensible. Literally frozen to his seat, he was revived only hours later, after a couple of ostlers had hauled him into an inn, bathed his feet in a tub of brandy and rubbed his body with astringents to restore the circulation. Cold re-animated the aggregated pains and injuries that on good days he could ignore, parcelling his body into fillets of deep aches striated by sharp, cartilaginous twinges. Having borne the brunt of a quarter-century of high leaps and heavy landings, the pain was worst in his legs. On winter mornings, his hamstrings were so tight he found it difficult to walk. Bone spurs in his heels and ankles felt like hot screws in his feet, while inside his knees grew the first signs of arthritic calcification.

The road never treated Joe well, but thankfully there was little travelling that spring, and by summer he was enjoying relative ease. Bettymania was finally over. His image tarnished, the gilt of adulation had peeled and blistered, helped on its way by John Philip Kemble who, sensing that the 'influx of pygmies' would surely induce an 'epidemic nausea', delivered a public emetic calculated to shame the people back to their senses. It had been administered in November, three weeks before the boy was due to return to Covent Garden, and came in the form of his very own infant phenomenon, an eight-year-old girl called Miss Mudie. Casting her as Peggy in *The Country Girl* (one of Dora Jordan's most popular roles), he treated the audience to the sickly spectacle of a child courted by a series of adult lovers, all of whom had to kneel to embrace her. The bounds of propriety had been pushed too far, and the disgusted audience hissed the child from the stage, although, to her credit, she refused to leave until she'd first come to the footlights to deliver a haughty rebuke. It was nasty and embarrassing, but it worked. The spell had been broken, the audience had been chastised, and no longer was the public willing to accept children playing adults.

Things were also running smoothly at the Wells, where the battle of Trafalgar was playing with the apotheosis of Nelson rising from the water and ascending into the clouds. Joe, meanwhile, had signed a new three-year contract worth twelve pounds a week and two clear benefits free from overheads, good for another two or three hundred pounds each. The water had pushed the pantomime to the front of the bill, which meant that, for the first time in his career, Joe's work had finished at the theatre before it was even dark. Hardly knowing what to do with himself, he took to ambling around the streets, taking in the sights and marvelling at the occupations of ordinary people 'in perfect astonishment at finding himself there'.

That summer, the Grimaldis took a cottage eight miles out of the city at Fallow Corner in the grounds of what is now Finchley Memorial Hospital. This small, agrarian community seated on the common a few miles above Kentish Town gave little JS the chance to enjoy the clean air and space his poor health badly needed. More than that, it reassured Joe to have his son as far away from the theatrical stews as possible. He didn't want his boy to go on the stage. He already had an apprentice in Mary's little brother, George, whom he had just taken on at the Wells, and Bettymania had only confirmed any lingering doubts. Instead JS lived quietly in the cottage with his mother for the duration of the summer season while Joe commuted, travelling between Finchley and Islington four or five times a week, spending the occasional night in Baynes Row when business detained him.

Having acquired a neat little gig and a wily old horse, 'a very steady one' who could find his own way home in the dark, Joe was at liberty to spend a few hours in the Sir Hugh Myddleton after every performance, and it became his custom to take a few glasses with his friends before falling asleep at the reins and waking up an hour later at his own gate where his fourteen-year-old servant, a boy named Richard Watts, would be waiting to help his master to bed. Sometimes Watts would also fall asleep, and there they would have stayed, dozing on either side of the fence, had not the horse woken them both with an irritated snort.

Everything seemed to be going well: the work was rewarding, the weather was good, and having had the satisfaction of reading in the press that 'Grimaldi's clown may, with justice, be said to be the best on the English stage', his status as a respectable citizen was confirmed when he was invited to sit on the jury of Highgate Manor Court.

But the tranquillity of summer turned with the leaves, and with his first season at Covent Garden approaching, the anxiety of business resumed. Working at Thomas Harris's theatre would be markedly different from life at Drury Lane. Covent Garden was the King's preferred venue for a reason, as during the almost forty years in which Harris had been associated with the theatre, he had built a commonwealth of such stability and sound principles that any monarch would have been proud to rule over it. Harris's reputation for fiscal probity, managerial efficiency and even-handedness was a far cry from the libertin- ism and perpetual chaos of Drury Lane, although it was the Lane that had always enjoyed a reputation as the more adven- turous and engaging of the two. This is not to say that Harris was immune to either novelties or faddishness, as the William Betty débâcle had shown, but by luring John Philip Kemble to Covent Garden, he aimed to seize the artistic laurels from his rival.

Free from the impecuniosity and financial brinkmanship that characterised life under Sheridan, Kemble set about as- sembling the biggest collection of talent Britain had ever seen, albeit one that strongly emphasised tragedy as opposed to Covent Garden's traditional strengths in innocuous modern comedies. In hiring Kemble, Harris dealt his rival a death blow, as Sheridan had neither the finances nor the focus to compete, and though granted the occasional reprieve in the shape of successes like Carlo the Wonder Dog, his theatre entered an irreversible period of decline that his reputation for flash and brilliance could do little to reverse.

There was no doubt about it: Joe was being inducted into the highest circle of British theatrical life, and he began to fret excessively about what role he should take for his impending début. This question brought him into contact with Covent

Garden's head of pantomime and melodrama for the first time, Thomas Dibdin's colleague and collaborator Charles Farley. Joe was set on playing Scaramouch in Delpini's *Don Juan*, a role he had successfully played at Drury Lane and which had the additional virtue of presenting him as a natural heir to one of the greatest pantomimists of them all. Farley, though, wasn't convinced, and made a suggestion that stopped Joe in his tracks: why not play the Wild Man in *Valentine and Orson*, the role synonymous with the malignant Frenchman Jean-Baptiste Dubois? Joe recoiled at the thought. After everything he had done, to open himself up to renewed accusations that he was nothing but 'a pupil and copyist of Dubois'? But Farley, who had played Valentine alongside Dubois many times, was convinced that Joe could do it better, arguing that the bigger, more extensive role was a vehicle far superior than the servile mugging of Scaramouch. Reluctantly, Joe allowed himself to be persuaded, but only on condition that Farley help him to reinvent the piece. Donning the lucky red cap he always wore to rehearsals, Farley coached him intensively long before the show had even been cast.

These sessions were a revelation. Joe was in awe of Farley's theatrical intelligence and his skill as a mime, taking so much from his instruction that in later life he was happy to say that if he had had any master at all it was Farley. Though older than Grimaldi by seven years, the two had a great deal in common. Like Joe, Farley was a local boy who had floated free of the slums through the power of a vividly phantasmagorical imagination. A life-long bachelor with a reputation for being exceptionally devoted to his mother, he had entered the theatre in childhood, working in a variety of menial capacities as he waited for his opportunities on stage. His choice of roles was hampered by a squat figure, an enormous nose and a curious voice said to sound either 'bubbling', as though with effervescent saliva, or as if his mouth contained a currant bun.

('His voice is against him,' claimed one review, 'and is not mended by over-exertion, which he seems to think it is.')

Ill-favoured by nature, Farley made the most of what he had, compensating for his physical shortcomings with a fund of talent and an ability to work without fatigue. He was 'remarkable', said Leigh Hunt, who served with him in the St James's volunteer corps at the height of the invasion threat, 'for combining a short, sturdy person with energetic activity'. His nose was later reduced by a primitive cosmetic surgery, and even the voice ended up working for him, particularly suited as it was to frothing madmen and giggling *bons vivants*. Farley's greatest gift, however, was for arranging pantomimes and melodramas, summoning scenes with the clarity of vision with which a child perceives the figures of its mind's eye. Though without formal education, Farley had an extraordinarily rich visual vocabulary and an eye for detail that he sharpened by spending hours browsing the artefacts of the British Museum or the prints in Signor Colnagi's Cockspur Street print shop, where he could often be found cramming information on flora, fauna, costume and geography.

Under Farley's instruction, Joe worked harder than he had for any other role. The play, which opened on 9 October, was performed in a mélange of dialogue, song and long sequences of action, and though Joe had no lines, as the Wild Man, he expressed his savagery through explosive movements and beast-like physicality. The piece opens with the return of the King of France from war, especially grateful for the heroism of Valentine, a foundling youth whose courage has assured their victory. Soon, a group of peasants arrives at court to petition for the King's protection from a wild man who is terrorising their woods, and Valentine is volunteered for the task of hunting him by envious courtiers who wish him out of the way. Accepting the challenge, Valentine enters the woods undaunted, encountering the Wild Man Orson just as he is out hunting for meat to feed the 'old weather-beaten she-bear' that suckled him. Valentine attacks him, but he proves a tenacious opponent, demonstrating the agility of an animal by leaping from bough to stage and back again, hurling rocks, ripping up saplings and wielding his club with monstrous rage. During the fight, the she-bear dies after drinking some wine left behind by Valentine's fleeing page, and weakened by grief, Orson submits himself to the warrior, who binds his hands and leads him back to court where, after various comic encounters with polite society, he is discovered to be the lost brother of his captor, and both of them the abandoned sons of the Queen of France.*

It was a watershed role for Grimaldi, the hardest part he had ever played, making physical demands that far outstripped anything he had tried before, while also fundamentally reshaping his sense of his career. The plaudits were many – as a representation of bestial man, William Hazlitt always preferred Grimaldi's Orson to any Caliban he had ever seen – but after only a few nights, his exertions caused significant pain, forcing him to 'stagger off the stage into a small room behind the prompter's box, and there sinking into an arm-chair . . . sob and cry aloud, and suffer so much from violent and agonising spasms, that those about him, accustomed as they at length became to the distressing scene, were very often in doubt, up to the very moment of his being "called" '. Grimaldi invariably

---

* The bear in *Valentine and Orson* was usually played by a man in furs, although on several occasions, Giovanni Belzoni, the 'Patagonian Sampson', chose to play Orson against a real bear. One night in Perth, Belzoni found his co-star in a particularly truculent mood during the death scene, biting and swiping and trying to get him into a potentially fatal clinch. Belzoni batted her off even as she was supposed to be dead. The result was booing and heckling from the Scottish audience, who berated him for his lack of respect and shouted, 'Why don't you gie your puir auld muther a wee kiss?' Belzoni retired from the stage and went on to become the most important Egyptologist of the early nineteenth century, excavating six major tombs in the Valley of the Kings, and bequeathing the British Museum many of its finest archaeological treasures.

conquered his pain in time to reappear, but in the contrast between the expansive candlelight of the Covent Garden stage and the 'small room behind the prompter's box', he uncovered the tension between public performance and inward despair that would become the defining principle of his career.

The idea went back to some of his earliest memories of childhood, such as a time in the green room at Drury Lane, where the Signor, having found him straying from his corner, took him on stage to beat him in front of the audience. As the *Memoirs* have it, the scene was taken 'as a most capital joke; shouts of laughter and peals of applause shook the house; and the newspapers next morning declared that it was perfectly wonderful to see a mere child perform so naturally, and highly creditable to his father's talents as a teacher'. While a search of the newspapers yields no such report, the intent of the anecdote was to lend weight to the idea that Joe was never more brilliant than when suffering. Such was the cornerstone of a personal mythology that became woven into the structure of the *Memoirs* themselves, ordering events within a carefully calibrated economy of punishment and reward where pleasures of any kind, professional or romantic, find an immediate counterweight in misery or pain.

It was an idea to which Joe would become superstitiously attached, in part because it was the only one that seemed to offer any explanation of his ability. Even at the height of his powers, Joe lacked a vocabulary to explain his performances accurately. Words eluded his critics, too. 'We can in no way describe what he does,' wrote one of the many delighted but baffled journalists who reviewed him, 'nor give any idea of the inimitable style in which he keeps up the ball from beginning to the end.' In the absence of any substantive grasp on what it was that made him so good, pain acted as talent's guarantee, proof that he was performing at the very limit of his abilities. In tears and panting in a backstage nook, stupefied by the

dilating fullness of his agonised body, Joe believed he had
uncovered the mysterious logic that guided his life.

~

Thomas Dibdin had never fully reconciled himself to his talent as a writer of pantomimes in spite of the quality of his
collaboration with Farley and the cachet it brought him with
Harris. To him it was the 'drudgery' that kept him from his
true vocation as a legitimate writer, and an annual affront to his
professional self-esteem. Kemble's arrival only served to make
matters worse, as now it was his turn to feel the Arctic chill
that for years had frozen out the pantomimists at Drury Lane.
The atmosphere deteriorated so badly that Dibdin decided
that if he was ever to have a chance of making it as a serious
writer, he had to distance himself from pantomime altogether.
Seeking out Harris, he petitioned for another assignment,
and was permitted to spend the summer of 1806 'free from
the everlasting dream of traps, flaps, daggers of lath, and parti-
coloured jackets' to provide Covent Garden with a farce.

Without Thomas Dibdin, pantomime was entirely ignored.
Preparations for Christmas usually began as early as July, but
by the end of October the carpenters hadn't built a single trick,
nor the seamstresses sewn a solitary spangle. Assuming that
Harris had other plans, Dibdin's *Reminiscences* recall how horrified he was when the manager came knocking on his door in
mid-November and announced, 'Well, my dear Dibdin! We
cannot do without a pantomime from you after all.' Appalled
that his newest bid to be taken seriously was dissolving before
his eyes, Dibdin protested in the strongest terms. There wasn't
nearly enough time, he said, but Harris would have none of it,
telling him to dust off some old ideas and get going. The only
script Dibdin had was a piece he'd been unsuccessfully pitching
for the past five years.

'What, that damned *Mother Goose*, whom you are so wedded to!' Harris exclaimed. 'Let's look at her again: she has one recommendation; there's no finery about her; and the scenery in general is too common-place to take up much time: so, e'en set everybody to work: I need not again see the manuscript. I will speak to Farley, and you must lose no time.'

'But, sir,' spluttered Dibdin, 'our late agreement, and the difficulties thrown in my way.'

'You are too good a fellow to talk about agreements when I want you to do me a service,' replied Harris, the pleasantry barely disguising the gravity of the command. Promising every resource within his power, he turned to go, saying, 'I cannot expect you to effect much, especially with such a subject; but do the best you can.'

Dibdin went to Farley, and the two set to work with lumpish hopes. The scenemen and carpenters shook their heads, tut-tutted, ran thick pencil marks through all the bits that would be impossible to make at such short notice and departed in a cloud of glue and turpentine. The big heads had to go and, given the paucity of time, the grand finale, the most anticipated scene in the whole theatrical calendar, must necessarily be austere. Next, they mustered the cast, who, looking at the outline of *Harlequin and Mother Goose; or, the Golden Egg!*, found it, in Joe's words, 'as plain as possible'. With 'neither splendid scenery, nor showy dresses . . . the apprehension of the performers', he recalled, was 'proportionately rueful'. With the script needing to be rewritten to accommodate production constraints, rehearsals began without it. (It didn't actually reach the Examiner of Plays to be censored until 18 December, and then only as an eight-page précis that contained no business of any kind, just the words to the songs.) There was another bad omen when Farley arrived on the first day without his lucky red cap, and had to be sent out immediately to get a new one.

For the next four weeks, the performers saw little but the Covent Garden cellars. Dressed in coarse linen toiles, they went carefully through their steps to the scraping accompaniment of the 'répétiteur', a dishevelled old gentleman with a violin. Fortunately, the cast worked well together. To say they were close significantly understates the degree to which families were at the heart of Georgian theatre. Joe was joined in the cast by Mary and her sister Louisa, while the Bolognas numbered no less than five: Jack played Harlequin, Louis played Pantaloon, Pietro was the Landlord, Barbara a fairy and Mrs Bologna a villager. Columbine was played by Miss Searle, whose little brother was also in the cast, as were representatives of four other long-standing Covent Garden families: the Tett brothers, the wives of John Follett and Whitmore, the scene painter, and Thomas Goodwin, the son of the music librarian. Connections also opened out beyond the theatre: Oddfish the sea monster was played by Monsieur Ménage, the father of Bella, the prepossessing Columbine of Drury Lane, and Master Ménage, Sadler's Wells's most popular monkey. King, Davis and Morelli were all Sadler's Wells regulars, the last also being an important theatrical agent, who acted as an intermediary between London managers and Italian acrobats.

There were also some connections for the future. Buried deep within the chorus was the journeyman actor Thomas Blanchard, who would later play Pantaloon to J. S. Grimaldi's Clown, although not so well: 'The fault of Mr. Blanchard', wrote *The Times*, 'is that he excites no sympathy. If he is knocked down, or jumped upon, or even killed, you are glad of it.' Blanchard's son, Edward, would eventually follow in the footsteps of Farley and Dibdin and become one of the foremost supremos of Victorian pantomime. He was also a manic depressive.

As rehearsals moved along and word got out that Covent Garden was preparing for Christmas, Drury Lane, determined, perhaps, to punish Grimaldi for his disloyalty, set to work on a spoiler, a pantomime even more hasty than Dibdin and Farley's, called *The Enchanters; or, Harlequin Sultan*. Opening on Boxing Day, it had Mr Montgomery as its Clown and Frank Hartland as its Harlequin. Joe and Jack went along to the opening night but found it nothing more than a dire assemblage of old scenery and borrowed airs. Montgomery, who clowned at the Royal Circus, had been called in a week before it opened, and even though he was being paid a much larger salary than any previous Clown at Drury Lane, he completely failed to get a handle on the business. It was, said Joe, 'so wretched that the audience began to hiss before it was half over, and eventually grew so clamorous that it was deemed prudent to drop the curtain long before the intended conclusion'.

Drury Lane's failure offered some encouragement to the cast at Covent Garden, though by the time *Mother Goose* was ready to open, the company had already resigned itself to the fact that Christmas 1806 would be a lamentable season for pantomime. Harris's tacit vote of no confidence was cast by his absence. Usually so diligent in his attention to all the productions in his theatre, he attended only one rehearsal, escorted by the man coming to be known as the pantomimists' albatross, John Philip Kemble. It was midnight on a Sunday, the only time Dibdin and Farley could get access to the stage for a full run-through with all its machinery, a rehearsal that would go until dawn. Harris enjoyed it well enough and even the sclerotic Kemble seemed to take it in good spirits, but both had enjoyed a long dinner and tucked more than a few bottles of wine under their belts. Certainly they found nothing in it to suggest that it was going to be one of the most important productions that either of them would ever live to see.

∾

Chains of lights converged on Bow Street on the evening of 29 December 1806, the trails of linkboys lighting the way from all corners of the mud-spattered city as theatregoers descended on the Covent Garden pantomime. Outside, hoarse hackney-carriage men shouted impatiently at their passengers, a slow-moving cargo of holiday groups adding to a crowd already swollen by the 'freshwater sailors' (fake beggars from the Holy Land), fruit women, playbill hawkers and men selling 'saloop', a hot concoction of sugar and sassafras, thought to be good for the guts. The opening of the pit doors signalled the customary dash for the front. With no central aisle or ticketed seats, it was a free-for-all, a steeplechase of men, women, knees and elbows, hurdling over the benches, jostling each other to shouts of 'Watch your pockets,' in a mad rush to get close to the stage.

Once the auditorium was full the bell rang twice, and in accordance with a fifty-year-old tradition, the audience settled in to watch John Philip Kemble's brother, Charles, appear in a constipated tragedy called *George Barnwell*. Playing it before the pantomime had originally been Garrick's idea, a means of salving his conscience by offsetting what he saw as the weightless amorality of laughter with stern admonitions to youth: 'We do not know a single drama', wrote the *Dramatic Censor* of this stodgy tale of a young merchant's vice-strewn path to the gallows, 'better calculated to place the youth of the metropolis . . . upon their guard against the snares, to which inexperienced innocence is but too often exposed from female seduction, and the dangerous allurements of fallen beauty.' The audience, however, tended to side with William Hazlitt, who thought it 'a piece of wretched cant', and showed their contempt by talking all the way through and applauding only when the green carpet that signalled the final scene of a tragedy was brought out.* By the time Barnwell was finally led to the scaffold, the mood in the house could not have been gayer. Safely back-stage, Charles Kemble, a strong, emerging actor in his own right, despondently brushed the orange peel from his shoulders, and made way for the pantomimists waiting in the wings.

Pieces of fruit made graceful parabolas across the auditorium as the scene-shifters set to work behind the heavy stage curtain, the hum of anticipation intensifying as the conductor stood in his pit and gestured to the orchestra. With a flick of his baton, as if throwing a lighted match into a tar barrel, he ignited William Ware's overture with a *whoof* that fanned out across the excited crowd. The curtain rose to a crack of thunder, revealing a village in the midst of a storm. In the distance were fields and a river with puzzled boats tossed on its swell. At opposite sides of the stage stood the gates of Squire Bugle's mansion and a simple country cottage, above which appeared Mother Goose riding on the back of her magic gander. Played by Samuel Simmons, a pocket-sized comedian (he 'can never lie *long* in bed'), who had initially cursed his luck but eventually came to see it as one of his greatest roles, she descended to the stage as the scenemen removed multiple layers of gauze to create the effect of dispersing clouds, simultaneously raising coloured lustres to show the sun breaking through and forming a rainbow. Now, bathed in glorious sunshine, a chorus of singing, dancing peasants poured into the village to celebrate the coming marriage of Squire Bugle to the beautiful young Colinette.

---

* Though it had been the practice to lay a green carpet for the final scene of a tragedy for many years, the origins of the custom are entirely unclear. It was practical inasmuch as it prevented those characters who were about to die from dirtying their costumes on the filthy boards, and was probably green because that was the colour most associated with the theatre with its green room, green curtain and green baize upholstery.

Grimaldi played Bugle, 'a rich widower with repulsive manners', whose name suggested a life devoted solely to the pleasures of the hunt. Bugle was representative of a country type much loathed in the metropolis for exploiting its tenants, enclosing their land and impoverishing them through inflated rents. It was not his authority they objected to so much as the way his exercise of it threatened the established order. If despotism was allowed to become cruelty, might it not imperil the nation by fuelling the kind of revolutionary discontent that had wrought such destruction in France? A disgrace to his class, the Squire was the polar opposite of the ideals of lordly paternalism that formed the supposedly benign foundation of the British social contract. His desire for Colinette, the unwilling bride pandered to by her sycophantic guardian Avaro, similarly represented his disregard for natural order.

Colinette is in love with Colin, a humble swain, played by Jack Bologna, seen pining from his cottage window at the beginning of the scene and cursing both the Squire and his intractable poverty. Bugle pulls Colinette towards him as she vainly protests, appealing to the Squire's own experience of young love by pointing to a gravestone at the centre of the stage that reads: 'In Memory of Xantippe, wife of Bullface Bugle, esq.' The lecherous old Squire just laughs, jovially singing, 'First wife's dead/There let her lie/She's at rest,/And so am I.' This is all too much for Colin: he suddenly rushes out to Colinette, who flies into his arms. A Beadle appears, as Avaro is pulling them apart, dragging Mother Goose in his wake. Accusing Mother Goose of witchcraft, the Squire condemns her to the ducking stool, despite Colin's pleas for clemency. But before the Beadle can lead her away, Colin pulls her free, running away as Mother Goose flies up to the clouds, and Avaro retreats with Colinette. Furious, the Squire cracks his whip at his first wife's tomb, accidentally summoning her ghost. Dressed in satin and ribbons, Xantippe – so named for the notoriously scolding wife of the philosopher Socrates – angrily chases her husband from the stage.

Safe in her cottage, surrounded by sprites, Mother Goose comes across the dejected Colin, and rewards him for his decency with a golden egg and the magic bird that lays them: 'This present shall her guardian's sanction gain,' she prophesies, before promptly disappearing. The astonished Colin carries both egg and gander (played by a small boy named Leonard) to the greedy Avaro, who now cannot give Colinette away fast enough. Consumed by avarice and too impatient to wait for another golden egg, he pulls out a knife to cut it from the goose and, though Colin stays his hand, he relents when the Squire reappears, suddenly fearful that he will again lose the right to marry his love. With the knife bearing down, the bird magically changes into Mother Goose, who launches the golden egg into a far distant ocean and transforms them all into the characters of the harlequinade – Bugle and Avaro become Clown and Pantaloon, and Colin and Colinette become Harlequin and Columbine. Scolding each in turn, Mother Goose gives Harlequin alone a chance to atone by handing him a magic sword and sending him on a quest: 'Regain the egg, and happy be,/Till then, farewell! Remember me!'

Such is the plot of *Mother Goose*, a simplistic rubric intended merely to kick-start the harlequinade. To a crowd like that of Covent Garden, well versed in Shakespearean comedy, its young lovers thwarted by cross-grained authority would have had a familiar feel. Shakespeare, however, affords his characters the chance to broaden their horizons by slipping into the woods and re-inventing themselves in a place of suspended laws and relaxed hierarchies, whereas the green world of pantomime is almost entirely punitive, a rapid succession of real and fantastic locations that subjected its characters to endless rehabilitative violence.

Mother Goose's harlequinade begins with two classic tricks: Harlequin leaping through a clock face in Avaro's hall, and a painting of a shotgun discharging itself into Clown's face. From here the lovers are pursued to a country inn, where Clown is scared off by a recruiting party who only manage to press a single drunken cobbler into service.

It was at this point during the performance of 27 January that a bottle was thrown from the two-shilling gallery, severely wounding a man below. A Mr Shepherd told how he and his brother had been watching the pantomime from the pit, about six rows back from the boxes, when he heard the sound of breaking glass, and turned to his brother, who had blood gushing from a wound in his head and was crying, 'I am a dead man.' Grimaldi came forward to try to calm the house as the victim was carried backstage. Farley, accompanied by two Bow Street officers, secured the gallery and offered sixty guineas to anyone willing to finger the culprit. A 'poor simple Welchman' named Davis was arrested and arraigned the following day, at which time it was doubtful that Shepherd would survive.

Back on stage, Joe as Clown and Louis Bologna as Pantaloon rough up the Landlord, while Jack Bologna as Harlequin disguises himself as a female fruit-seller. Joe moves in on Jack's fruit basket, pilfers a couple of items and, changing tack, tries to seduce him. The pair begin a burlesque *pas de deux*, parodying the latest fashions in dance, their leaps and twirls becoming ever more ludicrous until they are both being 'flung and floundered, and flounced and bounced, and shuffled and scuffled, and draggled and wiggle-waggled, shambled, gambolled, scrambled, and skimble-skambled'. It's typical of Joey's off-beam sexuality that he should entirely ignore Columbine yet be passionate for a man in drag. For Harlequin, Columbine is the ultimate reward. Helplessly feminine, the allure of this almond-eyed innocent is found as much in the fragrant rustle of satin and gauze as it is in flesh and bone.

While he pursues his goal with a rigid determination, ceaselessly seeking the egg, which is the key to her sexual possession, Clown is staunchly his opposite, the epitome of meandering sexuality and libidinous digression that embodies itself as an oblique ardour for a man disguised as a fruit-laden woman.

The lovers are chased inside the inn, where Clown and Pantaloon are distracted by a meal of wine and pies. When they sit down to cut into one, a live duck flies out, presenting Harlequin with the opportunity to bat the chairs and tables, sending them eight feet into the air. With a shout of terror, Joe, Pantaloon and the Landlord are flung up and down, propelled on long poles pushed through the stage from the cellars, bumping and buffeting their passengers, who have to cling on for dear life. When the furniture finally lands, there's a pause in the action as the audience are treated to a display of morris dancing, before the scene changes to reveal a young lad dressed in the navy blue coat of a cabin boy standing at the door of a humble Woodcutter's cottage. The boy, Master Smalley, plucked from the gutter by Thomas Harris, launches into a sentimental ballad that describes how he had been driven to sea by poverty and, having filled his purse after many cruel hardships, was shipwrecked in sight of land. His song over, he knocks at the cottage door in search of his mother and father, only to find them being turned out by a Bailiff and his constables, at which point Harlequin enters and transforms a broken coach wheel into the goddess Fortune, who showers the family with gold. This affecting portrait of the deserving poor, a father and son whose work accrues virtue rather than profit, restates once again the piece's antipathy to the politics of Squire Bugle. Heart-warming though it is, it's insufficient to prevent Clown trying to steal food from the Woodcutter's wife.

A garden of flowers and a moonlit pavilion provide transitional scenes before the harlequinade arrives in London. Joe is shot again and caught in a bear trap, and Columbine dances a reflective *pas seul* that conveys the tremulous mix of love and apprehension that defines her, entwining herself in a long garland of flowers that looks like a skipping rope made of roses. Columbines were not the greatest ballerinas, certainly not equal to the svelte foreign beauties who danced in the élite companies of Haymarket or King's, yet they had an air of erotic availability that those more polished ladies lacked. Generally local girls with milky complexions and saucy reputations, like the well-made Bella Ménage, denounced by Mrs Siddons as 'a naughty little dancing girl' for seducing her nephew, they had the devotion of large sections of the crowd. On occasion, this popularity translated into factional warfare, such as the trouble that broke out over the Surrey's rival Columbines, Miss Giroux and Miss Taylor, whose supporters fought pitched battles that landed both ladies in court. Columbines were not just for Christmas. When Byron first came down from Cambridge, he took full advantage of the sybaritic pleasures offered by the pupils of James d'Egville, who, it seems, supplemented his Drury Lane salary with a little procuring.

Now that the harlequinade had reached London, it called first at a house in Golden Square, where Joe falls from a balcony that suddenly disappears under the auspices of Jack Bologna's sword. Next they appear at St Dunstan's church, where Harlequin and Columbine hide by disguising themselves as figures on the clock tower. A Jewish milliner enters and is instantly robbed of two hats by Clown and Pantaloon, which Harlequin turns into enormous bells the moment they place them on their heads. He and Columbine then use them to ring the chimes.

Thus reeling, the scene is transplanted to Vauxhall Gardens, and the most spectacular of all the changes in this 'plain' pantomime, a view of the pleasure gardens during a midsummer gala. Vauxhall was a celebrated site of fashionable resort, offering music and dining, and romantic garden walks decorated with pergolas and fountains. The stage is filled with stylish extras dining in a sumptuous pavilion, while behind them the glamour of the evening is rendered in minute scenic detail, down to the tiny illuminated Chinese lanterns that line the receding walkways and the distant orchestra whose animated violinists bow in time to the music. The gorgeous vision is completed by the entry of the Pandean Minstrels, five handsome young Italian men engaged at Vauxhall to serenade the paths and bowers with astral music made on Pan pipes, triangles and tabors, each playing two instruments at once.

Yet the instant this study in elegance has had time to compose, it is upset by Joe, who starts his own serenade on a tin fish kettle, before somehow cajoling the entire company to join him in a crude country dance. With everyone up on their feet and dancing, he adds to the chaos by whipping off the tablecloths, like a cheap magician, and inexpertly juggling the crockery. Waiters charge frantically from side to side as plates smash and live birds splutter skywards from beneath the dinner platters, confusion that increases in speed and intensity until it reaches a crescendo of pandemonium, at which point the curtain drops and a cheesemonger, ruddy sort of fellow with back-bacon forearms and a new black smock, steps from the wings and awkwardly takes a bow. It is Mr Whitmore, the scene designer. The audience bathes him in its approval, and the harlequinade moves on.

The curtain rises to reveal something altogether more sedate: a grocer's shop and country post office. In a show that had so many well-loved scenes, this is probably the most famous, largely for Grimaldi's mordant pun, when, having stolen the letters from the postbox, he opens one, pulls out a small rope tied in a noose and reads, 'Sir, I'll trouble you with a line.' This done, he thrusts his hand back into the postbox just as Harlequin appears and turns it into a lion's mouth. Joe shrieks, snatching out his hand, and bringing with it an angry midget postman who menaces him with his bell. A baker appears, sets down his basket and enters the shop. Joe takes a loaf of bread and throws it to Pantaloon, who covers the postman's head with a basket. As the postman struggles, Joe comes to Pantaloon's aid, but as he does so, a 'Blackamoor's head' rises from the top of the basket and scares him out of his wits. Reaching for a plank, he tries to beat it back, but succeeds only in breaking it over Pantaloon's pate.

It's a surreal scene, indulging humour that raises the spectre of more than one anxiety, but has the postal service simply gone wild, or is Joe drawing out some of the dangers that lurk beneath the surface of the everyday – capital punishment, for example, or the European's fear of the Orient? Might all this business about letters and boxes even indicate a subtle sexual subplot that, in contradistinction to the hymnal destiny of Harlequin and Columbine, indicates the reproductive dead-end that is Clown and Pantaloon, attacked by a fanged orifice, a *vagina dentata* and a sexually threatening African? It's all too much for Joe and Louis, who take solace in the discovery of magically refillable bottles of wine. Having drunk themselves silly, they go off (presumably to pee), at which point Harlequin torments them further by turning the bottles into beehives. Through the power of suggestion, the grocer's shop is instantaneously transformed into a farmyard, into which Clown and Pantaloon stagger, and, taking up the beehives/bottles, are chased off, each with a swarm of bees around his head. They exit, 'bellowing'.

The harlequinade is nearing its end, and the scene changes to a mermaid's cave, where Mother Goose appears among her attendant fairies to announce, 'Your task concludes, your mistress' rage is o'er,/These wandering mortals, I'll perplex no more.' Harlequin has only one more obstacle to overcome before he can enjoy his reward: Oddfish, a queer aquatic monster that rises from the sea, guzzling oysters and spanking the unruly serpents that coil around his legs and terrorise Columbine. Harlequin dispatches him in the most hospitable way, deploying his sword as a yard of wine that he pours directly into the monster's mouth before sending him off to retrieve the golden egg. Oddfish obeys, and though his first foray produces only seaweed, his second bears the prize. Mother Goose restores order and, in what would usually have been the *coup de grâce* that brings about the most lavish scenic tableau of the year, turns Oddfish's Palace into a cut-price Eden, described as 'simply a pair of flats, and . . . no "blaze of triumph" whatever', whose most diverting feature is a pod of cheerful dolphins and some mermaids brushing their hair. The dancers rush back on for a final number intended to distract the eye from the woeful scenery, before the lovers come forward, their hands joined by the newly reformed and appropriately paternal Squire, as Mother Goose begs the audience's indulgence with her parting words:

> Ye patrons kind, who deign to view,
>   The sports our scenes produce,
> Accept our wish to pleasure you,
>   And laugh with Mother Goose.

To which Grimaldi adds,

> And let no critic stern reject
>   What our petitions beg,
> That we may from your smiles collect
>   Each night some Golden Egg.

The crowd's acclaim was deafening, and the following morning, the critics were universal in their submission to Joe's injunction. From beginning to end, they reported, the show had 'set the young . . . and old folks, too, in a roar'. It was received (said *The Times*) 'by JOHN BULL with that clamorous expression of his feelings to which he is accustomed on the view of an old favourite'. If the show seemed familiar, it was because, in one form or another, they'd probably seen much of it before. As Joe himself admitted, there wasn't 'a trick or situation in the piece to which he had not been well accustomed for many years'. From Harlequin's first escape to his last, *Mother Goose* proved the maxim that the old ones are the best, as some of the tricks and business, such as the flying tables and chairs, can be dated to at least 1685, when they appeared in a prototypical pantomime, William Mountford's *The Life and Death of Doctor Faustus Made Into A Farce*.

Not that anyone seemed to mind. 'We have not for several years', wrote the *European Magazine*, 'witnessed a Pantomime more attractive than this; whether we consider the variety and ingenuity of the mechanical devices; the whim, humour, and agility of the Harlequin, Clown, and Pantaloon; or the admirable dexterity with which the scenery is managed.' This 'dexterity' was one of its greatest virtues: as the machinery was relatively simple, there were none of the long delays and backstage mistakes audiences were used to.* A description of the show, printed within days of the début, had it that the first night '(which is generally only looked upon as a public rehearsal) was as perfect a performance, as need be wished'.

---

* The diary of James Winston, acting manager of Drury Lane from 1820–27, affords an acute sense of the degree to which pantomimes were constant works in progress. 'Dec. 26th, 1820: . . . The pantomime failed principally for the want of tricks . . . Two and a quarter hours first night. Dec. 27th, 1820: Much altered – much hissed. Dec. 28th, 1820: Pantomime much curtailed – went better.'

It was as if the pantomime had been presented as the answer to the question 'What is entertainment?', while the very definition of what it meant to be entertained was being redefined in the light of what the audience saw. Its nineteen scenes offered a full range of textures and tempos that blended comedy with spectacle, the two bound together by music of 'unceasing vivacity' that ran through the piece 'like the pattern in a watered gown'. The form provided the framework for what was essentially a variety show, a piece of extended slapstick dotted with guest slots for morris dancers, Master Smalley, and the Pandean Minstrels.

At the centre of it all was Joe. 'His very excellent clown', wrote one critic, 'obtains universal sufferance, his figure is neither too tall or too short, and . . . so irresistibly comic, as to put dullness to flight, and make a saint laugh, his acting and manner . . . leaves all competition at a very humble distance.' Even Lord Eldon, the Lord Chancellor, a major political player and sober establishment man who had never even seen a pantomime *Mother Goose*, could not contain his enthusiasm: 'Never, never,' he insisted emphatically, 'did I see a leg of mutton stolen with such superhumanly sublime impudence as by that man.' So impressed was he that he returned eleven times that season just to watch Joe steal. There was even praise from Kemble, who said that Grimaldi had 'proved himself the great master of his art', though most gratifying of all must have been the words of the inestimable Mrs Jordan, who called him simply 'a genius . . . yet unapproached'.

'Grimaldi's career until this Christmas', wrote one critic, 'may be regarded as the novitiate of his Saturnalian priest-hood,' and from that point on, he was a fully fledged star. Even the *Monthly Mirror*, the vehicle of unfailingly bad reviews, whose last mention of Joe had been to say of his Orson that 'we are inclined . . . to prefer his predecessor, Du Bois', conceded the fact, and by February, it was writing,

The Clown of Mr. Grimaldi is the principal cause of crowded lobbies and scarcely standing room. Many of our second- and third-rate tragedians would give their ears to meet with half the plaudits which are every night conferred on Grimaldi for his inimitable exertions. His Clown has not been equalled – we never expect to see it surpassed. He has arrived at an acme of all clownery.

Yet even in the first blush of celebrity Grimaldi had few opportunities to enjoy his success. Most popular actors threw themselves into the social whirl, dining out and holding forth in the salons of the affluent newly open to them. By contrast, Joe found that fame threatened his domesticity, even when it appeared to complement it. The clearest example of this was the appearance of a man who arrived on his doorstep after *Mother Goose* had played only eight times. The *Memoirs* remember him as Mackintosh, although in fact he was called John Mackoull. Joe had met him several times through the auspices of Jack Bologna around the time that Jack had been re-engaged at the Wells.

Jack knew him as a regular at the London theatres, a care-free bachelor of independent means who had once invited him to his house in Kent for a few days' shooting. He had asked Joe to come along and, thoroughly looking forward to a stylish country weekend, they were surprised to be greeted by a scruffy, bald, asthmatic driving a tax-cart. This was Mackoull in his natural habitat. A recreational impostor, he saw no harm in letting his London friends think he was much grander than he was. His lame horse led the way to his house, actually a dirty roadside pub two miles out of Bromley called the George Inn. This vexed Jack considerably, and he complained angrily at the deception, although, as their host cheerfully pointed out, the pub belonged to Mackoull's mother, a doting old woman who worked while he idled, so he was indeed a gentleman of leisure.

Jack seethed, but Joe saw the funny side, at least until Mackoull's delusions got them into serious trouble. Having calmed his guests with food and beer, he equipped them for shooting, declining himself to take a gun, and brought them to a wheat-field where, in tones of great excitement, he pointed out the game. But instead of the partridges and pheasants the sportsmen were expecting, Mackoull had indicated a flock of common pigeons, hundreds of them. 'I invited you to shoot birds,' he said, sensing their irritation, 'and pigeons are birds.'

'The fellow's a humbug,' whispered Jack, 'kill as many of his pigeons as you can,' and, opening fire, he blasted into the field without even bothering to aim. In spite of his great love of the breed, Joe joined in, and 'the slaughter was very great'. By the time their muzzles fell silent, the field was littered with corpses, and Mackoull immediately began to fuss, hurrying them to collect them up so they could get off as quickly as possible, confessing that neither field nor pigeons belonged to him but to a neighbour, 'and precious savage he'll be when he finds out how you have been peppering them'. Speechless at having been duped into committing a capital crime, the accidental poachers ran back to their gig and fled the country-side. Even in town, they weren't safe: before the week was out they got word that a constable was in London looking for them, hired by Mackoull's neighbour, using names and descriptions conveniently furnished by Mackoull himself.

Strange, then, that two and a half years later this contrary oddness should be sitting in Joe's parlour much transformed. Immaculately dressed, impeccably polite and betraying no sign of the fustian eccentric who had nearly got them hanged in Kent, he begged forgiveness so genteelly that Joe lacked all resolve to bear him a grudge. In the interim, Mackoull had established himself in business, taking rooms behind the Bank of England where he invited Joe to dine with him before the play. Joe found him easy and humorous company. There were several such dinners over the next few weeks, and a genuine friendship began to emerge. There were no objections, therefore, when Mackoull called with an invitation from friends of his who were keen to make Clown's acquaintance one night after the pantomime. Joe was reluctant to break his habit of taking supper with Mary at the end of the day, but eventually agreed and, on the night appointed, took a coach from Covent Garden to an address near Fitzroy Square where they stopped in front of one of the tallest, whitest, most brilliantly illuminated Queen Anne mansions on the street.

Convinced they had the wrong address, he was debating directions with the driver when Mackoull suddenly appeared from a passage and took his friend into a magnificent supper room, papered and gilded and lined with exquisite rugs. Around a large table set with fine crystal and silver stood six smiling couples, as impeccably presented and richly bejewelled as the room itself. Mackoull introduced the host and hostess, Mr and Mrs Farmer, who, shaking Joe's hand and paying earnest compliments to his abilities, introduced him to the others before they all sat down to a supper of succulent dishes and vintage wines. Once he had overcome his initial shock at being in such refined company, Joe enjoyed himself immensely, eating, drinking and regaling the table with songs and stories until at last liveried servants helped him to a coach at five in the morning.

Mary was beside herself when Joe described the night he'd had. Like her sisters, she loved nothing more than clothes, gossip and the doings of people of fashion, and when a second invitation arrived hard on the heels of the first, she demanded to come. The party reconvened with repeated success, and the nights in Fitzroy Square became regular events.

The Grimaldis were much taken with their convivial new friends, whose midnight suppers brightened the first dreary months of the year. Joe, in his cups, even invited them to dine at Baynes Row, much to the annoyance of his wife, who complained that they had 'not one quarter so many spoons as the Fitzroy Square people, and no chandeliers at all'. Even so, something was not quite right: despite their obvious wealth, neither Mr Farmer nor any of his guests ever spoke of business or trade, yet their liberal hospitality, easy manners and apparent lack of ceremony suggested they weren't aristocrats – at least not like any of the aristocrats Joe had ever encountered at the theatre. Mackoull was no help, saying only that they were people of substantial means and leaving it at that.

The dinners continued until early March, when Joe was asked to play Scaramouch for the benefit for his old friend Lund. As the show was at the Woolwich theatre, requiring an overnight stay, Mr Farmer proposed that the men of the group make a night of it. They all agreed, except a man called Jones, who regretted that he had to keep an appointment. The party went off in exceedingly high spirits, making Lund's benefit memorable not only for the performances but for the cheerful, talkative group in the box who dressed finely and spent freely.

It was the last Joe and Mary ever saw of their smart new friends, and neither did they hear from Mackoull, until several weeks later when a man named Harmer appeared at Baynes Row. Introducing himself as Mackoull's solicitor, he sat down and, fixing Joe with a grave stare, announced that his client was in custody, accused of robbing the Edinburgh mail coach, a crime for which he would almost certainly be put to death.

8

THE FORTY VIRGINS

He that does any one thing better than all the rest of
the world, is a genius. GRIMALDI has done this.

Oxberry's Dramatic Biography (1825)

KEMBLE CALLED TIME ON the Covent Garden season on 23 June
1807, thanking the audience for the generous patronage that
had seen *Mother Goose* play for ninety-two performances. It
had not been an entirely uninterrupted run, as Harris, unable
to believe his luck, had insisted they capitalise on their good
fortune by bringing forth a piece that employed all the opulence they had previously spared. The result was, predictably, a
disaster. *Ogre and Little Thumb* débuted at Easter, written by
Joe's schoolmate, Harris's son, Henry. It was his first stab at
pantomime and bore all the marks of someone trying too hard.
No amount of spectacle and over-complicated scenery, which
included a real waterfall dropping nine tuns of water a minute,
and an army of 'skipping children', could make up for its dreadful plot, a story described as so 'wretchedly managed' that it
'would disgrace a booth at Bartholomew Fair'. This was some
criticism, given the general standards of the time, but it was,
said *The Times*, a piece of 'brilliant stupidity . . . the worst piece
of mummery that has ever been privileged to disgrace a stage'.
Fortunately, Grimaldi's stock was bountifully high, and when he
and his colleagues went straight into a revival of *Mother Goose*,
it was embraced with a passion more ardent than before.

Over at Sadler's Wells, it was a summer of great business, due largely to Charles Dibdin's policy of giving the audience more of what they already liked. The hit of the season was an aquadrama called *The Ocean Fiend*, which featured an infant being hurled from a bridge, a daring rescue by a heroic New-foundland dog, and the spectacular immolation of a palace augmented by a brand-new effect called 'redfire', a chemical compound that, when burnt, produced an intense crimson light that reflected thrillingly against the pool. Joe's miraculous form also carried over from Covent Garden to Islington, even culminating in a bona fide miracle.

In July, another of Thomas Harris's sons, George, captain of the *Sir Francis Drake*, had arrived in Plymouth after a long voyage and, paid up, he and his crew went straight to London in search of a good time. Their first stop was Sadler's Wells, where they drank freely, ogled the water, and enjoyed London's premier clown, appearing in a pantomime called *Jan Ben Jan; or, Harlequin and the Forty Virgins*, an Orientalist confection with scenes set in China, Persia, London and Margate. Though geographically baffling, the business was particularly good. Clown, carried in a box and supposedly dead, pinched swigs of wine from two unsuspecting porters who accused each other and angrily started to fight, before introducing a new comic song, 'Don't I Look Spruce on My Neddy?', in which Joe lampooned the fashion for aristocratic jockeys while riding a charger fashioned from a bench, a broomstick and a donkey skull; and a half-sung, half-spoken 'chaunt' comparing the beasts of Pidcock's menagerie to men of different professions.

With Joe on top form, the house was in fits, not least Harris's men, including an old deaf-mute who sat through the entire performance red-faced and rocking with silent laughter. Gag after gag left him doubled up until, finally looking fit to burst, he turned to one of his shipmates and, with tears trickling down his cheeks, said, 'What a damned funny fellow.'

'Why, Jack,' said his thunderstruck comrade, 'can you speak?'

'Ay,' said the sailor, suddenly aware of what he'd done, and equally astonished. 'That I can, and hear, too.'

❧

Had Grimaldi been able to perform miracles off the stage, he might have been able to enjoy this period of unprecedented success. As it was, he found himself constantly fending off trouble, most urgently the business with Mackoull, which had taken a sinister turn. The visit paid by Mackoull's solicitor, Mr Harmer, had been for the purpose of enlisting Joe in his client's defence. Mackoull, he insisted, was innocent, and only Joe could save his neck. The coach he had supposedly robbed had been held up in the early hours of 13 March, when Mackoull was several hundred miles away in Woolwich, attending the benefit at which Joe had played. As a witness to that fact, it was imperative that he speak up. Joe agreed readily, but asked why, given how large the Woolwich party had been, the burden of an alibi fell to him alone. Harmer said nothing, and after taking down his testimony as well as Mary's, promised to get back in touch the moment there was news.

Harmer had been gone only a short while before a second visitor called, a young under-clerk from the Bow Street magistrate's office, who stayed long enough to warn Grimaldi that if he valued his reputation, and that of his wife, he should drop Mackoull at once. The threat left Joe in a state of high anxiety that refused to settle until Mackoull made bail and presented himself at Baynes Row. Joe demanded an explanation, again putting the question that Harmer had so neatly avoided: why was his testimony so all-important when he had friends like

Mr Farmer, men of rank and influence whose word alone would surely be enough to quash any charges? Mackoull blushed and hung his head, but not with shame. His shoulders were shaking as if he was trying to suppress a laugh.

'Besides – the ladies,' continued Joe. 'Dear me . . . the appearance of those gentlemen's wives would be almost enough to acquit you at once.'

This was too much for Mackoull, who burst out laughing. 'Mr Grimaldi,' he said, 'none of those women are married.'

Joe stared incredulously as the truth came boiling out. The women, Mackoull confessed, were all prostitutes, expensive courtesans hired to escort six professional criminals, a gang that specialised in robbery and forged bills. Farmer, their leader, had already been sentenced to death at the Old Bailey, and each of the others was similarly notorious in his own line of work, be it as burglar, highwayman or counterfeiter. This certainly explained their wealth and why they kept their own company, but Joe was less prepared for the revelation that followed. The attack on the Edinburgh coach had been their handiwork, and the Woolwich excursion contrived to cover it up. With the money safely put away, they had framed Mackoull, a dispensable booby tolerated simply because he claimed to know the famous Grimaldi. Joe had been made an unwitting accessory and, with Mackoull's nervous laughter ringing in his ears, he found his hands instinctively reaching for the man's throat and slamming him against the wall.* How dare he abuse their friendship by bringing him into criminal company, he demanded, and, even worse, induce him to bring his wife?

---

* This rare act of Grimaldian violence is one of only two recorded in the *Memoirs* – the other is the only instance of co-operation between him and Dubois. It happened after Joe had been falsely accused of driving an ox across Spa Fields by a corrupt parish constable named Lucas. When Lucas came to the theatre to arrest Grimaldi, Dubois threatened to throw him into the New River. When he tried a second time, Joe knocked him to the floor. When the incident came before the magistrate, Lucas was fined for false testimony.

With Joe's grip tightening, Mackoull turned from giggling idiot to beseeching wreck. A seasoned implorer, he fell to his knees, pouring forth sufficient 'entreaties for mercy and protestations of regret' to blunt his assailant's rage. Released, he fled at once, but by letting him go, Grimaldi had already hinted at what Mackoull must have hoped: the Clown was as honest as one of Dibdin's stage sailors and, however aggrieved, was incapable of abandoning a man when his life hung in the balance.

The following week there was another visitor to Baynes Row, the courtesan who had posed as Mrs Farmer. She was past dissembling and, dispensing with the mask, addressed Joe as a man of the world who had understood the nature of his Fitzroy Square hosts from the start. Surely 'Grim' could see that this was simply business? 'It's everybody's turn on time,' she said, 'and Jack's had a very long string.' The matter-of-factness with which she proposed Mackoull's sacrifice was chilling, and with the queasy feeling of a conspiracy folding in about him, Joe showed Mrs Farmer the door.

That August, Mackoull's trial took place in Stafford and, taking their leave of the Wells, Joe and Mary travelled north in the company of Harmer. In spite of everything, Joe helped the impoverished defence, even assisting a local clerk to transcribe the piles of documents that landed on Harmer daily. The unhappy picture that emerged from his schoolboy hand told the story of a troubled fantasist, a man with little sense of consequences or responsibility, in constant trouble with the law. The company he kept was insalubrious, he had indictments for keeping a disorderly house, and was known to frequent the theatre and pick pockets in the pit. Naturally, Mackoull denied everything, vigorously insisting that his 'former irregularities' had been renounced at least a decade before. He was, he claimed, the victim of a protracted campaign of police harassment, begun after he had refused to become an informer during a corruption case in 1800. Whatever the truth of it, his was a murky past, and when nine witnesses took the stand, each of them claiming to have seen him pass stolen bills in Cheshire, the jury had no trouble believing them. In actuality, the witnesses had been picked up off the streets only days before, and paid for their perjury by the prosecutor, himself in the pay of the Fitzroy Square gang. For most of them, it was the first time they had ever seen the man they identified, and by the time Grimaldi came to give his evidence, it seemed certain that justice would desert Mackoull.

The snarling boy who had menaced him on his doorstep had made no idle threat. The prosecutor tore into him, hoping to discredit his testimony by destroying his reputation, calling him an inveterate deceiver, a strolling player, 'a man reared in and ever accustomed to vice in its most repulsive and degrading forms – a man who was necessarily a systematic liar – and, in fine, a man upon whose word or oath no thinking person could place any reliance'. The abuse continued when it was Mary's turn to take the stand. Vilified in the witness box, she was insulted from the gallery, and leered at by ruffians who followed her out of the court.

Mackoull would surely have been destined for the gallows, were it not for the resourceful Constable Trott, the same dependable Hatton Garden officer who had delivered the Grimaldis and Lewises from murderous Pentonville burglars many years before. Trott had been recruited to the case by Harmer, who was convinced that the Bow Street office was corrupt. This was undoubtedly true, as the combined factors of low pay and a reward system for convicting felons not only provided officers with a financial incentive for framing people, but encouraged traffic in minor felons between the police and organised criminals, who were granted immunity in return for delivering a regular supply of decoys. Trott's investigations unearthed a suspect called Treble, very likely the same man introduced to Joe in Fitzroy Square as Jones, the only one to have excused himself from the Woolwich excursion. Treble had held up the coach and passed the money to be laundered by an associate known only as 'the Squire'. Treble, however, didn't live to harvest the fruits of his crime as the following day he was found dead, believed to have run mad and killed himself, though more than likely disposed of by the gang.

Trott turned his attentions to uncovering the identity of the Squire and eventually came to suspect a provincial actor named Robert Knight. Taking the stand in Stafford, he revealed that he had tracked Knight to a safe-house in Southend where he had arrested him in possession of banknotes stolen from the Edinburgh mail. With the real culprit dramatically pulled from thin air, the case against Mackoull collapsed, and the jury had no choice but to set him free.

Yet Mackoull's trials were far from over as even after his acquittal his tormentors continued the transmission of false-hoods, among them that Grimaldi had been paid handsomely to lie. He moved from his mother's pub to Worthing, where he found employment as a music-seller, but was still unable to outrun the rumours. Forced from town to town, into obscurer places and meaner professions, his arrivals were inevitably followed by anonymous letters that drew his neighbours into insinuating silences. Not even Knight's trial served to clear his name as, thanks to the mischief of the Fitzroy Square gang and the obstructions of a well-placed banker who might well have been an instrument of the initial crime, the case failed.

Driven to distraction by two years of whispers, Mackoull holed himself up to draft a long account of his case, spending whatever money he had to place his final plea before the public. It, too, fell on deaf ears, and Mackoull was never heard from again.

Thanks to Constable Trott's diligence, Joe returned to London earlier than expected, discovering to his great annoyance that he would not be required at the Wells because Dibdin had engaged a man called Robert Bradbury in his stead. Bradbury had first appeared at the Wells in 1803, performing an act with a pig. He was an excellent animal trainer, even travelling for a while with a bear he kept as a pet, one of several flamboyant habits he maintained as a way of attracting attention. According to those who knew him, Bradbury was 'ambitious of the society of gentlemen' and to that end kept a tandem, cultivated his speech (his letters show that he wrote well) and sported dandy fashions to the extent that he was dubbed the 'Brummell of Clowns'. But beneath the veneer lay a reputation for brawling and bullying that had followed him from his native Manchester, and a latent aggression that persistently appeared in his clowning. Henry Downes Miles was not a fan, calling him 'a man of great strength' but 'very dreary merriment', who relied too heavily on stunts and danger that amounted to 'an intense anxiety to meet with some severe, if not fatal accident'. Even by the deranged standards of the brotherhood of clowns, Bradbury was considered something of a loony although, to be fair, he wasn't entirely suicidal as he always went on stage protected by eight thick horse-hair pads, which he strapped to his knees, elbows, heels and hips, and a specially reinforced hat.

Bradbury had done well in his short stint at the Wells, entertaining the audience with routines that included leaping from the fly-tower to the stage, balancing on ten-foot crutches at the top of an unsupported ladder, and resting a sixteen-stone anvil on his chest while three burly blacksmiths set to it with hammers. The pure, exhilarating brutality of his showmanship was miles away from the carefully crafted clown-world Joe had built around Joey, and the positive reception he was getting served to convince the uncertain Joe that his own success had been just another fad. Believing that Bradbury 'had thrown him completely out of favour with the public', he despaired of ever winning back his place, confiding to his friend Richard Lawrence that 'it was all up with him'.

Dibdin did nothing to allay these fears, preferring to capitalise on his sudden clown surplus by proposing that Joe and Bradbury perform together, just as Joe and Dubois had done years before. Joe agreed because he needed the money, though the *Memoirs* confess that he 'yielded his consent with very ill grace', convinced that he would be heckled from the stage. In fact, the opposite was true. The Wells faithful were as pleased as ever to see him and, energised by their applause, Joe doubled his efforts. This in turn brought out the competitor in Bradbury, who in his zeal overstepped the mark, thus upsetting the audience, who hissed him off the stage 'in great disorder', leaving Joe to finish the piece alone.

Secure in the public's favour, Joe's summer season nevertheless came to an abrupt end on the night of 15 October. Having performed his service in the pantomime, he was already in bed when a volley of fists was heard hammering at his door. Downstairs he found a pale and breathless group. There had been an accident at the theatre, they said, and so much confusion and so many bodies that they were worried he was among them. Joe went immediately up to the Wells to find an enormous crowd outside, hordes of people in states of horrid anticipation, those pushing to get in met with equal force by those hoping to get out. With no chance of getting through, Joe ran around to the opposite bank of the New River, swam across to the back of Richard Hughes's house and jumped in through his parlour window. There, according to the *Memoirs*, he found himself surrounded by corpses. The parlour door was locked and, panicking, he began banging and shouting to be let out, thus terrifying Hughes's daughters, who were using the room as a mortuary. This detail, though, would appear to be a piece of Gothic embellishment, as by the time

Joe arrived, the scene was still too chaotic for a tally of the dead to have been made.

Be that as it may, once inside the theatre proper he would have come across a scene that resembled the aftermath of battle. Men and women with broken limbs and bleeding heads lay wailing all around, nursed by their traumatised friends. Among them was Joe's old friend Bob Fairbrother, who explained that he had been in the treasury office at around a quarter past ten when he had heard a terrific noise in the auditorium. Running to the stage to see what the matter was, he heard a cry of 'Fire! Fire!' that spread throughout the house, causing panic in the galleries and a sudden rush for the doors. Yet with no evidence of smoke or flames, and with a tankful of water on stage, it was clearly a mistake.

When Dibdin emerged with a speaking trumpet to try to calm the audience and get them to return to their seats, it was already too late. The first to take flight had been the ladies in the boxes, followed by the people in the gallery, the throng becoming a stampede, knocking over those at the front and trampling them under the feet of those who came behind. The people nearest the rails decided to jump for it, breaking down the sides of the gallery and either leaping directly into the pit or on to the chandeliers, which came crashing down with their weight. Two children were caught, but another severely damaged her spine. Most of those who died either fell from the galleries or were killed on the stairs.

The first doctor on the scene was Mr Sharp, who lived just three hundred yards away on Islington Road. He set about doing what he could, bleeding some corpses in the hope of reviving them, assisted by the heroic Constable Trott, so often in the background of Grimaldi's story — later he received special press attention as 'by his exertions, many lives were saved that night'. Soon, a stream of doctors arrived from St Bartholomew's Hospital, setting about the bodies with 'electricity, tracheotomy, and inflation of the lungs'. Largely, it was to no avail, although one man believed dead was revived when a vein was opened, only to become hysterical at finding himself beside his wife's corpse.

As word of the accident spread, many people hurried to the theatre, anxious for their loved ones. The building, meanwhile, was sealed to allow treatment of the injured and a count of the dead, and the Clerkenwell Volunteers had to be called to hold back those outside. One of the distraught onlookers was the mother of eleven-year-old Benjamin Price. He had been given permission to attend the theatre with neighbours, though his parents became concerned when his sister reported seeing him in their kitchen. When she called to him, he disappeared and, certain that she had seen his ghost, his mother flew to the Wells to discover that he was indeed dead.

The eventual tally was miraculously low, given that it had been standing-room only in the Wells that night. Eighteen had been killed, the details of the victims presenting a vivid picture of those who inhabited the galleries of Sadler's Wells. With an average age of less than nineteen, the eldest, James Phillipson, was thirty, while the youngest was a nine-year-old nursery-maid attending the theatre in the company of her employer and her employer's baby. Uniformly of the working classes, some held trades, one was a 'woman of the town', and another an unemployed errand-boy. None of them carried money or watches, although it was supposed that their bodies had been robbed.

The following day, the public were admitted into the Hugheses' parlour to identify the victims. As distraught mothers let out anguished groans, unsightly scenes were played out in the adjacent rooms, where lost property had been left out to be claimed, causing brawls among corvine opportunists and ghoulish fashion hunters. By this time, further details of the accident had come to light. It seemed that the trouble had been caused by two men and two women, belligerent drunks who had spent the night in the pit trying to provoke the people around them with threatening behaviour and foul language. One of the women had slapped another's face. The constables on duty warned them to stop three times, until eventually, with the help of some men from the audience, they were forcibly removed. During the scuffle, a shout of 'Fight! Fight!' came from the pit, which was interpreted in the boxes as 'Fire! Fire!' The misapprehension 'passed through the whole house in an instant, like an electric shock'.

The following day, the four accused were brought before a coroner's court set up in the bar of the Sir Hugh Myddleton. They were Sarah Luker, an old milk-woman with three children; Mary Vyne, her young, unemployed neighbour; and two brothers, John Pearce, a Wiltshire farm labourer, and Vincent Pearce, a servant who worked for the famous brewer, Samuel Whitbread. The evidence against them contradicted itself in places, and it was difficult to tell whether they had been fighting among themselves or, as Dibdin suspected, deliberately trying to provoke their neighbours in order to rob them in the confusion. The magistrate was unable to find them guilty of having 'wilfully occasioned the fatal and lamentable catastrophe' and ruled that the deceased had died 'casually, accidentally, and by misfortune'. This displeased Dibdin immensely, and when a report appeared in *The Times* suggesting that the management could have done more to save the victims, he pressed hard for the prosecution to prove their culpability. In time, Dibdin got his wish, and the sorry quartet appeared at Hatton Garden, charged with causing a commotion. Vincent Pearce received six months in Coldbath gaol, and his brother four months; three years later he was hanged for a theft at Salisbury. Sarah Luker got fourteen days, and Mary Vyne absconded.

After such a horrific event, it was impossible to continue the season. Sadler's Wells closed immediately, save for two nights at which the proceeds were given to the families of the bereaved. The actors, meanwhile, took their benefits at the Royal Circus and, within twelve days of the tragedy, Joe was falling from the balcony for laughs again as *Mother Goose* reopened at Covent Garden. A further twenty-nine performances guaranteed that by the time it made way for the new Christmas production, it had become the longest-running pantomime in history, eclipsing even the run of John Rich's *Harlequin a Sorcerer*, the all-conquering 1727 pantomime so often held up as the epitome of the form.

Mother Goose had also been inordinately profitable, heralding the age of mass entertainment by selling more than three hundred thousand tickets (enough to seat at least a third of the London population) and netting a profit of more than twenty thousand pounds. They were profits that would go unequalled by a pantomime for three decades, although Joe saw little of them. Instead, he shared a summer benefit with Jack Bologna that netted £300, and received a gold watch from Harris, along with the rare privilege of shaking his entire hand. It was perhaps just as well that the management weren't more extravagant, as soon, Harris and Kemble would be needing every penny they could find.

~

It was a nervous management that reopened the Wells on Easter Monday 1808. They were relieved to have been granted a licence in the wake of the accident, but it had been issued only on condition that the theatre stopped selling wine. Dibdin was content if it meant an end to vandalism, vulgar oaths and the quarrels of 'crack brained Boys', but it also absolved him from paying stipends to soldiers in lieu of billeting them, as he was required to do in accordance with wartime ordinances that placed servicemen in all establishments serving alcohol. Nevertheless, wine had been one of the only reliably profitable aspects of their business, and so entwined with the revellous and rubicund atmosphere of the Wells that he was genuinely worried for a future without it.

Still, the season opened steadily enough as Grimaldi brought audiences out to Islington in record numbers. Joe's renown was reaching undreamt-of heights, propelled by an array of merchandise and memorabilia that used his iconic visage to sell prints, song-sheets, board games, children's colouring books, painted wooden statuettes, chinaware, toby jugs, cruet-sets and pocket watches. A cup-winning racehorse was named after him, and his circle of acquaintance grew to include no less a person than Lord Byron. Joe had met the poet after he and Jack Bologna had been hired to entertain guests at the Waiters' Masquerade, a huge masked ball held at Burlington House on 8 July 1808. Once the performances had concluded at one o'clock in the morning, the sixteen hundred revellers sat down to supper in a covered garden of orange trees, after which Joe and Jack were invited to meet Byron, who was dressed as a monk. Byron was a huge fan of pantomime, later taking Delpini's afterpiece as the inspiration for his best-known narrative poem, *Don Juan*, and a long night of jocose carousing concluded with the poet asking the clown to reserve him a box every time he took a benefit.

But though Joe 'did what he liked with the town', his new-found celebrity was making it difficult to move around the city with the freedom he'd previously enjoyed. The regular dash he made from Sadler's Wells to Covent Garden while the seasons overlapped was suddenly dogged by fans and gawkers who wanted to stop and stare or shake his hand. When pressed for time, he'd been accustomed to making the trips in full slap and motley, but this had to be abandoned after he was chased by a rabid group who tried to tear at his costume for keepsakes. It was a good thing he knew Spa Fields much better than they did, hopping through its obstacle course of clothes-lines and water-pipes while they toppled behind him. Even taking a cab was no protection. Henry Downes Miles remembered standing in a crowd watching either a horse die or a man have a fit (he had forgotten which), when he heard a coach rattle past and caught a flash of Joe inside. Having seen the motley blur, the crowd completely forgot their previous diversion (leaving the man/horse to 'practise his contortions, writhings, and foamings in solitude') and set to the chase.*

In a previous age, experiences like these would have been reserved solely for saints and kings, but Joe was caught up at the epicentre of a growing phenomenon – modern celebrity, a culture of personal fascination that was born in the first decade of the nineteenth century. It was, in some respects, a by-product of Romanticism's focus on the individual, reinforced by the perception of men like Bonaparte, popularly thought to have devoted his existence to the possibilities of the self, with the result that the world was entirely remade. Celebrities were credited with a superabundant individuality, a surplus of self that lifted them above the common people and made others want to talk about them and pry into their personal lives. This in itself was by no means a new thing, but suddenly celebrity found that the commercial apparatuses were in place to exploit such urges on a massive scale by, for

---

* That fame altered personal relationships had been shown by the re-emergence of Mackoull, but even the Sir Hugh Myddleton was no longer the sanctuary it had been. Joe discovered this one night when he was held up at gunpoint on the Finchley Road. Frightened out of his wits, he blabbered that his tormentors wouldn't dare mistreat him if they knew who he was, to which came the reply, 'Oh, we know you well enough, Mr Grimaldi. We have been waiting for you these three nights.' One of the robbers turned out to be a drinking friend, a jeweller named George Hamilton, who had set his criminal friends on Joe after his business had failed. His identity was established the moment Joe passed him his pocket watch – Hamilton only had two fingers on his left hand.

example, distributing images cheaply and efficiently, or using their notoriety to sustain a large and competitive press.

With fame came a resurgence of Grimaldi's depression, although undoubtedly it also helped to cement his fame. Joe's melancholic personality had first come to the attention of the public during the run of *Mother Goose* when one periodical noted how he had 'resolved to betake himself to *sack cloth and ashes*!' as soon as the pantomime closed. The image of a melancholy clown was one that Joe himself had taken on, playing with it in his oft-repeated quip 'I make you laugh at night but am Grim-All-Day', thus ensuring that the double life of public laughter and private pain was in turn adopted by his audience. They took to it with great enthusiasm. The inevitable curiosity about the ways in which a performer's personal life might be reflected in his or her public persona resulted in the production of stories that made sensational use of the stark dichotomy, the most abiding of which had Joe paying a visit to a famous physician who advised him to combat his melancholia with 'relaxation and amusement'. Thomas Goodwin takes up the tale:

> 'But where shall I find what you require?' said the patient.
> 'In genial companionship,' was the reply; 'perhaps sometimes at the theatre; – go and see Grimaldi.'
> 'Alas!' replied the patient, 'that is of no avail to me; I am Grimaldi.'

Though undoubtedly a fable, the popularity of this anecdote, coupled with the fact that it still does the rounds – albeit with Grimaldi's name substituted for that of more recent comedians – suggests that it is thought to reveal a higher truth about the comedic personality. Indeed, the entire concept of the 'tears of a clown' might be traced back to Grimaldi and the popular image of him as a comic Midas, cruelly denied access to the one thing about him that gives others most pleasure.

It's a myth with its roots in the period's concept of creativity, especially the view that depression or melancholia, the indescribable sadness styled by Coleridge as 'a grief without a pang – void, dark and drear', was a symptom of heightened sensibility that inspired and ennobled its sufferers. Nowhere was this idea more evident than in the literary fad known as 'Wertherism' after Johann von Goethe's novel *The Sorrows of Young Werther* (1774), which immortalised emotional torture in its story of a poetic youth's self-destruction at the hands of unreciprocated love. Wertherism rejected stoic masculine roles in favour of a taut sensibility that quivered at the edge of illness, irrationality and hysteria; its breakdowns were not signs of weakness as much as their victim's superior emotional capacity.

Some, like the dramatist August von Kotzebue, embraced it as a gift that spurred him on to greater achievements. 'Never . . . either before or since,' he wrote of his depression, 'did I feel such a rapid flow of thoughts and images; and I firmly believe that there are some maladies, especially those by which the irritation of the nerves is increased, which stretch the powers of the mind beyond their usual reach: just as, report says, *diseased muscles'* [sic] *shells produce pearls.'*

Depression was mysterious, glamorous even. It was the price of talent, the mark that confirmed him as a superior artist, and the biggest legacy Joe would leave the world of comedy.

~

Sadler's Wells had been fortunate to recover from the accident without any obvious damage to its business, but when tragedy struck at Covent Garden in the early hours of 20 September 1808 the results were devastating. Smoke and fire had been spotted coming from the theatre at around four in the morning, but by the time the alarm had been raised, and the men of the Phoenix Fire Company had arrived, the blaze was of such magnitude that the interior was already destroyed. A further two hours were lost as the firemen searched frantically for sufficient water to fight the flames, having to make do with the feeble flow they procured from the pumps of the Bedford Coffee House. With the theatre already lost, nearby residents turned their attentions to saving their own homes, sprinting across the square in their nightshirts holding buckets and wet cloths they used to stuff their windows, while boys and servants scurried up to the rooftops with heavy mats to smother the fiery flakes that were being blown in their direction. As they craned their necks to see the frantic activity above, some of the crowd might have witnessed a bizarre scene – the goose from *Mother Goose*, canvas and feathers on a light wicker frame, hovering serenely above their heads, borne by thermal winds and making a stately progress from an attic window before floating off in the direction of Lincoln's Inn Fields.

Twenty-three people died in the fire, including twelve firemen killed by a falling ceiling as they tried to fight their way into the auditorium. The sun had long risen by the time the flames were finally quenched, revealing a smoking ruin whose roof and eastern wall were entirely demolished, along with all the adjacent houses on the Bow Street and Hart Street sides. Besides the damage to the building, the management had to reckon the loss of all its scenery, instruments and properties, including Mrs Siddons's entire wardrobe, put together over the course of thirty years, which included a rare bolt of lace that had belonged to Marie Antoinette. Other lost treasures included an organ bequeathed by George Frideric Handel for the oratorios in Holy Week, original scores by Handel and Thomas Arne, prompt-books and play scripts, and the Beef Steak Club's entire wine cellar, said to be worth more than fifteen hundred pounds. With the whole insured for less than a quarter of the total, there was little comfort to be had from that which could be salvaged: the charred remains of the procession from Kotzebue's Peruvian tragedy, *Pizarro*.*

Kemble, aged fifty-one, had lost everything, but bravely promised to raise a greater theatre even as the day broke on the ashes of the old. The company took up residence at the Haymarket while Harris and Kemble did the rounds raising money and engaging an architect, and Joe took the opportunity to play in Manchester and Liverpool, returning in time for Boxing Day, when the 'lucky old hag' *Mother Goose* was revived with a new scene showing the ruins of the old theatre magically rebuilt.

In his absence, Joe found that fickle London had turned to Drury Lane's Clown, Jean-Baptiste Laurent, whom many were claiming as his equal, if not his superior. Laurent was the Signor's last remaining apprentice, so Joe knew him well, his father's imprint still clearly visible in Laurent's portrayal of Clown as a blank-faced clodpate with a limitless capacity to absorb abuse. He even had something of the old goat's stamina: at fifteen years Joe's senior, he had far more agility than the younger man. Laurent, though, was more than just an imitator, and was held in such high regard by his summer employer, Philip Astley, that when he had once absconded, it was the manager himself who hunted him down and brought him back

---

* The cause of the fire was never resolved. It was initially thought to have started in the shilling gallery where, according to the papers, 'there had been much riot and confusion the preceding night', although it was later decreed to be the work of wadding fired from a gun. Neither theory was proven, and it was just as likely that the fire was the work of simple convection. A German stove had been left burning in the property room all night, and while it had no naked flame, the simple fact of it continuing to dry the air may have been sufficient to ignite a spark. Dry air was a constant hazard in the theatres, where lamps and candles removed the moisture from the atmosphere, causing particular problems in the fly-towers where, without constant vigilance, frayed ropes, exposed beams and the edges of scenery might easily start to glow with embers.

after tracking him to a puppet show on the Pont Neuf. Laurent also deserves special mention in the history of clowning for a particular innovation that has been emulated ever since: his singular pair of huge, flapping shoes.

The Frenchman's sudden burst of popularity induced the same doubts that had gnawed at Joe with the appearance of Bradbury, and fearing he had once again lost ground, he was greatly relieved that Harris and Kemble's fundraising came to quick fruition. Four days after the performance at the Haymarket, the entire company was assembled on the sodden cobbles of the piazza to watch the Prince of Wales, dressed in full Masonic regalia, lay the foundation stone for the new theatre. He spread the mortar with a silver trowel, hit it three times with a ceremonial mallet and emptied cups of corn, wine and oil over it for good luck. The company sang 'Rule Britannia' to the accompaniment of the band of the Coldstream Guards, and tried not to flinch through a twenty-one-gun salute.

As if jealous of its rival, on 24 February 1809, Drury Lane was itself levelled by fire. Sheridan, seeing the blaze from a window in the House of Commons, watched in mounting horror as he realised that the huge, unbroken flame that measured 450 feet across was his. The same frantic hunt for water followed, though it would have proved hopeless even had it been in plentiful supply as a strong north wind finished the job in hours, making day of night as far west as Fulham. It being a Friday in Lent, there was no play and no rehearsal so no lives were lost, a fact that seemed so convenient it might have been arranged. The finger of suspicion naturally pointed to its delinquent proprietor, whose years of unclassifiably tangled finances and felonious debts made a case in the public imagination for writing the whole thing off.

Sheridan's apparent composure in the face of ruin did little to quell the rumours: he had at first refused the Speaker's offer to adjourn the House when the fire was initially spotted, and shortly thereafter, watched the flames from the Piazza Coffee House, where he sat with his reprobate drinking partner, Michael Kelly. 'A man may surely be allowed to take a glass of wine by his own fireside,' Sheridan had said.

If arson it was, it was terribly ill-conceived as Sheridan was pitifully under-insured and had no money to rebuild. Furthermore, when the job of reviving the theatre was considered in the wake of the fire, he found it impossible to interest investors in anything that had his name attached to it. It was a fall from grace as dramatic as that of the statue of Apollo that had come crashing through the dome of Drury Lane as he and Michael Kelly looked on. Pushed aside in favour of an officious committee under the chairmanship of Samuel Whitbread, Sheridan quickly became yesterday's man. It was the close of another long chapter in the history of London theatre. Drury Lane would not reopen for three and a half years, exactly half the time Sheridan had left to live.

~

By contrast, the new Covent Garden was ready in record time. It was an unlovely building, big and boxy with an enormous Doric portico that, wrote James Boaden, 'astonishes by its ponderous inutility', giving the impression of nothing more than a dour Midlands pottery. Financed by a public subscription, insurance money and a generous gift from the Duke of Northumberland, the budget still fell short by almost £164,000, and to cover costs, Kemble and Harris looked to increase profit directly from the point of sale, raising ticket prices across the board and refitting the third gallery as a series of expensive private boxes that could be purchased for an entire season. The changes, announced in advance, caused an outcry, and 'the new theatre, born from misfortune', in the words of

Thomas Dibdin, 'was nursed in fresh calamity' as angry jere-miads accused the proprietors of forgetting their duty as custodians of a national institution to act like chiselling landlords. The theatre, they argued, was an extension of the democratic franchise exempt from tawdry economics. For the proprietors to assert their right to charge whatever they liked while privatising access to certain parts of it was nothing less than an attempt to reverse the balance of power in which the management served at the audience's pleasure.

Special anger was reserved for the Italian singer Angelica Catalani, hired from the Haymarket at a phenomenal fee. Cata-lani was supposed to usher in the new era, but the suspicion was that the higher prices were subsidising her pampered and allegedly immoral lifestyle. Immorality became a key theme of the protests, as the management was accused of practically installing a suite of brothels in the new boxes, whose privacy facilitated 'the playing of a play which does not endure witnesses'.

At first the controversy confined itself to a lively exchange of views, but when Covent Garden reopened on 18 September 1809, two days before the first anniversary of its destruction, it erupted into three months of vociferous and frequently violent protest that amounted to nothing less than a battle for the soul of the stage. Not that Harris felt any of it: a few months before the opening he decided to scale down his involvement and pass on his duties to his son, Henry, leaving Kemble to bear the full brunt of the opposition. Even as he drew breath to begin a laudatory prologue on the opening night, his voice was lost in 'a roar of disapprobation . . . a volley of hisses, hootings, and execrations', noise that continued from the opening address to the final curtain and beyond. In a heady state of belligerence, the house refused to clear until two in the morning, ignoring even the magistrates who arrived flanked with officers and tried unsuccessfully to read the Riot Act. The following night was the same. The auditorium was festooned with placards and banners proclaiming 'Old Prices' and not a single performer could be heard above the din. At the end of the performance, the audience again stayed put, hissing and shouting, 'God Save the King', 'No foreigners', 'No Catalani' and 'No Kemble'.

On the third night, Kemble came forward to entreat with them, but they gave him no quarter. The disturbances quickly took on a distinct identity, rallying the struggle under the initials 'OP' and adopting all the slogans and accoutrements of a political rally – OP medals, OP fans, OP handkerchiefs, OP waistcoats and caps – while the perpetrators evolved their tactics from straightforward shouting to incorporate singing, howling, barking, throwing sticks, running up and down the benches, waving rattles, blowing horns, ringing dustman's bells, sitting with their backs to the stage, cross-dressing, staging mock fights, pinching live pigs and performing a tribal dance, which involved monotonously jumping backwards and forwards and shouting, 'OP, OP,' while knocking the floor with staffs. Rival performances took place in the boxes until Kemble had spikes put along the sills to stop people jumping in and out of them, and orations were delivered from every quarter. 'Even women tried to speak,' wrote an amazed visitor from Sweden, 'and these speeches were regularly reported next day in the papers with the same exactitude as the parliamentary debates.' OP was all the rage.

On the sixth night, Kemble abandoned his Coriolanus-like hauteur, and agreed to a ceasefire. Catalani fled to Ireland, happy to be paid off, and the theatre's accounts were turned over to a committee to assess whether the price rises had been justified. That night a coffin was carried through the pit, celebrating the demise of the new prices, 'an ugly child, and base born, who died of the *whooping-cough* . . . aged six days'. But the funeral meats were scarcely reheated before the committee's report came back in support of the proprietors.

Theirs was not an isolated view, for a sizeable minority existed, including the editors of *The Times* and writers like William Cobbett, who upbraided the OP for obstructing free trade. To the protesters, however, the idea that theatre was commerce and they were its customers was straightforwardly repugnant, and they returned to the pit with their wrath redoubled. Kemble was furious and sought to fight fire with fire, hiring the pugilist Mendoza and a gang of prize-fighters to quell the tumult and intimidate the trouble-makers, though this merely led to an escalation of anger and an anti-Semitic backlash against the predominantly Jewish boxers.

Things got further out of hand when James Brandon, Covent Garden's doorkeeper and head bouncer for more than forty years, started wading into the audience, snatching banners and grabbing peaceable protesters to put them before the magistrates in the hope of harassing OP into non-existence. The strategy backfired after one sally collared a prominent ringleader, the respected barrister Henry Clifford. Not only were the charges against him swiftly dropped, but when he moved to counter-sue for wrongful arrest, the move-ment was suddenly re-energised around the sanctified values of liberty, free speech, and John Bull against John Kemble. Crowds began to follow Kemble to his house beside the British Museum, hollering until dawn and throwing stones at his windows, agitating his frayed nerves even further and terrify-ing Mrs Kemble so much that she slept next to a ladder in case she had to make her escape through the garden.

The rejuvenated protesters, replenished each night by the fresh hordes that flooded the pit when they were let in at half price, finally induced Kemble to abandon spoken drama and just show pantomimes. Yet *Hamlet* or Harlequin, the audience was indifferent, 'more than usually uproarious' throughout Kemble's chosen piece, *Oscar and Malvina*, one protester even managing to hit Jack Bologna with a tin horn.

At least the noise gave Kemble a new appreciation for the pan-tomimist's art – he is supposed to have said of Bologna, 'If that man could speak as well as he acts pantomimes, I would never again appear on the stage.'

Eighteen days later, Kemble threw Grimaldi into the maw, instructing him to play Scaramouch in *Don Juan*. It was his first night after a lengthy lay-off. Intermittently ill throughout the summer season, he had recovered only to injure his knee in the Sadler's Wells pantomime, *Castles in the Air*, which kept him offstage for the whole of August. There had been a spot of domestic bother too. Joe was required to testify again in court, as his young Finchley servant, Richard Watts, was tried at the Old Bailey for rustling sheep and selling their skins. Miracu-lously, instead of playing to rows and rows of sullen backs, Joe was greeted by warm applause, the audience permitting him to perform the entire show without disturbance. This brought an even more than usually haggard Kemble scurrying up back-stage. 'Bravo, Joe!' he said, enthusiastically shaking his hand. 'We have got them now.' But it was not to be. *Don Juan* played the following night, but the OP had had their holiday, and the pit was as turbulent as ever.

～

The OP war lasted a total of sixty-seven nights, nearly four months of riot and misrule that ended only with the complete capitulation of John Philip Kemble. Meetings were organised between him and Clifford, and articles of peace drawn up demanding the restoration of old prices, the demolition of private boxes, the dismissal of James Brandon, and all outstanding prosecutions dropped. As the exhausted Kemble delivered the terms of the truce from the stage with his own forced apology, a large placard was raised from the pit that read, 'We are satisfied.'

There were a few spats still left in it, but hostilities were largely over, having taken an enormous toll on everyone involved, not least Kemble, who was more dependent on opium than ever. Thomas Dibdin also decided to leave. His wife was pregnant and, having already lost two daughters, he elected to enter semi-retirement in a cottage in Betchworth, Surrey, devoting his time to his pet project, the 'Metrical History of England'. After thirty-five years in the choruses of Covent Garden and Drury Lane, Joe's mother, Rebecca Brooker, finally hung up her pumps, looking forward to spending more time with her only grandchild.

OP claimed another victim in the family as well: Joe's sister-in-law Louisa Bristow, for whom the season had brought an intense but fleeting fame. None of the Bristows had come to much in the profession, although Louisa had an uncommon beauty that had already been noted in the press, which is possibly why Kemble had decided to promote her from supernumerary to leading lady just as the riots began. It was the harshest introduction imaginable for such a young and untested actress, and the constant commotion, with the burden of learning more than twenty major roles, left her looking nervous and unprepared. Perhaps he had banked on any inadequacies being masked by the tumult, although the *Monthly Mirror* managed to catch enough of 'Mr Kemble's favourite' to conclude that 'a prettier Cordelia was never seen, but to do her justice, a worse was never heard'. Even in this oddest of seasons, Louisa's promotion had caused a stir in the company, with rumours suggesting that she owed her sudden elevation to the backstage favours she bestowed on her patron, suspicions that seemed to carry even more weight following her abrupt expulsion before the season closed.

Following her dismissal, Louisa was unable to get another job in London, but when she eventually found work at the Birmingham theatre the following year, she continued to cause rancour in the ranks of Covent Garden, albeit from a distance. Taking a benefit at the end of November 1810, she had begged her famous brother-in-law to swell the treasury with a performance. Grimaldi agreed and, once there, was invited by the manager, Mr Macready (father of the famous tragedian), to stay and perform for an additional three nights. But by entering into this arrangement, Joe unwittingly offended one of the most important actors in the company, John Fawcett, a comedian and significant star in his own right, who had only recently asked Grimaldi to perform at his own benefit but had been rebuffed on the grounds that he had asked him to play a character in a farce. Why Grimaldi should turn down this senior performer is a mystery, but he justified it as an unwillingness to intrude on 'legitimate' drama and thereby endanger his standing in his own 'branch of the profession'.

Whatever the reason, Fawcett took the refusal and Joe's subsequent trip to Birmingham as a gross insult, and determined to take his revenge by having *Mother Goose* announced in his absence to make him lose face with the public and risk censure by the management. A friend's note alerted Joe to the plot in the nick of time, telling him that his name had been published in the bills for the following night, 'and as they know you have not returned from Birmingham, I fear it is done to injure you'. Joe pleaded with Macready to let him go, but as the performance had sold out and the audience were expecting him, he was made to stay lest the house be torn apart.

It was past midnight by the time he finally took his seat in the coach for another bitterly cold and uncomfortable journey, made even more excruciating by the drunkenness of the coachman who kept getting lost. Nineteen miserable, sleepless hours put him beyond the point of exhaustion, but as the coach pulled into Salt Hill, a mile outside Slough and the last major staging post before London, he had no choice but to jump directly from the first coach into another that took him straight to the stage door. Rushing to his dressing room as the first bars of the overture were playing, he frantically dressed and pushed past an astonished Farley, who was waiting in the wings, preparing to take his place. Sitting in his box, Fawcett visibly soured as Joe arrived to take his cue, and for the next three years, he would neither speak to him nor look him directly in the eye. For Joe, however, it was another battering he could ill afford.

PART THREE

[1811–1837]

9

HARLEQUIN IN HIS ELEMENT

What a strange court! What a queer privacy of morals and manners do we look into! Shall we regard it as preachers and moralists, and cry, Woe, against the open vice and selfishness and corruption; or look at it as we do at the king in the pantomime, with his pantomime wife, and pantomime courtiers, whose big heads he knocks together, whom he pokes with his pantomime sceptre, whom he orders to prison under the guard of his pantomime beefeaters, as he sits down to dine on his pantomime pudding.

William Makepeace Thackeray, *The Four Georges* (1855)

SIR HENRY HALFORD WAS the one to tell him, although at first the King seemed not to understand. He sat listening in his purple dressing-gown, his beard and hair grown long and white, like an Old Testament prophet's, but it took a while for the severity of the news to cut through the thick briar that entangled his reason. When at last he became more lucid, he merely sighed and said, 'Poor girl.' The death of Princess Amelia, his youngest and dearest daughter, was the final burden the King's fragile mind would have to bear. Withdrawing into solitary sadness, he dabbed at the keys of a harpsichord as his thoughts ran inconsequentially on and the world around him began to dim. The Queen discontinued her visits, leaving her husband to mutely wander the labyrinth of his memory, and the cares of state devolved entirely to his eldest son, the Prince of Wales, the fat pasha who had waited hungrily for this moment since it had first been denied him twenty-three years before.

George III had spent much of his adult life battling with his sons, none of whom, with the exception of his seventh, Adolphus Frederick, had shown themselves to be anything but morally deficient. When not shacking up with actresses or consummating clandestine marriages, they were ruinously indebted or flogged the regiments under their command. None, though, outdid the villainous Ernest Augustus, Duke of Cumberland, who, having already distressed his parents with rumours of an incestuous affair with his sister Sophia, was at the heart of a much greater scandal in the summer of 1810 when his Sardinian valet, Joseph Sellis, was found lying in his apartments with his throat cut. The Duke, who had a head wound, claimed that a deranged Sellis had attacked him before retreating to his bedroom to kill himself. Informed gossips declared that it was Sellis who had been attacked for daring to defend himself from the Duke's sexual advances.

Compared to his siblings, the riotous and hedonistic George Frederick, Prince of Wales, was not that bad. It was true that he had pointedly snubbed his dutiful upbringing by embracing all the people and vices his father abjured, yet even in his dissipation he remained a hugely impressive man: his charm, his looks, his girdled Falstaffian girth, the outrageous gilt frogging on his dress-coats, which was said to weigh two hundred pounds, and his passionate connoisseurship of and support for the arts, all bespoke an individual committed to life with wide-open senses. The Prince, said the poet Percy Bysshe Shelley, was an 'overgrown bantling', convivial, but tending to excess, brimming with fellowship, yet often inconstant, chivalrous, romantic and lascivious too. In person, said the Duke of Wellington, he was 'very blackguard and very entertaining', with a keen sense of humour forged in company both male and bibulous that delighted in the complex rituals of torture and humiliation that flourished in English public schools. A lover of puns, swearing, sarcasm and scatology, he liked to dress in extravagant costumes and pull elaborate pranks, such as painting his friend's black mare white and presenting it to him as a gift. He was also an excellent mimic who did John Philip Kemble so well that the dandy Beau Brummell thought he should turn professional.[*]

In youth, the Prince's passion for the theatre had manifested itself as an erotic obsession with the actress 'Perdita' Robinson, but even in middle age, he was infused with the spirit of illusion to the degree that pageantry and opulence often seemed to constitute the limit of his statecraft. This, though, he understood exceptionally well. The party he threw at Carlton House to celebrate his accession as Regent, for example, an Asiatic fête festooned with lights and flowers, was, gushed the Irish poet Thomas Moore, an assemblage of 'beauty, splendour and profound magnificence': 'Nothing was ever so magnificent,' he wrote to his mother, 'it was in *reality* all that they try to imitate in the gorgeous scenery of the theatre.' Not everyone was so impressed. When George Tierney described the centrepiece of the two-hundred-foot-long dinner table, a stream made of silver that contained real fish sporting along 'faintly waving, artificial banks . . . covered with green moss and aquatic flowers', he also noted a theatrical likeness, dismissing it as 'that Sadler's Wells business'.

The Prince and the pantomime were made for one another, and during the period from the declaration of the Regency in 1811 to his coronation as George IV nine years later, the form reached its zenith. At Covent Garden, Charles Farley presided over a golden age. The company was the strongest it had ever

---

[*] Despite their reputation for wit and composure, the dandies themselves liked nothing better than a spot of slapstick. The funniest among them was generally held to be a Colonel Mackinnon, who, according to Brummell's great friend, Colonel Gronow (so short they called him 'Colonel No Grow'), 'used to amuse his friends by creeping over the furniture of a room like a monkey'. Even Grimaldi offered deferential praise of his ability, telling Gronow that 'Mackinnon has only to put on the motley costume, and he would totally eclipse me.'

been, 'a vast body of conjoined talent', said Frederick Reynolds, outstripping even Garrick's in the heyday of Drury Lane. For Robert Elliston (known as 'the Great Lessee' for the large amount of theatres he acquired and managed), it was simply 'the best body of performers that had ever been got together, in the memory of the living'. Its pantomime troupe, known as the 'pantomimic wonders', had been joined by several new performers since 1811, and two in particular made enormous contributions.

The first was James Barnes, a short Enfield cobbler whose otherwise bland face bore eyes as sharp as thorns, a Pantaloon with a 'mode of playing that anomalous character', wrote Charles Dibdin, who also hired him for Sadler's Wells, 'as completely original as Grimaldi's Clown'. Together, Barnes and Grimaldi transformed any scene in which they appeared into the 'acme of pantomimical drollery'. Barnes was followed by the Harlequin Thomas Ellar, who arrived at Covent Garden via Dublin's Crow Street Theatre and a number of travelling circuses to work as Jack Bologna's stunt double, performing all the jumps and tumbles in *Harlequin and the Swans* (1813) after Jack had broken his collarbone. Ellar moved so lightly he appeared barely to touch the ground ('His legs twinkle, rather than dance,' wrote *The Times*, 'he moves like a sprite') and he would complete his transformation from lovelorn youth to Harlequin by spinning his entire body with remarkable velocity, 'as if the masked face was only a whirling teetotum revolving on the centre of his frilled neck'. Like Joe and Jack, Barnes and Ellar became the best of friends, and remained so for the rest of their lives, travelling together, sharing the same room, and competing for the same women. As Harlequin, Ellar cut the finer figure, though this didn't stop Barnes deploying his natural wiles to win an advantage: on a trip to Paris, he managed to thwart a romance between Ellar and their landlady by emptying a box of maggots into Ellar's bed and carefully explaining to the repulsed lady in his pidgin French that the poor man couldn't help it as 'he was subject to them' three or four times a year. Overseeing them all was Charles Farley, dubbed 'the king of melo-dramas and high-priest of Christmas sports', who managed his troupe with paternal pride, treating them to a dinner at the Piazza Coffee House every Boxing Day afternoon. There, he would gee them up like cup-finalists, focusing their minds on the job ahead and entreating them to 'enjoy their evening as much as possible, but, at the same time, to remember "whom they have to cope withal" – viz. the good folks at Drury'.

Not only were Farley's performers the best available, but ever since *Mother Goose*, pantomime had gone from seasonal afterthought to the most eagerly anticipated production of the year. It had also become increasingly topical, taking on the role of an unofficial national review, a comic gallimaufry that examined manners, dances, current affairs, popular singers, victories in battle, notable public works, inventions like gas light, steam engines and macadamising, developments in industry, progress in mining and manufacture, events on the stock exchange, sporting events like hunting, rowing, boxing matches and horse-racing, the plight of the poor, the emancipation of slaves in the colonies, and all the latest trends in skirts, collars, boots and hats, each element introduced, laughed at and discarded, like a child opening presents on Christmas Day. Pantomime was a cultural audit, a great summing-up, or, in the words of *The Times*, 'a running commentary – an annual one, upon the whims and speculations of the year'.

More money than ever was being sunk into productions, and with the reopening of Drury Lane in 1812, competition between the rival houses pushed production costs steadily upwards, until by the late eighteen-teens a show could hardly be staged for less than a thousand pounds. The money went on lavish costumes, grand scenery and increasingly complicated tricks, but also one-of-a-kind novelties calculated to sink the opposition. Farley's first Regency pantomime, for example, *Harlequin Padmanaba; or, the Golden Fish* (1811), one of the many pantomimes heavily spiced with eastern aromatics to reflect the Regent's taste for chinoiserie, introduced to the stage Chunee, the largest Indian elephant ever seen in Britain. An unwilling spectacle, he consistently refused to play his part, turning his backside on the audience, making unscripted exits, rearranging the scenery with his flailing trunk, and trying to unseat a terrified Barnes and Mrs Parker, who were on his back dressed as the Sultan and Sultana of Kashmir. Chunee was booed until Farley finally got him to co-operate by feeding him bribes of rum. It worked for actors, why not elephants?*

---

* Chunee the elephant was killed in a hail of gunfire in March 1826, after the frenzy of his annual musth, exacerbated by the pain of a rotting tusk, had driven him into such a violent rage that he threatened to break out of his cage and kill his keepers. A decision was taken to destroy him, and Joe's friend Edward Cross, who had owned Chunee since 1812, as an attraction at the Exeter Change Menagerie, called in surgeons to administer poison. This had no effect. Next, a pair of marksmen were called to shoot him while his keepers held him back with ten-foot spears topped with double-edged blades, but their bullets merely made a hissing sound as they pierced his skin, which only served to enrage him further; he threw his entire weight against the bars of his cage, buckling the ironwork and threatening to open the cages of the lions and tigers next door. The report of musketry, combined with the elephant's furious trumpeting, set the other beasts into a cacophony of animal terror, their squawks and roars causing shoppers in the Strand to stop in their tracks and run towards the noise. A detachment of soldiers was called from Somerset House to execute him by firing squad, but the ill-trained men seemed incapable of correctly loading their rifles and their inept fusillades emptied over a hundred bullets into the elephant at close range before he began to show even the first signs of pain. All of a sudden, reported the *Mirror of Literature*, 'his eyes instantly appeared like balls of fire; he shook his head with dreadful fury, and rushed against the front of his den, and broke part of it, and it was expected every moment that the massy pillars, strengthened with plates of iron, would have given way'. They called for a cannon as the failed carnage got further out of hand, though in the end, there was no need: one of Chunee's keepers completed the destruction by piercing his stomach with a harpoon. As Cross wept inconsolably, Chunee fell to his knees in disbelief, like Caesar before the Forum, and, with a last, loamy exhalation, collapsed into a lake of blood. A hundred and fifty-two bullets were pulled from his corpse.

In all his obstinate, weighty pointlessness, Chunee might have been a metaphor for the Regency's own otiose, wastrel ways. The fact is that he probably was, for even as the pantomime was becoming increasingly glutted, its satirical instincts sharpened. Not that pantomime hadn't always been satirical – J. P. Malcolm, writing in the age of Dubois, had heartily commended it for 'ridiculing the follies of the age' – but the early nineteenth century saw a willingness to tackle increasingly political themes, as evinced by productions like Drury Lane's 1808 anti-slavery pantomime, *Furibond; or, Harlequin Negro*. Once the connection had been made, theatres leapt on the opportunity to discuss matters of substance behind the smokescreen of laughter, and side-step the censorship that made the stage the most politically neutered arena in Britain. It was this oppressive gagging that caused Leigh Hunt, writing in the *Examiner*, to declare pantomimes 'the best medium of dramatic satire', as their want of speech left the audience free to interpret the action however they pleased. 'Our farces and comedies spoil the effect of their ridicule by the dull mistakes of the author,' he argued, 'but the absence of dialogue in the Pantomime saves him this contradiction, and leaves the spectators, according to their several powers, to imagine what supplement they have to the mute caricature before them.' It was also an opportunity for the 'lesser stupid' to chastise the greater:

> a whole train of them . . . the worldly, the hypocritical, the selfish, the self-sufficient, the gossiping, the traitorous, the ungrateful, the vile-tempered, the ostentatious, the canting, the oppressing, the envious, the sulky, the money-scraping, the prodigiously sweet-voiced, the over-cold, the over-squeezing, the furious, the resenter of inconvenience who has inconvenienced, the cloaker of conscious ill by accusation, the insolent in return for sparing.

With this added bite, Joe Grimaldi went from being England's best-known simpleton to its premier visual satirist, 'Hogarth in action', the ideal mascot of a jostling, intemperate world, rattling off oaths in its creaking boots and gorging on beef and oysters. The easiest targets were the fastest moving. Regency style was fleet and capricious, giving each new production a host of things to laugh about. *Bang Up; or, Harlequin Prime!*, the Sadler's Wells pantomime of 1811, made fun of the dandies, raffish slang and the popularity of the Four-in-Hand Club, the coaching fraternity who aimed to outdo each other with the finery of their liveries and equipage. ('Bang up' meant both 'smart' and 'alert'.) *Harlequin Gulliver* (1817) saw Joe don a plum pudding, a coal scuttle and an iron stove-pipe to turn himself into a female dandy, a 'dandizette'.

Fashionable pastimes were also parodied: in *Harlequin and the Swans*, Clown performed with the popular Indian jugglers and, while trying to emulate their sword-swallowing, put a sword into his mouth that came out of the back of his head. In *Harlequin Whittington* (1814) he went on a balloon ride through the proscenium and over the heads of the audience. *Harlequin and the Red Dwarf; or, the Adamantine Rock* (1812) made fun of the famous Epping Hunt where East End traders and Essex grandees risked their necks trying to pass themselves off as sportsmen. Its hunt consisted of three laps round the stage with a real pack of hounds, Pantaloon riding a bedraggled pony and Clown a curious shaggy-haired horse, pursuing their stag, a bemused llama procured from Bullock's menagerie. *The Red Dwarf* also demonstrated how the pantomime might cast a critical eye over topics of more substance than excessive surtouts in a scene in which Joe used the detritus of a stable to transform himself from Clown to Hussar. As *The Times* described it:

Two black varnished coal-scuttles formed his boots, two real
horse-shoes shod the heels, and with jack-chains and the help
of large brass dishes or candlesticks for spurs, equipped his legs
in an uniform almost as clattering unwieldy, and absurd as the
most irresistible of our whiskered propungnatores ['champions'
or 'defenders']. A white bear-skin formed his pelisse, a muff his
cap, and a black tippet finished his toilet, by giving him a beard,
whiskers, and pendant moustaches.

It is odd to think that, in a time of war, jokes at the expense
of élite soldiers should have been so well received, but according to *The Times*, the audience 'roared with laughter, as they
saw the buffoon of a Theatre turn the favourite invention of
the mighty, and the wise, and the warlike, into merited ridicule'. The paper's approval stemmed from a 'general contempt
for these miserable imitations of foreign foppery', adding that
the joke was given special relish by the presence of a group of
genuine Hussars sitting in the stage box, 'covered *de cap à pied*,
with chains and cat skins'. While the British worshipped their
navy, they were at best ambivalent about their land forces, who
did not begin to gain popular support until after Wellington's
victory at the battle of Vitoria in the summer of 1813. Pantomimes showed them to be either a rabble and inept, as in
Harlequin and the Swans or *Harlequin's Jubilee* (1814), where
Joey inspected shabby regiments built from the dregs of
the alehouse garden, or as posturing, entitled braggarts, more
interested in their uniforms than their duty.

To be the constant butt of Grimaldi's jokes left the officers
unamused, and Harris once received a note direct from the
Horse Guards' mess saying that unless Clown desisted from
'his d—d infernal foolery' they would withdraw their patronage
en masse. But the pantomime happily practised double standards, for even as it chided the army for its vanity, it continued to
revel in its glories, presenting all manner of patriotic parades
and tableaux to honour heroes in the struggle against France.

This was demonstrated in the way that Joey the coal-scuttle Hussar applauded the feats of the men he ridiculed by seizing a midget dressed as Napoleon and dashing him into the jaws of a passing Russian bear – an allusion to Bonaparte's disastrous retreat from Moscow. The only rule was that nothing was sacred. No pretensions of excellence or claim to gravity were exempt from the cartoon world.

≈

Throughout this period, Joe became increasingly known for his tricks of construction, the production of a novel whole from a selection of found objects. One of their earliest uses came in *Harlequin in His Element; or, Fire, Water, Earth and Air* (1808), the show that followed *Mother Goose* and which Joe considered 'one of the best pantomimes in which he ever played'. One of its scenes found Joey idling at the side of a road, pilfering produce from the assorted tradespeople who passed him there. His trawl amounting to a fresh salmon, a pair of gloves, a hatbox, a pair of boots and the broad-brimmed hat of the constable sent to arrest him, he decides to stand the boots on the floor and rest the hatbox on top of them. His interest engaged, he next 'attaches a long glove on each side for arms, the piece of salmon for the head, and the whole is surmounted by the BEADLE's hat'. As he steps back to admire his curious, fish-headed figure, Harlequin appears, transforming the salmon into a 'perfect face', which nods a greeting to Clown, who is struck with terror and flees the scene.

In *Harlequin Asmodeus* (1810) he made the vegetable man that may have sown the seed of *Frankenstein*; in *Harlequin Padmanaba* he made a carriage from a child's bassinet and four wheels of cheese and hitched it to a team of springer spaniels. Tricks of construction provided a broader comic palette than he'd previously been able to use, offering something akin to sketch comedy rather than the freneticism of the circus ring, making the audience wait as he developed what critics called his 'sleepy style' of 'quiet humour and busy intensity'. Describing a piece of coach building in *Harlequin and the Ogress*, one wrote of how 'no one can *be at a loss* like Grimaldi. No one can suddenly hit upon a remedy like himself. He really seems never to have had a notion before how he was to make his carriage, but appears to build on the inspiration of the moment.' By letting things unfold at a more measured pace, and adopting 'the delightful assumption of *nonchalance*', he heightened the audience's anticipation and, in so doing, doubled the effect. Sometimes the routines were accompanied by a rare morsel of speech, short, elliptical utterances, like 'Here we are again', as he first came on, 'Nice moon', as he took in the nocturnal scenery, 'Nice', when eating biscuits, or 'Don't', when about to be tortured. Sparse and seemingly redundant though they were, they dripped with character and contained, in one critic's words, 'a world of concentration' that left nothing to be said. 'The audience drank in oblivion of all their grievances with the first tones of their old friend Joe's voice,' wrote William Hazlitt, 'for which indeed he might be supposed to have a patent.'

Clown was becoming more vocal in general, singing more and more songs, many of which included spoken sections of nonsense, mimicry or double-talk. Most of them came from the indefatigable pen of Charles Dibdin, who, near the end of his career, claimed to have written close to five thousand. Dibdin himself admitted that they were of little consequence: 'Unless sung by the Clown of the Pantomime, in Character, [they] lost half their effect.' Favourites included Joe partnering a horse-size starling in *Harlequin Gulliver*, or, in *Harlequin and the Swans*, singing a trio with a giant cod's head and a morose giant oyster recently jilted by its lover. Songs like 'What'll Mrs Grundy Say?', featuring a polyphony of unconnected snippets of London conversations, and 'Betty Brill', which incorporated the cries of a rebarbative fishwife, presented opportunities for Joe to delve into different characters. One of the most famous was called 'Tippitiwichit: or Pantomimical Paroxysms'. First sung in 1811, it was merely an excuse for him to engage in outlandish yawns, coughs and sneezes:

> This very morning handy,
>   My malady was such,
> I in my tea took brandy
>   And took a drop too much.
> (Hiccups) *Tol de rol*, etc.
>
> Now I'm quite drowsy growing,
>   For this very morn,
> I rose while cock was crowing,
>   Excuse me if I yawn.
> (Yawns) *Tol de rol*, etc.
>
> But stop, I mustn't mag hard,
>   My head aches – if you please,
> One pinch of Irish blackguard
>   I'll take to give me ease.
> (Sneezes) *Tol de rol*, etc.
>
> I'm not in cue for frolic,
>   Can't up my spirits keep,
> Love's a windy colic,
>   'Tis that makes me weep.
> (Cries) *Tol de rol*, etc.
>
> I'm not in mood for crying.
>   Care's a silly calf,
> If to get fat you're trying,
>   The only way's to laugh.
> (Laughs) *Tol de rol*, etc.

When the song went well, Joe was able to induce the entire theatre to yawn and sneeze along with him, 'A most remarkable instance of control over a large audience by means of the purely comic element,' said Thomas Goodwin.

Though the words were Dibdin's, the effect was Farley's, whose earlier instruction had provided Joe with the tools that enabled him to mature into a fine actor. Increasingly, his pantomimes came to feature scenes in which he took the stage alone for a virtuoso display of comic acting. Again, it was *Harlequin in His Element* that featured one of the first, a bit of business in which Clown stole a bottle of wine from a sleeping watchman, drank it, then played at being the watchman himself. Having tired of that game, he discovered that he was suddenly too drunk to find his mouth and so entered into a long quarrel with his mutinous body that could only be resolved by holding up the watchman's lamp to his cheek to light the bottle's way.

The scene was instantly popular and led to further opportunities to showcase his talents as a mime. One was witnessed by William Robson, a long-standing fixture of the London theatre scene, who had been particularly impressed by the emotional range Joe portrayed in Charles Dibdin's melodrama *The Wild Man* (1809). Recalling a scene in which Joe played an Orson-style beast about to kill an infant, he described the transformations that fell upon him when the child's despairing father used music to try to calm the beast. Robson wrote,

> The first fierce glance and start, as the sound struck upon his ear, were natural and fine – the hands hung as if arrested, the purpose was at pause. As the plaintive air of the flageolet continued, it was really wonderful to watch that which you felt as the natural effect of the music upon such a being – and when, at length, the savage heart became so softened that his whole frame shook convulsively, and he clasped his hands to his face in an agony of tears, he never failed to elicit the proudest triumph of the actor's art – the sympathizing drops from the eyes of every spectator. And, when the measure was changed to a livelier strain, the picture became almost frightful, for his mirth was in as great an extreme as his grief – he danced like a fury!

Such was Joe's reputation as a mime, he was said to have provided instruction to John Philip Kemble, and there were many who urged him to make the transition into legitimate drama. An 1812 letter from the radical politician Thomas Perronet Thompson to his sister sums up the feeling: 'It is greatly to be regretted', he wrote, having seen Joe perform in *Perouse; or, the Desolate Island*, 'that he did not make his appearance in Touchstone in *As You Like It*. He would have had John Kemble in Jaques; and I have no doubt that Grimaldi would throw great light upon the fool who was the delight of our forefathers, and deserve well of all lovers of Shakespeare.'

Joe had already taken a tentative step into legitimate drama in 1811 when, in a move that was sure to infuriate his enemy John Fawcett, he performed Bob Acres in Sheridan's *The Rivals* for his own Covent Garden benefit. It was one of two legitimate parts he would keep in his repertoire until his retirement. The other was a cross-dressing role, a kind of pantomime dame *avant la lettre*, the blowsy Moll Flaggon in Burgoyne's *The Lord of the Manor*, one of Fawcett's own parts.

The combination of singing and acting freed Grimaldi to move away from physical clowning and experiment with other types of comedy, especially scenes played at a slower pace than normally allowed by pantomime. It was this evolution that in *Oxberry's* judgement made him 'the only purely intellectual *Clown* we ever beheld', though by the same token, it was an adaptation he needed to make in order to survive. Finding ways to be funny while slowing the tempo was imperative if Joe was not to end his career prematurely. His Christmas pantomimes were regularly running into June, by which time Sadler's Wells had been open for two months, requiring him to do double duty on twenty-eight consecutive nights, fifty-six performances, each of which was equivalent to running several miles, dancing a ballet and doing a couple of rounds with a wrestler. Celebrity meant that the pantomime was increasingly being built around him, requiring that he appear in more scenes as the size of shows swelled in response to their popularity.

When Joe's health was flagging, new characters were invented to help share the load, as in *Harlequin Asmodeus'* introduction of a character called 'Dandy Lover', a self-regarding fop and Pantaloon's favoured suitor for the hand of Columbine, who exists, in the words of Thomas Dibdin, 'for no other earthly reason than to be knock'd about, trod upon, and pitch'd in to the Pit'. But whether due to the pressure of expectations or professional pride, Joe would never entirely abandon the fundamentals of physical comedy that had made him famous. He crossed the stage in four enormous strides, and when slapstick was called for, he held nothing back: 'It is absolutely surprising', wrote a correspondent for *The Times* in 1813, 'that any human head or hide can resist the rough trials which he volunteers. Serious tumbles from serious heights, innumerable kicks, and incessant beatings, come on him as matters of common occurrence, and leave him every night fresh and free for the next night's flagellation.' And, unlike Robert Bradbury, this 'most assiduous of all imaginable buffoons' refused to wear padding.

It was a style that Mirza Abul Hassan Khan, the Persian ambassador to the British court who had visited Covent Garden in 1810, likened to that of the acrobats of his native country. Hassan had been particularly impressed by a routine in *Harlequin Asmodeus* in which Joe would leap 'from a high window and just as easily leap back up again, returning each time as a different character . . . causing the noble audience to laugh uncontrollably'. It is no surprise, then, that a risky manoeuvre of any kind, whether it be personal, political or military, came to be known as 'Grimaldi's leap'. Confided Hassan Khan to his journal, it was 'an act I shall never forget'.

Throughout this period of ascendancy, Joe remained in the same precarious financial position he had been in since he and Mary had married. Henry Harris made sure to treat his miracle troupe well, bearing the expense of mending, pressing and washing their costumes, all of which at most theatres was the responsibility of the performers, and putting a pint of wine in their dressing room each night. Still, though, his weekly wages were meagre enough for one correspondent to claim that 'Grimaldi, worth his weight in gold, is kept on bread and water.' Other performers seemed to manage perfectly well. At Drury Lane, Jean-Baptiste Laurent received the same ten pounds a week as Joe and took the same number of benefits each year. Unlike Joe, he managed to save three thousand pounds, enough to lease part of the Lyceum and set up his own theatre, the Theatre of Mirth, although, admittedly, the venture did not end well.

Things were particularly difficult in 1812, when Joe was close to bankruptcy, despite clearing £625 in benefits. As always, naïvety and lack of oversight were at the root of his misfortune. Constantly the victim of his own poor judgement, he would think nothing of entrusting his entire provincial earnings to an unnamed associate and be surprised when he robbed him. Then there was the cost of supporting the rural lifestyle that he wanted for his son, 'the great expense consequence upon keeping a country as well as a town house', as the *Memoirs* put it, not to mention the 'great extravagance' of Mary, 'who although an excellent woman, had . . . a love of dress which amounted to a mania'. Though Joe blamed Mary for having to give up the lease of the Finchley cottage, there had been a run-in with the bailiff who had seized all the furniture at Baynes Row several months before they even took it. Such visits were becoming unnervingly familiar, and Joe took to having himself smuggled out of the theatre in a suitcase to avoid them. In time, he came to make light of his pitiful finances by transforming them into a piece of street-theatre: every afternoon he strolled to a pawn shop at the corner of the Liverpool and Islington roads and perched on a shelf until the manager came in to redeem him.

The pinch on his finances forced Joe to accept whatever provincial engagements he was offered, though it made him doubly indignant as he hated travelling and longed for nothing more than the routine of London. In the autumn of 1812, he accepted an offer to play in Cheltenham in spite of Richard Hughes's warnings that it was a 'bad theatrical town', unlikely even to cover his expenses. He arrived to find that he had just missed William Betty, on the come-back trail at twenty-one. Though still extremely young, Betty had been manhandled by time, transformed from a golden youth into a 'hippopotamus' with a voice like 'the gurgling of an Alderman with the quinsey'. One critic who had seen him perform Alexander the Great described him as a 'fat, fair, ranting, screaming fellow who might much better represent a Persian eunuch'; the *Theatrical Inquisitor*, meanwhile, thought he looked puzzled and out of his depth: 'Judging from his manner of delivery we should think that a greater portion of what he is repeating remains a mystery to him.'

Cheltenham was far kinder to Joe and even afforded an invitation for a day of hare-coursing in the Malvern Hills close to Berkeley Castle, the home of the keen amateur dramatist Colonel Berkeley, 'a local deity, whose word was law'. A real-life Squire Bugle, a million miles from your typical stage-struck day-dreamer, Berkeley was coarse, bluff, devoted to his hounds, and had once horsewhipped a newspaper editor in his own living room for writing a critical article. He invited Joe to stay for dinner before the evening's show, as he was entertaining a number of guests, including Lord Byron, there to take the waters – 'very medicinal and sufficiently disgusting' – and seek professional advice for his various complaints. Byron had chosen Cheltenham over the more established Tunbridge Wells as, under Berkeley's influence, it had earned a reputation as a gay, fast-living town, where society could afford to be a little more liberal, thanks to its transient population of provincial heiresses and wife-hunting officers who had only a few short weeks to make a favourable impression.

Byron and Grimaldi had met several years before, and though the intervening years had seen them both ascend the Olympus of celebrity, it was perhaps Grimaldi, and especially the vegetable monster of *Harlequin Asmodeus*, who had made the greatest impression. Byron greeted the Clown with appropriately pantomimic deference, 'making several low bows' and expressing 'in very hyperbolical terms his "great and unbounded satisfaction in becoming acquainted with a man of such rare and profound talents", etc.' Joe played along, aware he was being lampooned and returning 'the bows and congees three-fold', before making a face behind Byron's back that 'mingled gratification and suspicion' and raised a hearty laugh at Byron's expense. This was tantamount to a challenge, and Byron saw to it that the score was evened at dinner, when he arranged for one of the guests to take Grimaldi aside and proffer a little friendly advice.

'Byron is very courteous at the dinner-table,' said this guest in a whisper, 'but does not like to have his courtesy thrown away, or slighted; I would recommend you, if he asks you to take anything . . . no matter whether it be to eat or drink, not to refuse.'

Grimaldi bowed his thanks, grateful for the chance to avoid committing an embarrassing *faux pas* at a table at which commoners were few.

With the trap set, Byron proceeded to offer him a Trimalchio's feast of wines and delicacies, none of which Grimaldi could refuse, until he was so utterly gorged that he doubted he'd be able to perform that night. It was then that Byron presented him with an apple tart, which Grimaldi eyed with dismay but to which, bravely, he set a fork nonetheless. Then Byron interrupted him: 'Why, Mr Grimaldi,' he said, 'do you not take soy with your tart?'

'Soy, my lord?' said Joe.

'Yes, soy,' said Byron, passing over a bottle of salty black sauce. 'It is very good with salmon, and therefore it must be nice with apple-pie.'

Joe searched questioningly around the table, but an urgent nudge from his neighbour told him to get on with it. He dutifully poured soy over his dessert, took a couple of exploratory mouthfuls, and found himself quickly struggling against a tide of nausea. On the brink of vomiting, he lowered his fork and, in the most humble and beseeching terms, praised the great lord's generosity but begged his forgiveness for his apparent display of ingratitude, a pathetic address that had Byron in stitches.

This was fairly typical of Joe and Byron's relationship. Back in London, they began to see each other regularly as the poet became increasingly involved in the London theatre scene with the resumption of productions at Drury Lane, for which he had been commissioned to write the opening address, and his subsequent election to its Sub-Committee of Management. He was drawn to the theatrical temperament and enjoyed its lifestyle and the intrigue of the green room, keeping the company of people like d'Egville, the dancing pimp, and the volatile Edmund Kean, who excited him greatly. It wasn't always clear, though, how one was supposed to behave in his presence. For all the reconfigurations of the OP war, an actor's social status remained far from certain, and fame provided little insulation against the social snobbery that meant even Dora Jordan had to put up with abuse from her cook, who would scold her and let it be known that she was too good to take orders from a mere player.

Joe, too, had suffered censure in the first swell of his celebrity, for the 'glaring instance of impropriety and indecency' he had committed 'by presuming to come into the *Salon* of the *Theatre* in his *zany habilments*, and perform his antics'. 'This', said the correspondent, 'is an insult which no Audience can tolerate; therefore, for the future, it may be prudent for Mr. Grimaldi, to play the fool – *only upon the Stage!*' Given that Byron was part-enthusiast, part-patron, buying up fistfuls of benefit tickets and giving Joe elegant gifts, it was only natural that his overtures of friendship should leave Joe feeling wrong-footed. Though greatly honoured by the poet's attentions – Byron sometimes sent for him in the early afternoon, stayed with him until the performance, then waited in the wings until the curtain so that they could continue their conversation – he intimidated him too. For a start, he was more in awe of the great man than might admit a truly equitable friendship, and often left stammering by the velocity of his language and strength of his oaths. He was also especially wary of the poet's famous sarcasm, making a special effort never to contradict him in anything and going to extraordinary lengths to discover his views in advance to save himself the embarrassment of Byron's scorn. And, despite being a fellow sufferer, he also found Byron's sudden mood swings and propensity for despair alien and disconcerting. Yet there was obviously substance to Byron's friendship with Grimaldi, for when he departed England for ever in 1816, he presented Joe with a fine silver snuff box inscribed with the words, 'the gift of Lord Byron to Joseph Grimaldi'.

~

In the summer of 1815, Joe performed Clown in three different theatres on a single night. The occasion was the benefit of Miss Dely, newly married to his friend Hayward at the

Surrey Theatre (the renamed Royal Circus). With a cab on hand and Jack Bologna to accompany him, he played first at the Surrey, then across the river and up through the City to the Wells, before concluding the evening at Covent Garden, stopping only to change costumes and reapply his rain-smeared slap. Joe was very proud of this accomplishment, considering it 'something out of the common way', for which he 'plumed himself very much'. For John Fawcett, however, it presented the opportunity to serve his long-awaited dish of revenge: he withheld Joe's salary for not seeking the proper leave to perform at another theatre.

Fawcett was not the only one losing patience with Grimaldi's multiple engagements, for at Sadler's Wells Joe was taking more and more nights off to recover from his various trips and benefit nights, and had just spent four weeks in bed at the end of the summer, suffering from chest pains and shortness of breath. Either this illness or another later in the year was sufficiently bad to result in a rumour that Joe had died. William Hazlitt, one of the many taken in by the news, searched London to find out if it was true: 'We looked at the faces we met in the street, but there were no signs of general sadness; no one stopped his acquaintance to say, that a man of genius was no more . . . without the clown at Sadler's Wells, there must be an end of pantomime in this country!' Charles Dibdin was particularly irked by the state in which Grimaldi would return to Islington, attempting to solve the problem by manipulating engagements behind the clown's back, warding off rival managers and even turning down work on his behalf. As early as 1810, he had refused to release him to Charles Farley. 'He has complained so much of being unwell lately,' he wrote to Farley, 'has omitted his songs one night and for the last 6 nights has not played in the afterpiece [and] altho' I have advertised him for Monday and following evenings I know not whether he will play.' It was an action motivated in part by the pressure he was receiving from the shareholders: 'They feel much hurt at it,' he explained, 'as it really does us injury, to put up his name and he not then play.' Ultimately, though, he was protecting himself, for if he relented and Grimaldi then failed to report to the Wells, 'our folks would naturally say he made himself ill by doing so much and would have an opening to censure me for giving him permission'.

There was more to it than simply protecting an asset: Dibdin appears to have been equally rankled by the threat Grimaldi's fame posed to his own influence. If the short and bilious memoir by the night watchman Richard Wheeler is to be believed, animosity between Dibdin and Grimaldi had been overt and long-standing, despite their working relationship: 'From the first meeting of the stage manager and Grimaldi there was nothing but war,' wrote Wheeler, 'either open or concealed.' Tensions had escalated following the death of Joe's father-in-law and mentor, Richard Hughes, at Christmas in 1814, leaving Dibdin in sole charge.* Dibdin's philosophy of management was simple – 'A Theatre should be like an absolute Monarchy,' he had written – and he resented Grimaldi's rising status within the company, a position cemented when Joe had been elected as the Chief Judge and Treasurer of the Sadler's Wells Court of Rectitude the previous year, a body charged with drawing up a code of conduct for the performers under its jurisdiction, and administering fines for offences that included drunkenness, swearing, arguing, stealing clothes from the dressing rooms, calling someone a 'bugger' and farting ('1d. for the first offence, and 2d. for the second'). Such

---

* Hughes's funeral was on Boxing Day, thus presenting Grimaldi with another gruesome juxtaposition as he ran from dress rehearsal to graveside and back again to prepare for that evening's début of *Harlequin Whittington*. This time, though, the backstage tears would not pave the way for rapturous applause, as he sang flat and out of key, and 'with all his nearly irresistible power of producing laughter, it was almost half an hour before he could, by his ludicrous exertions, do away with the stupefying effect of his ballad'.

influence made it harder to submit Grimaldi to the various petty house rules that included prohibiting performers from speaking to each other except on stage and forbidding female singers to take encores and sacking others on the orders of Mrs Dibdin, who could 'bear no rivalry'. Meanwhile, he cavilled at every expense, though living in rent-free accommodation, paying himself and his wife generous salaries with two free benefits a year, and issuing free admission to local tradesmen in exchange for personal discounts.

With Grimaldi's successes threatening to spoil Dibdin's feudal comforts, conflict seemed certain, although without Wellington's victory at the battle of Waterloo it might never have been so calamitous. Victory turned the people away from their familiar pastimes, and embracing the boom in Napoleonics, they devoured every wartime artefact they could find. Three separate museums opened near Piccadilly to meet the demand for memorabilia, everything from weapons, medals and uniforms, to Napoleon's slippers, Josephine's furbelows and the emperor's knackered old charger, Marengo, who still had a bullet in his tail. The greatest draw was undoubtedly Napoleon's bulletproof travelling carriage. Originally presented to the Prince of Wales by the Hussar General Blücher, it had been sold by the cash-strapped Prince to the showman William Bullock, who exhibited it first at his Egyptian Hall before taking it on a tour of the provinces, where he claimed it had been seen by more than eight hundred thousand people.

In the glorious sunlight of peace, the old amusements looked worn and shabby. 'All Theatres are bad now,' complained Dibdin. 'Drury Lane is a very ruinous Concern – the others struggling with every Difficulty.' His was no exception, being pitched into a 'state of declension' before the battlefield could even be cleared of its dead. Economies needed to be made and the expensive aquadramas were the first thing to be cut. The drought proved only temporary, however, and the tanks were replenished after Dibdin discovered another talented Newfoundland, called Bruin, for whom he wrote an aquadramatic vehicle called *Philip and His Dog*. Bruin managed to turn a profit in 1816, but with things so uncertain, Dibdin was convinced that the water had to go. Expense was not the only problem. His aquatic inspiration was deserting him, and the novelty had worn off with the public who had long stopped marvelling at the effect and now saw only quarrelling perspectives, toy ships running aground and boys floundering in knee-high water. Added to the fact that Astley's was rumoured to be installing a tank of its own, Dibdin decided to put his faith entirely in Bruin, and drafted in four more performing dogs to support his 'Dog Star'.

It was against these difficulties that Grimaldi began negotiations for a new contract, requesting two benefits, his salary raised from twelve pounds to twelve guineas a week, and leave to undertake a six-week tour of the provinces every July. Dibdin refused this last point flat out, and countered by agreeing to the salary increase, but only on the condition that the two benefits be reduced to one. Locked in a battle of wills, Joe stood firm, confident that as senior performer and 'unquestionably the lion of the theatre', Dibdin would have no choice but to accede. Instead Dibdin fired him, giving the job of Clown to Signor Paulo, the son of Paulo Redigé and his mistress La Belle Espagnole, the Sadler's Wells funambulists who had been so kind to Joe as a boy.

Dibdin's move not only shocked Grimaldi, it came as a complete surprise to the Sadler's Wells faithful, a faction of whom fly-posted the neighbourhood with bills proclaiming, 'No Paulo!' and 'Joey for ever!' Some accused Joe of pasting them up himself, though if he had, his plan backfired when they were answered by bills that read, 'No Grimaldi!' In the event, the mob failed to mobilise on behalf of either clown, and when Joe slipped into the boxes on Paulo's first night expecting to address a riot, he found the house only a quarter full. Conveniently ignoring the effects of the post-war recession, he took it as evidence of his own popularity, no doubt drawing additional pleasure from the tepid comments his rival received in the press. Paulo 'stood his ground ably', they said.

Yet their indifference was to prove short-lived, as within a few weeks, Paulo had not only won over the critics but had been confirmed 'a universal favourite' at the Wells. To add insult to injury, he performed as a replica Joey, using the same costume and makeup Grimaldi had devised in the dressing rooms from which he was now an exile.

10

THE ORPHAN OF PERU

Grimaldi, he's getting old; what would you? One can't do anything else — neither pills nor rhubarb taken at the astrologic, star-predicted, Hicksian hour can impede the fatal progress of the years.

Letter of William Beckford (14 January 1819)

ON 2 DECEMBER 1816, a crowd of almost twenty thousand assembled outside the Merlin's Cave, a pub on Rosoman Street, Islington, just around the corner from Joe's house at Baynes Row. Composed of distressed manufacturers, sailors and artisans, working men impoverished by the economic crisis that had followed the victory against France, they had come to hear the radical orator Henry Hunt call for universal male suffrage and a range of tax, land and parliamentary reforms. Having addressed the crowd from a first-floor window, Hunt ceded the platform to a failed apothecary and agitator called James Watson, who for many years had been advocating violent insurrection as the means to secure change. Watson's speech was short but effective. Using martial rhetoric, he persuaded about three hundred men to march on the City, with his mentally unstable son at their head. The mob signalled its intent by looting a gun shop in Clerkenwell and shooting one of its customers in the groin, and by the time it reached Cheapside, swelled by more armed men, it mounted an assault on the Tower of London. A skirmish ensued with the regiment in residence, and the mob was quickly repulsed, dispersing into smaller, even more destructive groups, who rampaged through the streets.

The Spa Fields riots, as they came to be known, marked the beginning of what would prove a protracted period of unrest in Britain as increasingly vocal reform movements were met by equally intransigent authorities happy to respond with force. The government, convinced of rampant sedition among the working classes, set about suspending rights and redrafting laws, billeting troops in 'disturbed districts' and loosing *agents provocateurs* on every pub and debating society. As the head of state, and its most corpulent symbol of social inequality, the Prince Regent was the focus of discontent. Already unpopular due to the cruel mistreatment of his wife, Princess Caroline, whom he had hypocritically put on trial for adultery and forced out of the country in 1814, he had become widely despised. People lined the streets to boo him as he made his way to open Parliament in January 1817, and attacked his coach in the Mall. The result was only a broken window, although it was never fully ascertained whether it had been shattered by a bullet or a stone.

The puckish wantonness of his earlier years seemed to have abandoned the Prince, with the recent departure of two of his most totemic allies, Lord Byron and Beau Brummell, who had separately left England the year before, the first to outrun rumours of sodomy and incest, the second to escape his debts. Even the weather colluded in the national despondency, another cold winter making way for a dreary spring and a particularly gloomy summer. 1817 was not a good year.

Though it was the first time in thirty-five years that Joe had not played a summer in Islington, he wasn't unemployed for long. The first offer came from William Murray, the young manager of the Edinburgh and Glasgow theatres, who retained strong connections to Covent Garden through his sister Harriet, daughter-in-law to Mrs Siddons. He knew Joe well, having been both a pupil of Charles Farley and a villager in the original production of *Mother Goose*. Once Joe had agreed to terms in Scotland, another offer came from Knight, manager of the Manchester and Liverpool theatres. Having in a few days arranged enough work for a short tour of the north, Joe turned his back on Sadler's Wells.

The trip was lucrative but gruelling, his trials beginning on the outward journey with a night-time collision between two coaches that left both vehicles on their sides, one on top of the other. Competition between coaching companies and the Regency fashion for fast driving had made this kind of accident shamefully common. There were no serious injuries, though Joe found himself buried beneath five stout men at the far side of the bottom coach. It was the harbinger of further blows to come: while his Scottish shows passed off without incident, in Manchester he fell badly during a performance of *Castles in the Air*. He was required to emerge from the centre of an enormous bowl of gooseberry fool placed over a rising trap, but the ropes snapped as he made his ascent and sent him crashing into the cellar with nothing to break his fall. Bruised but with nothing broken, he managed to play on.

The following day the company decamped to Liverpool, forming a caravan that drove the thirty miles to the new venue. Joe showed the scenemen his injuries and begged to be spared a second fall, but his entreaties came to nothing: the same accident happened again. This time, though, it was worse, for when the ropes gave way Joe tried to catch the edge, but slipped; the narrowness of the trap forced his arms above his head and almost pulled them from their sockets before he fell to the cellar floor. Somehow he managed to finish, but had to be carried to bed at the final curtain. The following morning, unable to stand, he was lifted into the coach for the long drive home.

Had the carpenters deliberately tried to injure Joe? Falls were common, but consecutive accidents across two nights suggested malicious intent, and Joe had certainly had problems with them before. While he was working in Birmingham for Macready, his fastidiousness over the detail of specific props had been interpreted as starry petulance, and when it came time to go on stage, the scenemen replaced the real props with a live pig, a goose and two ducks and told him to get on with it. Scenemen and carpenters were a proud, tight-knit fraternity, a proto-unionised body who could halt a production if they felt aggrieved, extort money from any actor who relied on them for their effects, and exact revenge on those who refused to pay. Sheridan's friend Michael Kelly, the singer, owed one of his finest moments to a carpenter's poor timing in *Lodoiska*, but when he feuded with stage-hands during the course of the melodramatic opera *Blue-Beard*, they 'forgot' to lift the skeletons that were meant to dissolve magically before him, leaving Kelly with no choice but to kick and punch the apparitions noisily to the floor.

Frederick Reynolds similarly recalled how a particularly nervous actor playing the ghost in *Henry VI* bribed the carpenters nightly to raise him through the stage with 'particular gentleness and caution'. The arrangement worked well until the carpenters decided to raise their taxes, and when the actor resisted they heaved him through the trap so quickly that the ethereal vision shot six feet into the air and landed on the stage with an ostentatiously loud bang that produced 'an instantaneous burst of laughter from all parts of the house'.

Humiliation was one thing, but for pantomimists, the stakes were considerably higher. Though the theatre's strict hierarchy forbade carpenters to fraternise with performers, in the lowly pantomime department questions of status were fraught and contentious. Pantomimists relied on the goodwill of the carpenters far more than anyone else, but they were simultaneously bound to keep their distance by the rules of the house, thus presenting them with a number of unique problems of etiquette. Once, while working in Paris, for example, James Barnes had to ask the carpenters not to sit so close to him during lunch. It was a particularly delicate mission that had to be seen as his sole initiative, for if Clown and Harlequin were implicated, both of whom needed the carpenters on their side to perform their jumps and tricks safely, there would almost certainly be consequences. As Pantaloon, Barnes was relatively safe.

When the relationship did break down, the repercussions could be terrible – Harlequin might dive at a trick flap that had not been unfastened, or, having made it through, discover that the men holding the carpet to catch him had chosen that moment to take a break. This was exactly what happened to Thomas Ellar in *Harlequin Munchausen* (1818). Ellar, who had already paid his catch money, snapped at the men when they came to him to complain that their carpet was still very 'dry', and when the time came for him to leap through the face of the moon, the men were there, but so far out of position that he landed short and broke his hand. A younger performer called Tom Ridgeway, subjected to the same treatment, grabbed a handful of hair as he sailed past one of the carpenters, making sure not to let go until he'd torn it from the man's scalp. He had a right to be angry – no one in the profession could forget the fate of Signor Paulo's father, Paulo Redigé, who had died when the top of his skull collided with the head of a protruding screw after the carpenters had failed to catch him.

Joe limped into London to be greeted by a further barrage of requests from provincial theatres keen to secure his services. A long, circular itinerary was compiled, over which he consulted at length with Mary. It was agreed that he should take JS along for company. At fifteen, the boy had already outgrown his father by a couple of inches, was lean and supple with black hair and striking features that revealed his Italian genes and full lips and drowsy eyes gave him the look of a young voluptuary. Having been sickly throughout childhood, whether from a fundamentally infirm disposition or his parents' projected hypochondria, he was used to being left behind, and it was uncertain whether he'd have the stamina to endure such a long trip. But JS was tired of his cosseted existence, watching his cousin George practise handstands and somersaults and play with swords at Sadler's Wells while he went muffled even in fair weather and was confined to bed at the first sign of a sniffle. For years, he had been trying to demonstrate his suitability for the stage, especially through music, for which he showed early promise.

Still Joe persistently refused to let him enter the theatre, sending him instead as a day-boy to his old school in Putney, and then to one in Pentonville, where he shared his enthusiasm for the theatre with his classmates Robert Honner and Thomas Hamblin, both of whom went on to become actors. JS excelled in his lessons, and by twelve was fluent in French and well read in French literature, yet no amount of formal learning could dislodge the combined forces of nature and nurture that had impressed themselves upon him, and at length Joe was forced to concede.

JS's début came at Sadler's Wells on 10 October 1814 when, aged twelve, he played Friday in Sheridan's *Robinson Crusoe* for Joe's last benefit of the season. His appearance had been kept secret until just a few days before the show, although a hint lay in the image printed on the ticket – a paternal Crusoe patting the head of a youthful Friday. The performance was prefaced by weeks of intense rehearsal that introduced him to a side of his father quite separate from the amiable man who slept late and sang 'tol de rol' while shaving. At the theatre, Joe was a perfectionist, proceeding slowly through the minutiae of each trick, finding countless reasons to perfect footwork, props and scenery, and always busy, as if he anticipated being accused of working insufficiently hard. These were the habits he had learnt from his father, and while Joe was conscious not to visit the same kind of tyranny on his own son, he still found himself drilling him harder than the others, both to spare him from accusations of favouritism and out of nervousness lest the public think worse of him for the boy's shortcomings. JS, though, was perfect on the night, receiving compliments from every quarter, greatly comforting Joe, who fondly imagined that 'when his own heyday of fame and profit was over, he should gather new life from the boy's success'.

Almost a year passed before JS was given a second opportunity, playing in the greatest tradition of clowning families a miniature Clown beside his father in Farley's *Harlequin and Fortunio; or, Shing-Moo and Thun-Ton.** Though not so miniature, this was the role he assumed as they passed through Glasgow, Edinburgh, Berwick, Liverpool, Preston, Hereford, Worcester and Birmingham, performing *Don Juan*, *Harlequin Whittington* and an olio compilation of greatest hits that included the *Mother Goose pas de deux*, the Vegetable Man from *Harlequin Asmodeus*, and both the Oyster crossed in love and dog-drawn curricle from *Harlequin and the Swans*. His reception was 'highly flattering' at every leg, and at the end of it, father and son headed off to Cheltenham for a few weeks' relaxation. As JS looked about him, suddenly alert to the world's size and full of the fervid longings of adolescence, Joe took long medicinal baths and passed some time with Jack Richer, the famous Sadler's Wells rope-dancer, now enjoying a prosperous retirement with his wife, the wealthy widow of a clergyman.

Joe returned to Baynes Row for long enough to deposit JS and be cheered by the news that Sadler's Wells was having its

---

* Coincidentally, *Harlequin and Fortunio* was the first pantomime to feature a Principal Boy – then still known as a 'breeches' role – played by Maria de Camp. The Principal Boy would not become standard in pantomime for another forty to fifty years.

worst season in living memory. Then he was called away again
– first back to Birmingham, then Leicester and finally Chester,
where he met up with Jack Bologna for a run of *Mother Goose*.
Jack and Joe, closer than brothers for many years, were now
officially family. Jack had married Mary's beautiful sister,
Louisa Bristow, in 1816, following the death of his first wife,
Harriet. Like all brothers, the men squabbled, and never more
so when forced to live at close quarters. Jack was careful with
his money, and considered Joe extravagant, while Joe thought
Jack cheap and skimping. Joe would leave a trail of money in
the towns through which he passed, sparing no expense on
room and board, touring the shops for new clothes and neck-
cloths for himself, ribbons and linens for Mary. Jack, by
contrast, shrank at the thought of spending a farthing, took
the outside seat on the coach, slept in the cheapest rooms
available, ate only Welsh rarebit, and deliberately provoked
coachmen and waiters to avoid having to give them a tip. His
thrift annoyed Joe so much that he found it immensely enjoy-
able when, on the last night of their trip, his brother-in-law's
bill came to exactly the same as his own. In spite of his economising, Jack had failed to realise that the hotel's tariff was
all-in.

~

Fifty-six summer shows brought in £1,743, a thousand pounds
more than Joe would have made in Islington and for a third of
the performances. Sadler's Wells, meanwhile, had lost more
than £2,500 that season, its roof was in danger of falling in and
the landlord was threatening to raise the rent. Dibdin worked
night and day to avoid disaster, but his wife had recently died,
and with eight children to provide for, he found himself
consistently defeated by the task before him. The proprietors
added to the pressure by demanding an increased say in how

the theatre was run, in total contradiction to Dibdin's view that 'as a Republic . . . the administration will get into confusion, and confusion is the forerunner of defeat'. His principal antagonist was the majority shareholder, Richard Hughes's widow, Lucy.

Having lost confidence in Dibdin, she came to see Joe in the spring of 1818 and implored him to return to the Wells. Joe found her impossible to refuse, but agreed to reinstatement only on condition that he, too, became a shareholder. The request was motivated by the events of last summer and his distaste at having to dance to Dibdin's tune, but it was also an investment from which he hoped to draw an annual dividend of several hundred pounds to shore himself up against the vagaries of health and fame. An intimation that his star might be on the wane had come in March, when an Easter panto-mime called *The Marquis De Carabas; or, Puss in Boots* closed after only a single night. Playing Grimalkin the cat, Joe had initially pleased the audience by mewing his lines and imitat-ing a feline sneeze with great exactitude, but things turned nasty when Grimalkin persuaded the Ogre to change him-self into a mouse, which he duly swallowed. This seemingly innocuous gag caused outrage among a faction of the audi-ence, who thought it immoral, and for the first time in his long career, Grimaldi found himself being booed on stage at Covent Garden. The noise continued until the end, and for half an hour afterwards as patrons pulled up seats, broke the footlights and tore a hole in the curtain, until Fawcett appeared and promised never to show *Puss in Boots* again.

Lucy Hughes agreed to Joe's condition, and he purchased an eighth share in the theatre for an unknown price, though given that Charles and Thomas Dibdin had paid William Siddons £1,400 for their eighth share in 1803, it would have easily consumed his provincial profits and then some. In addi-tion to this agreement, he was re-employed as a performer on the terms he had previously proposed, twelve guineas a week, and the liberty to work for the highest bidder in July. Though his return 'was hailed with shouts of applause; and all, before and behind the curtain, appeared happy at seeing him "at home"', the theatre Joe was buying into bore only a few traces of its former glory.

In-fighting, financial depletion and a chronic lack of imagination had left the Wells without obvious direction, a lack of appeal that was reflected in the quality of the houses. The regular crowd seemed bored and was becoming decidedly rougher. Concomitantly, the titled dignitaries and ladies of quality who had been legion during Joe's ascendancy were travelling to Islington less and less often. There was evidence of this on the first night of the 1818 season. The house was filled to capacity for Joe's return, dangerously so – the rush for seats in the galleries caused a surge from the back that pushed some of the front row over the railings, and knocked a young man down between two benches where he was trampled to death. Fearing a repeat of the 1807 accident, Joe mounted the slips of the boxes and managed to be heard. This time, with their hero standing before them, the audience responded to the appeal for calm and, notwithstanding the fatality, the curtain went up at the advertised time.

The evening barely improved. Two women started fighting in the interval, while the performances themselves were thought so dismal as to be 'beneath the notice of criticism'. It was with some relief, therefore, that Joe took to the road for his summer excursion, clearing £682. On his return he was greeted with the news that the houses had been 'dead failures' that had left each proprietor owing £333.

Given the parlous state of British drama, it took Joe a surprisingly long time to realise that being a proprietor meant working doubly hard to subsidise a losing concern, though as soon as he did, he wanted out. His shares proved impossible to sell, and as his resentment grew, he joined with the other proprietors in blaming Dibdin for the Wells's ills, rejecting his talk of a routine slump and demanding change. A furious encounter followed that resulted in Dibdin throwing it all in ten days before the start of the 1819 season, and only with the greatest difficulty was he persuaded to come back for long enough to finalise the arrangements for the opening week. It was then that he gave Joe his most famous song, 'Hot Codlins', an audience-participation ditty about an apple-seller who gets disastrously drunk on gin. Dibdin never worked at Sadler's Wells again, although this was the least of his worries: following his resignation, he was imprisoned for debt and spent the next three years confined within the rules of the King's Bench prison. He was joined shortly thereafter by Thomas Barfoot, a boon companion and fellow Wells shareholder who had succumbed to penury after marrying one of the many actresses he pursued. She ended her days at the Clerkenwell workhouse where, according to Wheeler, 'worn out with drink and dissipation, she had become a spectacle'.

~

For someone whose career had been so inextricably linked to Dibdin's, it was inevitable that Joe should also go into a decline. Thrust into Dibdin's shoes in the absence of a more suitable candidate, he was confronted with all the problems of management while being far less equipped to deal with them. For a start, he had none of his predecessor's superhuman prolificacy, and even after employing a number of London's army of surplus dramatists, he still had difficulty furnishing all the necessary pieces, a problem perhaps best illustrated by the fact that this was the year in which he authored his first, and only, pantomime, *The Fates; or, Harlequin's Holy Day*. The entire family were pressed into service – JS, Mary, Louisa and

Jack Bologna all performed at the Wells, the latter for the first time in ten years – but still the responsibilities of management proved too much. Productions required his constant attention, and money became tight because he had to call off his provincial engagements. JS did not help by coming home one day and asking his father to pay off a significant debt he had accrued to a certain Mrs Price, although what for is unclear. The boy had definitely inherited his father's poor financial sense along with his talent.

The family moved to a smaller house nearer the theatre, at 8 Exmouth Street, just paces away from the Signor's grave at Northampton Chapel, where Joe's health began to deteriorate with the stress of each passing week. He endured regular bouts of breathlessness, gastric spasms and a constant low fever attended by rheumatoid aches that stiffened his joints and weakened his muscles. With his spirits desperately low, and his 'heavy and painful infirmities' impeding his ability to work, Joe had no choice but to resign at the end of the year.

Change was everywhere as, within a few short weeks, the darkness wound a terminal fold around the mad King, and the Regency came to a formal close with the accession of George IV. Grimaldi, Barfoot and Dibdin all decided to put their shares up for auction. Dibdin and Barfoot, desperate to be released from debtors' prison, sold theirs to Mr Dixon of the London Horse and Carriage Repository for a bargain price, but Joe, having either had a change of heart or, more likely, failed to receive his asking price, kept his. Without a manager to represent their interests directly, the proprietors decided to find a lessee to rent it for one or two seasons and share the risk. It was an increasingly popular expedient in these tough times, and effectively brought the age of era-defining owner-managers like Richard Brinsley Sheridan to an end.

Sadler's Wells's first lessee was an American, Howard Payne, a talented actor and industrious writer who had left

New York to soak himself in the atmosphere of the Anglophone world's most important theatrical town. Arriving full of artistic intent, he began by sacking the entire company save for Grimaldi, Barnes, Bologna and one or two others, and turning one of the workshops into a green room, something the performers had never had under Dibdin and joked that they didn't know what to do with. Payne made some interesting changes, bringing German melodrama and Astley-esque equestrianism to the Wells. But while the provisions were different, the state of the accounts was not. The Wells lost even more money and Payne, too, found his way into debtors' prison.

A new lessee was found in Daniel Egerton, but there were grounds of contention between him and Joe before he was even in place. Egerton wanted to retain him only on the understanding that he could loan him to other theatres as and when he wished, presumably having worked out that he stood to make more money by taking a percentage of Joe's one-off 'specials' than he did by paying him a weekly salary with all his unreliability. The proposition offended Joe immensely, and he refused to sign a contract. On 5 October 1820, he took his benefit with no idea that it would be his final regular appearance at the Wells. The following week, by pure coincidence, every person in the pit was presented with a commemorative portrait of their beloved clown.

Blissfully unaware that he'd reached the end of an era, Joe took off for an engagement in Dublin in the company of Ellar and JS, sailing on a brand-new steam-packet that cut the voyage time in half. He still had the syrup, even if it was getting harder to pour, and the trip went well. At Christmas he returned to Covent Garden to give his strongest performances for years, in *Harlequin and Friar Bacon*. The first gag didn't work – an updated version of one of the Signor's routines in which he imbibed gas instead of water from the Aldgate pump and became a human balloon – but the scene in which he invaded a lady's boudoir dressed as a chimney sweep, leaving his sooty imprint all over her white chairs, bed and toilet, had the house in stitches, including George IV, who rocked in his box and threatened to herniate the royal corset. There was also an exploding steam coach and an exemplary piece of dumb-show in which Joe performed *Macbeth*'s dagger scene in full motley, mimicking Kemble's manner and action so precisely that a dead silence descended on the audience, who 'seemed to vibrate with the effect upon the imagination'. This was followed by a taste of things to come with the introduction of a new piece of machinery, a moving diorama painted with views of the Irish Channel that turned on rollers to accompany Harlequin and Columbine's voyage across the stage from Holyhead to Dublin Bay.

The return to form was to prove short-lived, and the months that followed were marred by ill health and further breakdowns. In May, Joe collapsed from exhaustion following a performance of Farley's melodrama, *Undine; or, the Spirit of the Waters*, passing the role to JS, who was now his official understudy. In September, he, Ellar and JS returned to Dublin, but 'an agony of mind perfectly indescribable' forced him to cancel his shows and call one of the city's most eminent physicians, who diagnosed him as suffering from 'premature old age'. With his arthritic legs barely able to carry him, and his spine curled with pain, Joe went home, arriving in London weaker than at any time in his life.

～

As one Grimaldi withered, another rose. At nineteen, JS had outgrown his pallid, sick-room hue to become an athletic young man with the ability to tackle a range of substantial roles, a view backed up by *The Times*, which believed that 'in the language of Hector . . . Young Grimaldi, like young

Astyanax, "– may transcend his father's name" '. *Harlequin and Friar Bacon* marked something of a turning point for him too, for at last he was free from the role of mini-Clown, a part that was fine for someone like Laurent's six-year-old son Philippe, but which infantilised the dashing and ambitious JS.* *Friar Bacon* saw him graduate to the role of 'Dandy Lover', with which he would become particularly identified over the next few years as Farley used him and Clown as a double-act. The *Birmingham Reporter*, however, claimed to see through the arrangement, viewing JS merely as a poultice that hid the old man's infirmities, 'an apology for loss of agility in the parent'.

Comparisons of this kind would be the bane of JS's life, defining his career before it had even begun. Any compliments he received were inevitably back-handed, and he never failed to see his name in print without it being placed beside his father's – young Grimaldi, wrote one reviewer, for example, was 'sufficiently lively and comic to amuse, even when his father (the Prince of Clowns) is present'. Frustration, and the desire to differentiate himself, may well have been behind an early incident at Christmas in 1821, when he was censured for indulging in 'certain gross vulgarities' in the course of *Harlequin and Mother Bunch; or, the Yellow Dwarf*. 'Indecency upon the stage is an insult to every individual in the house,' thundered the correspondent, 'and . . . if he expects to be tolerated, he must considerably restrain his propensity to be coarse and indelicate; he has not merit enough to play such tricks with impunity.'

It was remarkably similar to an event that had taken place at Drury Lane the previous year when Robert Bradbury, the 'Brummell of Clowns', had caused outrage by lampooning a

---

* Years later, Philippe Laurent became an eminent Harlequin in the Parisian Théâtre des Funambules, and right-hand man to Jean-Gaspard Deburau, who popularised the tearful, iconic, white-faced Pierrot.

recent case of child abduction, compounding it by insulting a member of the audience, and then threatening to kick him in the backside when he rose to complain. Bradbury's immediate replacement by the ever-ready Frank Hartland caused further controversy when protests were staged by some of Bradbury's friends.* (Poor Hartland was an underdog even to the day of his death – killed by a falling beam while out strolling on the Westminster Road.)

JS's desire to develop a distinct identity of his own had been intensified by the constant travelling and performing in the company of his father, and if he had found Bradbury's lewd and rebellious style appealing it was probably because it was so far removed from Joe's. JS also emulated Bradbury's well-documented addiction to fashion, and similarly cultivated a streetwise affect that he inflected with the *louche* nonchalance and studied dishevelment of the Byronic dandies. Its fullest manifestation came in his idiosyncratic speech, a blend of his father's topsy-turvy colloquialisms, theatrical patois, and the inexhaustible slang of the late-Georgian 'Corinthians' or

---

* Joe did not see Bradbury for several years following his brief engagement at the Wells, until one day he received an unexpected note from a private madhouse in Hoxton. He took Richard Lawrence along for support, and the two men were led deep inside the asylum where they found him bound in a strait-jacket with his head completely shorn. Uncertain how to behave, Joe spoke slowly and carefully, which made Bradbury roar with laughter. He was only feigning madness, he claimed, having caught a young man trying to steal his gold pocket watch. The man turned out to be a member of a rich and powerful family who, to avoid a blot on their honour, had paid him handsomely to withdraw his prosecution. His 'lunacy' was only temporary, a means to defray any suspicion that the course of justice had been perverted. He had asked Joe to come in order to ask him a favour – the next day, he was due to be released, and wanted to know if Joe would play for his benefit at the Surrey. Happy to believe everything he'd heard, Joe agreed, and the next evening, things proceeded normally until it was Bradbury's turn to take the stage. 'Impelled by some strange and sudden whim', he suddenly turned nasty, performing 'a disgusting piece of irreverence and impertinence', too shocking to be named, that left the entire audience stunned.

'swells'. 'If he had had a companion to cope with him,' wrote one contemporary, 'in six weeks they would have forgotten the English language and framed an entirely new tongue. He . . . *never* used any phrase recognised by society.' So peculiar was his argot that members of the older generation frequently failed to understand him, such as the time Thomas Dibdin enquired after Joe, and JS said, 'The old buffer's as stiff as pitch':

> 'Good God, sir,' said Dibdin, 'you don't – you cannot mean to say he is no more!' 'No more!' said Grimaldi, 'he's more than you are, he's all drawn up of a heap.' 'Am I to infer that he is better?' 'Why, don't I tell you so? – he's as right as a trivet.' 'Shall we have the pleasure of seeing him this evening?' 'Course you will,' replied Joe, 'he's coming at darkey just to see the beauty of things.'

Bradbury was only a temporary role model, if he was ever one at all, as, following his ejection from Drury Lane, the eccentric Mancunian left the stage to travel the country as an itinerant Methodist preacher. But JS would not want for long because, as it would transpire, an unblushing reprobate was waiting in the wings and, like him, he hailed from theatrical royalty.

~

Joe would have nothing to do with Egerton's Wells, which was still failing to make a profit despite offering punters the sight of real Eskimos and sledge rides down an iced track that ran from the back of the stage to the back of the pit. Too unwell to travel, he found it impossible to live on the meagre ten-pound weekly salary Covent Garden had been paying him for years, so when an offer came through for six weeks' work at Vauxhall's Coburg Theatre 'at a considerable sum . . . and a free benefit', he rounded up his son and together they crossed the Thames.

Named for Prince Leopold of Saxe-Coburg-Saalfeld, son-in-law to the Prince Regent, and later father to Leopold II, scourge of the Belgian Congo, the Coburg owed its existence to Waterloo Bridge, completed in 1817. Its opening had been heralded by a publicity stunt performed by the clown Dicky Usher, who sailed from Southwark Bridge to Cumberland Gardens in a wash-tub drawn by four geese. Landing two and a half hours later, he swapped his tub for a carriage lashed to eight tomcats, which he then intended to drive to Waterloo Road, although the size of the crowd made it impossible, and he had to be carried on the shoulders of several watermen.

Situated in the growing but ramshackle neighbourhood of St George's Fields, the Coburg quickly acquired a reputation as the roughest and most disorderly theatre in town. Its managers had made every effort to offset the outside squalor by fitting its interior in sumptuous style, achieving an effect that *The Times* snidely described as 'rather gorgeous than elegant', although by the time the Grimaldis arrived, they had removed their gaudiest decoration, a mirrored stage curtain that allowed the audience to gaze upon themselves through the smears and finger marks in which it was constantly covered. At forty feet high, thirty wide and weighing five tons, it had to be taken down due to the strain it put on the roof, it was later dismantled and recycled as a looking-glass ceiling.

Joseph Glossop, the Coburg's manager, was a wealthy chandler who had come to London after stints managing Milan's La Scala and the San Carlo in Naples. Wily and active, he bent the rules and abjured authority, skipping off without paying his bills, punching one of the Drury Lane managers in the street and threatening to shoot the other, and being arrested for forgery after attempting to flee the country. For all his crazy bravado, Glossop was highly strung and had a nervous stomach that meant even the slightest anxiety caused him to vomit. Odd, then, that he should be at the vanguard of a growing movement among minor theatre owners who sought to challenge the terms of the theatrical monopoly and test the patent's resolve by staging legitimate dramas in thin melodramatic disguises. The Coburg's *Richard III; or, the Battle of Bosworth Field*, for instance, was essentially Shakespeare's history staged with minor revisions and a musical accompaniment inaudible beyond the front row. Joe even gave evidence in Glossop's defence at the subsequent prosecution, though nothing he could say could avert a hundred-pound fine, which in turn only served to make Glossop even more evangelical about reform. Yet the Coburg didn't get its nickname 'the blood-tub' from artistic adaptations of Shakespeare, as its stock-in-trade remained lurid, plot-free melodramas with titles like *The Temple of Death* and *Thalaba the Destroyer*, trading on a constantly regurgitated mix of murder, madness, apparitions, demagogues, prophecies, war and monsters.

Performing at the Coburg was an experience unlike any other. The audience was rarely, if ever, quiet, barracking the actors with their 'petulant cockneyism and vulgar slang', producing an atmosphere so hostile that Hazlitt described it as 'a Bridewell, or a brothel, amidst Jew-boys, pickpockets, prostitutes and mountebanks'. 'The object was not to admire or to excel,' he continued, 'but to vilify and degrade everything. The audience did not hiss the actors (that would have implied a serious feeling of disapprobation, and something like a disappointed wish to be pleased), but they laughed, hooted at, nick-named, pelted them with oranges and witticisms, to show their unruly contempt for them and their art.' Those performers included Ramoo Samee, a mystical Indian snake-charmer; 'Jew' Davis, turfed out of Sadler's Wells for his brutish manners and the 'practical and dirty jokes' he played on the foreign rope-dancers; and T. P. Cooke, an ex-sailor who would go on to become one of the biggest stars of the era and the first actor to play Frankenstein's monster.

From the Grimaldis' point of view, the most influential cast-member in residence, though neither the most talented nor the most famous, was Henry Stephen Kemble, son of Stephen George Kemble, nephew of John, Charles, and Sarah Siddons. Henry had little natural aptitude for acting, and seems to have come to it from a lack of imagination as much as anything else. At thirty-three, he was a distinctive-looking fellow, flamboyant, with a shock of snowy-white hair and a handsome face that was lined and gaunt. Said to have 'the strongest lungs and weakest judgement' of any performer in his station, Henry Kemble was a ranter and a ham, and thus ideally suited to the Coburg, where he was showered with walnuts and 'peals of derision'. He was playing the young Mogul revolutionary Tippoo Sahib when the Grimaldis arrived, an exotic outsider who possessed all the qualities he wanted people to see in himself. In reality, people didn't see much heroism in Henry Kemble, just biting wit and a reputation for raising hell.

Joe's first performance at the Coburg was an olio called *Salmagundi; or, the Clown's Dish of All Sorts*, puffed in the bills as 'a splendid comic pantomime with entirely new scenery, machinery, tricks, dresses and decorations in which Mr Grimaldi will sustain the character of Clown, and Mr Barnes that of Pantaloon'. It played for only a week before being replaced by *Disputes in China; or, Harlequin and the Hong Merchants*. Six days later Joe fell ill, and the bills proclaimed that 'The public is respectfully informed that in consequence of the continued and dangerous Indisposition of Mr Grimaldi, the Pantomime is unavoidably postponed. Due notice will be given of its next representation.' Due notice never came, as Joe found himself too ill to carry on.

Two weeks was all it took for JS to be fully inducted into the riotous world of Henry Kemble. He had idolised the rascally white-maned tumultuary, thirteen years his senior, from the moment they met. Incapable of discretion, and filled with mocking scorn for the feats of his famous family, he was someone with whom JS could share the alienation of being eclipsed by one's own name, concealing their insecurities behind huge amounts of drinking. 'The irregularities and drunkenness of this man were unpardonable,' wrote Charles Whitehead, the original editor of the *Memoirs*, of Henry Kemble, going on to accuse him of being 'the instigator of young Joe's follies and misconduct'. JS did not remain an apprentice for long for, as Whitehead soon conceded, 'which was the worst of the two was hard to be decided'.

With his father laid up, JS and his new confederate went on the rampage, drinking, gambling and baiting the Watch, the generally ineffective 'Charleys' who had become a popular target for drunken assaults ever since 'larking' had been made popular through the ribald adventures of Jerry Hawthorn and Corinthian Tom in Pierce Egan's comic novel *Real Life in London*. But for all that JS and Kemble used their cynicism and extravagance to ease the burden of pedigree, they, too, were paying homage to the most talented, maddening and ill-behaved incendiarist in contemporary theatre, the origina-tor of 'the Bedlamite system of acting', and every young actor's idol, Edmund Kean. Ironically, Kean was a great admirer of Joe Grimaldi, and claimed to have based his famous death scene in *Richard III* on Joe's own desperate retreat from the oncoming Tartars in Drury Lane's *Lodoiska* almost a quarter of a century before. Kean had also played Harlequin, and was so fond of pantomime that his father had dismissively claimed 'he would be a second Grimaldi – if anything'.

All this was forgotten once Kean had made his début as a leading tragedian, arriving with the impact of a falling meteor that made John Philip Kemble's 'majestic dryness and deliber-ate nothings' seem stiff and histrionic, and eventually led the old Roman, retiring to Lausanne, to live an ascetic life where, it was rumoured, he was jealous of the attention paid to Mont Blanc. Off stage, Kean lived as intensely as he acted on it. Stories circulated of an insatiable sexual appetite and taste for self-destruction, of whores lining up to service him between acts, and backstage rivers of booze. Seething with rage at his childhood abandonment, he was sullen and rude, especially to members of polite society, whom he accused of being fakers and hypocrites. He had tantrums and made threats, complained of being treated like a carthorse when he worked more than four nights a week, and once excused his late arrival on stage by explaining, 'I always take a shag before the play begins.'

Kean's example was literally intoxicating. He made it fashionable to be bad, and many sought to emulate his lifestyle in the hopes of tapping his talent. Though heavy drinking was a theatrical constant, Kean lent it a new Byronic glamour, raising it to the status of demonic compulsion as if it were the only sanctuary from a gift that might otherwise flay him alive. By establishing the Wolf Club at the Coal Hole Tavern in the Strand, he not only founded a brotherhood of actors similarly devoted to alcohol, but he cemented his own mythology by instituting the bond between genius and excess that would be taken up by an entire generation. Aspiring Wolf Clubs sprang up close to every theatre in every town, and in South London the Lambeth triangle that was home to the Coburg, Astley's and the Surrey theatre boasted more than any other place on earth. Lambeth had been a thespian ghetto even in the Signor's day, but now, with three large theatres and a growing transpontine population, it was known as the 'theatrical barracks'. Mount's Place, the home of Thomas Ellar, was an outpost of equestrians and pantomimists, while St George's Circus at the end of Blackfriars Road gave shelter to a colony of melodramatists, and Philip Astley's Hercules Hall on Westminster Bridge Road was said to house a theatrical family in every apartment, including that of the clown Dicky Usher.

With such a demographic, the taverns spilled over with performers in the clutch of intemperance, and when *Oxberry's Dramatic Biography* took its readers on a tour of them, it found 'an excellent actor, who, from a love of intoxication, has reduced himself (although a young man) to a state of pauperism', along with many others 'striving, with all their might, to destroy themselves the same way'. None could survey their 'emaciated countenances,' it concluded, 'with all its alloy of dissipation and vulgarity, without feeling a sincere regret'.* The managers were no better. Robert Elliston, the man who employed Kean and nursed his ego, drank copiously, pursued actresses and rarely went to bed until nine in the morning. His partner, James Winston, once claimed he'd been drunk for ten consecutive days. The only place where this was forbidden was Astley's Amphitheatre, where Philip Astley detested drunks and withheld the pay of any performer who, in his opinion, imbibed too much. Astley, though, had died in 1814 of stomach gout in Paris, and was succeeded in the family business by his son John, an angry alcoholic who ran up copious debts before following his father into a Parisian grave.

Drinking was not the only aspect of a profession that had fundamentally changed with the arrival of Kean. Angry posturing and complaints of overwork were endemic among young actors, while the irresistible force of celebrity had continued to erode the idea of actors as public servants, replacing it with a sense of them as a special breed, a delusion greatly encouraged by innovations in lighting, such as the introduction in 1817 of gas lamps that could be lowered to darken the auditorium, and the invention of 'limelight', a cone of incandescent lime that could be used as a directional spotlight on the performer.

---

* Interestingly, *Oxberry's* also claims that 'If any persons have an excuse for indulging at the shrine of Bacchus, it is those who are engaged in pantomime: the exertions they are compelled to make, require that they should resort to the use of stimulants.'

Drawn by the promise of being bathed in bumptious glory, celebrity became its own motivation and the stage an avenue to acclaim, transforming, in the opinion of Alfred Bunn, Macready's successor at the Birmingham theatre, the once-noble institution of Garrick into a refuge for the feckless and attention-seeking. 'An actor's position is very seldom obtained by education, by study, and preparation,' wrote Bunn despairingly. 'In nine cases out of ten he has tried his hand at some honest trade, and having failed or being disgusted, as a *dernier ressort* he flies to the stage, without possessing any of the qualifications considered essential.' Nowhere was this 'heartless indifference and contempt' for the craft more apparent than at the Coburg, where Hazlitt was disgusted to observe how the actors slurred their parts and behaved 'as if ashamed to be thought to take any interest in them, laughed in one another's faces, and in that of their friends in the pit, and most effectually marred the process of theatrical illusion, by turning the whole into a most unprincipled burlesque'.

~

Following his relapse, Joe spent August taking the Cheltenham waters, feeling well enough to accept two weeks in the local theatre, which had been leased by Farley. Yet his health was far from restored, and the visit took its place in the long-running cycle of breakdown and recuperation that had dogged him for years. As he neared his forty-fourth birthday, he had already subjected his body to almost two hundred thousand performances, yet he still remained unwilling to acknowledge his limitations or the extent of his chronic injuries, seeing every small improvement as a 'token of a real and permanent change for the better'. The situation persisted for almost a year, until things finally came to a head in the pantomime *Harlequin and the Ogress; or, the Sleeping Beauty of the Wood*. Rehearsals had been cut short to accommodate his diminishing strength, but ever the master of concealing pain from public view, Joey appeared before the holiday crowd 'all grin and good humour', and 'full of humorous whim', a deception so convincing that one reviewer even praised his 'singular faculty of appearing younger every year': 'Time seems to pass harmlessly by him,' he said, 'except to increase the rich lubricity of his face.' The journalist Theodore Hook was likewise deceived. 'The strength of Grimaldi, the Garrick of Clowns,' he wrote, 'seems like that of wine to increase with age.'

But the greatest act of denial was reserved for himself when, in January, Charles Kemble replaced Henry Harris as manager of Covent Garden and Joe signed a contract for three more years. He would only work for a fraction of that time as by Easter 1823, when *Harlequin and the Ogress* was replaced by a Farley melodrama called *The Orphan of Peru*, he was fast approaching the end. For twenty-four nights, Joe struggled painfully through his part, collapsing between scenes into the arms of men positioned in the wings where they laid him on a table and vigorously rubbed the muscles that had 'gathered up into huge knots'. On 3 May, *Harlequin and the Ogress* was announced again, but though he reported for duty, Joe's body would not comply. Seized with agony, he collapsed backstage, only to recover his senses with the heavy realisation that it was impossible to continue. Pain gave way to a wave of anguish 'to which all his bodily sufferings were as nothing', and alone in his dressing room, Joey the Clown buried his face in his hands 'and wept like a child'.

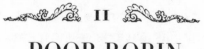
POOR ROBIN

Lastly, be jolly, be alive, be light,
 Twitch, flirt and caper, tumble, fall and throw;
Grow up right ugly in thy father's sight,
 And be an 'absolute Joseph' like old Joe.

> Joseph Grimaldi, 'Adieu to the Stage,
> and Advice to His Son' (1823)

IT ALL BEGAN WITH a blow to the head that would open the vents of hell.

JS had taken over his father's role in *The Orphan of Peru*, learning the part in a day and performing it superbly for the remainder of the run. He then joined the old man in Cheltenham, and while Joe sipped the restorative waters, JS indulged in something more sulphurous. Having just been offered the role of Drury Lane's principal clown at a salary of eight pounds a week, he had cause for celebration. At Cheltenham they met Alfred Bunn, frequently in town as a guest of Colonel Berkeley, the hardened roué who was conducting an affair with Bunn's wife. Bunn, likened to a cat thrown from an attic window for his propensity to land always on his feet, encouraged the affair, even installing his wife at Berkeley Castle the moment Berkeley had ditched his previous mistress, the beautiful actress Maria Foote, 'a divinity just lighted on the earth', whom he had seduced at seventeen and given two children.

Perhaps to avoid such salacious gossip, the conversation soon fell to business and, sure enough, Joe found himself agreeing to appear in Birmingham for two nights. Two nights became three, at the end of which, said the *Birmingham Reporter*, 'Mr. G. seems much the worse for wear.' Also appearing in Birmingham was Charles Kemble, whom Joe approached with news of JS's offer from Drury Lane, hoping to use it as leverage to persuade Kemble to keep him on. A negotiation began, at the end of which JS had been retained at Covent Garden at a weekly salary of six pounds.

Those three nights in Birmingham had cost JS two pounds a week and an opportunity to embark on a career of his own, and Joe a month in bed, victim of a 'severe and alarming illness'. Angry at his father's interference, JS was left with nothing to do but loiter around Cheltenham, waiting for their next engagement. Loitering meant only one thing – immersing himself fully in the excesses of the town. Too sick to pay attention to a young man's carousing, Joe only came to be aware of his son's drinking when it was already too late. Having raised himself painfully from bed one morning, he was brought to the door by the knocking of the Watch and told that JS had been locked up 'for some drunken freaks committed overnight'. Pulling on his coat, he accompanied the constable to the Watch-house, paid a fine and was taken to his son's cell, where he found him draped lifelessly across the bench, his face covered with blood and his hair matting about a severe head wound. Like so many of his metropolitan larkings, the previous night's revels had concluded with a fight with the local Charleys, although this time it was JS who had come off worst, felled by a Watchman's quarterstaff that had crushed his hat and knocked him unconscious.* The wound would eventually heal, but it was only the beginning of JS's troubles.

---

* Newspaper reports reveal that clowns and constables were evenly matched. In 1831, Henderson, a clown at Astley's, single-handedly beat up two police officers on account of 'being uncommonly active on his pins'. The clown of Saunders' Equestrian Troupe was not so lucky, killed by a cutlass-wielding Watchman in the early hours while walking home drunk.

With father and son both invalided, they prolonged their stay in Cheltenham for another two months in order to be well enough to appear in the Christmas pantomime. Returning to London in October, Joe began a long round of visits to leading doctors, many of whom had been recommended by the well-heeled patrons of Covent Garden. They included the plain-speaking John Abertheny, the physician who gave Joe a prescription to see himself perform; Sir Astley Cooper, Professor of Comparative Anatomy at the Royal College of Surgeons, whose patients included the Duke of Wellington and the King (who had made him a baronet for removing a painful cyst from his scalp); and James Wilson, an expert on nerve and muscular diseases, whose father had performed the post-mortem on Samuel Johnson. Many others could be added to this list, but as Joe hobbled from one consulting room to another, the opinions they gave remained emphatically the same. He was suffering from a series of ailments – a respiratory complaint that left him breathless and gasping for air, recurrent digestive problems, and a number of chronic long-term injuries to his back and knees that had resulted in crippling rheumatoid arthritis. Full recovery was impossible, and though he had expected the news for years, he still took it very badly, refusing to make a final decision about whether or not he should appear in the upcoming pantomime until the last possible moment. At the beginning of December Joe finally faced the truth, and the next day a short, apologetic note appeared on the desk of Charles Kemble, explaining that he would not be able to fulfil the terms of his articles.

JS was not the first choice to fill the vacant position. Kemble was reticent, and may have instructed Farley to make enquiries about the availability of more experienced clowns, like Paulo and Laurent. But Joe pressed on behalf of his son's claim, and after a number of discussions, it was eventually agreed that JS would make his début as Clown. The news was

immediately taken up by the press, and some, like the anonymous author of 'Grimaldi: a Jeu D'esprit', chose to dramatise
the passing of the pantomimic baton in verse:

> The Pantomime was all rehears'd,
>   And puff'd off in the bill,
> When, full of grief, in Fawcett burst,
>   To Kemble crying 'Hear the worst,
> Great Joe Grimaldi's ill.'

> 'Grimaldi ill!' the monarch cried,
>   'Say, what then shall I do?
> Had I Macready at my side,
>   Clown's part with him I would divide,
> And show folks something new.

> But is it true, my Fawcett, say
>   Has Fate thus spoke her will –
> Is all we've done, for many a day,
>   Cut up – our hopes all cast away –
> Is Joe Grimaldi ill?'

> 'He is, he is – that woeful brow
>   Declares my piteous lot;
> But come, cheer up, and tell me how
>   To act in this dire moment now,
> For someone must be got.'

> 'I've heard,' said Fawcett – as he spoke,
>   Great Kemble felt less pain
> 'He hath a son, all full of joke;
>   Could he be got, 'twould take the spoke
> Out of our wheel again.'

> Cried Kemble, 'Bring him hither straight,
>   Then puff him in the bill;
> The son will share the father's fate –
>   Be grinned at; I'm with joy elate,
> Though Joe Grimaldi's ill.'

While this poet took obvious comfort in the transmission of the role from father to son, others feared for the future of the form. 'His name is not in the bills,' wrote one. '"Clown, Mr. J.S. Grimaldi." Oh, villainous, J.S.! It should be "Clown, Mr. Grimaldi" – or Pantomime should betake itself to its weeds – and pine in perfect widowhood. We will say, without fear of contradiction, that there not only never was such a clown, but that there never will be such another.' The author went on to imagine Joe sitting by the fire with a glass of Madeira 'and J.S. (good in his way, but no Joe) listening to the clownish reminiscences of his inestimable Papa'.

Yet as JS prepared to assume tenancy of the horizonless tract of Joey's pockets, relations between the two men were far from cosy. Following the fight in Cheltenham, JS had begun to suffer epileptic seizures, episodes exacerbated by the constant cycle of heavy drinking and withdrawal he subjected himself to with the aid of an increasingly debauched circle that now included the great Edmund Kean. Three days before JS made his clowning début, the two men could be found drunk together in JS's Covent Garden dressing room, Kean in particularly petulant mood, throwing his weight about and shouting that if Elliston did not come to him immediately, he would leave for America the following day. Joe, meanwhile, fretted over the succession and bombarded his son with advice. When JS stopped listening, he published it in the form of doggerel verse:

> Hand Columbine about with nimble hand,
>   Covet thy neighbour's riches as thy own,
> Dance on the water, swim upon the land,
>   Let thy legs prove themselves bone of my bone.
> Cuff Pantaloon, be sure – forget not this;
>   As thou beat'st him, thou'rt poor, J.G. or funny!
> And wear a deal of paint upon thy phiz,
>   It doth boys good and draws in gallery money.

By the time of his début, JS had managed to shelve his problems, even showing some of the exceptional promise of which he was capable. 'His voice is thickening into that ancestral and sonorous tone,' wrote one reviewer of his Clown in Farley's *Harlequin and Poor Robin; or, the House that Jack Built,* 'his eye lacks none of its parental luster and wickednesses and his indescribable turn for mischief and humour is genuine Grimaldi-ism.' *The Times* wrote,

> Without being equal to his father just yet, Mr Grimaldi, jun. shows a great deal of cleverness; and his attempt may be considered as decidedly a successful one. He had great activity, and some humour. Tolerably light of finger, and uncommonly light of foot. He avoids, and with very good judgment, any servile imitations, and gets on rather by a juvenile vivacity, than by that sleepy style of humour which Mr Grimaldi, sen., latterly relied upon. Upon the whole, he is, at least, as good a clown as any now upon the stage; and if he takes pains, and avoids breaking his neck, we see no reason why he should not be as great a man as his progenitor.

~

Charles Kemble continued to pay Joe a half-salary until the end of the 1823–4 season, after which he found himself without an income and still unable to perform. 'In my present state of health,' he wrote to Richard Hughes junior, 'I fear I shall not be able to accept any engagement anywhere,' and pinned his hopes on selling his shares on the expiration of Egerton's lease. Disappointed to find their market value was still far below what he'd paid for them, he carelessly let them go in dribs and drabs, 'consequently rising every morning a poorer man'.

Another lessee appeared in Llewellyn Watkin Williams, son of the proprietor of the Old Bailey Boiled Beef House. Williams proposed to hold the leases to both the Wells and the

Surrey simultaneously, but proved no more capable of steering the theatre to profitability than any of his predecessors, despite a plan to divide his costs by splitting his company, having one half open at the Wells and closed at the Surrey, and the other doing the same in reverse. A special carriage was equipped to shuttle the cast between venues, but the experiment still failed and, predictably enough, Williams took his place in the King's Bench prison.

Forced to bear another loss on the Wells, Joe had no choice but to look about for work, and with little prospect of making money beyond performing, he put his health aside and offered himself out as a cameo performer in various pantomimes. One taker was Richard Brinsley Peake, son of the Drury Lane treasurer – his name betraying his father's devotion to the Sheridean cult of personality – who was dramaturge at the English Opera House. Peake proposed to place him in a piece called *Monkey Island*, describing his plan in a letter in which he sketched out a gallery of clowns that included portraits of Dubois, Paulo, Follet, Bradbury, Bologna and Laurent. The largest was covered with a curtain that read 'Grimaldi'. 'Grimaldi junior as Clown, and the other characters come on with catalogue to view the pictures,' Peake explained. 'Grimaldi junior draws the curtain of the centre picture and discovers his father – the "*ne plus ultra*" of pantomime – Harlequin touches the picture and Grimaldi descends – is received warmly by the audience and his friends – sings a song – and goes through the two last scenes of the pantomime.' In the event, Joe was too unwell even for this commitment, and the scene was excluded, leaving JS to take the engagement alone. 'Young Grimaldi is the best Clown,' read the review with demoralising predictability, 'excepting his father.'

Instead of liberating him, Joe's retirement from the stage only served to make JS's behaviour worse. At home, he was glowering, moody and withdrawn, and when out, kept the company of prostitutes, abandoning himself 'to every species of wild debauchery and riot'. To his epilepsy and seizures were added episodes of foaming mania in which he became 'a wild and furious savage', a seeming reincarnation of the Signor that so intimidated Joe he was unable to speak to his son for fear of provoking a violent confrontation. Joe and Mary watched helplessly as his drinking became increasingly reckless and compulsive, heedless of neither health nor consequences. Indeed, drink may have been responsible for the injury to E. J. Parsloe during the run of *Harlequin and Poor Robin*, when Parsloe, standing in for Barnes as Pantaloon, was stabbed in the face during a scene with JS, resulting in a lost eye and a dangerously high fever. JS's alienation continued to grow, until at last he turned his back on his family entirely, leaving home and refusing to speak to his parents, even to the extent of crossing the street if he saw them coming. For the next four years, say the *Memoirs*, Joe and Mary only saw their son on stage.

What had bred such animosity in the young man? Was the fight in Cheltenham entirely to blame, as Joe and Mary believed, or was it a legacy come to pass, the latest mutation of an atavistic madness that had coursed through the family's veins for generations? The reality was probably much more mundane: JS was simply smothered by his father's success and, with a resentment fed on narcotic fumes, his efforts to break free manifested themselves as a spiteful and misshapen rejection. With his good looks, swagger and swordsmanship, so skilful that it set the visiting King and Queen of the Sandwich Islands on the edge of their seats, JS was perfectly cut out for a life in straight acting and melodrama, a fact his father overlooked in his desire to see him inherit Joey. But while Joe had been able to impart techniques, he could do little to induce in his son a genuine love for the role, or convey a means to channel the inspiration that he himself could explain only through some mystical transaction with pain. Lacking that feeling of authenticity no doubt left JS feeling like a fraud, deserving of the comparisons that would superficially flatter before inevitably concluding with some assessment of the gulf between his abilities and those of Joe. One reviewer summed it up when he said that, 'Time and experience may do much [though] we will not at the expense of sincerity put this young gentleman in competition with the transcendent talent of his father.'

It was a familiar story in the theatrical world, where dwelling in the shadow of a famous parent had cursed both Fanny Bland, Dora Jordan's eldest daughter, who had tried and failed to establish herself as an actress and taken solace in doomed affairs and drugs, and her half-brother George Fitzclarence, who shot himself for want of recognition. And if the child is the parent to the man, then for Master William Betty the burden was even more acute, given that the legend he had to contend with was his own. Though able to live quite comfortably on the money he had earned as a boy, he found it impossible to quiet the demons that stemmed from those early years, and in 1821, a has-been for decades, he cut his own throat. He survived the attempt, and the following year invited all his old theatrical colleagues to a gala dinner for which he hired a large auction room. Only eleven people came. The year after that, he attempted suicide again by throwing himself through a closed window, but though he managed to break the glass, his bloated body was caught in the frame, and had to be pulled out by some Bow Street officers who noticed him dangling from the street. 'Most men', wrote Leigh Hunt, 'begin life with struggles, and have their vanity sufficiently knocked about the head and shoulders to make their kinder fortunes the more welcome. Mr Betty had his sugar first, and his physic afterward . . . I wish with all my heart we had let him alone.'

Worry over JS was compounded by worry about the fate of Sadler's Wells. Its lessees had universally failed, and with its dwindling audience and worthless shares, its business was on the brink. With no one willing to take it on, the proprietors were forced to look for a manager and, inevitably, they turned to a Dibdin.

Retirement had been unreasonably hard on Thomas Dibdin. The offer of fifteen pounds a week to work at the Surrey had tempted him from sequestration and reignited his taste for the theatre, which in turn led to him filling the position of prompter at Drury Lane before going back to the Surrey as manager and lessee. Denounced before the Police Committee as 'one of the greatest nuisances in the metropolis, being resorted to solely by thieves and prostitutes', the Surrey was a cash-consuming bunghole, which, when levelled with the mangy state of theatre in general, resulted in years of trouble, prolonged by the occasional glimmer of false hope proffered by an infrequent hit. In 1822, his association with the place ended in bankruptcy and a debt of more than eighteen thousand pounds, and what was supposed to have been an Elysian retirement became an Acherontic hell: Thomas was forced to take two jobs to pay off his debt, working at both the Haymarket and Drury Lane, where he clashed repeatedly with both managements. At fifty-two, he cut a bitter and careworn figure, mocked by the younger generation of performers, who considered him a relic, haunting the Drury Lane green room wreathed in pompous self-pity and telling anyone who would listen that 'twenty years ago [he] was a great man at Covent Garden'.

Airs and graces only served to make a bad situation worse, and when his play *The Chinese Sorcerer* did not get any laughs, he placed a note in the green room forbidding the actors to ad-lib lines. They responded with a note of their own, insisting that they were forced to ad-lib as theirs were the only decent jokes in the whole piece. When his pantomime *Gog and Magog*

Joe on the brink of nationwide celebrity: Portrait by John Cawse, painted in 1807 to commemorate the success of *Mother Goose*.

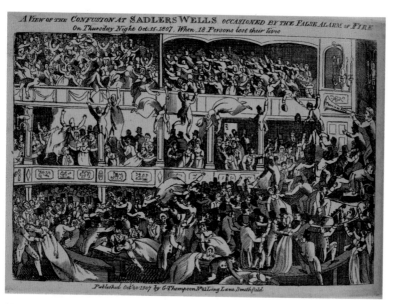

'A View of the Confusion at Sadler's Wells': Eighteen members of the Sadler's Wells audience died on October 15, 1807, during a stampede caused by a mistaken belief that the theatre was on fire. Onstage, Charles Dibdin can be seen holding a speaking trumpet and calling 'there is no fire'.

Covent Garden Theatre in 1809 following its controversial rebuilding after being destroyed by fire.

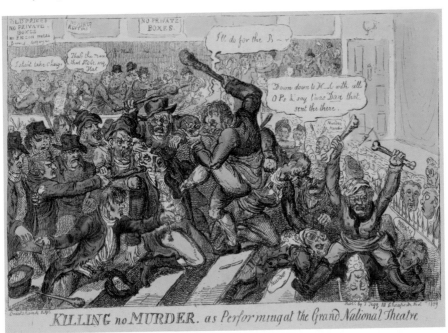

The OP War comprised sixty-seven nights of riotous disorder. Early on, Kemble tried to quell the unrest by having protestors violently removed, as in this print, which depicts the doorman James Brandon and his bouncers attacking respectable members of the audience. Right of centre, Daniel Mendoza, the 'father of scientific boxing', can be seen laying into a protestor prostrate on the bench. That Mendoza and many of the other boxers Brandon hired were Jews caused an anti-Semitic backlash that further cast John Philip Kemble as an enemy of John Bull.

The 1809 fire that destroyed Drury Lane Theatre burned with such violent intensity that it illuminated the sky for miles around. Seen here from the Chelsea Waterworks, many thought the circumstances of the conflagration too convenient to be entirely accidental.

'Mr Grimaldi and Mr Norman in the Epping Hunt': A scene from *Harlequin and the Red Dwarf* (1812), in which a llama was chased around the stage by a motley group of huntsmen on a bizarre array of steeds.

GRIM JOEY DASHING LITTLE BONEY
into the Jaws of a Russian Bear.

'Grim Joey Dashing Little Boney into the Jaws of a Russian Bear': Also from *Harlequin and the Red Dwarf*; Joe, dressed as a Hussar with coal-scuttle boots, throws a miniature Napoleon into the mouth of a passing bear.

MR. GRIMALDI, as *CLOWN*

in the Popular Pantomine of *HARLEQUIN & ASMODEUS*, now Performing at the Theatre Royal Covent Garden, Setting to with a Grotesque Figure which he makes up of a series of Vegetables, Fruit &c. and which becoming Animated beats him off the Stage.

'Joe Frankenstein': Grimaldi and the Vegetable Man from *Harlequin Asmodeus* (1811), one of his most noted 'tricks of construction', and a scene that would have certainly been known by Lord Byron and may also have had a subtle influence on the imagination of Mary Shelley. Note Joe's southpaw stance, which suggests that he may have been left-handed.

Grimaldi's last night: Too ill to stand, Joe
made his final public performance seated in
a chair, from which he sang 'Hot Codlins',
before rising to give a speech of thanks and
being led from the stage by his son.

MR GRIMALDI.
AS HE APPEARD
WHEN HE TOOK HIS FAREWELL BENEFIT
AT DRURY LANE THEATRE ON THE 27ᵗʰ of
JUNE 1828

The 'pantomimic wonders': Joseph Grimaldi as Clown, Thomas Ellar as Harlequin
and James Barnes as Pantaloon.

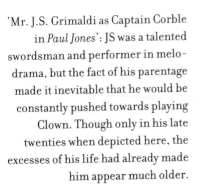

Henry Stephen Kemble: 'The irregularities and drunkenness of this man were unpardonable', wrote Charles Whitehead.

'Mr. J.S. Grimaldi as Captain Corble in *Paul Jones*': JS was a talented swordsman and performer in melodrama, but the fact of his parentage made it inevitable that he would be constantly pushed towards playing Clown. Though only in his late twenties when depicted here, the excesses of his life had already made him appear much older.

Mᴿ J.S. GRIMALDI.

(as Scaramouch)

'Mr. J.S. Grimaldi as Scaramouch': Not only was Scaramouch one of his father's greatest roles, it was also one that JS was engaged to play the night he died. Caught in the throes of hallucinations, he garbled snippets of its dialogue and attempted to dress for the part right up to the moment of his death.

Mr GRIMALDI, as Clown.

N° 42

Pub by DYER, 55. Bath Street City Road.

Joseph Grimaldi as 'Joey', the most significant comic creation of the nineteenth century. 'If to be loved by a whole nation in his lifetime and to live in all men's fancies a hundred years after is a true sign of greatness', wrote the pantomime historian Maurice Wilson Disher in 1925, 'then Joseph Grimaldi has a right to be reckoned among our famous men.'

was hissed and he looked to blame the carpenters, he lost the confidence of the management and the respect of the entire company, who ganged together to try to force him out. Dibdin clung doggedly on, resorting to a court order to enforce his contract. At the Haymarket, meanwhile, he was directed to write a play for a herd of reindeer, but by the time he had finished a piece he called *The Laplanders*, the reindeer had all died, and the management withheld his salary. Dibdin ended up back in court and having to borrow money from criminal extortionists to put food on his table.

It was, then, a ragged and miserable Thomas Dibdin who returned to Islington, a spot he found transformed as thoroughly as if it had been a pantomime trick. The once-bucolic Wells now stood in the 'centre of a large town', consumed by the metropolitan sprawl encouraged by a Tory government that had been spooked by the 1816 Spa Fields riots. Eager to brick over any space of dissident congregation, the expansive fields and pastures that had once surrounded Rosoman's wine-room were now reduced to fugitive rectangles, or overlaid with paving stones on which were planted rows of houses, squares and streets.

Though the world outside stood as proof that the epoch of Dibdin and Grimaldi had irrevocably passed, the new manager thought only of restoring the Wells to its former glory. Joe was appointed his assistant, for which he drew a salary of four pounds a week, and together they cut the prices and reinstated the wine, converting the Hugheses' old residence into a saloon and, for the first time in Sadler's Wells's history, offering half-price admittance after half past eight. Next Dibdin set to plundering his vast catalogue of melodramas, burlettas and pantomimes to shore up the repertoire, though the season succeeded only in sounding a stale note of nostalgia: the performances lacked spark. 'Mr T. Dibdin's talent has oozed away with a vengeance,' wrote one visitor, having endured a night of dreary pieces that failed to contain 'even any of the happy absurdities of his former productions'. As the season faltered, the bills began to promise that 'Mr Grimaldi will occasionally appear,' although the principal appeal of this promise was not the songs he sang or the patter he delivered, but simply 'once more witnessing the famed Joey' before it was too late. It was bad sport, wrote one observer, watching 'poor old Joey Grimaldi dragged from a sick bed, with a view to prop up the falling fortunes of this former scene of his early fame', and many might have boycotted his appearances entirely, had they been aware of their true cost.

Thomas Dibdin's first season ended with a deficit of fourteen hundred pounds, but still the proprietors persevered, slashing the budget to accommodate the loss, and reducing Joe's already meagre salary to a paltry two pounds. This prompted Mary to return to the Covent Garden chorus, while Joe wrote to JS to beg for money. A reply was long in coming, and would never have appeared at all had it not been for the urging of many acquaintances. When it did arrive, it took the form of a solitary line that read, 'At present I am in difficulties; but as long as I have a shilling, you shall have half.' No charity ever came from that quarter, but things at the Wells eventually improved sufficiently to keep Joe and Mary from the workhouse. Persuaded that Islington's enormous growth would provide them with an audience hungry for seasonal entertainments 'without compelling the inhabitants to plod through sleet and rain to the patents', the proprietors decided to take the unprecedented step of offering a winter season. No minor theatre had ever attempted such a move, but it went unchallenged despite an outstanding 1787 licence that restricted Sadler's Wells's operation to the months between Easter Monday and 19 September.

The additional season gave Thomas Dibdin the chance to make a second major contribution to the history of pantomime when, following the practice of the royal theatres, he ceased to offer new pantomimes at Easter and Whitsun and saved them solely for Christmas. Pantomime has been a yuletide entertainment ever since.

Fortunes were better served the following summer when a heat-wave convinced Dibdin to bring back the ponies, re-fence the coachyard and clear its outhouses to make way for 'Newmarket in Miniature', a racecourse that offered races by the light of a thousand lamps. It was quintessential Sadler's Wells – races were interspersed with exhibitions by 'the female jockey', Mrs Fitzwilliam, and sack races billed as if they were prize fights: 'a pedestrian from Berkshire' versus Wiltshire's Paddington, 'who has never been beaten'. Musical interludes were provided by military and Pandean bands, the evening concluding with a 'fire balloon, thirty-six feet in circumference and a parachute attached to it with two pigeons'. Though the profits were not staggering, it at least put them in the black.

When the receipts were good, Joe could at last enjoy some of the overdue fruits of retirement. These included making his annual pilgrimage to Bartholomew Fair, and taking a more prominent role in the activities of the Drury Lane Theatrical Fund, where in 1826 he had been elected one of its twelve directors, which also required him to act as a steward at its grand annual dinner. Less formally, he was installed as the president of the Crib Club, a friendly society that held its meetings in the Sir Hugh Myddleton, and whose membership included the illustrator George Cruikshank, and the pub's landlord, the appropriately named Dickey Wells. Pantomime, though, was intractably in his blood, and as he wrote to a friend in the Christmas season of 1826, he was 'quite ashamed of looking at himself in the Glass this season without his original painted Mug'.

His son, meanwhile, maintained his voluntary estrangement. Even in the face of such unwarranted rejection, Joe continued to dote on the boy and did everything he could to indulge him, hiring him at the Wells at five pounds a week along with his reprobate crony Henry Kemble. In a generational echo of the way he had always tried to please the ferocious Signor, Joe's acts of love served merely to make JS more contemptuous.

Having lost his son, Joe began to work with Tom Matthews, a bow-legged young man with a mouth 'like Piccadilly Circus' who was almost the same age as JS and desired nothing more than to study the craft with the man he was happy to call master. Dedicated and irreproachable as Matthews was, Joe continued to yearn for his wastrel son, constantly searching for ways to repair their relationship, acting in his benefits, and asking Dibdin to write them a duet, in the hope that, if they could not be reconciled in life, they might at least be reconciled on stage.

In the event, JS would not return home until September 1827, when Joe and Mary were roused by a noise outside their house. Going to investigate, Joe found his son shivering in the doorway, his eyes rolling into his head from the effects of a high fever. Together, they carried him in, laying his pale and emaciated body on the bed and covering him with blankets. His hair was lank and thinning, his straggly moustache and sideburns failing to compensate for an expansively tonsured dome that made him look considerably older than his twenty-five years. JS offered no explanation for how he had come to be in such a dangerous state, though the newspapers claimed it was the result of a drunken argument with a lover they called 'a female of a certain class, styled by a contemporary "a young lady"'. According to the *Morning Herald*, which erroneously reported his death,

> On Friday evening, he went, rather intoxicated, to the house of
> a young lady, and informed her that he had occasion to go out,

and she, being remarkably attached to him, persuaded him not to go, and flew to the door, in order to prevent him leaving, when he struck her a blow in the eye, and left her, which she took so much to heart that she went into the kitchen and drank a large draught of vitriol, upon which she was immediately taken to hospital, where she now lies in a most precarious state, and without the slightest hope of recovery.

'Mr. Grimaldi, jun., is not dead,' countered the *Globe*, 'but at the house of his father in Exmouth Street. His illness is a brain fever.' The *Globe* also revealed that his lover, 'although not quite out of danger', was expected to survive. In the days that followed, JS got worse. He began to suffer from hallucinations and apoplectic fits so severe that the doctors required him to be put in a strait-jacket. He stayed like this for two months, upstairs in a room in Exmouth Street, confined and raving. The moment he was recovered, he left Islington to go back to his lover, turning his back on his parents for another year.

∼

Some comfort was to be found in the friendship of Fanny Kelly, the beautiful niece of the singer Michael Kelly. Fanny had been apprenticed to her uncle as a little girl, and actually managed to prosper under her famous name in spite of his neglect, developing a talent that was admired by Sheridan and Sarah Siddons, and winning countless hearts, including those of the essayist Charles Lamb, whose offer of marriage she declined, and a manic obsessive called George Barnett, who bombarded her with ardent letters before attempting to shoot her from the pit of Drury Lane. A piece of the cartridge landed in Caroline Lamb's lap.

Besides her obvious gifts, Fanny Kelly was caring, sweet-natured and scrupulously honest. She had known Joe for almost thirty years, although the two only became close following his retirement. He was now entirely reliant on crutches to walk, and consequently left the house much less often. Fanny would call in to see how he was doing and take tea with him, and it was during one of these visits that the conversation undoubtedly turned to Joe's boyhood hero Carlo Delpini, the old pantomimist who had finally realised his life-long fear of the number eight by dying in February 1828, aged eighty-eight.

Delpini's last years had been spent in an 'obscure lodging' off St Martin's Lane, dogged by ill health and grinding poverty that was caused to some degree by the burden of having been the King's favourite. He had been bankrupted years before by the then Prince of Wales's inability to reimburse the three thousand pounds he had laid out on his coming-of-age ball, and the Prince had failed to repair Delpini's finances by refusing to intercede in his attempts to gain a licence to produce plays at the Little Theatre, Haymarket. After Delpini had resorted to picketing the gates of Carlton House, the Prince advised him to join the Drury Lane Theatrical Fund, commanding Sheridan to provide him with some dialogue that would permit him to qualify. Given that Delpini had terrible English and was only engaged for pantomime, this presented Sheridan with a considerable problem, until a solution was hit upon whereby Pantaloon could come across Harlequin and Columbine in a stolen embrace and cry, 'Pluck them asunder.' Delpini practised his line for weeks, intoning the words in every conceivable formulation, performing them before every member of the company and badgering them for their opinion, while they in turn made mischief by giving as much contradictory advice as possible.

When the big moment at last arrived, Delpini ran on, discovered the lovers and instantly dried, staring dumbstruck into the audience, deaf to the urging of the prompter. Tension rose and a shuffling, uncertain silence descended on the house, until Delpini suddenly blurted out a piece of gibberish that sounded like, '*Masson dire plock et*,' that caused the entire company to dissolve into a fit of convulsive laughter. 'Nevare you mind,' said Delpini, marching off. 'Dose may laugh dat lose . . . by Gar! I 'ave gained de Pension, ha! ha!, and I care not'ing at all for nobody.' He couldn't have been more wrong, as while the Fund made him a number of small individual payments, he never acquired a pension. A solitary gift of two hundred pounds was all he received from the King in his final years, and though it went some way to recognising the many hours of loyal service, it came too late to alleviate his suffering. When Delpini died, his widow, who had spent her own declining years lovingly devoted to her husband's care, was left penniless and destitute.

Delpini's death proved a salutary moment for Joe. No Clown had ever died rich, and given how worried he was by his own potential destitution, Fanny Kelly urged him both to apply to the Fund for a pension, and to fill his pockets by taking a proper farewell benefit at Sadler's Wells. Within days she had established an organising committee and was making the arrangements. The proprietors agreed to loan the theatre at no cost, and Thomas Dibdin likewise convinced the performers to offer their services for free. A date was set for the next St Patrick's Day, 17 March. 'O yes! O yes! O yes!' announced the bills. 'Mr Grimaldi's Last Appearance on the Islington Stage', followed by a few lines of Joe's appalling doggerel: 'For "forty years" they've back'd him,/'*Til Sickness* and *Old Time* attack'd him –'

The crowd numbered two thousand by lunchtime on the day of the benefit, their noise reaching the open windows of Joe's bedroom in Exmouth Street, where he lay, unable to move. A friend of William Oxberry called at the house in the afternoon and, finding him in 'a dreadful state of debility', pleaded with him not to perform. 'I pressed him not to think of it,' said Oxberry's friend, 'but I found him inflexible; and upon my further entreaty, he exclaimed, "I'll play to-night, if it costs me my life!" – and he was in so weak a state, that he burst into tears.' Whether visited by a spasmatic seizure, or simply unable to face a final journey to the Wells, he did not leave for the theatre until the doors had already been opened and the house filled in a single forward rush.

In the company of his doctor, the clown who used to run from Islington to Drury Lane in under eight minutes took an age to walk up the short hill from his house to the theatre, seemingly growing older with each laboured step. He arrived looking hollow and distracted, apparently oblivious to the energising buzz of the crowd, dressing himself for his first appearance as if in a dream. Performances began with Dibdin's melodrama, *The Sixes; or, the Fiends*, in which Joe performed the role of Hock, a German soldier, 'who being shut up in prison, finds plenty of consolation in a flask of wine', a piece Dibdin had written specially for the occasion. It was the sole piece of acting he would attempt that night as there would be no appearance as Clown. At last he came alive, keeping the audience 'in a roar of laughter' with his impression of a drunken sailor, until he tottered off, exhausted. The audience sat restlessly through a number of other pieces in which Joe played no part – a burletta, *Humphry Clinker*, some songs and rope-dancing – until he returned to sing a duet with his estranged son, though he was unable to manage the encore the audience called for so vociferously, retiring instead to the wings, where he sat tearfully watching JS and Tom Ellar perform the famous *pas de deux* from *Mother Goose*.

It was almost midnight by the time the entertainments finished, and Joe returned to the stage, dressed in a black dinner jacket with white waistcoat and white gloves. All the performers filed out from the wings to form a guard of honour silently around him as he advanced to the footlights, and the house rose in unison as he took his long, final look around the auditorium that had sustained him for almost half a century. The cheering and applause were deafening, but Joe could focus only on the finality of the moment, and when at long last he came to speak, his 'many-toned voice' was so weighted with emotion that it threatened to fail him entirely. Recalling the years he had appeared on the stage, he thanked them for their faithful patronage and announced, 'My race is ended,' as shouts of 'No! No! No!' rained from the crowd. When they at last fell silent, Joe gratefully acknowledged the generosity of the proprietors ('They ought to have given you a pension for life,' cried a voice from the gallery), and the performers and musicians who had donated their time. Wishing 'uninterrupted health' upon the assembly, he clasped his hands together and took his leave, saying, 'God bless you all! Farewell!'

As the ovation seemed never-ending and Joe could hardly stand, the performers closed around him and bore him away. Fireworks were lit, illuminating the words 'GRIMALDI'S THANKS' at the upper end of the stage. The applause had not abated by the time he reached the green room, utterly distraught and weeping (according to the *New Monthly Magazine*), 'with an intensity of suffering that it was painful to witness and impossible to alleviate'. Prior to the show, he had planned to distribute mementoes from his costume as favours to the apprentices, but he was too inconsolable to manage it and quit the theatre limp with exhaustion, and 'in a high state of fever'.

He was carried from the Wells and taken home to bed, where he lay sick for several days, unable to see the crowds of well-wishers who came to his door, and reading the reviews that sounded like obituaries. 'Wearied out with struggling against ill health for more than four long years, and finding no hope of amendment,' wrote one, '[Grimaldi] quietly resigned his theatrical life at twelve o'clock last Monday night.' Another said, 'That clown of clowns, and most classical clown that ever raised a laugh in this care-corroded world, has bid farewell to the stage for ever. He is, as the learned would say, *theatrically dead.*' Was there any other kind?

But Joe was not quite ready to be precipitately interred, and Sadler's Wells proved only to be a dress rehearsal for an even grander and more emotional farewell to come. A week after the benefit, partially recovered with the aid of receipts totalling £230, plus a host of anonymous gifts that amounted to an additional £85, Joe was persuaded to plan a second benefit for Covent Garden. Before anything could be arranged, however, there was one last insult to endure from the Kembles. Joe had called on Charles Kemble to ask if he might take the theatre for a night as he had done at the Wells. Kemble, in the midst of a financial crisis that had arisen from the non-payment of rates and taxes that had resulted in the theatre being put into the hands of the Court of Chancery, paid him little mind, ignoring follow-up enquiries until many weeks later when an answer arrived second-hand: the management apologised but, given present difficulties, regretted that they were unable to accommodate his wishes. Chancery or no, Fanny Kelly interpreted it as a calculated snub, a gesture of rank imperiousness, and made her displeasure known directly to its source.

Joe, of course, was immensely wounded, retreating into the familiar state of persecution that the Kembles so often inspired. 'So much for my long and faithful services,' he wrote to his friend, Richard Norman. 'Oh! my poor master, Mr Harris; God bless him! had he still been in possession, I should not have asked such a favour a second time.' A note then arrived from Stephen Price, the American lessee of Drury Lane, who had heard of Joe's predicament from Colonel Berkeley, himself apprised of the situation via the good offices of Fanny Kelly.

Keen to oblige 'so distinguished a veteran', Price offered his theatre free of charge for the penultimate night of the season, an offer Joe not only accepted but shoved in Kemble's face, making a special visit to Covent Garden to show him a copy of a bill he had printed that contained numerous damning allusions to the short shrift he had received from his former employer.

Kemble was furious, going so far as to vindicate Joe's feelings of persecution by declaring that 'You should have had a night for nothing, sooner than you should have gone there,' an admission that he had been happy to refuse when he had thought Joe had no other options. The moment was made all the better by the fact that John Fawcett, also present, magnanimously took Joe's side and, in the version offered in the *Memoirs* at least, the meeting culminated with Joe delivering a dressing-down that went some way to redressing a career's worth of injury. He would count himself lucky if he never met another Kemble again.

In spite of Kemble's slight, there was an auspicious circularity to ending his career at the theatre in which it had begun and, with the Drury Lane benefit set for 27 June, Joe was intent on delivering a farewell address to befit the occasion. Not trusting his own powers of composition, he looked around for an author and hit on the young poet and journalist Thomas Hood, a Londoner with a genuine regard for the city's popular culture, who three years earlier had published a valedictory verse on the clown's withdrawal from the stage in a collection of poems called *Odes and Addresses to Great People*. It was a commission Hood was happy to accept, especially as Joe stipulated that it be short — after all these years, he professed to still being a 'bad study'.

Joe's visit made a big impression on Hood, who was struck first by the beam of delight that fell across his housemaid's face when she opened the door to him, giving him reason to reflect on Joe's ability to exorcise care with a simple hello. It was followed by a much sadder realisation. He recalled,

> Slowly and seriously my visitor advanced and with a decided stoop. I could not forget that I had seen the same personage come in with two odd eyebrows, a pair of right-and-left eyes, a wry nose, a crooked mouth, two wrong arms, two left legs, and a free and easy body without a bone in it, or apparently any centre of gravity. I was half prepared to hear that rare voice break forth smart as the smack of a waggoner's whip, or richly thick and chuckling, like the utterance of a boy laughing, talking, and eating custard, all at once; but a short interval sufficed to dispel the pleasant illusion, and convinced me that Grimaldi was a total wreck . . . The lustre of his bright eye was gone – his eloquent face was passive and looked thrown out of work – and his frame was bowed down by no feigned decrepitude.

Hood was not alone in finding Grimaldi's condition distressing. The epitome of the *élan vital*, famously invulnerable to the assaults of death, he had become his own opposite, an abject symbol of time's unstoppable creep that made an entire generation pause for thought. 'We who have laughed long and hard at his drollery', wrote one commentator as the bills went up, 'are suddenly reminded of our approach into the vale of years by his chilling advertisement for a farewell benefit.' Prompted by shades of mortality, scores of envelopes began to arrive at Exmouth Street as the day of the Drury Lane benefit drew near, fans and well-wishers from all over the country sending cash, mementoes and expressions of thanks, like those of Richard Brinsley Peake, whose note conveyed the sentiments of thousands of pantomime-goers: 'If I was a rich man,' he wrote, 'the enclosed would have been ten times its amount, and I consider that I am your debtor in begging your acceptance of it – I have laughed to the *full value*, and the best recollections of my life are the merry hours you have caused to one who considers that a slice of solid pudding is better than empty praise.'

It was a sentiment echoed by the full house that packed Drury Lane, declared neutral territory for the evening as it contained almost the entire company and backstage staff of Covent Garden, whose season had ended the night before. The entertainments provided not only a celebration of Grimaldi's life, but a celebration of pantomime itself, performed by the greatest collection of pantomimical talent ever to be assembled on a single stage, including JS, James Barnes, Tom Ridgeway, William Southby (a pupil of Laurent and Clown at Astley's), and 'such a concatenation of Clowns and Columbines, Harlequin and Pantaloons' that it was hard to keep track. The only obvious omission was Jack Bologna. Louisa had recently given birth to a son, prompting the family to leave London and tour the provinces with an attraction built from one of Jack's designs, described by Charles Dibdin as 'a very ingenious mechanical and philosophical Exhibition'.

The pieces began with *Jonathan in England*, and then *The Adopted Child*, but the fun really started with Thomas Dibdin's parody of pantomime, *Harlequin Hoax*, in which Fanny Kelly re-created the argumentative and unwilling Columbine she had played in the original production fourteen years ago. It was in the middle of this that Joey appeared in full motley for his final outing, flanked by five other Clowns, all identically dressed, though 'nobody failed to recognise Grimaldi'. 'His entrée was the signal for a shout enough to rend the roof,' reported the *New Monthly Magazine*, as 'he stood up, his knees tottering, and every feature of his face convulsed'. Waiting in the wings was John Pritt Harley, director of the Drury Lane Theatrical Fund, who tried to run on and support him, but was restrained by JS, 'who knew that his father had taxed his energies for a last effort, and that those energies would not desert him'.

Having stood for his applause for as long as possible, Joe fell backwards into a chair that had been brought up against the footlights for his only scene of the evening, a bit of business from *Harlequin Captive; or, the Magic Fire*, a pantomime he had not performed since briefly replacing Dubois as Clown back in 1796. It was chosen, no doubt, because it called for Clown to be seated while a barber worked busily around his chops (a part filled by his devoted apprentice, Tom Matthews). Holding a tub of soapy water between his knees and 'much affected', he gave 'Hot Codlins' for the very last time although, according to *The Times*, he bore 'unstiffly' against the pain and emotion 'with so much humour, that the audience laughed as lustily as of old'. They called for an encore, which he was unable to give, tearfully acknowledging their applause from his chair until JS finally permitted Harley to lead him off.

Next, the audience were treated to a pantomime retrospective, an olio of favourite scenes for 'which the entire pantomimic strength of the metropolis assisted', including JS playing the Watchman scene from *Harlequin in His Element*, and Wieland and Chikini, two young Clowns from Drury Lane, dancing a comic *pas de deux*. As the last notes of music drained away, and the last performers ran offstage, Joe returned, divested of his motley, one hand hanging on to Harley, the other clutching Hood's speech. When the noise had finally died down, he said,

> Ladies and gentlemen, I appear before you for the last time. I need not assure you of the sad regret with which I say it; but sickness and infirmity have come upon me, and I can no longer wear the motley! Four years ago I jumped my last jump, filched my last custard, and ate my last sausage. I cannot describe the pleasure I felt on once more assuming my cap and bells tonight – that dress in which I have so often been made happy in your applause; and as I stripped them off, I fancied that they seemed to cleave to me. I am not so rich a man as I was when I was basking in your favour formerly,

for then I had always a fowl in one pocket and sauce for it in the other [*laughter, cheers, and applause*]. I thank you for the benevolence which has brought you here to assist your old and faithful servant in his premature decline. Eight-and-forty years have not yet passed over my head, and I am sinking fast. I now stand worse on my legs than I used to on my head. But I suppose I am paying the penalty of the cause I pursued all my life; my desire and anxiety to merit your favour has excited me to more exertion than my constitution would bear, and, like vaulting ambition, I have overleaped myself. Ladies and gentlemen, I must hasten to bid you farewell; but the pain I feel in doing so is assuaged by seeing before me a disproof of the old adage, that favourites have no friends. Ladies and gentlemen, may you and yours ever enjoy the blessing of health is the fervent prayer of Joseph Grimaldi — *Farewell! Farewell!*

The old friends rose to stamp and cheer and wave their hats, but the thunderous noise could not shake Joe from the trance into which he had fallen. His feet refused to move, and he stood at the lamps 'swaying to and fro as if fascinated, rooted to the spot', until JS forced his way on and 'taking the veteran by the hand, half led, half-carried him from the stage'. Backstage, Joe was taken into a private room where he was helped into a chair and fortified with a couple of glasses of Madeira. As a token of gratitude, he handed Mr Harley the new wig he had worn for the performance and the original copy of Hood's address, before a delegation of performers formed a line in the room to give him their farewells and good wishes.

At the stage door, the street was thronged with people waiting for him to emerge. They gave him three cheers and followed his coach all the way home, where they cheered him again as he went in, and refused to disperse until he had come out again and made a bow from the top of his steps.

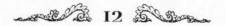

12

THE LIBERTINE DESTROYED

Don Juan, with frantick obduracy, seizes the mouldering bones of the murdered father; fractures them, and casts them at the feet of the Phantom, and in a paroxysm of wickedness, tramples on his skull! Horrid thunders roll! The vision vanishes! The earth yawns! The ministers of vengeance arrayed in flaming sulphur ascend from the chasm! – The Libertine, in all the agony of guilt, casts himself upon the ground to avoid the terrors which encompass him, but in vain! His momentary slumber is awakened by the demons which surround him; and, HELL, with all its HORRORS, bursts open to receive him!!!

Carlo Delpini, *Don Juan; or, the Libertine Destroyed* (1790)

THOUGH JOE HAD BID the stage farewell, the Grimaldi name remained on the bills through the efforts of JS. Joe's support for his estranged son did not falter, his attention to the boy's career fuelled by a desire to see his own work live on. Passing the baton from father to son was as important to him as it had been to the Signor, and the succession seemed secure when JS appeared as Clown in *Harlequin and Little Red Riding Hood* at Covent Garden on Boxing Day 1828. His performance was roundly praised, even if it failed to dislodge comparisons with the old man himself. 'Young Grimaldi – now, alas! our only Grimaldi,' wrote *The Times*, 'is evidently improving. The rawness of his boyhood is going off; he grows more like his father in manner . . . and therefore grows better. His activity is equal to anybody's, his grimace is very masterly . . . and his humour is getting generally rounder and more solid.' With both critics and audiences happy to give him time,

JS had every right to feel secure in his position, yet still the weight of expectation proved unbearable. Trapped in a role he had not chosen, he quickly reverted to his old ways, finding a solution to his problems in a self-sabotaging cocktail of drink and anti-social behaviour. After only three days, Charles Kemble sacked him from the pantomime and replaced him with the ever-dependable Signor Paulo.*

Ejection from Covent Garden was the cue for the acceleration of JS's decline. Tortured and alcoholic, he fell into a pattern of behaviour that saw him moving quickly from theatre to theatre, never staying longer than a couple of months before another relapse would compound the misery of his self-destructive ways. In the summer of 1829, he was taken back by the Wells to perform in a pantomime his father had produced called *Three Wishes*, comprised of twelve of the most popular scenes from his repertoire. Yet even the great love the Wells felt for Joe could not induce its management to tolerate his son's appalling behaviour, and JS was sacked after only a few weeks, replaced by the one whose dearest wish would have been to call Joe father, Tom Matthews.

Joe and Mary moved to a smaller house at 23 Garnault Place, just around the corner from their old one at Exmouth Street, where they intended to live a quiet retirement with the proceeds from his benefits and an annual pension of a hundred pounds granted by the Committee of the Drury Lane Theatrical Fund. Even now Joe's name retained the power to attract a crowd, as evinced by a practical joke that advertised an attempt by 'Grimaldi' to repeat Usher's trick of riding a wash-tub pulled by four geese down the Thames from Westminster to Vauxhall Bridge. The bill, announcing 'a Grand

---

* Paulo did not remain in the part for long. At the end of January he was injured when his carriage was hit by the drunk driver of a brick cart, throwing him out of his seat and 'upon the stones with great force', whereupon he was run over by a coal wagon.

Naval Aquatic Exhibition' in the best style of Charles Dibdin, claimed that Joe would win a hundred sovereigns if he could do it in less than forty minutes. Anyone who knew him was aware that it would take Joe that long to climb the stairs, but nevertheless an enormous crowd gathered to find tub and geese waiting, but no Grimaldi. The hoaxers had bet each other how many people would turn out.

Drury Lane's charity extended as far as providing JS with one last chance. In October 1829 he was cast in a melodrama called *The Greek Family*, and at Christmas he played Clown in the pantomime *Jack in the Box; or, Harlequin and the Princess of the Hidden Island*. 'Of Mr. J. Grimaldi,' wrote *The Times*, unrelenting in its familial theme, 'it is sufficient praise to say, that he very often reminded us of his never-to-be-forgotten father.' JS completed the season, but after that he disappeared from London, apparently on tour. He certainly visited Manchester and Edinburgh, where he was plagued by fits and insanity and 'not infrequently arrested'. 'Young Grimaldi arrived a few days since,' reported a Scottish newspaper in 1830, 'had scarcely landed when he was seized with feverish symptoms, and is at present in a most precarious state, and quite delirious.'

His itinerary was curtailed before the close of the year, when he voluntarily entered prison in London by invoking the Insolvent Debtors Act to rid himself of his many creditors. In court, he answered questions in 'a very candid manner', and listened to a citation that shed some light on his recent movements and turbulent lifestyle, listing addresses in Edinburgh, Glasgow, Ayr, Greenock, Stourbridge, Worcester and Cheltenham, and a long roll of lodgings in London that included four different addresses in Islington, three off Theobald's Road, one in Martlett Court, Drury Lane (where his great-grandfather had once pulled teeth), and one each in Mile End Road, Borough High Street, and the New Cut, Lambeth, next to the Coburg. It is unknown which of these addresses he returned to following his release from prison on 3 March 1831, aided by his father's expenditure of forty pounds on court costs and the expenses he incurred during incarceration, but by May he was employed at the Pavilion, an even more tawdry version of the Coburg, situated in an old clothes factory in Baker's Row, Whitechapel. Prison had obviously done nothing to reform JS, as he lasted less than three weeks in his new job before being sacked and presenting himself at his parents' door in 'the lowest form of wretchedness and poverty'. 'His dress had fallen to rags,' say the *Memoirs*, 'his feet were thrust into two worn-out slippers, his face was pale with disease and squalid with dirt and want, and he was steeped in degradation.'

Mary didn't want to let him in. She had suffered too long at the hands of his 'gross and violent abuse', but Joe was lonely and unable to turn him away. Only infrequently at the Wells, he had been spending long hours at home, arranging his folders of cuttings, manuscript plays and ideas for pantomime tricks, while Mary toiled in the Covent Garden chorus from ten in the morning until midnight. Unable to pursue any of his former hobbies, his greatest pleasure lay in theatrical politics and gossip, and he took an especially keen interest in the growing struggle between the patents and the minor theatres, who were making increasingly bold incursions into the province of legitimate drama.

As a proprietor, Joe was firmly on the side of the minors, a partisanship that was buttressed by the great delight he took in watching minor managers and impresarios inflict heaps of aggravation on his foe Charles Kemble. In concert with the managers of Drury Lane, Kemble had bankrolled a network of spies to inform him when any of the minor theatres were presenting pieces that might flout the law. In 1830, this had led to a prosecution against Chapman, the manager of the Tottenham Street theatre, a case that Joe attended with many

other notable men of the profession, whose enthusiastic support for the Tottenham reflected a growing dissatisfaction with
the anachronistic and oppressive terms of the Licensing Act.
Public opinion was almost entirely on the side of the minors,
and when the Tottenham escaped prosecution, despite being
unequivocally guilty of all charges, the court was overjoyed,
especially as Kemble was universally vilified as both a monop-
olist and a sneak.

Taking JS back provided Joe with a new focus: he concen-
trated on his son's rehabilitation and keeping temptation at
bay while looking to repair their bond by arranging outings. 'I
know it is a great favour to ask,' he wrote to a friend, probably
the manager of the Exeter Change Menagerie, Edward Cross,
looking for free tickets to see a show and visit the lions, 'but
as I cannot *now* put my hand in my pocket, have taken this
liberty, which if complied will add an additional obligation.' JS
seems to have made progress: the autumn and winter of 1831
proceeded quietly and with no major ructions. He even found
time for a little correspondence, although a letter written in
reply to a request from the theatrical autograph hunter
Charles Brantiffe Smith reveals either his affected nonchalance
or genuinely patchy memory: 'My Dear Sir,' he wrote, 'I cannot
remember in what year, or in what Pantomime I first appeared
at Covent Garden Theatre, all I can inform you of is that
when First I play'd the Principal Clown, the name of the Piece
was *Harlequin and Poor Robin; or, the House that Jack Built*, with
regard to dates, Mr Farley is I think the only person who can
give you the information you are in Search of.'

In the spring of 1832, the Wells was leased to the female
jockey, Mrs Fitzwilliam, who, having no room for Joe, let him
go soon after. Now that he had lost his small weekly stipend,
and with no further reason to live close to the Wells, the
Grimaldis decided to leave the Islington conurbation and enjoy the clean air and space of a riverside cottage in Woolwich,

close to the Royal Naval Dockyard. JS came with them – an encouraging sign – and, buoyed by his general improvement, Joe helped his son look for work. Easter 1832 saw him rewarded with a contract at the Coburg where, by accident or design, he was fitted to roles that perfectly reflected his notoriety: 'Gallows Charley, an ungovernable Kid' in *Paul Clifford or the Highwayman of 1770*; 'Desperetto' in *The Maid of Genoa*; and a 'Celebrated Drunken Combat' in *The Bandit of the Blind Mine*. But Joe's hopes for his son's recovery proved premature, as JS was off the bills in less than a week.

On 8 May, he appeared at a benefit for the orphans of his sometime Harlequin, the one-eyed E. J. Parsloe at the Surrey. Parsloe had died while playing Clown in the first ever production of *Mother Goose* to be performed in America. A company had travelled to play at the Bowery Theatre, New York, but Parsloe had fallen and injured his spine during the voyage, and after two nights of performing painfully before a bemused American audience, who had no idea what to make of this unusual form, he suffered a mental breakdown and had to be led from the stage. He was found dead the following morning.* Superstitious pantomimical circles noted that *Mother Goose* had never been successful without Joe Grimaldi. To try it was to court disaster.

Still Joe struggled on behalf of his son, writing to Alfred Bunn, as Christmas approached, in his new position as lessee of Drury Lane. Bunn was unable to help: 'Being as lost to the stage as he was to his family,' he wrote of JS, 'a compliance

---

* The tour company went their several ways following Parsloe's death. According to the Victorian pantomime producer E. L. Blanchard, the Harlequin, played by John Gay, 'wandered on to the West, after vainly endeavouring to establish himself in Boston and Baltimore; and, appearing one night at an Indian encampment in his Harlequin's dress, was taken by the red men for a great medicine man, and lived with them a year, till he had parted with all his spangles. He eventually found his way back to England and Whitechapel.'

with his wish was utterly impracticable.' He did, though, enquire whether the services of the father were available as arranger of that year's pantomime. Seeing a negotiating opportunity, Joe refused to concede, offering some of his tricks, scripts and designs in return for a place for JS. He wrote back to Drury Lane:

> I sincerely regret that nothing can be done for my son as I am confident that you would find him a valuable acquisition in every department. Salary, as I previously stated, would be a secondary consideration, as a permanent situation is all that is required. An article perhaps for three or five years might still (by your kind interference) not be objected to, commencing at 3*l*. per week. Should an opportunity present itself, I hope and trust you will interest yourself in his behalf for the sake of *Old Joe* and *Auld Lang Syne*. With regard to myself, I cannot express myself in terms sufficiently to return you my sincere thanks for the good opinion you still have of me, and of my poor humble abilities. It is certainly a great consolation to know in my solace that I am as much respected and esteemed in my retirement as when in my public character. Your kind offer to me to superintend the forthcoming pantomime (*however gratifying to my feelings*) I shall never forget but must decline. I could no more sit in an arm-chair to instruct a pantomime than I am capable of jumping out of a garret window without injury to myself – for this reason, should anything go contrary to my wishes all ailments would for a moment vanish, for I must exert myself, which in all probability might end in a bed of sickness, and might terminate my existence. All that I can offer is this – I have as many models and tricks as would furnish six or seven pantomimes, of which you may select what is necessary for your *Christmas Novelty*. Independent of which I have a good opening which you may inspect, and also can, upon a pick, assist you with a comic scene or two of business, if required. Thus I can promise without *fee or reward*, provided an arrangement can be made for my son.

However much he wanted to oblige old Joe, Bunn could not afford the liability, and JS did not appear on stage again until November, when he was called to appear at another benefit. The long hiatus and Woolwich air seem to have done him some good as his performance was faultless, and when he returned to his parents the following day, he brought with him the news that he had been re-engaged at the Coburg for the Christmas season.

The next day he celebrated his thirtieth birthday in modest style, and in the afternoon received a note inviting him to play at the Tottenham Street theatre in *Don Juan*, and a melodrama called *The Slave's Revolt*, based on *Oroonoko*, Aphra Behn's novel of a noble African taken into slavery. After borrowing some money, JS left to take the engagement on Sunday, 24 November, and on Wednesday Joe went up to town and found his son in high spirits. They dined, and JS left for the theatre. The following Sunday, however, he did not appear for dinner with his parents as he'd said he would. A few days later, the news arrived in Woolwich that their son was ill, prompting Joe to write to a friend to enquire whether it was necessary to send for a doctor. For two days he heard nothing, although, given JS's binges, this was far from unusual.

In the meantime, Mary fell dangerously ill and was confined to bed. 'She has had a Paraletic attack,' wrote Joe to Richard Norman, 'which has deprived her of the use of Limbs and Speech and is confined to her bed, and is assisted out of Bed and in Bed by 3 persons – her Speech has partially recovered but the Limbs I fear never will . . .' On 11 December, Joe was upstairs tending her when he heard a knock at the door. He went downstairs to open it and was greeted by a sombre-faced friend who informed him, 'with great care and delicacy', that JS was dead. The press notice read:

On Tuesday morning died after a sudden illness at his lodgings, 24 Pitt Street, Tottenham Court Road, Mr J.S. Grimaldi,
the successful successor, as it was once thought, of his talented
father. The deceased performed last week at Tottenham Street
Theatre, the parts of Scaramouch in *Don Juan*, and Black Caesar
in The Slave's Revolt, and then appeared in his usual health.
On Monday, however, he became delirious, but dressed himself
and assumed one of his principal characters, he was then mildly
restrained and medical aid called in, but all proved ineffectual,
and at nine o'clock yesterday morning he breathed his last. The
deceased was unmarried and in his 30th year.

On the Saturday following his death, an inquest was held
at the Hope public house. Before the coroner, Mr T. Stirling,
Mrs Walker, the landlady at 24 Pitt Street, explained how JS
had come to lodge with her a week before his death, making
nightly appearances at the theatre until the Monday night
when he had been seized with violent vomiting. She had called
for Dr Langley, who in turn told the jury how he had found JS
in 'a very weak and debilitated state', which had been caused,
in his opinion, by 'violent vomiting and inflammation'. Shortly
thereafter he was taken by a delirium in which he insisted on
dressing himself for the theatre and, convinced that he was
before an audience, began to drift in and out of the characters
of Oroonoko and Scaramouch, his own speech interleaved with
the parts he had been hired to play. A distressed Mrs Walker
and Mr Langley forcibly restrained him as he tried to leave the
house, attempting to put him back to bed, but it was no use. JS
kept rising, as if mesmerised, acting 'snatches of the parts to
which he had been most accustomed'. For the next several hours,
his hallucinations became increasingly vivid, his mumbling
speech an epigrammatic lattice of quotation and incoherence.
In the early hours of the following morning he died.

The events that had immediately preceded JS's sudden
illness were described by Mr Burton, the box-keeper at the

Tottenham Street theatre, Catherine Elliot, a fellow performer there, and her sister, the stage manager. The night before he had died, JS had asked Burton to provide him with a pass for a female friend. Burton had agreed, and 'allowed an elegantly attired lady to pass to the boxes'. A little later JS reappeared in a state of breathless excitement, begging for a private box where he and his lady friend 'would not be publicly observed'. At rehearsal the following morning, JS approached Catherine Elliot with the words, 'Old woman, I was nicely in for it last night,' to which she replied that she supposed he was, even though she was unable to decipher exactly what he meant and simply assumed he'd been drunk. 'It was a great row,' continued JS, at cross-purposes, 'but I was not aware it could be heard onstage.' If Miss Elliot now realised that something violent had transpired in the boxes, her suspicions were confirmed when JS removed a piece of material from his sleeve that looked to have been torn from a lady's nightgown. 'That,' he said, 'unless a dickey [shirt] . . . was all the linen she had on.'

Having boasted of an apparent sexual conquest, he next began to complain of pains in his left side, which he asked Miss Elliot to feel, but could not bear the pressure of her hand when she did. They were injuries for which her sister, the stage manager, offered an explanation: earlier that day, JS had slipped down the ladder going through a trap and fallen on his side, bruising his ankle, ribs and knee. Mr Langley, the surgeon, then told the court that, even though he had not made a detailed examination of the body, he did not consider these injuries to have been of significance in the matter of his death.

Having heard the available witnesses, Mr Stirling, the coroner, seemed satisfied with Langley's opinion. He asked the jury whether they required any further information. They declined, and he discharged the court. The press, however, was more sceptical, largely because JS's body had been buried a day before the inquest had begun. As one journalist wrote:

> This is a strange business. Pray what does Mr Stirling mean by holding an inquest where there is no dead body? There were marks of violence externally, and every symptom of violence internally: yet neither for the aidance of justice, nor for the interests of medical science did the said surgeon Langley seek to examine the lesion. How did Mr Langley know that the bruises did not occasion the death of the deceased? And if *they* did not, what did? Poison? We have only to say that the public have a right to know more about the matter. The cause of Grimaldi's death has *not* been inquired into, and he *did not die a natural death*.

This was not the only paper to voice suspicion, and its invocation of poison seems particularly suggestive, given the events of 1827 that had left JS at his parents' door in a state of intense agitation. Poison had been a factor then, insanity and hallucinations similarly preceded by high passions and violent arguments, and though JS had a history of mental illness, the onset of the vomiting and delirium that prefigured his death would certainly be consistent with sudden toxicity. A similar thing had happened to Thomas Ellar in 1835, when a jealous lover poisoned him with mercury, the effects of which turned his face blue for the remainder of his life. Who, though, might have poisoned JS? Was the 'elegantly attired lady' whom he had taken into the boxes that evening, possibly one of the many prostitutes who did business in the theatre, exacting revenge for an assault in which he had literally ripped the clothes from her back? Or was she, perhaps, the same 'young lady' of 1827, a long-term mistress with whom he was locked in a sadistic and mutually destructive passion?

The *Gentleman's Magazine* certainly seemed to think so, although it offered quite a different account of the death, claiming it was common knowledge that JS had died of the bruises Langley was so ready to dismiss, acquired in 'a drunken fight with a professed pugilist, the lover of his pretended wife, who was a young courtezan of excessive vulgarity and little pretension to beauty'. No clarification ever came forward, as while the *Morning Chronicle* reported that JS's body had been exhumed from its resting place in the burial ground of White-field's Tabernacle, Tottenham Court Road, on 17 December, an autopsy report was never filed. The case closed, and the sordid mystery of J. S. Grimaldi's death at thirty faded quickly from public view, barely commemorated save for the appearance of an anonymous little verse that spat the same venom on his memory that Anthony Pasquin had once expended on his grandfather. Its final stanza ran,

> Ev'ry act of each day brings thee hatred and Shame,
> Strews thy path with the thorns of disgrace,
> In Infamy's books writes the tale of your fame,
> And bids us retreat from your deeds and your name!
> The debts paid – if you can – rest in peace.

~

JS was the last of the Grimaldi line, but he left no will, no possessions, and a theatrical legacy that amounted to three small prints of himself in character and a bust of his likeness that his parents kept in their front room, covered with a sheet. Yet four years after his death (and two years before he edited Joe's *Memoirs*), Charles Dickens remained sufficiently affected by his fate to grant him a cameo appearance in a story called 'The Stroller's Tale', which comprised one of the earliest instalments of *The Posthumous Papers of the Pickwick Club*. In this story, the assembled Pickwickians are listening to a character called 'Dismal Jemmy', himself a down-at-heel actor, recalling the fate of a fellow performer, 'enfeebled by dissipation and emaciated by disease', who has squandered his talent and destroyed his career through drink. All the details are consistent with the facts of JS's life – the wasted promise, the intractable alcoholism, the downward mobility and serial expulsions from increasingly depressing venues – although in *Pickwick*, his fictional double, 'John', is embellished with a wife he habitually beats and a child he neglects to the point of starvation. One night, Jemmy comes across him on the stage. It is late and the theatre is dark. Jemmy recalls,

> I was dressed to leave the house and was crossing the stage on my way out, when he tapped me on the shoulder. Never shall I forget the repulsive sight that met my eye when I turned round. He was dressed for the pantomime, in all the absurdity of a clown's costume. The spectral figures in the Dance of Death, the most frightful shapes that the ablest painter ever portrayed on canvas, never presented an appearance half so ghastly. His bloated body and shrunken legs – their deformity enhanced a hundred fold by the fantastic dress – the glassy eyes, contrasting fearfully with the thick white paint with which the face was besmeared: the grotesquely ornamented head, trembling with paralysis, and the long skinny hands, rubbed with white chalk – all gave him a hideous and unnatural appearance of which no description could convey an adequate idea, and which, to this day, I shudder to think of.

John asks Jemmy for alms and, being granted them, disappears until a few days later when Jemmy receives word that John is dangerously ill. He goes to his bedside and discovers him raving and insensible and on the brink of death, menaced by phantom insects, frightful reptiles and faces peering from the walls 'searing him with heated irons, and binding his head with cords till the blood started'. Convinced that his wife was planning to murder him to avenge herself for his mistreatment, he begs Jemmy to keep her at bay, though all Jemmy can do is watch in pity as he dies, writhing through agonies and menaced by delusions that re-enacted the final hours of JS – quoting lines of verse, reciting parts from melodramas, singing snatches of songs and, most unsettling of all, laughing 'the clown's shrill laugh'.

That Dickens found a theme of deep personal significance in the circumstances of JS's death is demonstrated by the fact that this episode in *The Pickwick Papers* is but the first of countless images of derelict performers that wend their sorry way through his fiction, as lost and beggarly as a solitary note wobbling across an empty auditorium. Like many boys of his generation, Dickens had idolised Joe in his childhood, fondly recalling trips up to London where he would offer his applause 'with great precocity', all the while storing up impressions that would come to influence his early work – his first book, *Sketches by Boz*, had been commended for demonstrating the 'spirit of Grimaldi'. The fall of JS not only represented the desecration of those honey-hued pleasures, but perfectly distilled what would become one of his major themes: a contemplation of the distance between the imaginative world of children and the mottled realities of adult life. But Dickens also conceded that his memories of Joe were 'shadowy and imperfect', liable to misrepresentation, and it could be that the homunculus emerging from the darkness and shivering with delirium tremens represented an alternative memory, the other side of childhood that is full of threats and terrors.

Either way, it's an important juncture for a clown's reputation inasmuch as its over-emphatic contrast of laughter and vice colludes to produce the very first example in British culture of clowns as dangerous and troubling figures. In other words, in his portrayal of the death of JS, Dickens invented the scary clown, the menacing predator pushing pleasure beyond its tipping point and curdling into something more twisted and sinister. In this respect, JS is with us even to this day.

~

It was the season for dying. Charles Dibdin died a month after young Grimaldi, and was buried next to his mother, his grandmother, his wife and five of their children in the churchyard of St James's, Pentonville. Dissipation completed its death work on Edmund Kean the following May, the polestar of celebrity denied a place next to Garrick in Westminster Abbey. The promising young Tom Ridgeway, 'allowed to be the best clown we have seen since the days of the celebrated Grimaldi', was next, succumbing to a lung infection at only twenty-eight years old, followed by Paulo, who died at forty-eight, leaving his wife and family 'totally unprovided for'. In an instructive contrast to the professional silence that followed the death of JS, such was Paulo's standing that, within a fortnight of his passing, a committee had been formed to provide his widow with an annual pension. 'Some may think the sufferings of buffoons unworthy of sympathy,' wrote the *Morning Chronicle*, as it sympathetically reported the news, 'but every man who devotes his mind or body energetically to the production of excellence in his art, if it be not a bad one, is deserving of esteem. A capital fool must be a very clever fellow; he must exercise high qualities of energy and resolution, to endure the strains, and kicks and thumps, which *Clowns* are heir to.'

Joe and Mary decided it was time for them to go too. The shock of their son's death, combined with their joint disabilities, sent them both into a mournful depression. Mary had not fully recovered from her stroke, and Joe had suffered another attack of the spasms, incurring a doctor's bill for £54 that he had to ask John Hughes, secretary of the Drury Lane Theatrical Fund, to help him discharge. Finding their lives bleak and burdensome, they also turned to poison, making a pact to end it all. According to the illustrator George Cruikshank, they made their farewells, drank a fatal dose and lay side by side to await their deaths. Minutes passed and nothing happened. Many more minutes passed and still nothing happened, until at last Mary turned to her husband and said, 'Joey, are you dead?'

'No, Mary,' he replied. 'Are you?'

'No.' The only symptoms were wind and an upset stomach, which they cured with a good, warm supper, over which they agreed to forbear from suicide and endure their lives a little longer.

Mary did not have long to wait. She died some time in 1834, although the exact month and day remain vague. This uncertainty emanates from the *Memoirs* themselves, which mention her death only in passing, thereby remaining consistent in their rendition of Mary Grimaldi as the mistiest of vignettes, even though she and Joe were married for more than thirty years. Joe seems to have viewed her death as something of a reprieve, for as soon as she was gone he desired to leave Woolwich and 'return from Transportation', as he put it to Ellar, asking an old servant of the Hughes family to find him a house in Islington where he could receive visits from friends and be closer to his beloved Wells. The servant, Mrs Arthur, rented to him the house next to hers at 33 Southampton Street, Pentonville, for the modest rent of twenty-eight pounds per year, although the deal turned out to be too good to be true Joe was soon involved in a dispute with the landlord, Mr Proctor, over who was responsible for the property's Land Tax. 'I am not to be duped or imposed upon,' Joe wrote high-handedly, after receiving an unexpected bill and issuing a half-hearted threat to vacate.

Annoyances aside, he was glad to be home in Islington. It was, said the *New Monthly Magazine*, 'sacred ground to him', conjuring the romantic view that he 'was wont to wander up and down beside the tall poplars and the narrow river and cogitate upon his by-gone glories'. In truth, Joe was largely immobile, and while he retained good use of his arms and upper body, his legs were completely paralysed. In retrospect, he wished he had withdrawn from the stage in 1819 after his stint in management, believing that if he had given himself one or two years to recover properly he would have been able to resume some kind of career. Idleness, though, had been beaten out of him in childhood, the threats of the Signor so internalised that they had crippled him through a compulsion to please.

At Southampton Street, he was alone save for his house-keeper, Susannah Hill, although there was a fairly constant stream of visits from friends, who included Richard Hughes, Richard Norman, Alfred Bunn, Edward Cross, Tom Ellar, to whom he sold a pair of fiddles for five pounds, and Fanny Kelly, who sought his advice when she considered adopting a baby girl. He also kept in touch with old comrades like Charles Farley, himself ageing and obscure and living in Hart Street, Bloomsbury, where his accomplishments were overlooked by a younger generation of dramatists for whom he had paved the way. 'The . . . name of *Joseph Grimaldi* is dear to *all*, who like myself remember you in your glory,' Farley wrote consolingly to Joe, 'a glory that must take an age since it can pass away.' Every night he was called for by William Cooke, the landlord of the Marquis of Cornwallis, who put him on his back and carried him the few doors down to his pub, where he would entertain the drinkers and enjoy a nightly nip of scotch ale or gin and water.

This still left many empty hours which he passed in pen-ning short, maudlin letters that he assured his friends were agony to write – 'I am afflicted with rheumatism so severely as to be scarcely able to lift my pen' – and filled with complaints about ill health, poor finances and with requests for advances on his pension, bottles of soothing 'mixture' and cheering visits to 'talk of old times when life was young and no one was happier than your old and true chum'. As the benefit season approached he would still be assailed with requests to appear, in spite of his well-publicised disabilities. To one applicant he wrote,

> I am sorry I shall not be able to oblige you this year by even making an appearance for an hour. I am very ill – so ill indeed that I can scarcely hold the pen in my hand to write this to you. I am rheumatised – goutised – puffised – and generally done up. No more for poor Joey the larks and games, the sausage and baggy breeks, the Little Old Woman and Hot Codlins. Eheu! My foot is swathed in bandages, my body is wrapped in flannel, and my heart is bandaged in calico. I am always in pain.

'Poor Joey's laid up in lavender,' he wrote to another, 'and will never again make Christmas folk grin with his anticks, his buffooneries, and his quips and cracks. No more concealment of sausages in his capacious pockets – no more bottles stowed away – no more merry songs and sayings and jibes.' 'O my heart grieves!' he wailed, concluding his letter with a performative gesture reminiscent of the Signor's famous skeleton scene: 'Oh that pain, it is coming on again, and I must drop the pen that quivers in my hand – come and see poor Joey – come dear friend, and talk of the day of yore. The sight of your jolly rubicund mug will mayhap ease me and drive for the nonce "dull care away", Yours as ever, Joey Grimaldi ("Grim-all-day") Joking till the last you see.'

In these idle hours, Joe began writing, or rather dictating, his memoirs, completing them on his fifty-eighth birthday, 18 December 1836. An 1874 auction catalogue describes the manuscript (sadly lost) as 'filling 400 closely-written pages' and being 'as genuine and faithful an autobiography as ever was written, full, frank, and delightfully clownish, childlike and simple'. A month later, Sadler's Wells put on a revival of *Mother Goose*, with Joe appearing in the bills as patron. They still called out for 'Hot Codlins' there, irrespective of what was playing on stage, exasperating the management to the degree that in 1832 they had taken the extraordinary step of banning it, announcing to the patrons that 'It being customary . . . for some few persons to call for an obsolete song called "Hot Codlins", much to the annoyance of the generality of the Audience . . . no Song, or Performance of any description, will be allowed to be introduced, but such as is announced in the Bills of the Day.' That night it was permitted, although Jefferini faltered in his part as Clown, for when he sang 'Hot Codlins' in the presence of the great man, the reviews denounced it as 'the least humorous we have ever heard'.

Joe must have known Jefferini for a while. His real name was Jeffreys, and he kept a tobacconist's on Joe's old street, Garnault Place, that doubled as an illicit gambling-house. He also knew what it was to suffer for his art. Being inordinately tall, he was hampered when attempting to perform stage acrobatics and consequently suffered terrible injuries that he tried to conceal with excessive gurning, 'facial contortions' that, wrote E. L. Blanchard, 'excited roars of laughter from the audience, [but] were only a vent for the tortures the poor fellow in motley suffered from internal pain consequent to his leaping and dancing'. Joe watched the show from the back of a box accompanied by his neighbour, Mr Arthur, but was duly called to the rail by the acclamation of the audience, where an improvised speech of thanks again ended in the customary flood of tears.

This was Joe's last visit to the Wells in any capacity. In the weeks that followed he tried unsuccessfully to sell his memoirs, abandoning the idea in March when he entered into an agreement with the journalist and playwright Thomas Egerton Wilks to 're-write, revise and correct' the entire thing. Wilks took additional notes and recorded further anecdotes to adorn the piece before taking it away and promising to be finished by the end of November. It was from this work, rather than the original manuscript, that Dickens compiled the *Memoirs of Joseph Grimaldi*, dismissing Wilks's text as 'dreary twaddle'.

Joe, however, didn't live to see the project get that far. On the afternoon of 31 May 1837, he complained to his house-keeper, Susannah, of tightness of the chest, but was recovered enough by evening to spend a few hours in the Marquis of Cornwallis, where he appeared in good spirits. William Cooke carried him home on his back, and was bid goodnight with the words, 'God bless you, my boy. I shall be ready for you tomorrow.' Everything appeared as usual when Susannah put him to bed and left a candle on his table, though later that night she was woken by 'an unusual noise, similar to loud snoring', but when she went in to check on him, she found him fast asleep. When she went in again between five and six in the morning, however, 'she was shocked at discovering her lamented master apparently a corpse'.

The body was placed in a coffin in the parlour of Sou-thampton Street while the coroner convened at Cooke's pub. His verdict: *'Died by the visitation of God.'*

Joe was laid to rest in the churchyard of St James's, Penton-ville, at one o'clock on the afternoon of Monday, 5 June 1837. Though the brow of Pentonville hill was choked with mourn-ers, the funeral itself was simple, consisting of a hearse and two coaches bearing an all-male mourning party of Richard Hughes, Mr Dixon, part-proprietor of the Wells, Mr Arthur, Joe's neighbour in Southampton Street, Mr Dayus, the treasurer at the Wells, Dickey Wells, landlord of the Sir Hugh Myddleton, and his childhood friend Richard Lawrence. His grave, dug 'far beyond the usual depth', a courtesy afforded gentlefolk as a precaution against body snatchers, lay close to the vault of his first wife, Maria Hughes, and at the foot of the grave of Charles Dibdin.

EPILOGUE

Pantomime's best days are fled
Grimaldi, Barnes, Bologna, dead!

J. R. Planché, *Harlequin Out of Place* (1847)

'WE DON'T KNOW WHY so much fuss has been made about the death of this certainly very clever mountebank,' ran the notice in *Figaro in London*, a journal akin to *Punch*:

His own habits had rendered him dead to the public for many years, during which, but for those habits, he might have been continuing his calling with profit to himself and a certain species of satisfaction to the public. But as by his own intemperance he has long deprived us of any pleasure we might have derived from seeing him perform, we cannot make out how he is any more lost to us now than he has been for the last ten years. The gin-drinking paper people twaddle vastly over the interesting fact, that of late years he has been obliged to be carried 'pick-a-back' by the landlord, to a gin-shop, in Pentonville, and all we can say is, that the landlord and Grimaldi ought both to have been ashamed of themselves, Joe for being such an inveterate tap-room frequenter as to be carried to it when he could not walk, and the landlord for taking an evidently unfair advantage of the mental imbecility of a customer. It appears it was the delight of Grimaldi to sit drinking and gossiping half the night in a public-house, and that he did so the night before his death as usual. He was consequently called into the presence of his Maker in a 'beery' state, and must have been more than half 'moppy' when the loud trump of death summoned him. And yet the public is requested to be very melancholy, and to go into the fashionable mourning of a long face upon the occasion. We regret him certainly as we should the sudden 'exit' of any confirmed toper, but as to anything more we are not prepared to recognize Grimaldi's disease by a lengthy lamentation. He certainly could cram more sausages down his throat, and make uglier faces than any man alive, but as he had for so long rendered himself unfit to do anything of this kind in public, we cannot look upon his death as a national calamity.

As obituaries went, it was far from typical. *Figaro* was a 'low periodical', peddling a 'heap of falsehood', thundered Henry Downes Miles, but while certainly guilty of moral superiority and indiscriminately collating father and son, its refusal to parrot the prevailing sentiment presaged changing times.

Fifteen days after Joe's funeral, the death of William IV saw Princess Victoria of Saxe-Coburg-Gotha ascend to the throne, heralding a new age for a country that had emerged from a dramatic period of industrialisation, colonisation and political upheaval as the most powerful, wealthy and advanced nation on earth – or so it believed – ready to gild its accomplishments with a reformation of manners so exemplary that it would truly lead the world. The renunciation of Regency licence was a necessary part of that reform, and within a few short years no generation was more ashamed of its past prodigality than those respectable mid-century citizens who looked back on their Regency youth and found themselves virtually unrecognisable: 'The manners of the middle class', wrote a disbelieving Henry Angelo, 'are marked by a mighty change, in favour of general decorum,' of 'a cast and character so dissimilar to modern habits, that . . . we may be said to be no longer the same people.'

To reform society it was necessary to reform its diversions, and while change moved slowly, one of the most symbolic alterations came almost immediately in the suppression in

1840 of the 'vicious amusements' at Bartholomew Fair. To the Corporation of London, within whose jurisdiction that event had taken place under Royal Charter since 1133, the fair had become a disreputable nuisance that detracted from the general progress that had been made among the city's working classes. By prohibiting the presence of theatrical booths at the fair, the Corporation effectively labelled an entire generation of Chinese jugglers, Scottish giants, pig-faced ladies, fat children and dancing dogs as unsuitable entertainments for the urban masses, banishing them to even more grim and disreputable quarters.

Reforming measures of this kind continued for several decades until at last that 'naughty, fox-hunting, badger-baiting old England' had been 'improved out of all existence'. 'Where are the amusements of our youth?' wrote Thackeray in 1855. 'I hear of no gambling but amongst obscure ruffians; of no boxing but amongst the lowest rabble. One solitary four-in-hand still drove around the parks last year; but that charioteer must soon disappear . . . He must drive to the banks of Styx ere long.'

The Regency pantomime, long reeling from the withdrawal of its greatest star, was another form on the verge of collapse. 'It is agreed on all hands', wrote Leigh Hunt, as early as 1831, 'that Pantomimes are not what they were.' Joseph Grimaldi *was* pantomime. No other form had grown so dependent on the skills of one man or been defined so thoroughly by the uniqueness of his style, and without him it could not prosper long. Not even the once-mighty 'pantomimic wonders' could save it, as one by one they fell into their own battles with age and illness before the eyes of a largely indifferent public.

Barnes, 'paralyzed by premature age and incurable decrepitude', drank pints of brandy to alleviate his pain, eating the bread of charity and appealing, as the papers put it, to 'the hands of humanity for some nourishment to feed the last vestiges of a lambent flame that nature, in her settled course, must soon extinguish'. On 6 September 1838, a farewell benefit was arranged for him at the English Opera House by Richard Brinsley Peake where, following Grimaldi's precedent, he was led to a chair by Ellar and George Wieland to receive the salutes of a procession of sixteen Clowns, Harlequins, Pantaloons and Columbines, a 'grotesque' scene, according to *The Times*, though 'not without some sentimental feeling'. Twenty-one days later he died, aged fifty. His final request was for his benefit earnings to be passed to his dear friend Tom Ellar, 'who always stuck to me like a brother'. Distant family members interfered, and Ellar got nothing, even though he could barely afford to feed himself.

Like Barnes and Bologna, Ellar had failed to qualify for the Theatrical Fund, a fact that left him extremely bitter. 'We may risk our necks night after night, to draw the only good houses of the season,' he complained to the journalist Thomas Marshall, 'and yet there is no relief for us – though we of all others mostly require it.' The Harlequin who had once appeared to glide above the stage now had a morbid blue complexion and walked with a 'staggering, shuffling gait, as if every sinew in his frame had been slackened by debility'. Released from Covent Garden in 1836, he slipped through the minors until he was finally sacked from the Standard in Shoreditch, more of a beer-shop than a theatre, for stooping to pick up the few halfpennies that had been thrown at him on stage.

Destitute and unemployed, he had taken to playing his guitar on the streets accompanied by a Skye terrier called Spangles who, from his great receptiveness to verbal commands and stubborn refusal ever to set foot on a stage, was generally believed to be a retired theatrical dog. In 1839, having seen his name in Grimaldi's *Memoirs*, he approached Charles Dickens to see if he would ghost his own autobiography, but Dickens, who had greatly disliked his commission as Grimaldi's amanuensis, refused, informing him that such an undertaking could only end in 'disappointment and vexation'. Harassed on the street by the police, Ellar ended up playing his guitar in a gin-house in Shadwell, where the coal-heavers knocked him about for sport. Convinced that it was his fate to die on a dunghill, he was finally picked from his misery by an engagement to play Harlequin at the Adelphi theatre, but died within a few weeks of taking it.

Jack Bologna was the last to go, and though spared the physical suffering of his comrades, he similarly joined them in a rearguard action against the workhouse. After the failure of his mechanical exhibition, he taught dancing until he was taken on as Ebony, the black-faced assistant to Anderson, the Wizard of the North, an inept and controversial magician who had shocked society with his exhibition of two disabled children he called the 'Aztec Lilliputians'. It was this camp and degrading position he held until his death in Glasgow in 1846, aged seventy-one.

With the heart of the pantomime cut out, a new generation of arrangers, like E. L. Blanchard and J. R. Planché, set to work adorning its peripheries, shrinking the denuded harlequinade until it constituted only a few paltry scenes and extending the fairy-tale openings until they came to dominate the piece. Slapstick comedy was replaced with hyper-inflated spectacle and extravaganza – processions, thunderous orchestration and a host of scenic innovations that included ever-more impressive panoramas, animated backdrops and travelogue scenes. Few were happy with the changes. 'Oh! poor old Joey!' wailed the *Theatrical Observer*, having lost its patience with such humourless show. 'One twist of thy mirth-moving countenance was worth all the moving panoramas in the world; – and we would gladly give the Poreibasilartikasparbosporas, with the Russians, Turks, and Dardanelles, the Ambuscade and Battle, the Castle of the Seven Towers, and view of Constantinople to boot to see thee again with thy old colleague, Barnes, in one of thy thousand and one scrapes.'

Commensurate to the rise in spectacle was a general decline in the willingness to tackle current affairs and topical issues. Even more than this, the satirical bite of Regency pantomime was replaced by a sententious creep that sought to impart moral lessons through instructive allegories. This was even the case at Sadler's Wells, where in the 1840s one unimpressed old stager was disheartened to find a Christmas piece 'with neither Harlequin, Pantaloon, Clown, nor Columbine in it; but, no doubt, with a weighty *moral*. One of old Joey's petty larcenies would do more good to the rising generation than twenty *morals*; but so it is – the march of intellect has banished mirth from Sadler's Wells. What will it not effect next?'

'Pantomimes seem to have become partakers of the serious spirit of the age,' concurred Leigh Hunt, 'waiting for the settlement of certain great questions and heavy national accounts to know when they are to laugh and be merry again.'

Those questions would not be answered by the emergence of a new comic force, but rather by the unlikely rulings of a parliamentary select committee. Chaired by Edward Bulwer-Lytton and charged with investigating the state of British drama, it led to the passing of the 1843 Theatre Regulations Act, which abolished the 183-year-old patent theatre system and freed all theatres to perform whatever repertoire they liked under licence from the Lord Chamberlain. No longer required to be mute by law, pantomime refused to be silent. The openings grew longer still until they finally swept away the speechless frolics of Clown, Harlequin, Pantaloon and Columbine, replacing the arts of mime and gesture with the buxom, garrulous puns of pantomime dames and principal boys. Cast into the shadows by the eye-catching glitter that surrounded him, the role of Clown gradually diminished until it finally dwindled into 'a mere mass of gratuitous absurdity without object', with clowns endeavouring, in the words of Dickens's friend, the pantomime historian Andrew Halliday, 'to recommend themselves to the public by dancing on stilts, by walking on barrels, by playing the fiddle with their knees, and by various other devices of the kind', while having 'really nothing to do with the business of the scene'.

Surplus to requirements in theatres, most clowns retreated to the sanctuary of the equestrian ring that had nurtured them in the days before Joey, performing the same balancing acts and circus tricks that had been their bread and butter before the King of Clowns had given them life and purpose. Early Victorian circuses were ramshackle affairs, a far cry from the many-trailered travelling circuses that flourished in America with the advent of the railroads. It was an inching and perilous existence, and that many suffered from chronic indigence and early death only served to reinforce the idea of clowning as a haunted, tawdry trade. Pantomime, meanwhile, struggled to find a new identity, but thanks to the contributions of era-defining music-hall comedians like Dan Leno, the consummate dame, by the end of the nineteenth century it had largely settled into the bizarre, beloved entertainment that abides with us today.

Of Joe, nothing remained except shadows and traces, elusive impressions of long-vacated moments and instants never to be repeated. Some, like Tom Matthews, were unwilling to let the impression fade, and tried to keep the spirit of Joe alive not only through a long and successful career at both Covent Garden and Drury Lane, but also in the form of a tribute act – possibly one of the first in entertainment history. Matthews's homage, worked up twenty years after his master's death, consisted of 'anecdotes and sketches of the history of Grimaldi and in his pantomime days', delivered in the character of Joey and 'wearing even a part of Grimaldi's own dress'.

Playing single-handedly through scenes that included the skeleton scene, and selections from *Mother Goose*, the evening concluded with a rendition of 'Hot Codlins' accompanied by his daughter Clara on the pianoforte. Audiences proved not to be as loyal to the great man's memory as the old apprentice ('owing doubtless to the unpromising state of the weather', reported the *Marylebone Mercury* tactfully), and Matthews discontinued the act. His devotion, however, continued in private, for among his possessions when he died in Brighton in 1889 after being bedridden for a number of years were a wig and a pair of shoes that had belonged to Joe, and the 'painting brush he used to paint that glorious comic face'.

~

Back in Hackney, the clown service was over. I took my suitcase and wandered out into the cold, thanking both the vicar and the Clowns' Chaplain, but declining the invitation to watch the children's show in the community centre across the street. The clowns had done important work, maintaining their community and diligently preserving Joe's memory, yet as I made my way towards the station, I couldn't help wondering whether they were truly the guardians of his legacy. The slap and motley seemed to me a distraction, as the versatility of Grimaldi and the nuances of the harlequinade found their real continuity in music hall, variety, sketch comedy and revue. 'Joey' had been the first great experiment in comic persona, and by shifting the emphasis of clowning from tricks and pratfalls to characterisation, satire and a full sense of personhood, he had established himself as the spiritual father of all those later comedians whose humour stems first and foremost from a strong sense of identity – Charlie Chaplin, for example, Laurel and Hardy, or Tommy Cooper.

There is another, far more significant, legacy that Grimaldi
has given us, an effect on the history of comedy so profound that
it transcends any lineage or transmissible skill: Grimaldi
brought into culture the figure of the sad comedian, the solitary being whose disproportionate talent to provoke laughter
is born of a troubled soul. It was a process helped on its way by
an unlikely source, the Italian psychologist and criminologist
Cesare Lombroso (1835–1909), the 'father of eugenics', best
known for proposing the theory that social deviance might be
predicted by taking careful measurements of a person's head
and comparing them with those of convicted felons.

Lombroso was also interested in the phenomenon of creativity, arguing in an 1891 book, *The Man of Genius*, that what
society recognised as brilliance was in fact the fruit of a split
personality. Of these dual personalities, one is the inverse of
the other, the lack of moderation in either field providing the
creative component with its exceptional force. Thus, radical
thinkers keep conservative habits, actors are withdrawn when
not on stage, and comedians, as illustrated by Lombroso with
the story of Grimaldi visiting Dr Abertheny, are depressed.

Having put the idea into scientific literature, it was taken
up thirty years later by Sigmund Freud, who wrote that
humour was 'among the great series of methods which the
human mind has constructed in order to evade the compulsion to suffer', methods, he adds, which include 'intoxication,
self-absorption and ecstasy' and can ultimately lead to the
madhouse. Like the tears of the clown, the view that laughter
is a diversionary tactic employed by the privately wretched is
a contemporary commonplace, yet without Grimaldi, its first
exemplar, such an analysis would have been inconceivable.

As such, Grimaldi represents the genesis of the modern
idea of comedy – comedy that is not defined by formal rules
of genre, costume or theatrical convention, but as the interlac-
ing shades of light and dark that constitute an individual

psychology. Read almost any interview with or biography of a contemporary comedian and you will detect his influence lurking in the inevitable questions that seek to understand why the subject is drawn to laughter, hoping to unearth some explanatory bullying, neglect, or the tragic death of a parent. This is not to discount the value of such analysis, but rather to recognise that, without Joe, we might not have made martyrs and stoics of those as famous as Tony Hancock, Spike Milligan, Peter Sellers, Lenny Bruce, John Belushi, Richard Pryor, John Cleese, Stephen Fry, Caroline Aherne, Robin Williams and countless others who are all believed to have wrought their humour through battles with their demons.

This is how Joseph Grimaldi has changed us, and if it's a shame that he's not known better for his songs or his jokes, then it should be remembered that it can hardly be any other way. Comedy performed is an untranscribable art, the very mode of transience, a mayfly living in the confluence of the moment that immediately dies. What kind of memorial could there ever be for someone who operated always in the present tense, whose very purpose was to catch his audience by surprise with a visceral alteration of the now? 'To those who never saw him,' wrote a contributor to *Bentley's Miscellany*, 'description is fruitless; to those who have, no praise comes up to their appreciation of him. We therefore shake our heads with other old boys, and say, "Ah! You should have seen Grimaldi!"' As with all the best comedy, you simply had to be there.

APPENDIX

HARLEQUIN AND MOTHER GOOSE; OR, THE GOLDEN EGG!

A Comic Pantomime
by
THOMAS DIBDIN

*First performed at the Theatre Royal, Covent Garden,
on Monday, December 29, 1806.*

The Overture and Music composed by MR. WARE. The Pantomime produced under the direction of MR. FARLEY. The Dances by MR. BOLOGNA, JUN. The Scenery by MESSRS. PHILLIPS, WHITMORE, HOLLOGAN, GRIEVE, HODGINGS, and their Assistants.

MOTHER GOOSE	MR. SIMMONS
COLIN (afterwards Harlequin)	MR. BOLOGNA, JUN.*
AVARO (afterwards Pantaloon)	MR. L. BOLOGNA
SQUIRE BUGLE (afterwards Clown)	MR. GRIMALDI
BEADLE	MR. DENMAN
LANDLORD	MR. P. BOLOGNA
WOODCUTTER	MR. TRUMAN
CABIN BOY (with a song)	MR. SMALLEY
SERGEANT	MR. BANKS
ODDFISH	MR. MENAGE

---

* Some of Jack Bologna's jumps were doubled by John King, a dancer who had been at Covent Garden since 1788.

Gardeners . . . Messrs. Davis, Dick and Morelli. *Waiters* . . . Messrs. Baker and Griffiths. *Villagers, &c.* . . . Messrs. Abbot, T. Blanchard, Brown, Burden, Everard, Fairbrother, Fairclough, Goodwin, Lee, Linton, Meyers, Monk, Odwell, W. Murray, Platt, Powers, Rimsdyck, Sarjant, Street, Tett, J. Tett. Thomas, and Wilde. *Fairies* . . . Masters Benson, Goodwin, Morelli and Searle.

COLUMBINE . . . .   MISS SEARLE
WOODCUTTER'S WIFE . . . .   MRS. WHITMORE

Villagers, Fairies, &c.: Mesdames Benson, Bologna, L. Bologna, Bristow, Cox, Cranfield, Findlay, Follett, Grimaldi, Iliff, Leserve, Masters, Price, Slader, Watts.

In the course of the Pantomime (among others) the following
NEW SCENERY will be introduced:

VILLAGE, with STORM and SUNRISE — (*Hollogan*)
MOTHER GOOSE'S HABITATION — (*Phillips*)
HALL IN AVARO'S HOUSE — (*Hollogan*)
COUNTRY INN. INSIDE OF DITTO. MARKET TOWN — (*Phillips*)
WOODCUTTER'S COTTAGE. PAVILION BY MOONLIGHT — (*Grieve*)
FLOWER GARDEN — (*Grieve*) ST. DUNSTAN'S CHURCH — (*Whitmore*)
ENTRANCE OF VAUXHALL GARDENS — (*Whitmore*)
INTERIOR OF DITTO — (*Whitmore*)
GROCER'S SHOP, Outside — (*Hollogan*)
GROCER'S PARLOUR — (*Phillips*)
MERMAID'S CAVE — (*Whitmore*)
SUBMARINE PAVILION — (*Hollogan*)

The Machinery by MESSRS. SLOPER, BOLOGNA, JUN.,
CRESWELL, and GOOSTREE.
The Dresses by MR. DICK and MRS. EGAN

MOTHER GOOSE;
OR, THE GOLDEN EGG!*

SCENE FIRST
A village, with storm, &c.

Sunset, on the **RIGHT** *are the entrance gates to Squire Bugle's Mansion, adjoining to it Colin's Cottage. A Church with the churchyard in front,* **LEFT**; *the perspective a distant view of a river and a bridge over it; moving objects both on the river and bridge.*

During the storm **MOTHER GOOSE** *has raised, she is seen descending from the skies mounted on a gander. After the storm the clouds disperse, and a Rainbow is seen, the Sun rises gradually, &c., &c.; its golden beams are finely reflected in the windows of the Church.*

A crowd of **MALE** *and* **FEMALE PEASANTS** *assemble, decorated with flowers, to celebrate the nuptials of the* **SQUIRE** *and* **COLINETTE**; *some dance while others sing the following:*

Chorus

Neighbours, we're met on a very merry morning,
    Lads and lasses dressed in all their pride so gay,
To celebrate the happy hour, when maiden shyness scorning,
    Sweet Colinette is married to the Squire to-day
        Old and young
        Join in the throng,
    Cutting nimble capers,
        Haste to the church,
        In the lurch

---

* The following text is based on Thomas Hailes Lacy's edition of *Harlequin and Mother Goose; or, the Golden Egg!*, published in London, undated, though most likely 1807. Some punctuation has been silently modified, and musical cues have been omitted, as have the direction of entrances and exits stage left or right. Emendations for the sake of clarity are marked by square brackets. Omissions are denoted by ellipses.

Leaving care and vapours.
    No one sad,
    Hey! go mad,
Man and maiden seem to say,
    If I know who
    Prove but true,
The next may be my wedding day.

Enter **AVARO**, *leading* **COLINETTE**.

Bugle solo. Enter the **SQUIRE** *from the mansion, equipped for hunting, preceded by* **HUNTSMEN**, **JOCKEYS**, **GROOMS**, *and* **SERVANTS**.

AVARO *presents* **COLINETTE** *to the* **SQUIRE**. *She turns from him and welcomes* **COLIN**, *who appears at the window of the cottage.* **[AVARO]** *interferes.* **COLINETTE** *approaches and points to the tomb of the* **SQUIRE'S** *late wife, which is seen in the centre of the churchyard, bearing the following inscription:*

In Memory
OF
XANTIPPE
WIFE OF
BULLFACE BUGLE, ESQ.

when the **SQUIRE** *jocularly sings the old air of*

First wife's dead
There let her lie
She's at rest,
And so am I.

The **SQUIRE**, **AVARO**, *and* **COLINETTE** *with* **HUNTSMEN**, *&c. march in procession, but are interrupted by* **COLIN**, *who enters from his cottage.* **COLINETTE**, *from an impulse of love, flies to him for protection. They are separated by* **AVARO**, *who with the* **SQUIRE**, **COLINETTE**, *&c. sing the following:*

Sestetto and Chorus

COLIN	When guardians break a promise due.
SQUIRE	Who dare our progress stop?
AVARO	When richer suitors come to woo.
SQUIRE	Such folks as you can hop.
COLINETTE	Yet listen to the injured youth,
AVARO (to SQUIRE)	Your dignity he mocks.
COLIN	I claim her hand.
SQUIRE	Indeed, forsooth! I'll put him in the stocks.
	Then merrily, merrily march away,
	For this shall be my wedding day.
CHORUS	Then merrily, merrily march away,
	It is the Squire's wedding day.
COLIN	This should have been my wedding day.

A **BEADLE** *and* **COUNTRYMAN** *enter, with* **MOTHER GOOSE** *in custody as a reputed witch. The* **BEADLE** *addresses the* **SQUIRE** *as follows:*

BEADLE	So please your worship e'er we go,
	Punish this wicked witch.
MOTHER GOOSE	O fie!
	Good neighbours, why d'ye use me so?
	Indeed, no wicked witch am I.
COLIN	Pity her age.
MOTHER GOOSE	Pray let me loose,
	Don't hurt poor harmless Mother Goose.
BEADLE (to COLIN)	Out of the way, officious fool!
SQUIRE	Go – take her to the ducking stool.
COLIN	Shame, neighbours, shame!
SQUIRE	Don't list to him;
	But try if she chance to sink or swim.
	Mean time merrily march away,
	Because this is my wedding day.
CHORUS	Merrily, merrily march away,
	And keep the squire's wedding day.

While they sing the chorus **COLIN** *rescues* **MOTHER GOOSE** *from the* **BEADLE** *and* **COUNTRYMEN**, *who makes her exit. She is seen to ascend as before.*

The **SQUIRE** *approaches his late wife's tomb and strikes it with his whip. The tomb opens and her ghost appears, which* **MOTHER GOOSE** *has raised, clad in white satin and poppy ribbons, follows the* **SQUIRE**, *shakes her hands at him, and descends through a trap. The* **SQUIRE** *runs off terrified.*

Meantime **COLIN** *and* **COLINETTE** *are conversing with one another. They both exit.*

SCENE SECOND
Mother Goose's Retreat

The front of a thick wood, on one side an entrance, on the other thick foliage, &c; an **OWL** *seated on branch, very prominent in the perspective; a clear blue sky with moon and stars, &c.*

MOTHER GOOSE *enters, and sings the following:*

> The grasshopper chirrups – listen, listen,
>   The cricket chimes in with the sound;
> On water and windows the moonbeams glisten,
>   And dewdrops bespangle the ground.
>
> Then haste from dog rose, briar and bell,
> From dingle, brake, or daisied dell,
> Collect each potent fairy spell
>   Our magic can produce.
>
> To plague yon squire, and to aid
> Young Colin to obtain the maid;
> And when my orders are obeyed
>   You'll laugh with Mother Goose.

CHORUS (*from without*) Ha, ha, ha! – ha, ha, ha!
We'll laugh with Mother Goose.

MOTHER GOOSE   Now softly see Aurora's blush,
Bids cease your revels – hush, hush, hush!

MOTHER GOOSE *waves her stick, when four* **SPRITES** *enter, they dance round her, and afterwards retire. The wood opens and presents* **MOTHER GOOSE'S HABITATION.**

MOTHER GOOSE *exits into her cottage.* **COLIN** *enters in a very desponding state.* **MOTHER GOOSE** *suddenly approaches to address him in these lines, with action appropriate:*

MOTHER GOOSE   Youth, why despair? The girl thou shalt obtain;
This present shall her guardian's sanction gain.

The **GOOSE** *appears*

Nay doubt not, while she's kindly used, she'll lay
A golden egg on each succeeding day;
You served me – no reply – there lies your way.

MOTHER GOOSE *exits.* **COLIN** *appears struck with surprise, feeds and makes much of the* **GOOSE,** *and on looking up his wonder is increased by the disappearance of her cottage. The scene during this period changes to her retreat as before.* **COLIN** *and* **GOOSE** *exit.*

SCENE THIRD
A Hall in Avaro's House

COLINETTE *enters followed by* **AVARO,** *and soon after,* **COLIN.** **AVARO** *endeavours to turn him out, when* **COLIN** *shows him the golden egg.* **COLIN** *brings in the* **GOOSE** *and explains what wealth he may possess; avarice gets the better of* **AVARO'S** *promise to the* **SQUIRE.** **COLIN** *presents him with the golden egg, and he joins* **COLIN** *and* **COLINETTE'S** *hands, but presuming he shall gain all the gold at once by destroying the* **GOOSE,** *he draws his knife, and is preparing to murder it, which* **COLIN** *prevents.*

SQUIRE *enters;* **COLIN,** *fearful of losing his prize, consents rashly to the sacrifice of the bird. The* **GOOSE** *now makes her exit through a panel in the back scene, which turns around and presents* **MOTHER GOOSE,** *who seizes the egg, addresses* **AVARO** *as follows:*

MOTHER GOOSE	Thou avaricious, selfish ingrate elf,
	Like other fools too cunning for thyself;
	Thy ward shall still perplex you by her flight –
	Lo! thus I change the lovers, motley white

(COLINETTE *is changed to* **COLUMBINE** *and* **COLIN** *to* **HARLEQUIN)**

Thou too shalt wander till this egg of gold,
Which in the sea I cast, you once again behold.

The Scene opens and discovers

SCENE FOURTH
The Sea

MOTHER GOOSE *throws the golden egg into the sea. Scene changes back to Avaro's Hall.*

MOTHER GOOSE	Stop, fool! Some recompense is yet thy due.
	(to the **SQUIRE***)* Take that *(changes him to* **CLOWN***)*
	(to **AVARO***)* While thou shalt wear my livery too.
	(changes him to **PANTALOON***)*

Air

For slighted kindness take your due;
    Yet mirth shall with your toils entwine;
Be Harlequin – while you pursue,
    Not Colinette, but Columbine.
(gives **HARLEQUIN** *the sword)* This gift receive, amend what's past,
And guard it better than the last;
    Regain the egg, and happy be,
    Till then, farewell! Remember me!

MOTHER GOOSE *retires, and the comic business begins here.*

*[**CLOWN** and **PANTALOON**] endeavour to secure **HARLEQUIN**, who eludes their grasp, and leaps through the face of the clock, which immediately presents a **SPORTSMAN** with his gun cocked. The **CLOWN** opens the clock door, and a little **HARLEQUIN** appears as the pendulum, the **CLOWN** saying 'Present! Fire!' The **SPORTSMAN** lets off his piece, the **CLOWN** falls down, during which period **COLUMBINE** and **HARLEQUIN**, who had previously entered through the panel, escape.*

*After some tricks, the **CLOWN** runs off in pursuit, with **PANTALOON** on his back.*

SCENE FIFTH
A Country Inn

In front of which is a signpost, 'Chequers', and on it a large puncheon, with the word 'Rum'; a garden seat is on one side of the door, &c.*

*Enter a **RECRUITING PARTY**. They beat up for **RECRUITS** and various characters enter, amongst which is the **CLOWN**, who runs off terrified at the drum. A drunken **COBBLER** is the only recruit gained, who with the **RECRUITING PARTY** enters the Inn.*

***HARLEQUIN** and **COLUMBINE** enter, and go into the Inn; and soon after **HARLEQUIN** is seen at the window of it. **PANTALOON** and **CLOWN** enter, place themselves on each end of the garden seat. **HARLEQUIN** waves his sword – they are thrown against each other off the seat. They change situations, and the like again takes place.*

*The **CLOWN** knocks smartly at the door. The **LANDLORD** appears with a full jug; the **CLOWN** strikes him on the belly as he comes out, upon which he throws the contents of the jug in his face; a fracas ensues; they perceive **HARLEQUIN** at the window, and they exit into [the] house.*

***HARLEQUIN** leaps from the window, smacks his sword, and the rum puncheon descends from the signpost, which he transforms into a fruit*

---

* puncheon: a large punch bowl.

barrow, and a painted puncheon, with a Bacchus* astride, ascends in its place. The **LANDLORD** comes out of his house, and is struck with the change, but wishing for his puncheon again, **HARLEQUIN** changes the painted one into a rum puncheon as before. The **LANDLORD** exits.

[**HARLEQUIN**] now throws off his Harlequin's dress, and appears as a complete St. Giles's **FRUIT GIRL**. The **CLOWN** is seen at the window, and wants to buy fruit. **HARLEQUIN** beckons him down. The **CLOWN** obeys, and endeavours to steal the fruit. **HARLEQUIN** prepares to treat him roughly. **PANTALOON** enters from the Inn, and intercedes for him. The **CLOWN** is forgiven; **PANTALOON** pays him, and exits.

CLOWN makes love to [**FRUIT GIRL**]; a dance is proposed, then a mock opera by the **CLOWN** and **HARLEQUIN**; they both exit. The Scene changes.

SCENE SIXTH
Inside of the Inn

The **LANDLORD** enters, followed by **SERVANTS**, who place chairs and a covered table, and exit. **HARLEQUIN** and **COLUMBINE** now enter and seat themselves. They are surprised by the **CLOWN**, on whom **HARLEQUIN** plays tricks, and he runs off.

HARLEQUIN rings the bell. The **LANDLORD** enters. **HARLEQUIN** asks for concealment. **HARLEQUIN**, **COLUMBINE**, and **LANDLORD** exeunt.

The **CLOWN** enters, followed by **PANTALOON** and the **LANDLORD**. The two latter seat themselves, and are thrown off their chairs. The **CLOWN** sits down at the table and drinks wine, and **PANTALOON** prepares to cut up a pie, when a live **DUCK** flies out of it, and walks forward on the stage, to the surprise of **PANTALOON**, &c., and the gratification of the **CLOWN**, who, with mimic attitude, follows it and seizes it, and runs off.

HARLEQUIN enters. **PANTALOON** runs to the door and shuts it. The **CLOWN** thrusts a chair at him, when **HARLEQUIN** leaps through some

---

* Bacchus: Roman god of wine and revelry.

*club rules.** **PANTALOON** *runs out of the door after him, which the* **CLOWN** *locks. The* **CLOWN** *sits down to regale.*† **HARLEQUIN** *enters from the opposite door, waves his sword, and the magic table ascends. The* **CLOWN** *for some time perceives not his situation, and narrowly examines, walking underneath and around where it stood. He now looks up and sees the table, utters a shout of surprise, and quietly seats himself again, when the table descends and the* **CLOWN** *and chair go up. He halloes.*

Instantly, **PANTALOON** *is heard knocking at the door. The* **LANDLORD** *enters and opens it, when* **PANTALOON** *is struck with amusement at the* **CLOWN'S** *situation. The* **LANDLORD** *exits, and returns with a saw to cut him down, during which time the chair and* **CLOWN** *have descended. The* **CLOWN** *and* **LANDLORD** *seat themselves at the table, when it ascends gradually, and presents a first, a second, and a third tier of tables, covered with cloths, furnished exactly as the first, with two wax lights on each. The* **CLOWN** *and* **LANDLORD** *separate them, when* **PANTALOON, LANDLORD** *and* **CLOWN** *place themselves at the respective tables, the* **CLOWN** *in the centre, and all three tables in line with* **PANTALOON, CLOWN,** *and* **LANDLORD,** *who ascend together to the height of six or seven feet, when the* **CLOWN,** *forgetful of his own situation, is laughing at his neighbours'.*

HARLEQUIN *and* **COLUMBINE** *enter, when another table, to represent a small dining one, is brought on.* **HARLEQUIN** *touches it, and a complete supper appears on it, lit up with six candles, at which instant the candles on the other three tables disappear.* **HARLEQUIN** *and* **COLUMBINE** *enjoy the elevated situation of their exalted friends and exeunt.*

SERVANTS *now appear, are equally surprised, when a humorous scene ensues, by the* **CLOWN** *pelting them with plates, &c. The* **CLOWN,** *during this fracas, catches a cocked hat,*‡ *which has been thrown at him, puts it on, and appears the President Odd Fellow*§ *of the high though not exactly free and easy situation. Scene changes to*

---

* club rules: a list of house rules affixed to the wall.
† regale: eat.
‡ cocked hat: a three-cornered hat with an upturned brim.
§ President Odd Fellow: head of a benevolent society, formed for largely social purposes, whose structure imitated the rites, orders and degrees of Freemasonry.

SCENE SEVENTH
View in a Market Town

A crowd of **VILLAGERS** *enter, singing 'Chorus of the Country Fair'.*

CHORUS   While pipes and tabors rend the air,
                    Neighbours, neighbours, haste to the fair.

MORRIS DANCERS *now enter and exhibit.* **HARLEQUIN** *and* **COLUMBINE** *enter, pursued; they claim protection of the* **MORRIS DANCERS**, *which they accede to.*

LANDLORD, PANTALOON, *and the* **CLOWN** *enter, they hustle them, walk on their hands with their heads downwards, which concludes this scene. Scene changes to*

SCENE EIGHTH
A Woodcutter's Cottage

A **SAILOR BOY** *comes forward and sings the following*

Song

The sea was rough, the clouds were dark,
          Far distant every joy,
When forc'd by fortune to embark,
          I went a cabin boy.

My purse soon fill with foemen's gold,
          I hastened home with joy,
But wreck'd in sight of port, behold
          A hapless cabin boy.

The **BOY** *knocks at the cottage door, his* **MOTHER** *appears, and shortly after the* **WOODCUTTER**, *returning from labour, they exit into cottage.*

HARLEQUIN *and* **COLUMBINE** *enter, pursued, they knock at the door,* **WOODCUTTER** *comes out, they entreat concealment, and their wish is granted.*

Shortly after, the **[BAILIFF]** and **CONSTABLE** come to distrain* the Woodcutter's goods for rent. **[WOODCUTTER** and **FAMILY]** enter, they lament their hard fate, and **HARLEQUIN** condoles with them, finds he has no money about him, but suddenly recollecting his power, he changes a wheel that is seen on the stage to Fortune moving on her axis,† who disperses out her golden favours from her cornucopia, to the gratification and relief of the poor **WOODCUTTER** and **FAMILY**.

The **CLOWN** enters and as usual plunders from the Woodcutter's **WIFE**. **HARLEQUIN** drives him off. **HARLEQUIN** and **COLUMBINE** exit. The **WOODCUTTER, WIFE,** and **BOY** exit. Change.

SCENE NINTH
A Pavilion by Moonlight

HARLEQUIN and **COLUMBINE** enter, dance, &c. He changes two banks‡ to a steel trap and spring gun.§

The **CLOWN** and **PANTALOON** enter. The **CLOWN** is caught by the trap, the gun goes off, and frightens **PANTALOON**, who leads off the **CLOWN** by the leg that is fastened in the trap, when the pavilion is changed by **HARLEQUIN** to

SCENE TENTH
A Flower Garden

GARDENERS bring in three tubs with trees, the centre of one of which is changed by **HARLEQUIN** to a sunflower, and **COLUMBINE** dances a pas seul.

HARLEQUIN, the **CLOWN** and **PANTALOON** appearing, changes the other two trees to statues of himself and Columbine, behind which

---

* distrain: seize property as punishment for non-payment.
† Fortune: the figure of Fortune was traditionally portrayed presiding over a wheel of fate, to which was affixed a cornucopia, or horn of plenty.
‡ banks: benches.
§ steel trap and spring gun: a jawed trap whose activation triggers a shot from a specially rigged musket. Used to ward off poachers and trespassers.

they conceal themselves. The **CLOWN** *knocks down* **PANTALOON***, when* **HARLEQUIN** *links them together, and makes them turn round and round, over head and heels, in which way they exit.* **HARLEQUIN** *and* **COLUMBINE** *exit. Scene changes to*

SCENE ELEVENTH
A View of Golden Square

The **CLOWN** *and* **PANTALOON** *enter. A house with lodgings to let attracts their attention . . . and here a number of whimsical tricks between the* **CLOWN** *and* **PANTALOON** *are displayed by them. They exit into the house.*

HARLEQUIN *and* **COLUMBINE** *enter.* **HARLEQUIN** *knocks at the door, the* **CLOWN** *looks out of the window.* **COLUMBINE** *exit[s].* **HARLEQUIN** *waves his sword and balcony falls. A bustle ensues.* **HARLEQUIN** *exits. The* **CLOWN** *and* **PANTALOON** *come out and exit. Change.*

SCENE TWELFTH
St. Dunstan's Church

A **CROWD** *are assembled to see the figures strike the bell,* [*] *amongst whom is a pieman whom the* **CLOWN** *robs of his pies.*

HARLEQUIN *and* **COLUMBINE** *enter, pursued. He waves his sword. The dial descends, they place themselves on it, and are conveyed to the recess, where the two figures with clubs give place to them. The* **CLOWN** *and* **PANTALOON** *enter, view them with wonder.*

HARLEQUIN *and* **COLUMBINE** *retire, and the two figures with clubs take their original situations. The* **CLOWN** *and* **PANTALOON** *appear entranced, and while they are lost in thought, a* **JEW** *enters. They parley.* **PANTALOON** *bargains for two hats, during which time the* **CLOWN** *pilfers a jacket from the Jew's bag, puts it on, and* **JEW** *exits.*

---

[*] the figures: the church of St Dunstan-in-the-West, Fleet Street, was famous for its clock – the first in London to have a minute hand – and its bell tower that contained the figures of two giants who rang the chimes.

The dial again descends with the two figures, who beat time with their clubs, terrifying **PANTALOON** *and* **CLOWN**, *whose hats are changed by* **HARLEQUIN** *into the two bells. The figures keep close to them, menacing to restore the bells, when* **PANTALOON** *mounts the dial and the* **CLOWN** *clings around it – ascending in this situation. Change.*

SCENE THIRTEENTH
Entrance to Vauxhall Gardens

Various characters now enter, **BEAUX, BELLES,** *and a great variety of mixed company, attended by* **WATERMEN, HACKNEY COACHMEN, LINK BOYS,** *&c.*

The **CLOWN** *enters and puts in practice his old tricks, he pilfers a* **GENTLEMAN** *of his hat and a* **LIGHT HORSEMAN** *of his sword, when the following catch is sung.*

Catch

VISITORS	Here we are, we'll all be merry;
	Vauxhall galas banish care:
WATERMEN	Hope you'll please to pay the wherry –
COACHMEN	Hope you'll pay poor coachee's fare.
1ˢᵗ VISITOR	Hang your nasty skulls and oars;
2ⁿᵈ VISITOR	Come, let's in and see the fun;
1ˢᵗ VISITOR	What's to pay? What monstrous bores;
	What's your number;
COACHMAN	Three and sixpence!
1ˢᵗ VISITOR	I'll take care of Number 1!
COACHMAN	I'll summon you all,
WATERMAN	To Waterman's Hall*
COACHMAN	To Somerset House†
CHORUS	A rare Vauxhall!

---

* Waterman's Hall: situated on the north bank of the Thames near London Bridge, Waterman's Hall was the administrative office of the Company of Watermen, incorporated in the sixteenth century.
† Somerset House: from 1779, the affairs of London's Hackney carriages were overseen by a sub-department of the Royal Treasury located in Somerset House, the Strand.

They all exeunt to the gardens. Changes to

SCENE FOURTEENTH
Orchestra in Vauxhall Gardens

The orchestra is fully illuminated as on a gala night. The **MUSICIANS** *appear in motion. The* **COMPANY** *consists of great variety, and the illusion is completed by the entrance of the* **PANDEAN MINSTRELS** *playing the favourite air.*

The **CLOWN** *enters, and excites much laughter by playing on a large tin fish kettle (which is hung round his neck) with a ladle and whisk, his chin resting on a hair broom, which he supports between his feet. Strikes up. The* **COMPANY** *form a country dance, after which the* **CLOWN** *throws the* **WAITER** *and* **COMPANY** *into confusion by stealing tablecloths, &c., and a scene ensues full of merriment and fun – plates thrown in all directions,* **FOWLS** *fly away off the dishes, &c., when the Scene closes, and all exeunt. Scene changes to*

SCENE FIFTEENTH
A Grocer's Shop and Post Office

The **CLOWN** *enters and steals the letter out of the box. He opens one and secretes some notes, then another – 'Sir, I'll trouble you with a line –' and exhibits a small [noose] which is enclosed in the letter.*

HARLEQUIN *enters, changes the letter box into a lion's head. The* **CLOWN** *advances, puts his hand in to get more letters, and is caught fast in the mouth of the lion. He endeavours to extricate himself, and draws out of the box a little* **POSTMAN**, *who annoys the* **CLOWN** *with his bell.*

A **BAKER** *comes on, sets down his basket, and enters the grocer's shop. The* **CLOWN** *steals a loaf, throws it to* **PANTALOON**, *who now enters and covers the* **POSTMAN** *with the basket. While* **PANTALOON** *and* **CLOWN** *are endeavouring to keep the basket over the* **POSTMAN**, *the top opens and a* **BLACKAMOOR'S HEAD** *appears and recedes. They are both terrified. The* **CLOWN** *goes in and returns with a board.* **PANTALOON** *pops up on one side of the basket, when the* **CLOWN** *breaks the board in two upon his head. They exit.*

Two **PORTERS** *then bring in a chairman['s] horse,*[*] *on which are two chests of tea.* **HARLEQUIN** *and* **COLUMBINE** *enter, pursued, he changes the chests into an elegant sideboard, furnished complete, behind which he and* **COLUMBINE** *hide themselves.* **HARLEQUIN** *changes the Scene to*

SCENE SIXTEENTH
Grocer's Parlour

The **CLOWN** *and* **PANTALOON** *enter, and they drink wine with the magic bottle. The* **CLOWN** *and* **PANTALOON** *go off.* **HARLEQUIN** *changes the sideboard into a bee-hive. Stand the whole of the scene, as if by magic, in one second presents the interior of*

SCENE SEVENTEENTH
A Farm Yard

HARLEQUIN *with* **COLUMBINE** *concealed behind the bee stand; when* **PANTALOON** *and* **CLOWN** *enter, each takes up a bee-hive. The bees swarm about their heads, and they exeunt bellowing. The Scene now changes to*

SCENE EIGHTEENTH
The Mermaid's Cave

The perspective shows the sea through the opening of the cavern.

MOTHER GOOSE *enters, attended by four* **FAIRIES***, whom she addresses in these lines:*

> Your task concludes, your mistress' rage is o'er,
> These wandering mortals, I'll perplex no more,
> Go wake the favourite of my sprites, who sleep
> Within the briny bosom of the deep;
> The spell-bound egg, from bondage to redeem,
> Reward true love, and end our magic dream.

---

[*] chairman's horse: a handcart or barrow.

MOTHER GOOSE and **FAIRIES** *exit when* **ODDFISH** *rises out of the sea. Pantomime for* **ODDFISH**. *Comes forward smacking the serpents that twine around his legs, and takes up two shells* and devours the fish. He then exits.*

HARLEQUIN and **COLUMBINE** *enter, as also soon after* **ODDFISH**. **COLUMBINE** *is terrified and* **HARLEQUIN** *pours wine into the mouth of*

ODDFISH *from his sword.* **HARLEQUIN** *now commands him to dive into the sea for the golden egg, he obeys, and returns with sea-weed which* **COLUMBINE** *receives. He goes a second time, and comes forward with the golden egg.* **HARLEQUIN** *receives it from him.*

CLOWN and **PANTALOON** *enter.* **HARLEQUIN** and **COLUMBINE** *take shelter behind* **ODDFISH**, *who keeps each at bay with his serpents.*

MOTHER GOOSE *enters.* **HARLEQUIN** *presents to her the golden egg, and she reconciles all parties with these lines:*

> The egg returned, receive thy lovely choice.
> The gift is sanctioned by her guardian's voice.
> You soon restored to person, house, and lands,
> Shall like a hearty English squire, shake hands.
> Meanwhile his magic dwelling you shall view,
> Furnished by fairy hands, to pleasure you.

MOTHER GOOSE *waves her stick. Changes to a view of the last scene, representing*

SCENE NINETEENTH
A Submarine Palace

The wings and sides of which are dolphins. In the perspective a tripod of them, and two recesses or alcoves, in each of which is seen a **MERMAID** *busily employed in combing her hair, and the whole terminated by a distant view of the sea.* **DANCERS** *approach habited to correspond with the scene, and at the finale, the* **SQUIRE** *joins the lovers' hands.*

---

* shells: oysters

Chorus – **MOTHER GOOSE, SQUIRE, PANTALOON,** *&c.*

Finale

MOTHER GOOSE	Ye patrons kind, who deign to view
	The sports our scenes produce,
	Accept our wish to pleasure you,
	And laugh with Mother Goose.
CHORUS	And laugh with Mother Goose, &c.
SQUIRE	And let no critic stern reject
	What our petitions beg,
	That we may from your smiles collect
	Each night some Golden Egg.
FULL CHORUS	Ye patrons kind, who deign to view
	The sport we'd feign produce,
	Accept our wish to pleasure you,
	And laugh with Mother Goose.
MOTHER GOOSE	Who humbly begs,
	On bended legs,
	That you, good lack,
	Her cause will back,
	And scorn to crack
	Her Golden Egg.
FULL CHORUS	Who humbly begs,
	On bended legs,
	That you, good lack,
	Her cause will back,
	And scorn to crack
	Her Golden Egg.

Curtain

ACKNOWLEDGEMENTS

NONE OF THIS WOULD have been possible without the friendship, guidance, and gin and ginger ale of my agent, Ben Mason, and the insightful and unfailingly excellent advice of my editor at Canongate, Nick Davies. Both have been a pleasure to work with, and this book would be immeasurably poorer without them. I am also grateful to Andy Miller, who embraced the project when it was just an idea, and Anya Serota, who helped it on its way. Big thanks also to Hazel Orme for her exceptional copy editing, to Elizabeth Lunn and Little Jim Allen for reading parts of the manuscript, and to the judges of the 2007 Jerwood/Royal Society for Literature Prize for non-fiction, Hermione Lee, John Stubbs and Sarah Wheeler, for being so generous and convivial in their assessment of it. More than anyone, I wish to thank my wife, Josie, for her boundless love, support, and willingness to spend at least part of each day discussing sad clowns. Thank you for being so lovely, thank you for our beautiful children, and thank you for largely resisting the inclination to stab me.

During the course of my research, I have been fortunate to encounter many people whose expertise and assistance have been invaluable. These include the Clowns' Chaplain, the Reverend Roly Bain, the Reverend Rose Hudson-Wilkin, of All Saints Church, Jane Moody, of the University of York, Don Nielson, of Arizona State University, Willibald Ruch, of the University of Zurich, Jennie Walton, of the Drury Lane Theatrical Fund, and a shadowy private detective named

Mrs Perkins. An especially large debt of gratitude is owed to transpontine impresario, Horatio Blood, for introducing me to the treasures of juvenile drama, and unreservedly sharing his vast knowledge, list of contacts and unbridled enthusiasm. For that, I remain enduringly grateful.

Thanks also to the many wonderful librarians I have met, especially Elizabeth Falsey of the Harvard Theatre Collection, Marcus Risdell of the Garrick Club Library, and most of all, Laura Taddeo, English Subject Librarian at the University of Buffalo, SUNY, without whose very practical help my research would have been conspicuously harder. I am also grateful for the helpful responses and many photocopied pages I have received from the staff at the Beinecke Library, Yale; the Print and Drawings Room of the British Museum; the British Library; the Brotherton Library at the University of Leeds; the trustees of the Huntington Library, San Marino (who were also kind enough to award me a fellowship); the Islington Local History Centre; the London Metropolitan Archive; the Mander and Mitchenson Collection at the University of Greenwich; the Museum of London; the Rare Book Room at Cornell University; the Thomas Fisher Rare Book Room at the University of Toronto; and the Victoria and Albert Museum.

Finally, as I was working on the last chapter of this book, my brother suffered an accident that left him in a coma. Thankfully, more than a year later, he is fully recovered, and I promise never to take him for granted again. I may not have had this opportunity were it not for the excellence of the doctors and nurses of the York ICU, the professionals at the Goole Neurorehabilitation Centre, and the many old friends and stonemasons who looked out for him, especially Danny Sampson. Most of all, I wish to acknowledge the unremitting care, loyalty and devotion shown by my parents during my brother's time of need, and for teaching me, a parent myself, the true meaning of selfless love.

NOTES

As BEFITS THE LIFE of a popular entertainer, the majority of material on Grimaldi is to be found in informal locations – newspaper reviews, gossip columns, letters, and collections of playbills, memorabilia and theatrical ephemera. In particular, much of what remains has been pasted into scrap-books and 'grangerised' editions of Dickens's *Memoirs* (the process whereby printed texts were dismantled and rebound alongside supplementary material, popular among Georgian and Victorian book-collectors since the 1790s). Specific references are found here in the notes, although my principal sources have been the British Library's Percival Collection of Material Relating to Sadler's Wells, 1683–1849 (14 vols) (hereafter 'Percival'), and three items in the Harvard Theatre Collection: a two-volume 'special copy' of the *Memoirs of Joseph Grimaldi* (London: Richard Bentley, 1846), 'illustrated with upwards of two hundred theatrical portraits, engravings, playbills, autographs, cuttings, etc.'; Augustin Daly's four-volume ex-illustrated edition of the *Memoirs* (also London, 1846); and the 'Grimaldi Scrapbook', whose final entry is dated 28 February 1858. Full details of these and other manuscript sources can be found in the Bibliography.

Introduction

xxi *Mary Shelley's* Frankenstein: See Dalton and Mary Gross, 'Joseph Grimaldi: An Influence on *Frankenstein*', *Notes and Queries*, 28:226, no. 5 (1981): 402–4.

xxii *primarily aimed at adults*: The fact that modern clowns are considered principally to be children's entertainers – an idea that would have appalled the many hardened acrobats and *forains* – is thanks largely to the alteration in audience demographics that were a result of Grimaldi's fame. As his celebrity grew, attendance at the Christmas pantomime increasingly became part of the holiday ritual of many middle-class families: 'not only hosts of holiday school-boys, and girls,' wrote Frederick Reynolds, 'but, grandfathers and grandmothers, and whole families of "children of larger growth"'. The pantomime learnt to accommodate itself increasingly towards its growing juvenile audience throughout the Regency, though it was not until the Victorian period that it became almost entirely infantilised, with clowns throwing sweets into the audience and various characters leading singalongs and playing call-and-response games with the children.

xxii *'a flying wagon'*: William Hazlitt, *The Complete Works of William Hazlitt*, ed. P. P. Howe, 21 vols (London: J. M. Dent, 1930–34), vol. 18, p. 323.

xxv *twenty thousand Londoners*: A mild inflation of David Worrall's 'conservative estimate' from *Harlequin Empire: Race, Ethnicity, and the Drama of the Popular Enlightenment* (London: Pickering and Chatto, 2007), p. 19.

xxvi *'half-idiotic . . . emblem of gross sensuality'*: Charles Dibdin, junior, *Professional and Literary Memoirs of Charles Dibdin the Younger: Dramatist and Upward of Thirty Years Manager of Minor Theatres*, ed. George Speaight (London: Society for Theatre Research, 1956), p. 89 (hereafter 'Dibdin, Memoirs').

xxvi *Grimaldi's lawlessness*: See David Mayer III, *Harlequin in His Element: The English Pantomime, 1806–1836* (Cambridge, Massachusetts: Harvard University Press, 1969), p. 262.

xxvi *'imbued with the spirit of peculation'*: 'Memoir of Joseph Grimaldi', in *Oxberry's Dramatic Biography and Histrionic Anecdotes*, ed. Catherine and William Oxberry, 5 vols (London, 1825–6), vol. 2, pp. 109–22, p. 119 (hereafter 'Oxberry (eds), "Memoir of Joseph Grimaldi"').

xxvi *'suffered under nervous irritation'*: Henry Downes Miles, *The Life of Joseph Grimaldi, with Anecdotes of His Contemporaries* (London: Christopher Harris, 1838), p. 190 (hereafter 'Miles, *Grimaldi*').

The Wonders of Derbyshire

3 *'very Pit or hole'*: Martin Lister, *A Journey to Paris in the Year 1698* (London, 1699), p. 180.

3 *'vast croud of people'*: Lister, *Journey to Paris*, p. 181.

4 *Armenian coffee . . . sweetmeats and pastries*: See Robert M. Isherwood, *Farce and Fantasy: Popular Entertainment in Eighteenth-Century Paris* (Oxford and New York: Oxford University Press, 1986) pp. 23–4, 30.

4 *Comédie-Française*: See Jeffrey S. Ravel, *The Contested Parterre: Public Theatre and French Political Culture, 1680–1791* (Ithaca and London: Cornell University Press, 1999), pp. 118–26.

5 *'deformed concert'*: Ravel, *Contested Parterre*, p. 115.

5 *'Buy my shit, it's fresh'*: (*Qui veut de ma merde? Argent de ma merde; c'est de la fraîche*), Isherwood, *Farce and Fantasy*, p. 32.

5 *'Spiritual Tyranny'*: Anthony Ashley-Cooper, Lord Shaftesbury, *Letter Concerning Enthusiasm* and *Sensus Communis: An Essay on the Freedom*

of Wit and Humour, ed. Richard B. Wolf (New York: Garland, 1988), p. 14. Spelling modernised.

7 *sauteur*: Isherwood, *Farce and Fantasy*, p. 38.

7 *Grande Troupe Étrangère*: See Émile Campardon, *Les Spectacles de la Foire*, 2 vols (Geneva: Slatkine Reprints, 1970), vol. 1, p. 385. According to Philip Highfill, Kalman A. Burnim and Edward A. Langhans, *A Biographical Dictionary of Actors, Actresses, Musicians, Dancers, Managers & Other Stage Personnel in London, 1660–1800*, 16 vols (Carbondale: Southern Illinois University Press, c.1973–93) (hereafter *BDA*) vol. 6, Giovanni was not the Grimaldi of 'Les Enfants Hollandais', as claimed by Findlater (*Joe Grimaldi: His Life and Theatre*, 2nd edn [Cambridge University Press, 1977] [hereafter, 'Findlater, *Joe Grimaldi*'] Appendix A, p. 24). That troupe belonged to an impresario (possibly a relative, also called Grimaldi) active in Germany in 1760. Les Enfants Hollandais published a book of their pantomime scripts.

7 *jump as high as the chandelier*: Campardon, *Spectacles de la Foire*, vol. 1, p. 385.

9 *'Surgeon Operator for the Teeth'*: Advertisements for 'Signor Grimaldi's Most Agreeable Dentifrice Powder' in use 'for years past' date as far back as 1737, along with the claims that he could painlessly draw teeth, fill cavities with lead and even make dentures, 'although this operation is so curiously difficult as to be questioned by many, and particularly some of the profession'. *BDA*, vol. 6; Dennis Arundell, *The Story of Sadler's Wells, 1683–1977* (London et al.: David and Charles, 1965), p. 23.

9 *'danced away on four horse-shoes to Dover'*: Henry Angelo, *The Reminiscences of Henry Angelo*, ed. H. Lavers Smith, 2 vols (New York and London: Benjamin Blom, 1969), vol. 2, pp. 116–17.

10 *a tattered Harlequin's costume*: Miles, *Grimaldi*, pp. 12–13.

10 *nor leaves anything to a son*: Will of John Baptist Grimaldi, 11 March 1760. PROB/11/854.

10 *'she could break chandeliers'*: Thomas Dibdin, *History of the Stage*, quoted in Miles, *Grimaldi*, p. 13.

11 *'the precise degree of relationship'*: *The Drama; or, Theatrical Pocket Magazine*, unidentified clipping, British Library; Miles, *Grimaldi*, p. 13.

11 *part of the retinue of George III's bride*: See *BDA*, vol. 6.

11 *regional tours*: Summer tours offered a particularly lucrative outlet for the Signor's sideline, and whenever he performed in the provinces, as he did in Liverpool in 1760, and Bristol in 1774 and 1775, he made sure first to place a notice in the local paper announcing 'Grimaldi, Surgeon-Dentist, who has had the Honour of attending her MAJESTY, the Prince of Wales, and the Prince and

Princess of Brunswic [sic], and the Happiness of having his Applications crow'd with Success'. *BDA*, vol. 6, pp. 388–97.

12 *'sublime et divin'*: Findlater, *Joe Grimaldi*, p. 46.

12 *'a man of genius'*: Charles Dickens, *The Memoirs of Joseph Grimaldi*, ed. and rev. with notes and additions by Charles Whitehead (London: Richard Bentley, 1846) (hereafter 'Whitehead *Memoirs*'), p. 4, fn.

12 *'Grimaldi is a man of great strength and agility'*: Whitehead *Memoirs*, p. 3, fn.

12 *'the best Clown we ever saw'*: Arundell, *Sadler's Wells*, p. 31.

13 *'symptom of a nation's degeneracy . . . the toil of thinking'*: *The Times*, 11 May 1785; John Corry, *A Satirical View of London; Comprehending a Sketch of the Manners of the Age*, 2nd edn (London, 1803), p. 238.

13 *'pantomimical'*: See John O'Brien, *Harlequin Britain: Pantomime and Entertainment, 1690–1760* (Baltimore and London: Johns Hopkins University Press, 2004), pp. 210, 213.

14 *leave a puppet show*: John de Castro, *The Memoirs of J. de Castro, Comedian*, ed. R. Humphreys (London, 1824), pp. 187–8.

14 *'I must give you Harlequin'*: Cyril W. Beaumont, *The History of Harlequin* (New York: Blom, 1967), p. 91.

14 *insisted on being paid*: Findlater, *Joe Grimaldi*, p. 35. For the jubilee procession, see Martha Winburn England, *Garrick and Stratford* (New York: New York Public Library, 1962), p. 67.

14 *'ye worst behav'd Man'*: *BDA*, vol. 6, p. 391.

15 *'cut his head into two parts'*: Maurice Willson Disher, *Clowns and Pantomimes* (Boston and New York: Houghton Mifflin, 1925), p. 90.

15 *'will not end so comically'*: Disher, *Clowns and Pantomimes*, p. 90.

15 *'a certain class of Londoner'*: C. A. G. Groede, *A Stranger in England; or, Travels in Great Britain* (London, 1807), vol. 2, p. 268. For a thorough account of the theatre career of Charles Dibdin, see Robert Fahrner, *The Theatre Career of Charles Dibdin the Elder* (New York, et al.: Peter Lang, 1989).

15 *'intended to act speaking pantomimes'*: David Worrall, *Theatric Revolution: Drama, Censorship and Romantic Period Subcultures, 1773–1832* (Oxford: Oxford University Press, 2006), p. 254.

15 *'conceived himself under the highest obligations . . . would rather die'*: Charles Dibdin, *The Royal Circus Epitomised* (London, 1784), p. 29.

16 *dangle for hours*: de Castro, *Memoirs*, p. 16.

16 *'playing at top'*: de Castro, *Memoirs*, p. 16.

16 *'a compleat investigation'*: Charles Dibdin, *Royal Circus Epitomised*, p. 29.

17 *to steal the lead from the roof*: *The Times*, 9 May 1785. See also George Raymond, *The Life and Enterprises of Robert William Elliston, Comedian* (London: Routledge, 1857), p. 157.

17 *'he knows, in himself, exactly, the degree of merit'*: Charles Dibdin, *The Professional Life of Mr. Dibdin, Written by Himself, Together with the Words of Six Hundred Songs Selected From His Works, Interspersed with Many Humorous and Entertaining Anecdotes Incidental to the Public Character*, 4 vols (London, 1803), vol. 2, p. 112.

17 *she just thirteen*: William Van Lennep, Emmett L. Avery, Arthur H. Scouten, George Winchester Stone and Charles Beecher Hogan (eds), *The English Stage, 1660–1800: A Calendar of Plays, Entertainments and Afterpieces Together With Casts, Box-Receipts and Contemporary Comment*, 11 vols (Carbondale and Edwardsville: Southern Illinois University Press, 1960–79) (hereafter *'English Stage'*), lists 'Miss' Blagden's first appearance in the bills as 1759 (pt 4, vol. 2).

18 *'began to behave cruelly towards her'*: This section draws heavily from, and is deeply indebted to, Richard Findlater's original research in the Greater London Council archive, then in County Hall. Some of this material, including copies of birth and marriage certificates and the signed papers in which the Signor devolves power of attorney to his solicitor, now resides in the London Metropolitan Archives, though sadly, I have been unable to locate the divorce petition itself. See Charles Dickens, *The Memoirs of Joseph Grimaldi*, ed. Richard Findlater (New York: Stein and Day, 1968), Appendix A, p. 296 (hereafter, 'Dickens, *Memoirs*').

18 *'very much abuse and ill-treat her'*: Dickens, *Memoirs*, Appendix A, pp. 296–7.

18 *affairs with the young dancers.* Arundell, *Sadler's Wells*, p. 19. Findlater (*Joe Grimaldi*, p. 38), states: 'In the Sadler's Wells seasons of 1761 and 1765, he publicly carried on affairs with three sisters, the Wilkinsons, of whom one at least (later Mrs Mountain), was his apprentice.' There is some confusion here, as, though Rosemund Wilkinson, later Mrs Mountain, was indeed the Signor's pupil at the Royal Circus, she wasn't born until *c.*1768, and would have been only four or five years old at the time of his association with Dibdin's project. It is also Findlater's assertion that Caroline Wilkinson gave Grimaldi syphilis.

19 *'chiefly lived in the kitchen'*: Dickens, *Memoirs*, Appendix A, p. 297.

19 *'occasional fairy'*: Gerald Frow, *'Oh Yes It Is!': A History of Pantomime* (London: BBC, 1985), p. 59.

19 *'exercises in music, dancing, oratory, etc.'*: *BDA*, vol. 6, p. 392.

19 '*contracting herself in matrimony*': Deed of Covenant between Joseph [Giuseppe] Grimaldi and Rebecca Brooker. Dated [by another hand?] October 1773. Grimaldi Scrapbook, Harvard Theatre Collection, p. 4.

20 '*Oh dear*': James Boaden, *The Memoirs of Mrs. Siddons, Interspersed with Anecdotes of Authors and Actors* (Philadelphia: Carey et al., 1827), p. 88; Alan Kendall, *David Garrick: A Biography* (London: Harrap, 1985), p. 208.

21 '*a great round cloud*': Louis Simond, *An American in Regency England: The Journal of a Tour in 1810–1811*, ed. Christopher Hibbert (London: Robert Maxwell, 1968), p. 33. Walter Besant, *London in the Nineteenth Century* (New York and London: Garland, 1985), p. 217. The houses in the Clare Market were so close together that it wasn't possible to build a sewer until 1802; until then, residents had to make do with a cesspit in their cellar.

21 *Islington Road*: The announcement that advertised the Signor's benefit night at Sadler's Wells on 18 September 1780 stated that tickets may be had 'of Mr. Grimaldi, at his house, opposite Sadler's Wells gateway, Islington Road'. Whether or not he moved there with Anne Perry is unknown. Percival Collection of Material Relating to Sadler's Wells, 1683–1849 [hereafter 'Percival'], 14 vols, vol. 1. For the Lambeth garden, see Dickens, *Memoirs*, p. 31.

21 '*in dis hose dere be no religion at all*': Angelo, *Reminiscences*, vol. 2, p. 116.

22 '*three or four female servants*': Dickens, *Memoirs*, p. 41.

22 '*three young Grimaldis*': Findlater, *Joe Grimaldi*, p. 49; *English Stage*, pt 5, vol. 2. More intriguing still, especially given the repetition of names across various generations of Grimaldis, is that 'William' was one of the names Joe gave his only son.

22 '*never known to be inebriated*': Dickens, *Memoirs*, p. 31. As Nigel Hamilton reminds us (*Biography: A Brief History* [Cambridge, Massachusetts: Harvard University Press, 2007], pp. 100–28), reputation was the all-important factor guiding biographical accounts in the Victorian period. Reputation was doubly important for a person like Grimaldi, who, though he had earned great celebrity and public affection during his lifetime, possessed very little in the way of material comforts that could define him as a middle-class gentleman. Indeed, with his disability and constant financial worries, it was only reputation that prevented him being aligned with the indigent urban poor.

22 *lifting them by their hair*: Dickens, *Memoirs*, p. 34.

23 '*trebled, or quadrupled the punishment*': Dickens, *Memoirs*, p. 41.

23 '*a street or two long*': Dickens, *Memoirs*, p. 40.

24 '*inexpressible torment*': Jacques-Bénigne Winslow, *The Uncertainty of the Signs of Death, and the Danger of Precipitate Interments and Dissections, Demonstrated*

(Dublin, 1746), pp. 44, 61. *The Uncertainty of the Signs of Death* is not just relentless gore, as by constantly scanning its pages the Signor would have picked up any number of useful tips, including detailed instructions on how to revive a drowned man by blowing tobacco smoke into his anus (p. 161).

24 '*appears as dead*': Findlater, *Joe Grimaldi*, p. 32.

24 '*safe for anoder month*': de Castro, *Memoirs*, pp. 192–3. Joe's *Memoirs*, however, claim the Signor was mortally afeared of the fourteenth of every month.

24 '*visitant from the world of spirits*': 'Reminiscence of Grimaldi, Written by Tom Matthews', *Kentish Independant* [*sic*], 29 May 1858, clipping in Grimaldi Scrapbook, no page number.

25 '*Honest Joe Miller*': J. Milling, 'Miller, Josias (1683/4–1738)', *Oxford Diction-ary of National Biography*, Oxford University Press, 2004; online edn, May 2005 (hereafter '*DNB*').

The Wizard of the Silver Rocks

27 '*serio-comic, prophetic, political, musical piece*': Advertisement in the *Morning Chronicle and London Advertiser*, 16 April 1781; Arundell, *Sadler's Wells*, p. 34. Joe danced with one of his stepsisters, though which one remains unknown. Mary, Findlater's candidate, is dismissed quite reasonably by *BDA* on the grounds that she had been married to Lascelles Williamson for three years by this time and was therefore no longer billed as 'Miss Grimaldi'. For Placido Bussart, see Percival, vol. 1, f. 215.

28 '*first bow and first tumble*': Dickens, *Memoirs*, p. 33.

28 '*eloquent legs*': Miles, *Grimaldi*, p. 5.

28 *début as Little Clown*: While both the *Memoirs* and Miles's *Grimaldi* state that Joe's pantomime début was in Sheridan's *Robinson Crusoe; or, Harlequin Friday*, I follow Findlater (Dickens, *Memoirs*, p. 33, fn. 4) in preferring *The Triumph of Mirth* as a more likely candidate, first for the date, as *Robinson Crusoe* débuted on 29 January 1781, when Joe had just turned two, and second, if we are to believe the many stories that Joe débuted as 'Little Clown', then *The Triumph of Mirth* makes more sense because Signor Grimaldi played Clown in that piece, and Friday in *Crusoe*.

28 *he was in his seventies*: BDA, vol. 6, p. 392.

29 '*a mere baby ting*': Miles, *Grimaldi*, p. 24.

29 *an apprentice of Iron Legs*: This claim is based on Miles's report of Delpini's assertion that he had been an apprentice of 'Nicolini'.

29 '*he runs all hazards*': *The Times*, 2 August 1788.

30 'dampened the remainder of the day's entertainment': Percival, vol. 2, f. 44.

30 'dat is your vortune': Dickens, Memoirs, pp. 37–8.

30 anchors of reason and authority: Modern studies into the family backgrounds of children identified as jokers or class-clowns reveal parents who, like the Signor, fall significantly short of the ideals of love and nurture. Specifically, these parents have difficulty maintaining a sense of consistency and adult equilibrium. They are prone to pettiness, physical or verbal bouts of aggression, and behaviour that seeks constantly to undermine other family members and score points against them. They will often emphasise the great sacrifices they have made on behalf of their children, encouraging them to be more independent while simultaneously criticising the child's lack of polish, and lament their own problems while remaining unsympathetic to other people's. Most importantly, indeed critically so, for the development of a sense of humour within the child is that they were found to hold views that were consistently inconsistent, frequently irrational, and liable to change with little warning. Funny children are used to contradictory instructions and information, such as receiving indiscriminate praise or blame irrespective of their behaviour, or engaging in conversations in which the terms of the discussion could be reshaped at any moment. Though immersion in a world of confused information and emotional volatility might be thought to result in deep anxiety, it appears that funny children grow quickly wise to the erratic behaviour of their parents and are able to see beyond it, learning in particular not to internalise their parents' views of them, but understand them as changeable whims rather than as fundamental truths. Although a healthy way of coping, it does mean that the child develops an understanding of the world as a shifting plane of ambiguities, void of the anchors of reason and the authority a parent conventionally provides, resulting in a heightened sense of the ludicrous. Such children become pathologically dedicated to maximising unpredictability, and thus naturally gravitate towards comedy as they find it exploits all the mechanisms to which they've been most consistently exposed: surprise and uncertainty, refused expectations, unexpected outcomes, paradox and suspended causality. See, for example, Seymour and Rhoda Fisher, Pretend the World is Funny and Forever: A Psychoanalysis of Comedians, Clowns and Actors (Hillsdale, New Jersey: Lawrence Erlbaum Associates, 1981) and Samuel Janus, 'The Great Comedians: Personality and Other Factors', American Journal of Psychoanalysis, 35:2 (1975): 169–74.

31 'opium is to the Turk': Miles, Grimaldi, p. 25.

32 systematically suppressing any theatre: The King's Theatre held a similar patent for opera, and the Haymarket for out-of-season summer shows.

32 'part of our political system': Fintan O'Toole, A Traitor's Kiss: The Life of Richard Brinsley Sheridan (London: Granta, 1997), p. 116.

32 'openly selling and delivering': Simond, An American in Regency England,

p. 45. Exposure to explicit solicitations and bawdy commentary was all part of the evening: 'Not a night passes but these wretched out-casts enter into a dialogue with the Gods of the galleries,' wrote a correspondent for the *Theatrical Inquisitor*, 'and the conversation is not managed with much delicacy on either side.' *Theatrical Inquisitor*, November 1812, p. 144. Auditoria were frequently used as metaphors for social stratification. 'We have three ... different and distinct Classes,' wrote one London guide, 'The first is called the *Boxes*, where there is one peculiar to the King and Royal Family, and the rest for the Persons of Quality, and for the Ladies and Gentlemen of the highest Rank, unless some Fools that have more Wit than Money, or perhaps more Impudence than both, crowd in among them. The second is call'd the *Pit*, where sit the *Judges*, *Wits* and *Censurers* ... in common with these sit the *Squires*, *Sharpers*, *Beaus*, *Bullies*, and *Whores*, and here and there an extravagant *Male* and *Female Cit*. The third is distinguished by the Title of the *Middle Gallery*, where the Citizens' Wives and Daughters, together with the *Abigails* [maids], Serving-Men, Journey-Men and Apprentices commonly take their places.' Roy Porter, 'Material Pleasures in the Consumer Society', in *Pleasure in the Eighteenth Century*, ed. Roy Porter and Marie Mulvey Roberts (Basingstoke: Macmillan, 1996), pp. 19–35, pp. 29–30.

33 *'imitating the lowing of a cow'*: A big laugh encouraged him to try a range of animal impressions, though none of them proved as popular as the first, prompting his friend Hugh Blair to advise, 'My dear sir, I would confine myself to the *cow*!' James Boswell, *Boswell's London Journal, 1762–1763*, ed. Frederick A. Pottle (Edinburgh: Edinburgh University Press, 1991), p. 236, fn. 1.

33 *'hush men'*: Boaden, *Memoirs of Mrs. Siddons*, p. 374.

33 *'unless the play is stopped'*: Linda Kelly, *The Kemble Era: John Philip Kemble, Sarah Siddons and the London Stage* (London et al.: Bodley Head, 1980), p. 84. This is quite probably one of those theatrical anecdotes that has been attributed to any number of well-known actors. It's certainly similar to one appearing in Thomas Dibdin's *Reminiscences*, though this time involving an eccentric actor named Newton, who performed on Mrs Baker's Kent circuit. Confronted by the crying child, Newton said, 'Ma-*dam*, I assure you, upon the veracity of a man and a *gentle*-man, that unless you instantly adopt some method of keeping the play quiet, it will be morally impossible for the child to proceed.' Thomas Dibdin, *The Reminiscences of Thomas Dibdin of the Theatres Royal Covent Garden, Drury Lane, Haymarket, etc.*, 2 vols (London, 1837), vol. 1, p. 226.

33 *'exuberance of liberty'*: Simond, *An American in Regency England*, p. 46.

33 *a piece of brass . . . apple skewered on a knife*: Charles Beecher Hogan, *The London Stage, 1776–1800: A Critical Introduction* (Carbondale et al.: Southern Illinois University Press, 1968), p. cc; Benjamin Crosby, *Crosby's Pocket Companion to the Playhouses, Being the Lives of All the Principal*

London Performers (London, 1796), p. 341. In 1789, a violinist was hurt at Sadler's Wells when a drunken sailor fell from the gallery and landed on his head.

34 *'a regular entertainment'*: Hogan, *London Stage*, p. ccv.

34 *thunderous laughter on its opening night*: Frederick Reynolds, *The Life and Times of Frederick Reynolds*, 2 vols (New York and London: Benjamin Blom, 1969), vol. 1, p. 110.

34 *a train of black velvet*: Linda Kelly, *Richard Brinsley Sheridan: A Life* (London: Sinclair-Stevenson, 1997), p. 88.

34 *'an eye of peculiar brilliancy'*: O'Toole, *Traitor's Kiss*, p. 196.

35 *'funeral pile'*: James Boaden, *Memoirs of the Life of John Philip Kemble, esq., Including a History of the Stage from the Time of Garrick to the Present Period* (Philadelphia: Small, et. al., 1825), p. 116.

35 *'pay us our salaries!'*: Kelly, *The Kemble Era*, p. 111.

35 *first borrow fifty pounds*: The particular victim of this piece of charm was Sarah Siddons, see Clare Tomalin, *Mrs. Jordan's Profession* (London: Penguin, 1995), p. 38, and Kelly, *The Kemble Era*, p. 86.

35 *'So cordial were his manners'*: Boaden, *Life of J. P. Kemble*, p. 117.

36 *'vat a clevare fellow dat Sheridan is!'*: According to Frederick Reynolds, who encountered the Signor when one day out walking with Tom King, the full story, straight from the horse's mouth, goes as follows: 'O vat a *clevare* fellow dat Sheridan is! Shall I tell you? *Oui*, yes, I vill. *Bein donc*. I could no never see him at de theatre, so *je vais chez lui* – to his house in Hertford Street, muffled up in great coat, and I say "*Domestique!* You hear?" "Yes." "Vell, den, tell you master dat M. –, de Mayor of Stafford, be below." *Domestique* fly – and on de instant I be shown into de drawing-room. In von more minute, Sheridan leave his dinner party, enter de room hastily, stop suddenly, stare, and say, "How dare you, Grim, play me such a trick?" Then putting himself in a passion, he go on, "Go sare! Get out of my house." "Begar," say I, placing my back against the door, "not till you pay me my forty pounds," and then I point to de pen, ink, and paper, on von small tables in de corner, and say, "Dere! Write me the check, and de Mayor shall go *vitement entendez vous*? If not, *morbleu*, I vill–" "Oh!" interrupted dis *clevare* man, "if I must, Grim, I must," and as if he were *très pressé* – very hurry – he write de draft, and pushing it into my hand, he squeeze it, and I do push it into my pocket. Vell den, I do make haste to de bankers, and giving it to de clerks, I say, "Four tens, if you please, sare." "Four tens!" he say with much surprise. "De draft be only for four pounds!" O! vat a *clevare* fellow that Sheridan is!' Reynolds, *Life*, vol. 2, pp. 231–3.

36 *'magnificent and appalling creature'*: See Leigh Hunt, *The Autobiography of Leigh Hunt, with Reminiscences of His Friends and Contemporaries*, 2 vols (New York: AMS, 1965), vol. 1, p. 158.

37 *'Was it a miserable day?'*: Reynolds, *Life*, vol. 2, p. 317.

37 *'the sobs, the shrieks'*: Boaden, *Memoirs of Mrs. Siddons*, p. 161.

38 *'conscience … conshince'*: See Hunt, *Autobiography*, vol. 1, p. 188.

38 *'It is ojus'*: Hogan, *London Stage*, p. cxiii.

38 *'part baby-talk'*: Amanda Foreman, *Georgiana, Duchess of Devonshire* (New York: Modern Library, 2001), p. 45.

39 *'persons who had rendered themselves … crime and danger for the gratification'*: James Peller Malcolm, *London Redivivum*, 4 vols (London, 1803–7), vol. 3, p. 233; Arundell, *Sadler's Wells*, pp. 21–2. A letter from Winifred Jenkins, the young Welsh maid in Tobias Smollett's novel *The Expedition of Humphry Clinker* (1771), provides us with a fictional visitor's view of the entertainment on offer, as well as the immoderate behaviour of its patrons: 'I was afterwards of a party at Sadler's-wells, where I saw such tumbling and dancing upon ropes and wires, that I was frightened and ready to go into a fit — I tho't it was all inchantment; and, believing myself bewitched, began for to cry — You knows as how the witches in Wales fly upon broom-sticks: but here was flying without any broom-stick … and firing of pistols in the air, and blowing of trumpets, and swinging, and rolling of wheel-barrows upon a wire (God bless us!) no thicker than a sewing-thread; that, to be sure, they must deal with the devil! — A fine gentleman, with a pig's-tail, and a golden sord by his side, come to comfit me, and offered for to treat me with a pint of wine; but I would not stay; and so, in going through the dark passage, he began to shew his cloven futt, and went for to be rude: my fellow-sarvant, Umphry Klinker, bid him be sivil, and he gave the young man a dowse in the chops.' Tobias Smollett, *The Expedition of Humphry Clinker*, ed. Lewis M. Knapp (Oxford: Oxford University Press, 1992), p. 108; Arundell, *Sadler's Wells*, p. 37.

40 *a blunderbuss*: See Dickens, *Memoirs*, p. 199, fn. 1.

40 *'throwing in their dogs, etc.'*: Arundell, *Sadler's Wells*, p. 31.

40 *'best made men in England'*: Malcolm, *London Redivivum*, vol. 3, p. 235.

40 *'roast beef'*: See Jane Moody, *Illegitimate Theatre in London, 1770–1840* (Cambridge: Cambridge University Press, 2000), p. 24.

41 *'orchestral twinklings'*: Moody, *Illegitimate Theatre*, p. 41.

41 *The Battle of Fockschau*: Arundell, *Sadler's Wells*, p. 46.

42 *'Opera House on a Saturday night'*: 'At the moment, when the gallant assailants seemed secure of victory, a retreat was sounded, and Moustache and his adherents were seen receding from the repulse, rushing down the ladders, and then, staggering towards the lamps, in a state of panic and dismay … These great performers having had no food since breakfast, and knowing that a fine, *hot supper*, unseen by the audience, was placed for them at the top of the fort, they naturally speeded towards it, all hope, and exultation; when just as they were about to commence operations, Costello, and his assistants commenced theirs, and by the smacking of whips, and other threats, drove the terrified combatants back in disgrace.' Reynolds, *Life*, vol. 1, pp. 262, 264. Arundell, *Sadler's Wells*, p. 37.

42 *a singing duck*: Arundell, *Sadler's Wells*, p. 38.

42 *'degrade a bagnio'*: Sir Walter Scott, 'Essay on the Drama', in *The Miscellaneous Prose Works of Sir Walter Scott, Bart.*, 3 vols (Edinburgh: Robert Cadell, 1850), vol. 1, pp. 615–16, Ian Kelly, *Beau Brummell: The Ultimate Man of Style* (New York: Free Press, 2006), p. 169.

43 *'perceptible change in his countenance'*: William Makepeace Thackeray, *The Four Georges*, in *The Works of William Makepeace Thackeray*, vol. xviii (New York: P. F. Collier, n.d.), p. 373.

43 *'My wine bills were very large'*: Michael Kelly, *Reminiscences*, ed. Roger Fiske (London: Oxford University Press, 1975), p. 210.

43 *'Composer of Wines'*: James Robinson Planché, *The Recollections and Reflections of J. R. Planché*, 2 vols (London: Tinsley Bros., 1872), vol. 1, p. 38.

43 *major lapses in judgement*: See Kelly, *Kemble Era*, pp. 104–5.

44 *'served up as a dessert'*: See Worrall, *Theatric Revolution*, pp. 254–5.

44 *'infant phenomenon'*: Charles Dickens, *Nicholas Nickleby* (London: Mandarin, 1991), p. 322. In 1880, after the introduction of numerous child labour laws, and a general attitudinal shift in relation to child performers, Augustus Harris, under the pseudonym 'Feraldt', still defended the practice of employing children on the stage: 'For all the School Board may advance, and serious families may oppose to the contrary, this engaging of children at the hardest season of the year helps many a father and mother over the winter, and without in any way doing harm to the child. They are fairly paid, look upon the whole thing, in spite of coercion and fatigue, as a game, and are taught their drill in addition to learning obedience and the pleasure of emulation.' Michael R. Booth (ed.), *English Plays of the Nineteenth Century, V: Pantomimes, Extravaganzas, and Burlesques* (Oxford: Clarendon, 1976), pp. 504–9, p. 506. In 1889, William Gardner, of the Crystal Palace Company, was fined 2s. 6d. at the instance of the London School Board for employing seven under the age of ten, and nine others over ten in the

Christmas pantomime and keeping them from their studies. *The Times*, 28 January 1889.

44 *'greatest Nursery of Misery and Vice'*: Tomalin, *Mrs. Jordan's Profession*, p. 50.

44 *children were everywhere*: See Tomalin, *Mrs. Jordan's Profession*, p. 149; Findlater, *Joe Grimaldi*, p. 98; Robert Shaughnessy, 'Siddons, Sarah (1755–1831)', *DNB*.

45 *flying chariot*: de Castro, *Memoirs*, p. 36.

45 *'they made such a terrible noise'*: Kelly, *Reminiscences*, p. 208.

46 *'an unfinished house'*: Andrew Halliday, *Comical Fellows; or, the History and Mystery of the Pantomime* (London: Thomson, 1863), p. 73. See also 'A stage-manager will tell you that it is as impossible to do without strong language during the performance of a pantomime, as it is to command a man-of-war without it, in a gale of wind', Halliday, *Comical Fellows*, p. 93.

46 *soles pressed flat*: See A. H. Saxon, *The Life and Art of Andrew Ducrow, and the Romantic Age of the English Circus* (Hamden, Connecticut: Archon, 1978), p. 40.

47 *intervened to stop one of the beatings*: Saxon, *Ducrow*, p. 41.

47 *'the avarice of unnatural parents?'*: Findlater, *Joe Grimaldi*, p. 29.

47 *a crank minority*: Not until 1879 did an act come into force barring circuses, theatres, music halls and 'other places of public amusement' from using children under fourteen in performances or exhibitions that might be dangerous to life or limb. Any parent or guardian found in violation of the act was to be fined, the amount 'not to exceed ten pounds'. See Brenda Assael, *The Circus and Victorian Society* (Charlottesville and London: University of Virginia Press, 2005), p. 159.

47 *'the infant son of Grimaldi '*: *English Stage*, vol. 6, pt 5, p. 703.

47 *'with the utmost velocity'*: Dickens, *Memoirs*, p. 37.

47 *'camphorated oil and spirits'*: Findlater, *Joe Grimaldi*, pp. 230–1, fn. 14.

48 *'like Bottom the Weaver'*: *Monthly Magazine*, August 1837, clipping in the Extra-Illustrated *Memoirs of Joseph Grimaldi* (London: Richard Bentley, 1846), Harvard Theatre Collection, 2 vols (hereafter 'Bentley ex-ill.'), vol. 1.

48 *'laugh, scream, and speech'*: William Robson, *The Old Play-goer* (Fontwell: Centaur, 1969), p. 239.

49 *'scanty mutton scrags'*: J. C. Drummond, Anne Wibraham and Dorothy Hollingsworth, *The Englishman's Food: A History of Five Centuries of English Diet* (London: Jonathan Cape, 1958), pp. 114, 227. Small beer had an alcohol content of between two and three per cent, and was drunk at every meal. Fermented alcoholic drinks were often safer than drinking water.

Harlequin's Frolics

51 *'extremely ill'*: *BDA*, vol. 6, p. 393.

51 *'partly new and partly selected from old'*: *London Stage*, pt 5, vol. 2, p. 766.

52–3 *John Williams*, pseud. Anthony Pasquin, *The Children of Thespis. A Poem*, 3 parts (London, 1786–8). On Pasquin, see *DNB*, James Sambrook, 'Williams, John (1754–1818)'. The full section devoted to Giuseppe Grimaldi reads:

> What monster is this, who alarms the beholders,
> With Folly and Infamy perch'd on his shoulders;
> Whom hallow'd Religion is lab'ring to save,
> Ere Sin and Disease goad the wretch to his grave,
> 'Tis —! Alas, Nature starts at the name;
> And trembles with horror, and reddens with shame!
> Like the Ocean which weeps, when the tempests allay'd,
> She shudders to look on the work she has made.
> I marvel that God does not open the place,
> To ingulph him, like Corah, and all his foul race.
> In their hate of his principles, all are agreeing,
> And the fruit of his loins curse the cause of their being.
> Like a pestilent breeze, he infects these sad times,
> A vile abstract of hell, and Italia's crimes!
> See Justice offended, exhibits a halter;
> And the crucifix shakes as he crawls to the altar:
> E'en Angels drop tears in such habits to find him:
> As he throws Retribution with horror behind him.
> When his soul disembogues each infernal transgression,
> Sweet Mercy revolts at the sable confession.
> And Honour and Truth form a strong combination
> To kick such a miscreant thro' the creation.
> Lo! Eternity's paths he with terror explores,
> As dæmons look up from sulphureous shores:
> While Tartarean bards chaunt the caitiff's encomium,
> And Satan sits hunger'd in deep Pandemonium.
>
> His touch is contagious and preys on our sanity,
> Offensive to life, and abhorr'd by humanity.
> Like the plague-fraught embrace of a foul Alepponian,
> Or the incrusted glove of a sick Caledonian;
> It nips Virtue's bud, like the winds from the east,
> Or Circe's fell wand, turns the fool to a beast:
> Or that hot-bed of vagabonds, rais'd on the breast
> Of fallen Britannia, to sing her to rest;
> Where anticks Discretion can kick till she winces,
> And rascal castratos strut prouder than princes:

Where Countesses fight, to kiss sapless Tenducci;
Or tie on the sandals of black Catenucci.

Is it wond'rous that you such antipathy see,
When the tyrant to Virtue's a tyrant to me?
Go, shew me the den where a scoundrel's confin'd,
I'll strike his black heart, and unnerve his base mind;
I'll goad him thro' life with the rod of Correction,
Till his scull pendant locks shall turn grey with reflection;
From the arm of a Titan I'd tear him elate,
Tho' guarded by all the artillery of Fate:
If I quit him, may Peace and my penitence sever;
And the smiles of Omnipotence leave me for ever.

It boots not with me if his infamous darings
Are hid by a star, or armorial bearings:

As Gregory made the proud Emperor wait,
Bare-footed and cold, at Canusium's gate;
E'en thus shall the haughty bend low at my nod,
Confess their allegiance, and honour my rod.

Nefarious island! oh, besotted nation!
Where Folly, to Vice, runs in studied gradation.
See Guilt on the judgment seat, mark'd by pollution,
To watch the degrees of a mean prosecution;
To determine the outlines of right and of wrong,
As manacled Honour is led thro' the throng;
To meet cunning Sophistry's wily position,
And the half famish'd sons of illicit Ambition.

Say, who shall be bless'd, if a Howard's unsainted!
Say, who is unsullied, if Curtius is tainted!
But his worth, like true gold, from the chemical fire,
Will rise less alloy'd, and be valu'd the higher;
And the lie of the moment, which Malice had sign'd,
Sweet Truth shall expunge from the national mind:
As the lion, awak'ning on Nemea's plain,
Indignant shakes off the dank dew from his mane (pp. 88–90).

53 *paid for his crimes in full*: I give the date as 14 March, rather than the 16 Findlater provides, after the unidentified clipping in the Islington Local History Centre that reads 'On Friday died Mr. Grimaldi ... .' 14 March 1788 was a Friday. Not only actors lived off Stangate Street. Rudolph Cabanel, the machinist who made all the elaborate stage equipment for Henry Holland's new Drury Lane, also kept his workshops there.

54 *clapping his hands*: Dickens, *Memoirs*, p. 42.

54 *'Don't be such a fool'*: Dickens, *Memoirs*, p. 42.

54 *'jumped from the bier'*: Dickens, *Memoirs*, p. 43.

54 *'fallen from the cliff at Margate'*: Thomas Goodwin, *Sketches and Impressions: Musical, Theatrical, and Social, 1799–1885* (New York and London: Putnam, 1887), p. 16.

55 *'disputes ... for the teeth'*: 'The Will of Joseph Grimaldy, otherwise Grimaldi', 25 February 1786, PROB 11/1163. See also *BDA*, vol. 6, pp. 388–97; Disher, *Clowns and Pantomimes*, p. 88.

55 *'disagreements with managers'*: 'Obituary: Joseph Grimaldi', *Gentleman's Magazine*, September 1837, p. 319.

55 *'Dancing Master, Dentist, Conjurer'*: Unidentified newspaper clipping, Islington Local History Centre.

56 *having had candles applied to their feet*: Winslow, *Uncertainty of the Signs of Death*, p. 25.

56 *'sever my head from my body'*: 'Will of Joseph Grimaldy'.

56 *'a headstone'*: Northampton Chapel, Exmouth Street, was demolished in 1886. The fate of the Signor's remains is unknown.

56 *'Grim-All-Day-at-Breakfast'*: Burney Collection of Theatrical Portraits, vol. 6, no. 7435. British Museum, Prints and Drawings.

56 *the Signor's estate*: In 1778, Sheridan purchased Willoughby Lacy's half of the lease to Drury Lane for £31,500. See F. H. W. Sheppard (ed.), *The Theatre Royal, Drury Lane and The Royal Opera House, Covent Garden*, in *Survey of London*, vol. XXXV (London: Athlone, 1972), p. 16.

57 *frequently changing address*: This point is made by the editors, *BDA* (vol. 6, p. 396), who note that the Signor's several addresses at that time included lodgings in the insalubrious Princes Street, Clare Market.

58 *'in the likeness of a Monkey'*: Findlater, *Joe Grimaldi*, p. 232, fn. 15.

58 *'Mind, John'*: Dickens, *Memoirs*, p. 46.

61 *'like a Spanish play'*: Foreman, *Georgiana*, p. 207. 'I do not mean to accuse him of duplicity,' wrote the Duchess of Devonshire, in addition, '... but he cannot resist playing a sly game.'

61 *'something undefined, if not undefinable'*: John Genest, *Some Account of the English Stage from the Restoration in 1660 to 1830*, 10 vols (Bath: Carrington, 1832), vol. 6, p. 522–3.

62 *'dare not innovate for my life'*: Thomas Dibdin, *Reminiscences*, vol. 1, p. 15.

62 *'To be critically exact'*: Kelly, *Kemble Era*, p. 70.

62 *it pained him greatly*: Which is not to say that Kemble was himself a miserable ascetic. Sir Walter Scott recalled how Kemble was one of the few people who could induce him into getting drunk.

63 *'LAUGHABLE, and VERY CHEAP'*: Thomas Dibdin, *Reminiscences*, vol. 1, p. 201.

63 *'Bastille must bring money'*: George Taylor, *The French Revolution and the London Stage, 1789–1805* (Cambridge: Cambridge University Press, 2000), p. 42.

63 *The remainder of the evening*: Dickens, *Memoirs*, p. 47.

64 *in less than eight minutes*: Dickens, *Memoirs*, p. 47.

64 *deathbed confession of Pietro Carnevale*: *English Stage*, vol. 2, pt 5, p. 1087, fn. 6.

64 *'he would inherit that clown's fame'*: *The Times*, 13 August 1790.

64–5 *'that excellent performer'*: *The Times*, 20 August 1788.

65 *'Goliath of clowns'*: Dibdin, *Memoirs*, p. 41; *The Monthly Mirror*, April 1797; *BDA*, vol. 4, pp. 483–5.

65 *a trick-riding clown*: See *BDA*, vol. 4, pp. 483–5; Findlater, *Joe Grimaldi*, p. 55; *The Times*, 24 April 1786.

65 *'in a manner far superior'*: *The Times*, 22 May 1787; *The Times*, 15 January 1787.

65 *'julking'*: See Saxon, *Ducrow*, p. 31.

66 *'dark, malicious and ambitious part'*: Dibdin, *Memoirs*, p. 118.

66 *'horror, guilt, confusion and revenge'*: Malcolm, *London Redivium*, vol. 3, p. 236.

67 *'human nature, debased'*: Malcolm, *London Redivium*, vol. 3, p. 236.

67 *'like a tiger of his prey'*: Malcolm, *London Redivium*, vol. 3, p. 236.

67 *'the Cymbals'*: *The Times*, 10 August 1799; Arundell, *Sadler's Wells*, p. 54.

68 *safely to Holyhead*: Dibdin, *Memoirs*, pp. 32–3.

68 *'amusements under Dubois'*: Bentley ex-ill., vol. 1, p. 10.

68–9 *'little Marmozet'*: *The Times*, 28 December 1789.

69 *failure to pay the rent*: Sheppard, *Survey of London*, p. 32.

70 *'a handsome Italian'*: Findlater, *Joe Grimaldi*, p. 54.

70 *'well behaved honest people'*: Arundell, *Sadler's Wells*, p. 39.

70 *flute through each nostril*: Arundell, *Sadler's Wells*, pp. 39–40. As a family, the Bolognas also did tableaux and posture work. *The Times*, 11 August 1792,

carries an advertisement for 'a pleasing Exhibition of Strength and Posture Work, entirely new called LE TABLEAU CHINOIS, by Signor Bologna and his Children. In which will be displayed a variety of curious and striking manoeuvres.'

70 'trick and expression': BDA, vol. 2, p. 191.

71 'Satan arraying his Troops': See Richard D. Altick, The Shows of London (Cambridge, Massachusetts et al.: Belknap/Harvard University Press, 1978), p. 121–2.

72 Bartholomew Fair: Altick, Shows of London, p. 86.

72 'manager is the monarch': Thomas Holcroft, The Life of Thomas Holcroft, ed. Elbridge Colby, 2 vols (New York: Blom, 1968), vol. 1, p. 153.

72 'not of the first rate': BDA, vol. 8, p. 28.

73 'the most inconvenient in England ': Findlater, Joe Grimaldi, p. 69.

73 'industrious to an extreme': BDA, vol. 8, p. 28.

73 'punctuality, propriety and attentiveness': BDA, vol. 8, p. 28.

73 'the most abject servility': Dibdin, Memoirs, p. 41; Arundell, Sadler's Wells, p. 77.

74 'St. James's Square': The Times, 28 June 1793.

74 armoury of fearsome weapons: Dibdin, Memoirs, p. 43.

75 capacity of almost four thousand: The actual seating capacity of the 1794 Drury Lane is only ever an estimated figure. Mine is based on the 3,919 cited in Sheppard, Survey of London, p. 52.

75 anticipation and intimacy: Boswell, London Journal, pp. 256–7.

75 'vast void ... a wilderness of a place': Torrington, quoted in Hogan, London Stage, pp. xliv-xlv; Siddons, quoted in Joseph Donohue, Theatre in the Age of Kean (Oxford: Blackwell, 1975), p. 18. One observer complained in 1810, 'Not a feature of the face can be distinguished, far less the variations and flexibility of the muscles, the turn of the eye and graceful action.' Donohue, p. 19.

76 'loud explosions': John Philip Kemble, Lodoiska: An Opera in Three Acts (London: n.d. [1794]), p. 56.

76 impromptu stunt: See Paul Ranger, 'Terror and Pity Reign in Every Breast': Gothic Drama in the London Patent Theatres, 1750–1820 (London: Society for Theatre Research, 1991), pp. 46–9.

76 feed this grandiosity: In his Memoirs, John Bannister wrote that Drury Lane 'was now become a sort of political, financial association. Large debts were contracted secured by renters' shares, with nightly payments and free admissions: the practice soon arose of engaging greater companies in every

department of the drama than could possibly be brought into action in any one night of performance; and often players, who were not wanted, were retained, that they might not increase the size of the rival establishment. All this had more the air of pushing a trade than promoting a liberal art, and the high estimation of theatres diminished in consequence.' John Adolphus, *Memoirs of John Bannister, Comedian*, 2 vols (London: Richard Bentley, 1839), vol. 1, p. 331.

77 *still earning less*: See Findlater, *Joe Grimaldi*, p. 67.

The Flying World

80 *sodomy*: Together, Dibdin and Bickerstaffe had written one enormously successful opera, *The Padlock* (1768), in which Dibdin had also starred as Mungo the comic African servant. The part, with its popular catchphrase 'Mungo here, Mungo dere', is notable for being the first comic blackface role in history and therefore a direct antecedent to later racist minstrelsy.

80 *'should not know him'*: Holcroft, *Life*, vol. 2, p. 238.

80 *a move that greatly angered his father*: See Dibdin, *Reminiscences*, vol. 1, pp. 10–12.

80 *'Write to Tom Dibdin'*: Dibdin, *Reminiscences*, vol. 1, p. 311.

80 *'the triplicate horrors'*: Dibdin, *Reminiscences*, vol. 1, p. 134.

81 *John Street Theatre*: Disher, *Clowns and Pantomimes*, p. 94.

81 *'Every ill my thoughts employ'*: Disher, *Clowns and Pantomimes*, p. 93.

82 *'heart and soul'*: Leigh Hunt, *Leigh Hunt's Dramatic Criticism, 1808–1831*, ed. Lawrence Hutson Houtchens and Carolyn Washburn Houtchens (New York: Columbia University Press, 1949), p. 88.

83 *'ate little, drank little, slept less'*: Dickens, *Memoirs*, p. 55.

84 *The table was carrying sixteen men*: Dickens, *Memoirs*, p. 59. See classified advertising for Sadler's Wells in *The Times*, 5 May 1796. Arundell (*Sadler's Wells*, p. 55) names one of the Sicilian strongmen as 'Signor Saccardi' although it is also possible that the performer was the 'French Hercules' of Sadler's Wells, mentioned by Henry Angelo in his *Reminiscences* (vol. II, p. 8): 'Lying upon his back, with his legs and arms he raised from the ground, and supported for half a minute, sixteen moderate-sized men, who were standing upon a long table.'

85 *tendency to mix up his words*: Findlater, *Joe Grimaldi*, p. 174, records several examples of Joe's malapropisms.

86 *the natural choice to succeed*: *English Stage*, vol. 3, pt 5, Drury Lane, 11 November 1796.

87 *starting to look fat*: BDA, vol. 2, p. 195.

89 *'a conjuror's study'*: Richard Wheeler's Memoir from the Clerkenwell Workhouse, Percival, vol. 4, p. 191.

89 *'hated Grimaldi'*: Dickens, *Memoirs*, p. 80.

91 *'come and welcome him'*: Dickens, *Memoirs*, p. 87.

91 *'winning the affections of a young lady'*: Dickens, *Memoirs*, p. 91.

92 *'a pretty young wife'*: Dickens, *Memoirs*, p. 110.

92 *'merry as a marriage bell'*: Dickens, *Memoirs*, p. 104.

93 *'buy anything'*: Dibdin, *Memoirs*, p. 17.

93 *'the Astleyian fancy'*: Dibdin, *Memoirs*, p. 18.

93 *'never let 'm have anything to eat'*: Alfred Bunn, *The Stage: Both Before and Behind the Curtain, from Observations Taken on the Spot*, 3 vols (London: Bentley, 1840), vol. 1, p. 59; Dibdin, *Memoirs*, p. 20.

93 *Astley was immovable*: Dibdin, *Memoirs*, p. 20.

94 *stayed for the next nineteen and a half years*: Dibdin, *Memoirs*, p. 21.

94 *pulled him aside*: Dibdin, *Memoirs*, p. 43.

94 *'peculiar whimsicality'*: Dibdin, *Memoirs*, p. 43.

94 *'majestic strength'*: *The Times*, 2 August 1799.

94 *performing academy for children*: BDA, vol. 4, p. 484.

95 *doubts about Charles*: BDA, vol. 4, p. 482. Charles Dubois's first appearance at Sadler's Wells was in *Meadea's Kettle* on 9 April 1792. My assertion that he was around eleven or twelve in 1800 is based on the conjecture that he made his début between the ages of three and four, as was the course for theatrical progeny.

95 *'more extravagant than it had been the custom'*: Dibdin, *Memoirs*, p. 48.

96 *'Come, ladies'*: Dibdin, *Memoirs*, p. 65.

96 *tax on wig powder*: George Rudé, *Hanoverian London, 1714–1808* (Berkeley and Los Angeles: University of California Press, 1971), pp. 236–7.

97 *'musical bagatelle'*: *The Times*, 21 April 1800.

97 *London's premier clown*: *The Times*, 14 April 1800.

97 *'I'll be damned if you do!'*: Arundell, *Sadler's Wells*, p. 62.

97 *suggestive looks*: *The Times*, 21 April 1800.

98 *'magic, quickness and variety'*: Disher, *Clowns and Pantomimes*, p. 97.

98 *'a Taylor's box'*: *The Times*, 21 April 1800.

98 *'dealing with the Devil'*: *The Times*, 26 April 1800.

99 *elbows jammed*: Dibdin, *Memoirs*, p. 44.

99 *'Nobility of the first rank'*: *The Times*, 5 May 1800. The bill, continued the correspondent, proves 'that after all, the priority of existence, and elegance of plan in amusements over other similar Theatres, will always give Sadler's Wells the decided preference in point of respectability; particularly when exertions like those which have been made this season are set on foot for the reception of the public ever mindful of those who study its satisfaction'.

99 *the clown fraternity*: *BDA*, vol. 6, p. 408.

99 *apprentices of the Signor*: See Disher, *Clowns and Pantomimes*, p. 90.

100 *hungry to acclaim raw and unaffected talents*: The greatest beneficiary of this urge was Edmund Kean, lauded as a force of nature when contrasted with Kemble's stiff, declamatory style. Jacky Bratton has called this phenomenon, first noted in Georgian theatre, 'the "natural" newcomer who suddenly exposes the theatrical establishment as stylised and old-fashioned'. Jacky Bratton, 'The Celebrity of Edmund Kean: An Institutional Story', in Jane Moody and Mary Luckhurst (eds), *Theatre and Celebrity in Britain, 1660–2000* (Basingstoke: Palgrave, 2005), pp. 90–106, p. 90.

100 *'as Clown and singer of Clown's Songs'*: Dibdin, *Memoirs*, p. 41.

101 *Childbirth had claimed another victim*: See Lawrence Stone, *The Family, Sex and Marriage in England, 1500–1800* (Harmondsworth: Penguin, 1979), p. 64.

101 *'poor Joe'*: Dickens, *Memoirs*, p. 111.

The Magic of Mona

105 *Coldbath gaol was*: among the first London prisons to be reformed, and its governors had introduced the mindless turning of the waterwheel 'to restore temperance and cleanliness, and to mend the morals of the profligate by restraining vicious intercourse'. Rudolph Ackermann, William Combe, W. H. Pyne, Augustus Pugin and Thomas Rowlandson, *The Microcosm of London; or, London in Miniature*, 2 vols (London: Methuen, 1904), vol. 1, p. 127.

107 *'interminable confinement'*: Dickens, *Memoirs*, p. 126.

107 *'silly'*: *BDA*, vol. 2, p. 458.

107 *a familiar face*: Byrne appears to have been paid the respectable salary of ten pounds a week. *BDA*, vol. 2, p. 458.

107 *'a large vessel'*: Adolphus, *Memoirs of John Bannister*, vol. 1, pp. 257–8.

108 *a freer and more balletic approach*: Beaumont, *History of Harlequin*, p. 110.

108 *fifty thousand spangles*: Thelma Niklaus, *Harlequin; or, the Rise and Fall of a Bergamask Rogue* (New York: George Braziller, 1956), p. 157.

108 *dandified masculinity*: On classical form in men's fashions of the 1790s, see Kelly, *Beau Brummell*, pp. 100–7.

109 *'big head' Punch*: Punch wore 'a large and heavy hump on his chest, and ... on his back; a high sugar-loaf cap, a long-nosed mask, and heavy wooden shoes'. Dickens, *Memoirs*, p. 118. Sheridan particularly appreciated his early scenes, offering the punning compliment, 'Your punch was so good, I have lost all spirit for the pantomime.'

109 *delivered Joe as their champion*: One theatrical correspondent described it thus: 'In consequence of a dispute, as *serious* as most of those from which our modern Duels originate, viz. *which could make the ugliest face!* which, after many vain appeals to the company present, ended in a mutual exchange of cards (another prevailing puppyism), and the meeting alluded to in consequence took place; but so completely had the circumstance been circulated as to become generally known; and, however the Gentlemen might have calculated upon privacy, notwithstanding the lateness of the hour, several hundreds of spectators were witness to the important contest, which ended in a mere *jack boot* business, creating the most convulsive effects of laughter. We suppose our readers smoke us by the time, and readily see that we allude to the very fine satire upon modern duelling, so well executed by Messrs. Dubois and Grimaldi, in the very entertaining Harlequinade of *The Philosopher's Stone*, by Mr. C. Dibdin, jun, at Sadler's Wells.' Percival, vol. 3, f. 89.

110 *'grew discontented'*: Dibdin, *Memoirs*, p. 45.

110 *transformed the art of clowning*: See Moody, *Illegitimate Theatre*, p. 212.

110 *'shone with diminished rays'*: Dibdin, *Memoirs*, p. 45.

111 *owed thirteen hundred pounds*: Tomalin, *Mrs. Jordan's Profession*, pp. 210–11; Kelly, *Kemble Era*, p. 62. Drury Lane salary and provincial tours meant that in the season 1799–1800, Kemble made a profit of £1,112 (*DNB*).

111 *ruthless economising*: Thomas Dibdin described her speech as 'idiomatic of Peckham-fair'. Dibdin, *Reminiscences*, vol. 1, p. 227.

112 *'Bonny Long'*: Though *Memoirs* refer to Mrs Baker's prompter as 'Bony Long', Dibdin's *Reminiscences* has him as '*Bonny* Long', a title that has more likelihood of being accurate, as Long was reputedly fat, and Dibdin was personally acquainted with the man in question, whereas Dickens was not.

112 *'no thumbs'*: Dibdin, *Reminiscences*, vol. 1, p. 98.

112 *'In gratitude for her kindness'*: Dickens, *Memoirs*, p. 127.

114 *William Powell*: Dickens, *Memoirs*, p. 125.

114 *travelling to the Continent*: Kemble had only resumed management on

the understanding that he would buy a share in the theatre and become part-proprietor. But after his lawyer had examined the documents pertaining to Sheridan's purchase of the theatre and declared that Sheridan's ownership couldn't be ascertained for certain, he gave up the idea.

114 *the Signor had kicked a man in the face*: 'We recollect the father of the old Grimaldi, the clown, having been had up to Bow-Street for kicking a gentleman in the street on the chin.' *Morning Chronicle*, 22 August 1826.

115 *a sustained conspiracy against him*: Of Joe's persecution complex, Miles wrote that, 'unmerited injury seemed ever-present to his imagination; and this medium magnified the animosity which he supposed the other party to bear towards him, until it positively absorbed every other idea, and every action of the party was attributed to this never-dying hate'. Miles, *Grimaldi*, p. 176.

115 *more than he was getting from Kemble*: In the 1801–2 season, Kemble was paying Joe £4 a week. He himself drew a salary of £56. Boaden, *Life of J. P. Kemble*, p. 458.

115 *'most antique theatre in London'*: Dibdin, *Memoirs*, p. 47.

115 *'penurious manner'*: Dibdin, *Memoirs*, p. 47.

115 *enlarged pit and gallery*: Arundell, *Sadler's Wells*, p. 64.

116 *'stood unrivalled'*: *Morning Chronicle*, 31 August 1802.

116 *'truly affecting'*: *The Times*, 21 August 1802.

116 *pony races*: Dibdin may well have taken the idea from Dublin's Theatre Royal, Crow Street, where a similar thing had been tried at the end of the eighteenth century. See Iain Mackintosh, *The Georgian Playhouse: Actors, Artists, Audiences and Architecture, 1730–1830*, Hayward Gallery Exhibition Catalogue (London: Arts Council of Great Britain, 1975), item 308.

117 *'a rustic booby'*: Dibdin, *Memoirs*, pp. 47–8.

117 *'lubberly loutish boy'*: Halliday, *Comical Fellows*, p. 35.

118 *'a whole pantomime in itself'*: *London Magazine*, 1823, Islington Local History Centre.

118 *'a thousand odd twitches'*: Findlater, *Joe Grimaldi*, p. 199.

119 *'clown atrocity ... New School'*: Miles, *Grimaldi*, p. 193; Dibdin, *Memoirs*, p. 47.

119 *There were influences*: See also Moody, *Illegitimate Theatre*, p. 214.

119–20 *'a grown child'*: Oxberry (eds), 'Memoir of Joseph Grimaldi', p. 119.

120 *'mincing affectation'*: Oxberry, (eds), 'Memoir of Joseph Grimaldi', p. 119.

121 *a stable of boxers*: *English Stage*, 20 December 1788, vol. 2, pt 5, p. 1120.

121 *if it was to end by midnight*: Richard Ryan, *Dramatic Table Talk; or, Scenes, Situations and Adventures, Serious and Comic, in Theatrical History and Biography*, 2 vols (London, 1835), vol. 1, pp. 19–20.

121 *it was impossible*: The exact date of this episode remains mysterious, as the *Memoirs* place it after his marriage to Mary Bristow and the second trip to Mrs Baker's (December 1801, and March 1802, respectively). The bills show that *Blue-Beard* was performed only twice in the 1802–3 season, on 28 May and 10 June. Its last performance in the 1801–2 season was 26 November. Similarly, Kemble had left Drury Lane for the Continent in July 1802, and could not therefore have been present at Joe's reinstatement the morning after the furore. To further muddy the waters, *Blue-Beard* was billed for 22 September 1801, which would allow for Kemble's presence, but would provide alternative problems of chronology. This entire episode marks a point of some confusion in both the *Memoirs* (unsurprisingly), and Findlater's *Joe Grimaldi*.

124 *'a liberal and magnificent scale'*: Dibdin, *Memoirs*, p. 54.

125 *'Corsican usurper'*: See Stuart Semmel, *Napoleon and the British* (New Haven and London: Yale University Press, 2004), pp. 38–71.

125 *'a nation of arms'*: Angelo, *Reminiscences*, vol. 2, p. 404.

125 *342,000 men across Britain*: Robert Harvey, *The War of Wars: The Great European Conflict, 1793–1815* (New York: Carroll and Graf, 2006), p. 354.

125 *John Barber Beaumont*: Angelo, *Reminiscences*, vol. 2, p. 407. Theatrical volunteers also included George Cooke and Charles Incledon.

126 *'theatres … prosper most during War'*: Dibdin, *Memoirs*, p. 119.

127 *'of gentlemanly appearance'*: The account of John Grimaldi's unexplained disappearance from Drury Lane in November 1803 can be found in Dickens, *Memoirs*, pp. 132–41.

130 fn. *the end of John Grimaldi's story*: See *World*, 30 November 1877, p. 1, and 1 December 1877, p. 5. An even more garbled version of this story appears in *The Times*, 24 December 1877.

The Spirit of the Waters

131 *Lord Nelson*: For Nelson's celebrity, see Kathleen Wilson, 'Nelson and the People: Manliness, Patriotism and Body Politics', in David Cannadine (ed.), *Admiral Lord Nelson: Context and Legacy* (Basingstoke: Palgrave, 2005), pp. 49–66.

132 *Napoleon supposedly credited them*: Anita Louise Press, 'Sadler's Wells Theatre Under Charles Dibdin the Younger from 1800-1819: When Britannia Ruled the Stage', unpublished doctoral dissertation (University of Toronto, 1994), p. 207.

132 *decorated for patriotism*: Press, 'Sadler's Wells', p. 209.

132 *Carlo the Wonder Dog*: Reynolds, *Life*, vol. 2, p. 351.

133 *'a pair of Tongs'*: Dibdin, *Memoirs*, p. 99.

133 *'baiting with a whale'*: Dibdin, *Memoirs*, p. 60.

134 *'and sit so for an hour or two'*: Dibdin, *Memoirs*, p. 80.

134 *'a pause of breathless wonder'*: Dibdin, *Memoirs*, p. 62.

134 *'in an extacy'*: Dibdin, *Memoirs*, p. 62.

135 *'the most novel, imposing and nationally interesting Exhibitions'*: Dibdin, *Memoirs*, p. 62.

135 *Archimedes' pump*: The proprietors eventually arranged with the New River Company to provide water direct from the mains for an annual fee of twenty pounds. See Dibdin, *Memoirs*, p. 63.

135 *'heat of Bengal'*: Boyd Alexander (ed. and trans.), *Life at Fonthill, 1807–1822: From the Correspondence of William Beckford* (Stroud: Nonsuch, 2006), p. 247.

135 *allowed to stand*: Richard Wheeler's Memoir from the Clerkenwell workhouse, Percival, vol. 4, f. 186.

136 *'Patagonian Sampson'*: The accuracy of this event may be called into question. Press, 'Sadler's Wells', p. 229, suggests it happened during the years of the Aquatic theatre, while Stanley Mayes (*The Great Belzoni: The Circus Strongman Who Discovered Egypt's Treasures* [London: Tauris Parke, 2003]), p. 44, asserts that as Belzoni did not appear at the Wells after 1803, the water alluded to must have been the chalybeate springs beneath the stage. It seems unlikely, however, that he could have fallen that far (and that accurately) without more serious injury to himself and his load.

136 *Betty's infatuation*: *The Times*, 2 May 1805.

137 *tickets sold out in seven minutes*: *The Times*, 3 December 1804.

137 *'drowned by the shrieks'*: *The Times*, 3 December 1804.

137–8 *People fainted*: James Boaden, *The Life of Mrs. Jordan, Including Original Private Correspondence and Numerous Anecdotes of Her Contemporaries*, 2 vols (London: Edward Bull, 1831), vol. 2, p. 170. A thorough description of the opening night can be found on pp. 168–75.

138 *'made him their divinity'*: Boaden, *Life of J. P. Kemble*, p. 485.

138 *Betty's fee was accordingly raised*: Reynolds, *Life*, vol. 2, p. 364.

138 *enough for Sheridan to pay the Duke of Bedford*: Boaden, *Mrs. Jordan*, vol. 2, p. 181; *Life of J. P. Kemble*, p. 487.

139 *'he has changed the life of London'*: Giles Playfair, *The Prodigy: A Study of the Strange Life of Master Betty* (London: Secker and Warburg, 1967), p. 73.

139 *'principally men'*: Dibdin, *Reminiscences*, vol. 1, p. 386.

139 *'Master Polly's and Master Jenny's'*: *The Times*, 5 December 1804.

139 *'all the smoothness of boyhood'*: See Julie A. Carlson, 'Forever Young: Master Betty and the Queer Stage of Youth in English Romanticism', *South Atlantic Quarterly* 95:3 (Summer 1996) 575–602; and Playfair, *The Prodigy*, p. 77.

139–40 *six stone three*: Playfair, *The Prodigy*, p. 81.

140 *'rubbing his naked body'*: Playfair, *The Prodigy*, p. 86.

140 *'young and girlish beauty'*: Carlson, 'Forever Young', p. 590.

141 *'frightful'*: Kelly, *Kemble Era*, p. 163.

141 *'coughing down his paramount opponent'*: Reynolds, *Life*, vol. 2, p. 364.

141 *'Infant Candlesnuffer'*: Allardyce Nicoll, *A History of Early Nineteenth Century Drama, 1800–1850*, 2 vols (Cambridge: Cambridge University Press, 1930), vol. 1, p. 20.

141 *'according to the calculations in different nurseries'*: Percival, vol. 3, n.p.

142 *'rather partial to the race'*: Dibdin, *Memoirs*, p. 110.

142 *'celebrated German Dwarf'*: Dibdin, *Memoirs*, pp. 97, 67, fn. 1.

142 *'town could not be kept at fever heat'*: Boaden, *Mrs. Jordan*, vol. 2, p. 184.

142 *'truly original Correspondence'*: Boaden, *Mrs. Jordan*, vol. 2, p. 190.

142 *'Peter Pangloss'*: See Carlson, 'Forever Young', p. 593.

143 *'Phantoscopia'*: See Altick, *Shows of London*, p. 218.

143 *London via Lisbon*: Theodore Fenner, 'Ballet in Early Nineteenth-Century London as Seen by Leigh Hunt and Henry Robertson', *Dance Chronicle*, 1:2 (1977–8), 75–95, p. 79.

144 *Jamie Harvey*: See Judith Milhous, 'The Economics of Theatrical Dance in Eighteenth-Century London', *Theatre Journal*, 55:3 (2003), 481–508, fn. 28.

144 *'astonishing attitudinarian'*: Hunt, *Autobiography*, vol. 1, p. 154.

144 *'offensively coarse'*: *Monthly Mirror*, January 1805, p. 338.

144 *'too base a metal'*: *Monthly Mirror*, May 1804, p. 56.

145 *Coaches moved at walking pace*: *The Times*, 6 November 1805.

145 *'on the decline'*: Dibdin, *Reminiscences*, vol. 1, p. 400.

146 *'a living magnet of attraction'*: Dickens, *Memoirs*, p. 154.

146 *'chip off the old block'*: Dickens, *Memoirs*, p. 155.

146 *official company notice*: Boaden, *Life of J. P. Kemble*, p. 219.

146 *'theatrical thermometer'*: Dibdin, *Reminiscences*, vol. 1, p. 289. Perhaps this was not so unusual for the period. Offering to shake hands with only one finger is one of the pompous affects of *Vanity Fair*'s Joseph Smedley.

147 *'Mr Peake … is a gentleman'*: Dickens, *Memoirs*, p. 155.

147 *'came off victorious'*: Dickens, *Memoirs*, p. 156.

147 *Graham threatened to sue*: See Raymond, *Life of Elliston*, pp. 107–8.

148 *'something more than a public calamity'*: Robert Southey, *The Life of Nelson*, 2nd edn, 2 vols (London: John Murray, 1814), vol. 2, p. 191.

148 *'darling hero of England'*: Southey, *Life of Nelson*, vol. 2, p. 237.

149 *'mad for Entertainment'*: Dibdin, *Memoirs*, p. 68.

150 *'slim boy'*: Dibdin, *Memoirs*, p. 66.

150 *'repaying its own purchase money'*: Percival, vol. 3, f. 171.

150 *'pantomimic talent'*: Dibdin, *Reminiscences*, vol. 1, p. 399.

151 *'as socially as friendship'*: Dibdin, *Memoirs*, p. 72.

152 *pirated by Parker's comedian*: Dibdin, *Memoirs*, p. 74.

154 *'Joey Grimaldi, 1805'*: Currently in the possession of the Museum of London, see M. R. Holmes, *Stage Costume and Accessories* (London: London Museum, 1968), p. 71, item 260.

155 *'English Rose'*: de Castro, *Memoirs*, p. 45.

155 *'not a man to be intimidated'*: Dibdin, *Memoirs*, p. 77.

155 *bound over to keep the peace*: Dibdin, *Memoirs*, p. 64.

156 *managed to break free*: See Boaden, *Mrs. Jordan*, vol. 2, pp. 133–4, and Marius Kwint, 'Philip Astley (1742–1814)', *DNB*; see also de Castro, *Memoirs*, p. 48.

156 *a dogged and fierce competitor*: Despite their rivalry, on 2 September 1803, Sadler's Wells held a benefit for Astley's performers put out of work by the destruction of the theatre, raising seventy pounds to be distributed among them (Dibdin, *Memoirs*, p. 96).

Mother Goose

157 *bathed his feet in a tub of brandy*: Dickens, *Memoirs*, p. 161.

158 *'influx of pygmies … epidemic nausea'*: Genest, *Some Account of the English Stage*, vol. vii, pp. 662–3.

159 *'in perfect astonishment'*: Dickens, *Memoirs*, p. 163.

159 *Fallow Corner*: See Frank Marcham, 'Joseph Grimaldi and Finchley', reprinted from *Transactions of the London and Middlesex Archaeological Society* (London, 1939), p. 49.

159 *He already had an apprentice*: Dibdin, *Memoirs*, p. 97, fn. 1.

159 *Watts would also fall asleep*: Dickens, *Memoirs*, p. 187.

159 *'the best on the English stage'*: Unidentified clipping in Robert Wilkinson and William Herbert, *Playhouses, Theatres and Other Places of Public Amusement in London and its Suburbs from the Reign of Queen Elizabeth to William IV* (London: R. Wilkinson, n.d.), extra-illustrated volumes, Library of the Garrick Club, vol. 6, p. 107; Marcham, 'Grimaldi and Finchley', p. 48.

161 *'a pupil and copyist of Dubois'*: Dickens, *Memoirs*, p. 163.

161 *devoted to his mother*: Dibdin, *Reminiscences*, vol. 1, p. 401.

162 *'His voice is against him'*: Percival, vol. 4, f. 245.

162 *'a short, sturdy person'*: Hunt, *Autobiography*, vol. 1, p. 148.

162 *Signor Colnagi's*: Farley's colleagues often made fun of his lack of formal education and want of foreign languages. James Robinson Planché recalled that 'So little did he know of the language of our lively neighbours, that he is reported to have waited day after day at the doors of one of the theatres in Paris in order to witness the first performance of a new grand spectacle, entitled, as he imagined, *"Relache"* [signifying the period between shows when the theatre was dark], mistaking the bills with that word only in large letters which he saw posted up there to indicate the production of some important novelty.' Richard Henry Stoddard (ed.), *Personal Reminiscences by Chorley, Planché, and Young* (New York: Scribner, Armstrong, 1876), p. 146.

163 *'she-bear'*: Thomas Dibdin, *Valentine and Orson, A Romantic Melo-drame* (London, 1804).

163 *preferred Grimaldi's Orson*: William Hazlitt, *Examiner*, 23 July 1815.

163–4 *'stagger off the stage'*: Dickens, *Memoirs*, p. 164. Grimaldi's suffering bears a remarkable similarity to that of the ballet-dancer Rudolf Nureyev (1938–93). Though working in different art forms, the demands they placed on their bodies were fundamentally the same. Nureyev's biographer, Julie Kavanagh, reports that, 'Since 1973, Rudolf had been dancing with a permanent tear in his leg muscle; he had destroyed his Achilles tendons by years of landing too heavily; he had heel spurs; the bones were chipped – so that even basic walking gave him pain. When he emerged from his dressing room, slowly limping in his clogs and full-length bathrobe, he looked more like a hospital patient than a ballet star, often making straight for the special chair put aside for him in the wings.' Julie Kavanagh, *Nureyev: The Life* (New York: Pantheon, 2007), p. 485.

164 *'a most capital joke'*: Dickens, *Memoirs*, p. 36. The performance in question, *The Triumph of Mirth*, was comprehensively overlooked by reviewers, save for the theatre critic for the *British Magazine and Review*, who on the opening night only managed to report that 'The piece was executed with fewer blunders than generally happen on the first representation of a pantomime, and was well-received.' *British Magazine and Review*, 1783, p. 57 (clipping in the collection of the Islington Local History Centre). On the structural function of this trope within the *Memoirs*, see Leigh Woods, 'The Curse of Performance: Inscripting the *Memoirs of Joseph Grimaldi* into the Life of Charles Dickens', *Biography*, 14:2 (Spring 1991), 138–52.

164 *an idea to which he would become superstitiously attached*: Jane Moody comments that 'Dickens's inclusion of this miniature narrative of histrionic sensibility highlights the way in which the dramatisation of savagery seemed to hold in perilous tension violent tenderness and innocent destructiveness, the gentle and the diabolic.' *Illegitimate Theatre*, p. 92.

164 *'We can in no way describe what he does'*: *Monthly Mirror*, January 1807; Joseph Munden said that 'It is impossible to describe what he did. A thousand masks would not portray the grotesque contortions of his countenance.' Thomas Shepherd Munden, *Memoirs of Joseph Shepherd Munden, Comedian. By His Son* (London: Richard Bentley, 1844), p. 127.

165 *'drudgery'*: Dibdin, *Reminiscences*, vol. 1, p. 397.

165 *'parti-coloured jackets'*: Dibdin, *Reminiscences*, vol. 1, p. 397.

166 *'do the best you can'*: Dibdin, *Reminiscences*, vol. 1, p. 398.

166 *'as plain as possible'*: Dickens, *Memoirs*, p. 165.

166 *'proportionally rueful'*: Dickens, *Memoirs*, p. 165.

166 *just the words to the songs*: See Larpent Plays, 1054, MS dated by Larpent, 23 December. For more on John Larpent's character and abilities as the Lord Chamberlain's Examiner of Plays, see Mayer, *Harlequin in His Element*, pp. 238–44.

167 *'If he is knocked down'*: *The Times*, 27 December 1828. The pantomime was *Little Red Riding Hood*.

168 *'so wretched'*: Dickens, *Memoirs*, p. 165.

169 *'We do not know a single drama'*: *The Dramatic Censor: or, Weekly Theatrical Report*, January 1800. Garrick first performed *Barnwell* before a pantomime in 1759 (Disher, *Clowns and Pantomimes*, p. 290).

169 *'wretched cant'*: William Hazlitt, 'George Barnwell', *A View of the English Stage*, in *Complete Works*, ed. P. P. Howe, vol. 5, p. 269; Hogan, *London Stage*, p. xlvii.

170 *'can never lie long in bed'*: Disher, *Clowns and Pantomimes*, p. 127.

170 *initially cursed his luck*: Boaden, *Life of J. P. Kemble*, p. 500.

171 *'a rich widower'*: Disher, *Clowns and Pantomimes*, p. 98.

172 *a small boy named Leonard*: Goodwin, *Sketches and Impressions*, p. 18.

172 *'Regain the egg, and happy be'*: All quotes are from Thomas Dibdin, *Harlequin and Mother Goose; or, the Golden Egg!* (London: Thomas Hailes Lacy, 18–).

173 *'poor simple Welchman'*: *The Times*, 27 and 28 January 1807.

173 *'skimble-skambled'*: Thomas Hood, *Hood's Own; or, Laughter From Year to Year* (London: Bailey, 1839), p. 263.

175 *'a naughty little dancing girl'*: *BDA*, vol. 10, p. 190.

175 *rival Columbines*: Raymond, *Life of Elliston*, pp. 172–5.

175 *sybaritic pleasures*: Fiona MacCarthy, *Byron: Life and Legend* (New York: Farrar, Straus and Giroux, 2003), p. 73.

178 *'simply a pair of flats'*: Halliday, *Comical Fellows*, p. 36.

179 *'in a roar'*: *Monthly Mirror*, January 1807.

179 *'JOHN BULL'*: *The Times*, 30 December 1806.

179 *'had not been well accustomed'*: Dickens, *Memoirs*, p. 166.

179 *'We have not for several years'*: *European Magazine*, vol. 51, January 1807, p. 54

179 *'dexterity'*: *The Times*'s correspondent, even as he commends the fluidity of the stage-management, rather overstates the complexity of the scenery: 'In the management of the scenery, which was very complicated, there was as little perplexity and mismanagement as could be expected on the first exhibition,' *The Times*, 30 December 1806.

179 *'as perfect a performance'*: John Fairburn, *Fairburn's Description of the Popular and Comic New Pantomime, called Harlequin and Mother Goose; or, the Golden Egg* (London, 1807), p. 29.

180 *'unceasing vivacity'*: Frow, *Oh Yes It Is!*, p. 70.

180 *'His very excellent clown'*: *Fairburn's Description of Mother Goose*, pp. 30–31.

180 *'sublime impudence'*: Findlater, *Joe Grimaldi*, p. 120.

180 *'the great master of his art'*: Boaden, *Life of J. P. Kemble*, p. 500.

180 *'a genius'*: Boaden, *Mrs. Jordan*, vol. 2, p. 201.

180 *'Grimaldi's career'*: Disher, *Clowns and Pantomimes*, p. 99.

181 *'the principal cause of crowded lobbies'*: *Monthly Mirror*, November 1806, February 1807.

182 *'pigeons are birds'*: Dickens, *Memoirs*, p. 146.

182 *'The fellow's a humbug'*: Dickens, *Memoirs*, p. 146.

182 *'the slaughter was very great'*: Dickens, *Memoirs*, p. 146.

182 *'precious savage'*: Dickens, *Memoirs*, p. 147.

184 *'no chandeliers at all'*: Dickens, *Memoirs*, p. 168.

184 *almost certainly be put to death*: John Mackoull, *Abuses of Justice*, 2nd edn (London: M. Jones, 1812), p. 74.

The Forty Virgins

185 *'disgrace a booth'*: *European Magazine*, vol. 51, April 1807, p. 294.

185 *'brilliant stupidity'*: *The Times*, 17 April 1807, 18 April 1807.

186 *'redfire'*: Redfire, a chemical compound of strontia, shellac, potash and charcoal, was to be used extensively in 'blow-ups' of this kind, the dramatic conflagrations and immolations that conventionally concluded many melodramas, and which were set to become all the rage in London's minor theatres. No respectable house could afford not to end the evening without the spectacle of exploding citadels and burning minarets acting as a visual metonym for justice served on tyranny. That said, the most famous 'blow-up' of all was at Covent Garden – the explosion that ended Isaac Pocock's *The Miller and His Men* (1813). See Dibdin, *Memoirs*, pp. 90–91; Moody, *Illegitimate Theatre*, pp. 98–106.

186 *'Sir Francis Drake'*: The ship's name is revealed by Dibdin, *Reminiscences*, vol. 1, p. 440.

186 *'chaunt'*: Charles Dibdin, *Jan Ben Jan; or, Harlequin and the Forty Virgins* (London, 1807).

187 *'That I can, and hear, too'*: Dickens, *Memoirs*, p. 176.

187 *if he valued his reputation*: Mackoull, *Abuses of Justice*, p. 66.

188 *'Besides – the ladies'*: Dickens, *Memoirs*, p. 172.

188 *'none of those women are married'*: Dickens, *Memoirs*, p. 172.

189 *'protestations of regret'*: Dickens, *Memoirs*, p. 174.

189 *'Jack's had a very long string'*: Dickens, *Memoirs*, p. 174.

189 *pick pockets in the pit*: Mackoull, *Abuses of Justice*, p. 165.

189 *'former irregularities'*: Mackoull, *Abuses of Justice*, p. 2.

190 *'ever accustomed to vice'*: Dickens, *Memoirs*, p. 177.

190 *Vilified in the witness box*: Mackoull, *Abuses of Justice*, pp. 186, 191.

190 *regular supply of decoys*: See Donald A. Low, *The Regency Underworld* (Stroud: Sutton, 2005), pp. 30–5.

191 *paid handsomely to lie*: Mackoull, *Abuses of Justice*, p. 191.

192 *'Brummell of Clowns'*: Percy Fitzgerald, *Chronicles of Bow Street Police-Office, with an Account of the Magistrates, 'Runners' and Police; and a Selection of the Most Interesting Cases*, 2 vols (London: Chapman and Hall, 1888), vol. 2, p. 11; Dickens, *Memoirs*, p. 184, fn. 1.

192 *'if not fatal accident'*: Miles, *Grimaldi*, p. 7; Dickens, *Memoirs*, p. 181.

193 *'it was all up with him'*: Miles, *Grimaldi*, p. 134.

193 *'yielded his consent'*: Dickens, *Memoirs*, p. 180.

193 *'in great disorder'*: Dickens, *Memoirs*, p. 181.

193 *a piece of Gothic embellishment*: Henry Downes Miles, who bases the merit of his own text on its willingness to take issue with Dickens's whenever it can, particularly relishes making this point (*Grimaldi*, pp. 137–8).

194 *'by his exertions'*: Percival, vol. 3, f. 191.

195 *'electricity, tracheotomy'*: *The Times*, 21 October 1807.

195 *beside his wife's corpse*: Percival, vol. 3, f. 184, and Dibdin, *Memoirs*, p. 94.

195 *When she called to him, he disappeared*: Percival, vol. 3, f. 184.

195 *None of them carried money*: Percival, vol. 3, f. 199.

195 *corvine opportunists*: Dibdin, *Memoirs*, p. 95; Dibdin, *Reminiscences*, vol. 1, p. 404.

196 *'Fire! Fire!'*: Percival, vol. 3, f. 193.

196 *'casually, accidentally, and by misfortune'*: Percival, vol. 3, ff. 192, 199.

196 *Mary Vyne absconded*: *The Times*, 1 August 1811.

197 *enough to seat at least a third of the London population*: The number of places sold is speculation based on the capacity of Covent Garden at three thousand seats, multiplied by 122 performances. For a similar calculation, see Mayer, *Harlequin in His Element*, p. 385, n. 9, and *Fairburn's Description of Mother Goose*, p. 58. The population of London in 1807 was just over one million.

197 *shared a summer benefit*: See *BDA*, vol. 6, p. 412.

197 *'crack brained Boys'*: Dibdin, *Memoirs*, p. 98.

198 *an array of merchandise*: *Mother Goose* was adapted as a board game by James Wallis's 'Instructive Toy Warehouse', at that time the most prolific producer of board games in Britain.

198 *sixteen hundred revellers*: *Morning Chronicle*, 14 July 1808.

198 *to reserve him a box*: George Gordon, Lord Byron, *Byron's Letters and Journals*, ed. Leslie A. Marchand, 12 vols. (Cambridge, Massachusetts: Harvard University Press, 1973–94), vol. 1, p.152.

198 *'did what he liked with the town'*: Miles, *Grimaldi*, p. 124.

199 *'foamings in solitude'*: Miles, *Grimaldi*, p. 128.

199 *modern celebrity*: See Leo Braudy, *The Frenzy of Renown: Fame and Its History* (New York: Vintage, 1997), and Tom Mole, *Byron's Romantic Celebrity: Industrial Culture and the Hermeneutic of Intimacy* (Basingstoke: Palgrave, 2007).

200 *'sack cloth and ashes'*: The same paper suggested that Grimaldi 'apply to the Foreign Office for the appointment of Ambassador or Missionary to some of the Continental States, as his powers are calculated to render them merry!' Unidentified clipping, Augustin Daly's *Extra-Illustrated edition of The Memoirs of Joseph Grimaldi* (London: 1846), Harvard Theatre Collection, 4 vols, vol. 2, p. 81, facing (hereafter, 'Daly ex-ill.').

200 *'Grim-All-Day'*: There are many formulations of this line, a line that first appeared in Oxberry (eds), 'Memoir of Joseph Grimaldi', p. 113.

200 *'I am Grimaldi'*: Goodwin, *Sketches and Impressions*, p. 14.

201 *Wertherism*: See Inger Sigrun Brodey, 'Masculinity, Sensibility, and the "Man of Feeling": The Gendered Ethics of Goethe's *Werther'*, *Papers on Language & Literature*, 35:2 (1999) 115–40, especially pp. 116, 137.

201 *'diseased muscles'* [sic] *shells produce pearls'*: Ryan,*Table Talk*, vol. 2, p. 39.

202 *hovering serenely*: Goodwin, *Sketches and Impressions*, p. 18.

202 *loss of all its scenery*: Kelly, *Kemble Era*, p. 170.

202 *Other lost treasures*: *Gentleman's Magazine*, vol. 78, 1808, pp. 845–7.

203 *'lucky old hag'*: Dibdin, *Reminiscences*, vol. 2, p. 422.

204 *huge, flapping shoes*: Disher, *Clowns and Pantomimes*, pp. 136–8.

204 *band of the Coldstream Guards*: See Boaden, *Life of J. P. Kemble*, pp. 523–4.

205 *'ponderous inutility'*: Boaden, *Life of J. P. Kemble*, p. 533.

205 *the budget still fell short*: All figures taken from Marc Baer, *Theatre and Disorder in Late Georgian London* (Oxford: Clarendon, 1992), pp. 21–2.

205–6 'born from misfortune': Dibdin, Reminiscences, vol. 1, p. 421. Erik Gustaf Geijer, Impressions of England, 1809–1810, trans. Elizabeth Sprigge and Claude Napier (London: Cape, 1932), p. 98–9.

206 'the playing of a play which does not endure witnesses': Baer, Theatre and Disorder, p. 19.

206 'roar of disapprobation': Geijer, Impressions of England, p. 97.

207 'Even women tried to speak': Geijer, Impressions of England, p. 97.

207 'whooping-cough': Ben Wilson, The Making of Victorian Values: Decency and Dissent in Britain, 1789–1837 (New York: Penguin, 2007), p. 200.

208 slept next to a ladder: Kelly, Kemble Era, p. 177–8.

208 just show pantomimes: 'Whenever there is Danger of a Riot,' Kemble had written in a memorandum to managers, 'always act an Opera; for Musick drowns the noise of Opposition.' Hogan, London Stage, p. ccv; Miles, Grimaldi, p. 161.

209 'If that man could speak': Disher, Clowns and Pantomimes, p. 295.

209 tried at the Old Bailey: See Marcham, 'Grimaldi and Finchley'.

209 'Bravo, Joe!': Dickens, Memoirs, p. 210.

209 'We are satisfied': Boaden, Life of J. P. Kemble, p. 548.

210 'Metrical History of England': Dibdin, Reminiscences, vol. 1, pp. 433, 435.

210 'a prettier Cordelia': Findlater, Joe Grimaldi, p. 136.

211 'done to injure you': Dickens, Memoirs, p. 190.

Harlequin in His Element

216 'overgrown bantling': Christopher Hibbert, George IV: Regent and King, 1811–1830 (London: Allen Lane, 1973), p. 6.

216 extravagant costumes: See Tomalin, Mrs. Jordan's Profession, p. 99.

216–7 elaborate pranks: See John Ashton, Social England Under the Regency (London: Chatto and Windus, 1899), p. 267.

217 Brummell thought he should turn professional: Kelly, Beau Brummell, p. 65.

217 'ever so magnificent': Hibbert, George IV, p. 3.

217: 'artificial banks': Steven Parissien, George IV: The Grand Entertainment (London: John Murray, 2001), p. 262.

217 'that Sadler's Wells business': E. A. Smith, George IV (New Haven and London: Yale University Press, 1999), p. 134.

218 *'vast body of conjoined talent'*: Reynolds, *Life*, vol. 2, pp. 401, 402.

218 *'the best body of performers'*: Raymond, *Life of Elliston*, p. 156.

218 *'pantomimic wonders'*: Thomas Marshall, 'Ellar, the Harlequin', in *Lives of the Most Celebrated Actors and Actresses*, ed. Thomas Marshall (London: 1848), p. 118.

218 *'original as Grimaldi's Clown'*: Dibdin, *Memoirs*, p. 104.

218 *'his legs twinkle'*: *The Times*, 27 December 1828.

218 *'a whirling teetotum'*: E. L. Blanchard, *The Life and Reminiscences of E. L. Blanchard, with Notes from the Diary of Wm. Blanchard*, ed. Clement Scott and Cecil Howard, 2 vols (London: Hutchinson, 1891), vol. 2, p. 581.

219 *'subject to them'*: Disher, *Clowns and Pantomimes*, p. 124.

219 *'the king of melo-dramas'*: Robson, *Old Play-goer*, p. 241.

219 *'enjoy their evening as much as possible'*: Oxberry (eds), 'Memoir of Joseph Grimaldi', p. 114.

219 *'a running commentary'*: *The Times*, 27 December 1825.

219 *a show could hardly be staged for less*: See Mayer, *Harlequin in His Element*, pp. 102–3.

221 *'ridiculing the follies of the age'*: Malcolm, *London Redivium*, vol. 3, p. 235; Dibdin, *Memoirs*, p. 103. *Furibond* was produced to celebrate the passage of the 1807 Slave Trade Act, legislation criminalising human trafficking within the British Empire, the first major victory in the movement towards abolition. It opened among the slaves of a Jamaican coffee plantation, who are eventually freed after the figure of Britannia descends from the skies and grants them their liberty (see *European Magazine*, vol. LIII, January 1808, p. 51). Mayer writes that liberal sentiments 'were not allowed to interfere with the comic possibilities which Drury Lane management felt their due when portraying Negroes on the stage. The pantomime's Clown had two scenes ... in which he pursued a Negro servant girl, attempting to make love to her. When Clown finally married her, he was immediately presented with horns and six children.' *Harlequin in his Element*, p. 254.

221 *'best medium of dramatic satire'*: *Examiner*, 26 January 1817.

221 *'a whole train of them'*: *Examiner*, 26 January 1817.

222 *'Hogarth in action'*: Miles, *Grimaldi*, p. 7.

222 *'Bang up'*: Dibdin, *Memoirs*, p. 105.

223 *'Two black varnished coal-scuttles'*: *The Times*, 15 January 1813, spelling amended.

223 *'roared with laughter'*: The Times, 15 January 1813.

223 *'general contempt ... with chains and cat skins'*: The Times, 15 January 1813.

223 *'ambivalent about their land forces'*: As Mayer explains, there was also a fear that in lieu of a foreign enemy, the army might be turned against the domestic population and domestic barracks be used to enforce monarchical tyranny. *Harlequin in His Element*, p. 55.

223 *'d—d infernal foolery'*: Gentleman's Magazine, vol. vii (1871), p. 91.

224 *'one of the best pantomimes'*: Dickens, *Memoirs*, p. 187. *The Times*, 30 December 1808, remarked that, 'in point of invention, of whim, and of variety, it is very far indeed below *Mother Goose* ... but the rich humour of GRIMALDI is capable of giving currency to a more meagre composition: the success of the performance is principally to be attributed to his exertions'.

224 *'BEADLE's hat'*: Thomas Dibdin, *Harlequin in His Element*, in Michael R. Booth (ed.), *English Plays of the Nineteenth Century*, vol. 5, 'Pantomimes, Extravaganzas and Burlesques' (Oxford: Clarendon, 1976), sc. x, p. 83.

225 *'sleepy style'*: The Times, 27 December 1823.

225 *'no one can be at a loss'*: clipping, London Magazine, 1823, Islington Local History Centre.

225 *'delightful assumption of nonchalance'*: Oxberry (eds), 'Memoir of Joseph Grimaldi', p. 119; *Leigh Hunt's Dramatic Criticism*, p. 110.

225 *'world of concentration'*: Moody, *Illegitimate Theatre*, p. 216.

225 *'their old friend Joe's voice'*: William Hazlitt,*Examiner*, 29 December 1816.

225 *close to five thousand*: 'My Father, Brother and self have written more Songs than not only any other three, but three score men put together—some thousands, of which for public, private and various occasions, I have written nearer 5,000 than 4,000.' Dibdin, *Memoirs*, p. 46.

225 *'Unless sung by the Clown of the Pantomime'*: Dibdin, *Memoirs*, p. 113.

226 *'A most remarkable instance'*: Goodwin, *Sketches and Impressions*, p. 14.

227 *Harlequin in His Element*: The stage directions are as follows: 'CLOWN makes free with the wine himself, till being quite inebriated he determines on a frolic, which he commences by stripping the WATCHMAN and clothing himself in the great coat and hat. Wishing to take another sup of his wine, he after many fruitless attempts at last gets hold of the bottle, but not being able to guide it to his mouth, he with the other hand feels for his mouth and tries again, in vain, to put the neck of the bottle into it. Being vexed he takes up the lantern and, holding it to his cheek, effects ... his purpose. He then shuts the sleeper into his box, and with the lantern and rattle parades the stage, crying

the hour in a ludicrous tone.' Thomas Dibdin, *Harlequin in His Element*, sc. iv, pp. 78–9.

227 *'The first fierce glance and start'*: Robson, *Old Play-goer*, pp. 240–1.

228 *provided instruction to John Philip Kemble*: *Gentleman's Magazine*, vol. vii (1871), pp. 91. The article also claims that he taught the dandy Charles Stanhope 'and other noblemen and gentlemen of the Court'.

228 *'It is greatly to be regretted'*: Letter of Thomas Perronet Thompson to Nancy Thompson, 25 June 1812. Brotherton Library, University of Leeds, SC MS 277/1/8.

228 *Moll Flaggon*: Percival, vol. 4, f. 78.

228 *'intellectual Clown'*: Oxberry (eds), 'Memoir of Joseph Grimaldi', p. 120.

229 *'to be knock'd about'*: Thomas Dibdin, *Harlequin Hoax* (Larpent MS, 1814); Mayer, *Harlequin in His Element*, p. 176.

229 *'It is absolutely surprising'*: Percival, vol. 4, f. 139.

229 *'an act which I shall never forget'*: Mirza Abul Hassan Khan, *A Persian at the Court of King George, 1809–10: The Journal of Mirza Abul Hassan Khan*, ed. Margaret Morris Cloake (London: Barrie and Jenkins, 1988), p. 92.

230 *'Grimaldi, worth his weight in gold'*: Daly ex-ill., vol. 2, p. 81 facing.

230 *entrusting his entire provincial earnings*: This had happened following his engagement in Birmingham at the behest of Louisa Bristow – the loss: £150. See Dickens, *Memoirs*, p. 191.

230 *'the great expense'*: Dickens, *Memoirs*, p. 212.

230 *run-in with the bailiff*: See Dickens, *Memoirs*, pp. 161–3.

231 *strolled to a pawn shop*: Unidentified clipping, Islington Local History Centre.

231 *'an Alderman with the quinsey'*: MacCarthy, *Byron*, p. 184.

231 *'a Persian eunuch'*: Paul Ranger, 'Betty, William Henry West (1791–1874)', *DNB*.

231 *'remains a mystery to him'*: *Theatrical Inquisitor* (1812), pp. 234–5.

231 *'a local deity'*: Grantley Fitzhardinge Berkeley, *My Life and Recollections*, 4 vols (London: Hurst and Blackett, 1865) vol. 2, p. 164.

231 *'very medicinal and sufficiently disgusting'*: MacCarthy, *Byron*, p. 183.

232 *'mingled gratification and suspicion'*: Dickens, *Memoirs*, p. 214.

232 *'Byron is very courteous'*: Dickens, *Memoirs*, pp. 215–16.

233 *'nice with apple-pie'*: Dickens, *Memoirs*, p. 216.

233 *too good to take orders from a mere player*: See Kristina Straub, *Sexual Subjects: Eighteenth-Century Players and Sexual Ideology* (Princeton, New Jersey: Princeton University Press, 1992), p. 157. Evidence that Grimaldi was beginning to see himself as something other than a performing servant is given in the anecdote concerning the clergyman who invited him and a singer called Higman to dinner with a large, convivial party. As soon as the dinner was over, the host turned to Higman, whom he 'commanded, rather than asked', to give a song. Higman obliged, and Grimaldi was next directed to do a turn, although when he demurred, begging some time to digest, the host haughtily informed him that he'd been invited solely to entertain the guests. Joe was incensed, angrily lecturing the clergyman on manners before asking to be excused. Dickens, *Memoirs*, p. 218.

234 *'an insult which no Audience can tolerate'*: Daly ex-ill., vol. 2, p. 81 facing.

234 *strength of his oaths*: Byron's flash and swagger was a version of masculinity with which Grimaldi identified, or so it would seem from a comment in the *Memoirs* that parrots one of Byron's own. It concerns the author Matthew Lewis, synonymous with Gothic literature thanks to the success of his deliciously indecent novel, *The Monk*, whose evident homosexuality unnerved the Clown. 'He was an effeminate looking man,' wrote Joe, 'almost constantly lounging about the green-room . . . and entering into conversation with the ladies and gentlemen, but in a manner so peculiar, so namby-pamby . . . that it was far from pleasing to a majority of those thus addressed.' Byron, who had a long acquaintance with Lewis, letting him stay at the Villa Diodati even though he thought him a 'jaded voluptuary', had similarly mixed feelings about his company. 'I will never dine with a middle-aged man', he once said, 'who fills up his table with young ensigns, and has looking-glass panels to his book-cases.' D. L. Macdonald, *Monk Lewis: A Critical Biography* (Toronto: University of Toronto Press, 2000), p. 60.

235 *'plumed himself'*: Dickens, *Memoirs*, p. 222.

235 *'We looked at the faces we met in the street'*: *Examiner*, 31 December 1815; Hazlitt, *Complete Works*, vol. 18, p. 208.

235–6 *'He has complained so much ... giving him permission'*: Letter from Charles Dibdin to Charles Farley, 9 August 1810, Harvard Theatre Collection.

236 *'there was nothing but war'*: Richard Wheeler's Memoir from the Clerkenwell workhouse, Percival, vol. 4, f. 193.

236 *Dibdin in sole charge*: Percival, vol. 4, f. 101.

236 *'A Theatre should be like an absolute Monarchy'*: Dibdin, *Memoirs*, p. 122.

237 *personal discounts*: Richard Wheeler's Memoir from the Clerkenwell workhouse, Percival, vol. 4, f. 189.

237 *Marengo*: Altick, *Shows of London*, p. 239.

237 *'All Theatres are bad now'*: Arundell, *Sadler's Wells*, p. 93.

238 *the water had to go*: Dibdin, *Memoirs*, p. 117.

238 *knee-high water*: For examples of unimpressed reviewers tiring of the aquatic drama, see Gillian Russell, *The Theatres of War: Performance, Politics, and Society, 1793–1815* (Oxford: Clarendon, 1995), p. 73.

238 *negotiations for a new contract*: Dibdin and Grimaldi disagree on this point. Grimaldi, who does not mention the time off for touring, claimed that the salary increase was agreed to, but only with the loss of one of his benefits (Dickens, *Memoirs*, p. 228), whereas Dibdin makes no mention of benefits, and recalls the problem purely revolving around the proposed absence (Dickens, *Memoirs*, p. 119).

238 *'lion of the theatre'*: Dickens, *Memoirs*, p. 228.

239 *'stood his ground ably'*: Percival, vol. 4, f. 71.

239 *'a universal favourite'*: Percival, vol. 4, f. 76.

The Orphan of Peru

243 *bottom coach*: At least they were saved the ordeal of some Wiltshire passengers the year before, who had their coach attacked by an escaped lioness. Ashton, *Social England*, pp. 354–6.

244 *told him to get on with it*: Dickens, *Memoirs*, p. 189.

244 *'instantaneous burst of laughter'*: Reynolds, *Life*, vol. 2, p. 321.

245 *not to sit so close to him during lunch*: See 'Journal of Old Barnes the Pantaloon, On a Trip to Paris in 1830', Percival, vol. 5, f. 112.

245 *that moment to take a break*: The *Morning Chronicle*, 29 December 1779, reported that 'The scene shifters last night spoilt the effect of [the scenery] and had nearly killed Harlequin (W. Bates) who twice broke the scene to pieces in attempting to jump through the head of an image, placed at the top of a water course, which he could have easily executed had not the scene men, through the most scandalous inattention, suffered the part of the scene which was to give way for the leap, to be fastened up.'

245 *broke his hand*: Dickens, *Memoirs*, p. 248.

245 *torn it from the man's scalp*: Oxberry (eds), 'Memoir of Joseph Grimaldi', p. 115.

245 *top of his skull collided*: Dibdin, *Memoirs*, p. 115.

246 *Joe's last benefit of the season*: See Percival, vol. 4, f. 101. There is a small possibility that JS's début was actually at Covent Garden on 12 July 1814. The event was a night of music to honour His Excellency Prince Platoff, the Cossack commander who had led his men with distinction eighteen months earlier, harassing Napoleon's vastly superior force on its miserable retreat

from Moscow. He had promised to give his daughter to any man who could bring him Napoleon's head. The bill was predominantly musical, including overtures from Mozart's *Magic Flute* and *Don Giovanni*, an opera, and songs on the death of Nelson, concluded by Sheridan's *Crusoe*. See Ashton, *Social England*, p. 88.

247 *'when his own heyday of fame'*: This wish no doubt lies behind the *Memoirs'* mistaken claim that this was the part in which Joe himself had been introduced to the stage by his father (it was in fact *The Triumph of Mirth*). The desire for continuity-through-symmetry expressed in this false memory was obviously too choice to resist. Dickens, *Memoirs*, p. 219.

247 *Harlequin and Fortunio*: Hazlitt described the pantomime as 'indifferent,' though 'better when Mr. Grimaldi comes in, lets off a culverin [a ten-foot cannon] at his enemies, and sings a serenade to his mistress in concert with Grimalkin', a cat. *Examiner*, 31 December 1815, Hazlitt, *Complete Works*, vol. 18, p. 208.

247 *'highly flattering'*: Percival, vol. 6, f. 6.

249 *'as a Republic'*: Dibdin, *Memoirs*, p. 122.

249 *tore a hole in the curtain*: Findlater, *Joe Grimaldi*, p. 191.

249 *consumed his provincial profits*: See Dibdin, *Memoirs*, p. 53, and Findlater, *Joe Grimaldi*, p. 192.

250 *'hailed with shouts of applause'*: Dibdin, *Memoirs*, p. 123.

250 *curtain went up at the advertised time*: Percival, vol. 4, f. 95.

250 *'beneath the notice of criticism'*: Percival, vol. 4, f. 95.

250 *'dead failures'*: Miles, *Grimaldi*, p. 171.

251 *'Hot Codlins'*: The humour of this song arose from Dibdin's device of leaving the final word of each verse blank. The audience was then able to shout the supposedly risqué rhyme back at Grimaldi, who would cry, 'For shame,' in mock outrage. That it became such a great favourite was no doubt due to the combination of audience participation and Grimaldi's peerless drunk act.

'Hot Codlins' (Charles Dibdin)

A little old woman her living she got
By selling codlins, hot, hot, hot;
And this little old woman, who codlins sold,
Tho' her codlins were not, she felt herself cold;
So to keep herself warm, she thought it no sin
To fetch for herself a quartern of —

Ri tol iddy, iddy, iddy, iddy,
Ri tol, iddy, iddy, ri tol lay.

This little old woman set off in a trot,
To fetch her a quartern of hot! hot! hot!
She swallow'd one glass, and it was so nice,
She tipp'd off another in a trice;
The glass she fill'd till the bottle shrunk
And this little old woman, they say, got —

Ri tol iddy, iddy, iddy, iddy,
Ri tol, iddy, iddy, ri tol lay.

This little old woman, while muzzy she got,
Some boys stole her codlins hot! hot! hot!
Powder under her pan put, and in it round stones;
Says the little old woman, 'These apples have bones!'
The powder the pan in her face did send,
Which sent the old woman on her latter —

Ri tol iddy, iddy, iddy, iddy,
Ri tol, iddy, iddy, ri tol lay.

The little old woman then up she got,
All in a fury, hot! hot! hot!
Says she, 'Such boys, sure, never were known;
They never will let an old woman alone.'
Now here is a moral, round let it buz —
If you mean to sell codlins, never get —

Ri tol iddy, iddy, iddy, iddy,
Ri tol, iddy, iddy, ri tol lay.

251 *King's Bench prison*: Although, by the time of his resignation from Sadler's Wells, Charles Dibdin, junior, had gained a reputation as a theatrical hack, there were those who were willing to credit his talents with more respect. An August 1819 biographical sketch in the *European Magazine*, for example, placed him in a series of writers that included Samuel Taylor Coleridge and Madame de Staël.

251 *'drink and dissipation'*: Richard Wheeler's Memoir from the Clerkenwell workhouse, Percival, vol. 4, f. 194.

252 *a certain Mrs Price*: Letter from Joseph Grimaldi to Mrs Price, 8 July 1820: 'Madam, I have seen my son who is most prepared to settle the whole of your account. But if you will call on me on Friday morning with a receipt for £10 on account I will give it you leaving the balance a little longer. Yours, J. Grimaldi. Ps. Let the receipt be given in Mr. J.S. Grimaldi's name.' Daly ex-ill., vol. 4, p. 103.

252 *'heavy and painful infirmities'*: Dickens, *Memoirs*, p. 252.

252 *Grimaldi, Barfoot and Dibdin all decided*: Though the sellers are not named, the bill of auction (Percival, vol. 4, f. 173) announces three lots: two of seven-fortieths (Dibdin and Barfoot's share), and one of five (Grimaldi's). See also Appendix C, 'Share Holdings in Sadler's Wells, 1799–1820', in Dibdin, *Memoirs*, p. 167.

253 *a commemorative portrait*: Whitehead, *Memoirs*, p. 149, fn.

254 *'vibrate with the effect'*: *Gentleman's Magazine*, vol. vii, (1871) p. 91.

254 *'agony of mind ... premature old age'*: Dickens, *Memoirs*, pp. 255–6.

254–5 *'Young Grimaldi'*: *The Times*, 7 January 1820.

255 *'infantilised the dashing and ambitious JS'*: In 1816, for example, JS played a 'pocket clown attendant on Harlequin' in *Harlequin and the Sylph of the Oak; or, The Blind Beggar of Bethnal Green* (Covent Garden).

255 *'loss of agility in the parent'*: *BDA*, vol. 6, p. 416.

255 *'certain gross vulgarities'*: *The Times*, 27 December 1821.

255 *'Indecency upon the stage'*: Unidentified clipping, Percival, vol. 4, f. 218.

255–6 *caused outrage*: *European Magazine*, January 1819, pp. 48–51.

256 *killed by a falling beam*: E. L. Blanchard, *Life and Reminiscences*, vol. 1, p. 97.

257 *'never used any phrase recognised by society'*: Unidentified clipping, Islington Local History Centre.

257 *'Good God, sir'*: Unidentified clipping, Islington Local History Centre.

257 *sledge rides*: Arundell, *Sadler's Wells*, p. 102.

257 *'at a considerable sum'*: Dickens, *Memoirs*, p. 257.

258 *Dicky Usher*: Ashton, *Social England*, pp. 413–14.

258 *'rather gorgeous than elegant'*: *The Times*, 9 April 1822.

258 *punching one of the Drury Lane managers*: James Winston, *Drury Lane Journal: Selections From James Winston's Diaries, 1819–1827*, ed. Alfred L. Nelson and Gilbert G. Cross (London: Society for Theatre Research, 1974), pp. 30, 46, 57.

258 *the slightest anxiety*: Winston, *Drury Lane Journal*, p. 49.

259 *evangelical about reform*: George Rowell, *The Old Vic Theatre: A History* (Cambridge: Cambridge University Press, 1993), p. 19; Moody, *Illegitimate Theatre*, p. 119; Dickens, *Memoirs*, pp. 267–8.

259 *'a Bridewell, or a brothel'*: William Hazlitt, 'Minor Theatres – Strolling Players', in *Hazlitt on Theatre*, ed. William Archer and Robert Lowe (New York: Hill and Wang, 1957), pp. 155–64, p. 162.

259 *'practical and dirty jokes'*: Richard Wheeler's Memoir from the Clerkenwell workhouse, Percival, vol. 4, p. 195; Cooke played the monster in R. B. Peake's *Presumption; or, the Fate of Frankenstein* (1823).

260 *'strongest lungs and weakest judgement'*: *BDA*, vol. 8, p. 335.

260 *Clown's Dish of All Sorts*: The Coburg's 1822 season was notable for featuring a comic burlesque called *Life in Paris*, one of the many 'larking' plays inspired by Pierce Egan's picaresque novel *Tom and Jerry; or, Life in London*. *Life in London* was the fad of the year, with shows based on it playing at the Adelphi, Surrey, Astley's and Sadler's Wells. The Adelphi, Wells and Astley's productions were all called *Life in London*. The Surrey's was titled *Tom and Jerry; or, Life in a Lark*. See *The Times*, 9 April 1822.

261 *'which was the worst'*: Whitehead, *Memoirs*, p. 156, fn.

261 *'Bedlamite system of acting'*: Percival, vol. 5, f. 23.

261 *'a second Grimaldi'*: *Examiner*, 7 October 1827.

262 *the attention paid to Mont Blanc*: Hunt, *Autobiography*, vol. 1, p. 183.

262 *'I always take a shag'*: Winston, *Drury Lane Journal*, p. 16.

262 *'theatrical barracks'*: Walter Thornbury and Edward Walford, *Old and New London: A Narrative of Its History, Its People and Its Places*, 6 vols (London: Cassell, 1873), vol. 6, p. 371.

263 *'without feeling a sincere regret'*: Oxberry (eds), 'Memoir of Joseph Grimaldi', pp. 161–2.

263 *drunk for ten consecutive days*: Winston, *Drury Lane Journal*, pp. 56, 62.

263 *Astley detested drunks*: de Castro, *Memoirs*, p. 36.

263 *'limelight'*: 'Lighting', in Phyllis Hartnoll (ed.) *The Oxford Companion to the Theatre*, 4th edn (Oxford: Oxford University Press, 1983). See also Mole, *Byron's Romantic Celebrity*, p. 19.

264 *'In nine cases out of ten'*: Bunn, *The Stage*, p. 58.

264 *'heartless indifference and contempt ... unprincipled burlesque'*: 'The play was indifferent, but that was nothing. The acting was bad, but that was nothing.

The audience was low, but that was nothing. It was the heartless indifference and contempt shown by the performers for their parts and by the audience for the players and the play, that disgusted us with all of them.' William Hazlitt, 'Minor Theatres – Strolling Players', in *Hazlitt on Theatre*, ed. William Archer and Robert Lowe (New York: Hill and Wang, 1957), pp. 155–64, pp. 162–3.

264 *'token of a real and permanent change'*: Dickens, *Memoirs*, p. 256.

265 *'Time seems to pass harmlessly by him'*: *The Times*, 27 December 1822.

265 *'The strength of Grimaldi'*: Percival, vol. 4, f. 181.

265 *'gathered up into huge knots'*: Dickens, *Memoirs*, p. 258.

265 *'wept like a child'*: Dickens, *Memoirs*, pp. 258–9.

Poor Robin

267 *likened to a cat*: Winston, *Drury Lane Journal*, pp. 26, 127.

267 *'a divinity'*: Percival, vol. 4, f. 245.

268 *'Mr. G. seems much the worse for wear'*: Dickens, *Memoirs*, p. 261, fn. 2.

268 *at a weekly salary of six pounds*: Joe consistently acted as JS's agent from this time until the boy's death. A letter from Joe to Mr Arnold of the English Opera House, dated 18 May 1824, reveals how keen Grimaldi was to shop his son around: 'My son Mr. J.S. Grimaldi at present being disengaged during the vacation of C G theatre, wishes should anything be in contemplation wherein his exertions can be brought into action to fill up that time – Exclusive of his pantomime requisites, he is an excellent swordsman and in every other respect you will find him worth attention. – I would offer myself in a slight degree but my health is so much impaired by the profession already that I am fearful of attempting too much, however, something might be done especially as Mr. J.P. Cooke is in your theatre, by the revival of Perouse, Don Juan etc. This however yr consideration and as speedy an answer as possible will greatly oblige, your humble servant, J. Grimaldi.' Loose leaf inserted into George Cruikshank, *Life of Grimaldi by Charles Dickens: Proofs of the Etchings by George Cruikshank* (1838), Harry Elkins Widener Collection, Harvard University.

268 *'severe and alarming illness'*: Dickens, *Memoirs*, p. 262.

268 *'drunken freaks'*: Dickens, *Memoirs*, p. 262.

270 *'Grimaldi: a Jeu D'esprit'*: 'Biography of the British Stage', undated clipping, Islington Local History Centre.

271 *'His name is not in the bills'*: Unidentified clipping, Islington Local History Centre.

271 *found drunk together*: Winston, *Drury Lane Journal*, p. 78.

271 '*Hand Columbine about with nimble hand*': Though the poem cannot categorically be assigned to Grimaldi, given its close resemblance to the doggerel versifying that Joe increasingly came to produce in his retirement, there is no reason to doubt its authenticity.

'Adieu to the Stage, and Advice to His Son'

Adieu to Mother Goose, adieu, adieu,
To spangles, tufted heads, and dancing limbs;
Adieu to pantomime, to all that drew
O'er Christmas shoulders a rich robe of whims.
Never shall old Bologna – old, alack!
Once he was young and diamonded all o'er –
Take this particular Joseph on his back,
And dance the matchless fling beloved of yore.

Ne'er shall I build the wondrous verdant man,
Tall, turnip-headed, carrot-fingered, lean –
Ne'er shall I on the very newest plan
Cabbage a body – old Joe Frankenstein
Nor make a fire, nor eke compose a coach
Of saucepans, trumpets, cheese, and such sweet fare
Sorrow hath ta'en my number – I encroach
No more upon the chariot, but the chair.

Gone is the stride, four steps across the stage
Gone is the light vault o'er a turnpike gate!
Sloth puts my legs into this tiresome cage,
And stops me for a toll – I find too late!
How Ware would quiver his mad bow about
His rosin'd tight ropes, when I flapped a dance!
How would I twitch the pantaloon's good gout
And help his fall, and all his fears enhance!

How children shrieked to see me eat! How I
Stole the broad laugh from the aged sober folk!
Boys picked their plums out of my Christmas pie,
And people took my vices for a joke.
Be wise (that's foolish), troublesome (be rich) –
And oh, J.G. to every fancy stoop!
Carry a ponderous pocket at thy breech
And roll thine eyes as thou wouldst roll a hoop.

Hand Columbine about with nimble hand,
Covet thy neighbour's riches as thy own,
Dance on the water, swim upon the land,
Let thy legs prove themselves bone of my bone.
Cuff pantaloon, be sure – forget not this;
As thou beat'st him, thou'rt poor, J.G. or funny!
And wear a deal of paint upon thy phiz,
It doth boys good and draws in gallery money.

Lastly, be jolly, be alive, be light,
Twitch, flirt and caper, tumble, fall and throw;
Grow up right ugly in thy father's sight,
And be an 'absolute Joseph' like old Joe.

272 *'voice is thickening'*: Unidentified clipping, Library of the Garrick Club.

272 *'Without being equal to his father just yet'*: *The Times*, 27 December 1823.

272 *continued to pay Joe a half-salary*: Winston, *Drury Lane Journal*, p. 102; Daly ex-ill., vol. 4, p. 100.

272 *'In my present state of health'*: Letter from Joseph Grimaldi to Richard Hughes, 11 February 1824, Daly ex-ill., vol. 4, p. 100.

272 *'rising every morning a poorer man'*: Dickens, *Memoirs*, p.266.

273 *'the "ne plus ultra" of pantomime'*: Grimaldi Scrapbook, Harvard Theatre Collection, p. 13.

273 *'Young Grimaldi is the best Clown'*: *The Times*, 5 July 1824.

274 *'every species of wild debauchery'*: Dickens, *Memoirs*, p. 266 (see also p. 262).

274 *stabbed in the face*: *Trewman's Exeter Flying Post or Plymouth and Cornish Advertiser*, 25 November 1824.

274 *King and Queen of the Sandwich Islands*: The Sandwich Islands' ruling couple were particularly impressed with JS's swordsmanship when they saw him perform in Farley's melodrama, *The Spirit of the Moon*. See *The Times*, 24 April 1824.

275 *'Time and experience may do much'*: Percival, vol. 5, f. 51.

275 *cut his own throat*: Winston, *Drury Lane Journal*, p. 34.

275 *Only eleven people came*: Winston, *Drury Lane Journal*, p. 50.

275 *dangling from the street*: Winston, *Drury Lane Journal*, p. 69.

275 *'I wish with all my heart we had let him alone'*: Hunt, *Autobiography*, p. 183.

276 *one of the greatest nuisances in the metropolis*': Percival, vol. 4, f. 132.

276 *great man at Covent Garden*': Winston, *Drury Lane Journal*, p. 67.

276 *placed a note in the green room*: Winston, *Drury Lane Journal*, p. 66.

277 *centre of a large town*': 'When I first went to Sadler's Wells,' wrote Charles Dibdin, 'there was scarcely a House near it, and when I left it in 1819 but a few. Now it is the centre of a large town; and when in the year 1826 I went to see my Brother, in Myddleton Square, which with a Church in the centre stands where the Boys used to play at cricket, I actually lost my way, on a spot where I had resided upwards of 20 years.' Dibdin, *Memoirs*, pp. 39–41.

277–8 *Mr. T. Dibdin's talent*': Percival, vol. 5, f. 52.

278 *witnessing the famed Joey*': Percival, vol. 5, f. 23.

278 *dragged from a sick bed*': *Weekly Dramatic Register*, 2 June 1827.

278 *At present I am in difficulties*: Dickens, *Memoirs*, p. 266.

278 *without compelling the inhabitants*': Percival, vol. 5, f. 50.

279 *a pedestrian from Berkshire*': Percival, vol. 5, ff. 50, 52.

279 *fire balloon*': Percival, vol. 5, f. 50.

279 *Drury Lane Theatrical Fund*: He had been first elected to the Committee in 1808, following the resignation of Charles Kemble, and voted on again intermittently for the next twenty years.

279 *quite ashamed of looking at himself*': Findlater, *Joe Grimaldi*, p. 206.

280 *like Piccadilly Circus*': Disher, *Clowns and Pantomimes*, p. 145.

280 *a female of a certain class*': Unidentified clipping, Daly ex-ill., vol. 1, p. 15.

280–1 *On Friday evening … hope of recovery*': Findlater, *Joe Grimaldi*, p. 218.

281 *Mr. Grimaldi, jun., is not dead*': Unidentified clipping, Daly ex-ill., vol. 1, p. 15.

282 *reimburse the three thousand pounds*: Delpini's memorandum to the Prince (undated, though possibly 18 December 1798) reads: 'For the performance of the Deserter (Louisa) ten nights at the Little Theatre in the Haymarket; Subscription tickets 1 guinea. Mr. Weltjie [Louis Weltje, proprietor of a St James's cake shop, entered the Royal service as 'steward and *maître d'hôtel*' to the Prince's accounts and became one of his closest friends and advisers] requested to have five for his Royal Highness … £63. His Royal Highness honored me every night with his presence, with company. According to the rules of the Theatre it is customary for the Royal Family not to pay at the door – but at the end of the season the Treasurer makes out his account. But by the order of Mr. Weltjie this was not to be delivered, as he said he would

settle it. Therefore, ten nights for his Royal Highness's Box, at £3 pr. night ... £30. The Masquerade of the Fair of Venice, at the Pantheon, which I made on purpose for his Royal Highness after seven weeks labor and study, was three hundred guineas out of pocket. Mr. Weltjie took the receipts of all the money, and promised to see everything made good to me by his Royal Highness. Ten tickets given to Mr. Weltjie for his Royal Highness for the above Masquerade, at two guineas each ... £21. My last two Benefits, at Covent Garden Theatre, his Royal Highness had twelve tickets the first year, and six, the next ... £4 10 0 [Total:] 118 10.' A. Aspinall (ed.), *The Correspondence of George, Prince of Wales, 1770–1812*, 8 vols (Oxford: Oxford University Press, 1967), vol. 4, p. 540. Delpini's picket of Carlton House: when the Prince emerged, Delpini reportedly exclaimed, 'Ah! Votre altesse! Mon Prince! If you no speak to my Lord Chamberlain, for pauvre Delpini, I must go to your *papa's* bench.' Ryan, *Table Talk*, vol. 1, p. 259.

282–3 '*Pluck them asunder ... and I care not'ing*': Findlater, *Joe Grimaldi*, p. 233, fn. 1.

283 '*Mr Grimaldi's Last Appearance ... attack'd him*': Percival, vol. 5, f. 81.

284 '*burst into tears*': Oxberry (eds), 'Memoir of Joseph Grimaldi', p. 121. See also Percival, vol. 5, f. 82.

284 '*roar of laughter*': Percival, vol. 5, f. 82.

284 *white waistcoat and white gloves*: Percival, vol. 5, f. 82.

285 '*many-toned voice*': Bunn, *The Stage*, vol. 2, p. 167.

285 '*God bless you all! Farewell!*': Percival, vol. 5, f. 82.

285 '*GRIMALDI'S THANKS*': Percival, vol. 5, f. 82.

285 '*with an intensity of suffering*': *New Monthly Magazine*, Percival, vol. 5, f. 87.

285 *planned to distribute mementoes*: Percival, vol. 5, f. 82.

285 '*in a high state of fever*': Oxberry (eds), 'Memoir of Joseph Grimaldi', p. 121.

286 *Fanny Kelly interpreted it*: Basil Francis, *Fanny Kelly of Drury Lane* (London: Rockcliff, 1950), p. 134.

286 '*my poor master, Mr Harris*': Whitehead, *Memoirs*, p. 186, fn.

287 '*so distinguished a veteran*': Dickens, *Memoirs*, p. 274; the relevant passage in the bill read: 'It is respectfully announced, that Mr. GRIMALDI, After more than Four Years of severe and unremitting Indisposition, which continues without hope of alleviation, is compelled, finally, to relinquish a Profession, in which, from Infancy, he has been honoured with as liberal a share of Public

Patronage as ever has been accorded to Candidates of much higher pretensions. Numerous Patrons having expressed surprise that Mr. GRIMALDI'S Benefit did not take place at the *Theatre Royal, Covent Garden,* he takes the liberty of stating, that after bidding farewell to his Friends and Supporters at *Sadler's Wells,* (the Scene of his favoured exertions from the Age of Three Years) he applied to the present Directors of *Covent Garden Theatre,* who, in the kindest manner, expressed their regret, that the well-known situation of the Theatre precluded the possibility of indulging their strong inclination to comply with the request he had ventured to prefer. On transferring the application to *Mr. PRICE,* the Lessee of the Theatre Royal, *Drury Lane,* Mr. GRIMALDI has the pleasure to say, that it was acceded to with a celerity which enhanced the obligation, and demands his most sincere acknowledgement.' Percival, vol. 5, f. 89.

287 *'You should have had a night for nothing'*: Dickens, *Memoirs*, p. 277.

287 *Odes and Addresses to Great People*: Hood's poem is as follows:

> Joseph! they say thou'st left the stage,
> To toddle down the hill of life,
> And taste the flannell'd ease of age,
> Apart from pantomimic strife –
> 'Retired – [for Young would call it so] –
> The world shut out' – in Pleasant Row!
>
> And hast thou really wash'd at last
> From each white cheek the red half-moon
> And all thy public Clownship cast,
> To play the private Pantaloon?
> All youth – all ages yet to be
> Shall have a heavy miss of thee!
>
> Thou didst not preach to make us wise –
> Thou hadst no finger in our schooling –
> Thou didst not 'lure us to the skies' –
> Thy simple, simple trade was – Fooling!
> And yet, Heav'n knows! we could – we can
> Much 'better spare a better man!'
>
> Oh, had it pleased the gout to take
> The reverend Croly from the stage,
> Or Southey, for our quiet's sake,
> Or Mr. Fletcher, Cupid's sage,
> Or, damme! namby pamby Pool, –
> Or any other clown or fool!

Go, Dibdin – all that bear the name,
Go Byeway Highway man! go! go!
Go, Skeffy – man of painted fame,
But leave thy partner, painted Joe!
I could bear Kirby on the wane,
Or Signor Paulo with a sprain!

Had Joseph Wilfred Parkins made
His grey hairs scarce in private peace –
Had Waithman sought a rural shade –
Or Cobbett ta'en a turnpike lease –
Or Lisle Bowles gone to Balaam Hill –
I think I could be cheerful still!

Had Medwin left off, to his praise,
Dead lion kicking, like – a friend! –
Had long, long Irving gone his ways
To muse on death at Ponder's End –
Or Lady Morgan taken leave
Of Letters – still I might not grieve!

But, Joseph – everybody's Jo! –
Is gone – and grieve I will and must!
As Hamlet did for Yorick, so
Will I for thee (though not yet dust),
And talk as he did when he miss'd
The kissing-crust that he had kiss'd!

Ah, where is now thy rolling head!
Thy winking, reeling, drunken eyes,
(As old Catullus would have said,)
Thy oven-mouth, that swallow'd pies –
Enormous hunger – monstrous drowth! –
Thy pockets greedy as thy mouth!

Ah, where thy ears, so often cuff'd! –
Thy funny, flapping, filching hands! –
Thy partridge body, always stuff'd
With waifs, and strays, and contrabands! –
Thy foot – like Berkeley's Foote – for why?
'Twas often made to wipe an eye!

Ah, where thy legs – that witty pair!
For 'great wits jump' – and so did they!

Lord! how they leap'd in lamplight air!
Caper'd – and bounced – and strode away! –
That years should tame the legs – alack!
I've seen spring through an Almanack!

But bounds will have their bound – the shocks
Of Time will cramp the nimblest toes;
And those that frisk'd in silken clocks
May look to limp in fleecy hose –
One only – (Champion of the ring)
Could ever make his Winter, – Spring!

And gout, that owns no odds between
The toe of Czar and toe of Clown,
Will visit – but I did not mean
To moralize, though I am grown
Thus sad, – Thy going seem'd to beat
A muffled drum for Fun's retreat!

And, may be – 'tis no time to smother
A sigh, when two prime wags of London
Are gone – thou, Joseph, one, – the other,
A Joe! – 'sic transit gloria Munden!'
A third departure some insist on, –
Stage-apoplexy threatens Liston! –

Nay, then, let Sleeping Beauty sleep
With ancient 'Dozey' to the dregs—
Let Mother Goose wear mourning deep,
And put a hatchment o'er her eggs!
Let Farley weep – for Magic's man
Is gone – his Christmas Caliban!

Let Kemble, Forbes, and Willet rain,
As though they walk'd behind thy bier, –
For since thou wilt not play again,
What matters, – if in heav'n or here!
Or in thy grave, or in thy bed! –
There's Quick might just as well be dead!

Oh, how will thy departure cloud
The lamplight of the little breast!
The Christmas child will grieve aloud
To miss his broadest friend and best, –

Poor urchin! what avails to him
The cold New Monthly's Ghost of Grimm?

For who like thee could ever stride!
Some dozen paces to the mile! –
The motley, medley coach provide –
Or like Joe Frankenstein compile
The vegetable man complete! –
A proper Covent Garden feat!

Oh, who like thee could ever drink,
Or eat, – swill – swallow – bolt – and choke!
Nod, weep, and hiccup – sneeze and wink? –
Thy very yawn was quite a joke!
Though Joseph, Junior, acts not ill,
'There's no Fool like the old Fool' still!

Joseph, farewell! dear funny Joe!
We met with mirth, – we part in pain!
For many a long, long year must go
Ere Fun can see thy like again –
For Nature does not keep great stores
Of perfect Clowns – that are not Boors!

288 *'Slowly and seriously my visitor advanced'*: Percival, vol. 5, f. 88. 'Of his sufferings,' Hood continued, 'he spoke with a sad but resigned tone, expressed deep regret at quitting a profession he delighted in, and partly attributed the sudden breaking down of his health to the superior size of one particular stage which required of him a jump extra in getting off. That additional bound, like the bittock at the end of a Scotch mile, had, he thought, over-tasked his strength.'

288 *'vale of years'*: Percival, vol. 5, f. 83.

288–9 *'If I was a rich man'*: Grimaldi Scrapbook, Harvard Theatre Collection, p. 12.

289 *'concatenation of Clowns, Columbines'*: Percival, vol. 5, f. 83.

289 *'ingenious mechanical and philosophical Exhibition'*: Dibdin, *Memoirs*, p. 47.

289 *'a shout enough to rend the roof'*: New Monthly Magazine, vol. vii (1871), p. 92.

289 *'taxed his energies for a last effort'*: New Monthly Magazine, July 1839.

290 *'laughed as lustily as of old'*: Percival, vol. 5, f. 83.

290–1 *'Ladies and gentlemen ... Farewell! Farewell!'*: Percival, vol. 5, f. 84.

291 *'half led, half-carried him'*: New Monthly Magazine, July 1839.

291 *made a bow from the top of his steps*: Dickens, *Memoirs*, p. 281.

The Libertine Destroyed

293 *'Young Grimaldi'*: The Times, 27 December 1828.

294 fn. *Paulo did not remain in the part for long*: The Times, 21 January 1829.

294 *Three Wishes*: The Times, 9 June 1829.

294 *annual pension*: Dickens, *Memoirs*, put the figure at £100, whereas the *Caledonian Mercury* (10 April 1828) suggests £130.

294–5 *'Grand Naval Aquatic Exhibition'*: Morning Chronicle, 29 July 1829.

295 *'very often reminded us of his never-to-be-forgotten father'*: The Times, 28 December 1829.

295 *'not infrequently arrested'*: Findlater, *Joe Grimaldi*, p. 216.

295 *'quite delirious'*: Unidentified clipping, dated 1830, Daly ex-ill., vol. 1, p. 13.

295 *Edinburgh ... next to the Coburg*: The Times, 4 March 1831. 'Upon the filing of the Petition and Schedule of Joseph Samuel William Grimaldi commonly called and known by the name of Joseph Samuel Grimaldi, formerly of Noble St. Islington, then of 18 Guildford Place Spa Fields then of 31 New North St. Theobald's Road, then of Devonshire St. Queen Square, then of the corner of Drake Street Theobald's Road then of Mile End Road then of Chade Row Bagnigge Wells Road then of Stourbridge Worcester and Cheltenham Gloucestershire of Chade Row aforesaid then of 5 Borough Road Surrey, then of Lloyd's Row Spa Fields Middlesex then of Edinburgh, Glasgow, Ayr and Greenock all in Scotland, then of Martlett Court, Drury Lane [where his great grandfather pulled teeth] Middlesex and later of 13 Mitre Street New Cut Lambeth and of the Coburg Theatre, Lambeth aforesaid comedian.' Daly, ex-ill., vol. 4, p. 139.

296 *'dresses had fallen to rags'*: Dickens, *Memoirs*, p. 284.

296 *growing struggle between the patents and the minor theatres*: Watson Nicholson, *The Struggle for a Free Stage in London* (New York: Blom, 1966), pp. 309–11; Moody, *Illegitimate Theatre*, pp. 42–3.

297 *'I know it is a great favour to ask'*: Charles Brintiffe Smith, *Original Letters of Dramatic Performers, Collected and Arranged by Charles Brintiffe Smith*, Library of the Garrick Club, c. 1850, 9 vols, vol. 2, p. 62.

297 *'I cannot remember in what year'*: Brintiffe Smith, vol. 5, p. 80.

298 *found dead the following morning*: Blanchard, *Life and Reminiscences*, vol. 1, p. 4, fn. 1. There is some disagreement over the details of this story. Blanchard's editors date it at 1829, although erroneously, as Parsloe was playing Clown at Drury Lane in 1830. Moreover, a clipping in the Percival collection suggests that the pantomime was not *Mother Goose* at all: 'A letter has been received in London from New York, stating that Parsloe, who went to America some time since, while performing in *Peter Wilkins* at one of the theatres there, was precipitated on the stage in consequence of some failure in the machinery, and killed on the spot.' Percival, vol. 2, f. 53.

298–9 *'Being as lost to the stage'*: Bunn, *The Stage*, vol. 2, pp. 162.

299 *'I sincerely regret ... provided an arrangement can be made for my son'*: Clipping, *Era Almanac*, 1883, Mander and Mitchenson Collection, University of Greenwich.

300 *'She has had a Paraletic attack'*: Findlater, *Joe Grimaldi*, p. 220.

301 *'On Tuesday morning ... in his 30th year'*: Unidentified clipping, 23 December 1832, Daly ex-ill., vol. 1, p. 13.

301 *seized with violent vomiting*: 'Extraordinary Inquest on Young Grimaldi', unidentified clipping, 23 December 1832, Daly ex-ill., vol. 1, p. 13.

301 *'snatches of the parts'*: Dickens, *Memoirs*, p. 287.

303 *'a strange business ... did not die a natural death'*: 'Extraordinary Inquest on Young Grimaldi', unidentified clipping, 23 December 1832, Daly ex-ill., vol. 1, p. 13.

304 *'a young courtezan'*: *Gentleman's Magazine*, 2:6 (June 1838), p. 417.

304 *Whitefield's Tabernacle*: *Morning Chronicle*, 17 December 1832.

304 *'Ev'ry act of each day'*: Unidentified clipping beneath a portrait of JS as Scaramouch, Daly ex-ill., vol. 3, p. 125.

> 'Epistle I. To JOE GRIM*****.'
> We all are thy debtors, detestable Joe,
> That debt with one voice we'll repay –
> In our ears you have clank'd the bodings of woe,
> While our hearts fought the cares of this life to forego,
> You turned the deaf vision away.
>
> Yet remark – nothing more than acknowledgements pure
> Of your gifts can our bosoms impart;
> Thy intentions towards us shall be laid at your door,
> We are barren in vice, so shall merely restore,
> Those evils which sprang from your heart.

Your wretched self-pride! Your assassin-like leer,
Shed on Mirth fell malignity's cloud –
Fair Mirth's placid voice seem'd discord in your ear;
For cruelly vicious and meanly severe –
In dark cares her chaste form you'll enshroud.

Ev'ry act of each day brings thee hatred and Shame,
Strews thy path with the thorns of disgrace,
In Infamy's books writes the tale of your fame,
And bids us retreat from your deeds and your name!
The debts paid – if you can – rest in peace.

* Watchman! – I give charge of those fellows.

305 *'dressed to leave ... shudder to think of'*: Charles Dickens, *The Pickwick Papers* (Harmondsworth: Penguin, 2003), p. 49.

305 *'searing him'*: Dickens, *The Pickwick Papers*, p. 50.

306 *'great precocity'*: Charles Dickens, 'Speech to the General Theatrical Fund Association', 6 April 1846, in *The Speeches of Charles Dickens*, ed. K. J. Fielding (Oxford: Oxford University Press, 1968), p. 76.

306 *'spirit of Grimaldi'*: Edwin M. Eigner, *The Dickens Pantomime* (Berkeley: University of California Press, 1989), p. 6.

306 *the scary clown*: Scary clowns are legion in popular culture, and some of the best-known examples include *Poltergeist* (1982), Pennywise, the Dancing Clown in Stephen King's novel *It* (1986), photographer Cindy Sherman's 'Psychedelic Clown' series of 2004, the movie *Killer Klowns from Outer Space* and, of course, *Batman*'s Joker. Mixing circus imagery with horror motifs is sometimes known as 'dark carnival'. For a discussion of this genre, see Mark Dery's chapter 'Cotton-Candy Autopsy: Deconstructing Psycho-Killer Clowns', in his *The Pyrotechnic Insanitarium: American Culture on the Brink* (New York: Grove, 1999), p. 73.

307 *'the best clown we have'*: *Caledonian Mercury*, 13 December 1834.

307 *'unprovided for'*: *The Times*, 31 July 1835.

307 *a committee had been formed*: Percival, vol. 6, f. 6.

307 *'the sufferings of buffoons'*: Percival, vol. 3, f. 212.

307 *doctor's bill*: Letter from Joseph Grimaldi to John Hughes, 19 March 1834, Daly ex-ill., vol. 2, p. 53.

308 *forbear from suicide*: This anecdote appears in Blanchard Jerrold's *Life of George Cruikshank in Two Epochs* (London: Chatto and Windus, 1883), p. 233: 'Joey and his much better half, one evening, disputing about precedency, resolved upon taking poison to end all contention, and to settle their differences of opinion for ever. But not taking enough, and forgetting the oft quoted maxim, now travestied "Drink deep, or taste not any poisonous thing," the feeble dose merely kept them awake and talkative, and lying in the same room, with a slight partition between them, sensations became unpleasant, and so they held a colloquy in their fears as follows: "Joey are you dead?" "No Mary – are you?" "No." And then they altered their minds, and felt disposed to live a little longer, arose, had a good supper and something warm and comfortable as a sedative and antidote, and then jogged on a little more in unison.'

308 *'return from Transportation'*: Disher, *Clowns and Pantomimes*, p. 115.

308 *'I am not to be duped'*: Letter from Joseph Grimaldi to Mr Proctor, 20 July 1836.

308 *'wont to wander up and down'*: Percival, vol. 3, f. 212.

309 *'Joseph Grimaldi is dear to all'*: Letter from Charles Farley to Joseph Grimaldi, 20 December 1836, Grimaldi Scrapbook, Harvard Theatre Collection.

309 *'afflicted with rheumatism'*: 'D.J.', 'Letter of Joseph Grimaldi', *Notes and Queries*, 7 Series, 24 November 1888, pp. 24–5.

309 *'no one was happier than your old and true chum'*: Letter from Joseph Grimaldi to unknown recipient, 9 December 1835, Daly ex-ill., vol. 1, p. 53.

310 *'I am very ill … always in pain'*: Findlater, *Joe Grimaldi*, p. 222.

310 *'Grim-all-day'*: Letter from Joseph Grimaldi to unknown recipient, 5 December 18??, Bentley ex-ill., vol. 2, p. 203.

310 *'400 closely-written pages'*: Unidentified clipping, Islington Local History Centre.

311 *'no Song, or Performance of any description'*: Disher, *Clowns and Pantomimes*, p. 146.

311 *'least humorous'*: Disher, *Clowns and Pantomimes*, p. 147.

311 *'roars of laughter'*: Blanchard, *Life and Reminiscences*, vol. 1, pp. 51–2, fn. 3.

311 *'re-write, revise and correct'*: Dickens, *Memoirs*, p. 299.

311 *'dreary twaddle'*: *Letters of Charles Dickens*, ed. Madeline House and Graham Storey (Oxford: Clarendon, 1982), vol. 1, p. 337.

312 *'Died by the visitation of God'*: 'Coroner's Inquest on Joseph Grimaldi, the Celebrated Clown', June 1837 clipping, Islington Local History Centre.

312 *His grave*: Despite a life spent perpetually pleading poverty, Joe left more than £500 to distribute among his family and friends. Louisa Bristow received £74, Charlotte Bryan, Mary's second sister, received £100 and all his household goods except plate and jewels, and Maria Neville, the youngest of the Bristows, got £50. His neighbour Mrs Arthur received £100 for her kindness, and Dayus, Norman, and another friend, James Banister of Deptford, each received £25 for 'old acquaintance' and 'kind attentions'. Richard Hughes, appointed Joe's trustee, was bequeathed his shares in Sadler's Wells and the rights to his memoirs, while Hughes's daughter Elizabeth received two patchwork quilts made by his first wife, Maria, and one by Maria's sister, Julia. Before he died, Joe promised Macready the snuff box he had been presented by Lord Byron. Some weeks after the funeral, Richard Hughes received a letter from a woman called Jane Taylor, who claimed to be Joe's sister and asked if she'd been remembered in his will. Even if he was aware of the Signor's many daughters, Hughes was convinced that it was a hoax, and after he had penned a polite reply, she was never heard of again.

Epilogue

313–14 *'We don't know why... a national calamity'*: Figaro in London, 10 June 1837.

314 *'manners of the middle class'*: Angelo, *Reminiscences*, vol. 1, p. 219.

315 *prohibiting the presence of theatrical booths*: Paul Schlicke, *Dickens and Popular Entertainment* (London: Allen and Unwin, 1985), p. 93.

315 *'naughty, fox-hunting'*: Andrew Lang, quoted in Vic Gatrell, *City of Laughter: Sex and Satire in Eighteenth-Century London* (New York: Walker, 2006), p. 418.

315 *'the amusements of our youth?'*: Thackeray, *Four Georges*, p. 377.

315–16 *eating the bread of charity*: The Times, 2 August 1838.

316 *'not without some sentimental feeling'*: The Times, 6 September 1838.

316 *'stuck to me like a brother'*: Blanchard, *Life and Reminiscences*, vol. 2, p. 584.

316 *'risk our necks'*: Marshall, 'Ellar', pp. 118–19.

316 *'slackened by debility'*: Marshall, 'Ellar', p. 118.

316 *'Spangles'*: Blanchard, *Life and Reminiscences*, vol. 2, p. 582.

317 *'disappointment and vexation'*: Marshall, 'Ellar', p. 123.

317 *died within a few weeks*: Marshall, 'Ellar', p. 122.

317 *'Oh! poor old Joey!'*: Mayer, *Harlequin in His Element*, p. 139.

318 *'with neither Harlequin ... not effect next?'*: Percival, vol. 5, f. 86.

318 *'serious spirit of the age'*: Tatler, 28 December 1831.

319 *'mass of gratuitous absurdity'*: *The Times*, 30 December 1830.

319 *'recommend themselves to the public'*: Halliday, *Comical Fellows*, p. 50.

320 *accompanied by his daughter*: Grimaldi Scrapbook, Harvard Theatre Collection, p. 24.

320 *'unpromising state of the weather'*: Grimaldi Scrapbook, p. 24.

320 *died in Brighton in 1889*: Blanchard, *Life and Reminiscences*, vol. 2, p. 632, fn. 1.

320 *'that glorious comic face'*: Findlater, *Joe Grimaldi*, p. 238, fn. 7. By the time Tom Matthews died, Joe's grave had fallen into weed-ridden disrepair. *Lloyd's News* paid to have it restored in 1909, but the briars soon returned, and when the headstone fell away from the plot, no attempt was made to reattach it. With the stone consigned to a workman's shed, Grimaldi remained forgotten to all but the most dedicated theatre historians until 1949, when a group of working clowns decided to hold a memorial service in his honour. St James's was the obvious choice, and the event took place annually for ten years at that location until the church was deconsecrated and the clowns were offered the service's current home at Holy Trinity, Dalston.

321 *'evade the compulsion to suffer'*: Sigmund Freud, 'Humour', in *The Standard Edition of the Complete Psychological Works of Sigmund Freud*, ed. and trans. James Strachey, vol. 21, pp. 161–6, p. 163.

322 *'You should have seen Grimaldi!'*: Anon., 'Reminiscences of Grimaldi', *Bentley's Miscellany*, 19 (1846), pp. 160–1.

BIBLIOGRAPHY

Anon., 'Reminiscences of Grimaldi', *Bentley's Miscellany*, 19 (1846), pp. 160–1

Ackermann, Rudolph, William Combe, W. H. Pyne, Augustus Pugin and Thomas Rowlandson, *The Microcosm of London; or, London in Miniature*, 2 vols (London: Methuen, 1904)

Adolphus, John, *Memoirs of John Bannister, Comedian*, 2 vols (London: Richard Bentley, 1839)

Altick, Richard D., *The Shows of London* (Cambridge, Massachusetts et al.: Belknap/Harvard University Press, 1978)

Angelo, Henry, *The Reminiscences of Henry Angelo*, ed. H. Lavers Smith, 2 vols (New York and London: Benjamin Blom, 1969)

Arundell, Dennis, *The Story of Sadler's Wells, 1683–1977* (London et al.: David and Charles, 1965)

Ashley-Cooper, Anthony, Lord Shaftesbury, *Letter Concerning Enthusiasm* and *Sensus Communis: An Essay on the Freedom of Wit and Humour*, ed. Richard B. Wolf (New York: Garland, 1988)

Ashton, John, *Social England Under the Regency* (London: Chatto and Windus, 1899)

Aspinall, A. (ed.), *The Correspondence of George, Prince of Wales, 1770–1812*, 8 vols (Oxford: Oxford University Press, 1967)

Assael, Brenda, *The Circus and Victorian Society* (Charlottesville and London: University of Virginia Press, 2005)

Baer, Marc, *Theatre and Disorder in Late Georgian London* (Oxford: Clarendon, 1992)

Beattie, James, 'On Laughter and Ludicrous Composition', in *Essays* (Edinburgh, 1776), pp. 253–66

Beaumont, Cyril W., *The History of Harlequin* (New York: Blom, 1967)

Beckford, William, *Life at Fonthill, 1807–1822: From the Correspondence of William Beckford*, ed. and trans. Boyd Alexander (Stroud: Nonsuch, 2006)

Berkeley, Grantley Fitzhardinge, *My Life and Recollections*, 4 vols (London: Hurst and Blackett, 1865)

Besant, Walter, *London in the Nineteenth Century* (New York and London: Garland, 1985)

Blanchard, E. L., *The Life and Reminiscences of E. L. Blanchard, with Notes from the Diary of Wm. Blanchard*, ed. Clement Scott and Cecil Howard, 2 vols (London: Hutchinson, 1891)

Boaden, James, *Memoirs of the Life of John Philip Kemble, esq., Including a History of the Stage from the Time of Garrick to the Present Period* (Philadelphia: Small et al., 1825)

—, *The Memoirs of Mrs. Siddons, Interspersed with Anecdotes of Authors and Actors* (Philadelphia: Carey et al., 1827)

—, *The Life of Mrs. Jordan, Including Original Private Correspondence and Numerous Anecdotes of Her Contemporaries*, 2 vols (London: Edward Bull, 1831)

Booth, Michael R. (ed.), *English Plays of the Nineteenth Century, V: Pantomimes, Extravaganzas, and Burlesques* (Oxford: Clarendon, 1976)

Boswell, James, *Boswell's London Journal, 1762–1763*, ed. Frederick A. Pottle (Edinburgh: Edinburgh University Press, 1991)

Braudy, Leo, *The Frenzy of Renown: Fame and Its History* (New York: Vintage, 1997)

Brodey, Inger Sigrun, 'Masculinity, Sensibility, and the "Man of Feeling": The Gendered Ethics of Goethe's *Werther*', *Papers on Language & Literature*, 35:2 (1999) 115-40

Bunn, Alfred, *The Stage: Both Before and Behind the Curtain, from Observations Taken on the Spot*, 3 vols (London: Bentley, 1840)

Byron, George Gordon Noel, *Byron's Letters and Journals*, ed. Leslie A. Marchand, 12 vols (Cambridge, Massachusetts: Harvard University Press, 1973–1994)

Campardon, Émile, *Les Spectacles de la Foire*, 2 vols (Geneva: Slatkine Reprints, 1970)

Cannadine, David (ed.), *Admiral Lord Nelson: Context and Legacy* (Basingstoke: Palgrave, 2005)

Carlson, Julie A., 'Forever Young: Master Betty and the Queer Stage of Youth in English Romanticism', *South Atlantic Quarterly* 95:3 (Summer 1996) 575–602

Cohen, David B., *Out of the Blue: Depression and Human Nature* (New York: Norton, 1994)

Coleman, Loren, *Mysterious America* (London and Boston: Faber and Faber, 1983)

Coleridge, Samuel Taylor, *The Table Talk and Omniana*, ed. T. Ashe (London, 1884)

Conolly, L. W., *The Censorship of English Drama, 1737–1824* (San Marino: Huntington Library, 1976)

Corry, John, *A Satirical View of London; Comprehending a Sketch of the Manners of the Age*, 2nd edn (London, 1803)

Crosby, Benjamin, *Crosby's Pocket Companion to the Playhouses. Being the Lives of All the Principal London Performers* (London, 1796)

Cruikshank, George, *Life of Grimaldi by Charles Dickens: Proofs of the Etchings by George Cruikshank* (privately published, 1838)

de Castro, John, *The Memoirs of J. de Castro, Comedian*, ed. R. Humphreys (London, 1824)

Dery, Mark, *The Pyrotechnic Insanitarium: American Culture on the Brink* (New York: Grove, 1999)

Dibdin, Charles, senior, *The Professional Life of Mr. Dibdin, Written by Himself, Together with the Words of Six Hundred Songs Selected From His Works, Interspersed with Many Humorous and Entertaining Anecdotes Incidental to the Public Character*, 4 vols (London, 1803)

—, *The Royal Circus Epitomised* (London, 1784)

Dibdin, Charles Isaac Mungo, junior, *The Professional and Literary Memoirs of Charles Dibdin the Younger, Dramatist and Upward of Thirty Years Manager of Minor Theatres*, ed. George Speaight (London: Society for Theatre Research, 1956)

—, *Jan Ben Jan; or, Harlequin and the Forty Virgins* (London, 1807)

Dibdin, Thomas J., *The Reminiscences of Thomas Dibdin of the Theatres Royal Covent Garden, Drury Lane, Haymarket, etc.*, 2 vols (London, 1837)

—, *Harlequin and Mother Goose; or, the Golden Egg!* (London: Thomas Hailes Lacy, 18–)

—, *Harlequin Hoax* (Larpent MS, 1814)

—, *Valentine and Orson, A Romantic Melo-drame* (London, 1804)

Dickens, Charles, *The Memoirs of Joseph Grimaldi*, ed. Richard Findlater (New York: Stein and Day, 1968)

—, *The Memoirs of Joseph Grimaldi*, ed. and rev. with notes and additions by Charles Whitehead (London: Richard Bentley, 1846)

—, *Letters of Charles Dickens*, ed. Madeline House and Graham Storey, 12 vols (Oxford: Clarendon, 1982)

—, *Nicholas Nickleby* (London: Mandarin, 1991)

—, *The Pickwick Papers* (Harmondsworth: Penguin, 2003)

—, *The Speeches of Charles Dickens*, ed. K. J. Fielding (Oxford: Oxford University Press, 1968)

Disher, Maurice Willson, *Clowns and Pantomimes* (Boston and New York: Houghton Mifflin, 1925)

'D.J.', 'Letter of Joseph Grimaldi', *Notes and Queries*, 7 Series, 24 November 1888, pp. 24–5

Donohue, Joseph, *Theatre in the Age of Kean* (Oxford: Blackwell, 1975)

Drummond, J. C., Anne Wibraham, and Dorothy Hollingsworth, *The Englishman's Food: A History of Five Centuries of English Diet* (London: Jonathan Cape, 1958)

Eigner, Edwin M., *The Dickens Pantomime* (Berkeley: University of California Press, 1989)

England, Martha Winburn, *Garrick and Stratford* (New York: New York Public Library, 1962)

Fahrner, Robert, *The Theatre Career of Charles Dibdin the Elder* (New York et al.: Peter Lang, 1989)

Fairburn, John, *Fairburn's Description of the Popular and Comic New Pantomime, called Harlequin and Mother Goose; or, the Golden Egg* (London, 1807)

Farley, Charles, *Harlequin Asmodeus; or, Cupid on Crutches* (London: J. Barker, Dramatic Repository, 1810)

Feltham, John, *Picture of London for 1805* (London, 1805)

Fenner, Theodore, 'Ballet in Early Nineteenth-Century London as Seen by Leigh Hunt and Henry Robertson', *Dance Chronicle*, 1:2 (1977–8), 75–95

Findlater, Richard, *Joe Grimaldi: His Life and Theatre*, 2nd edn (Cambridge: Cambridge University Press, 1977)

Fisher, Seymour and Rhoda, *Pretend the World is Funny and Forever: A Psychoanalysis of Comedians, Clowns and Actors* (Hillsdale, New Jersey: Lawrence Erlbaum Associates, 1981)

Fitzgerald, Percy, *The World Behind the Scenes* [1881] (New York: Blom, 1972)

—, *Chronicles of Bow Street Police-Office, with an Account of the Magistrates, 'Runners' and Police; and a Selection of the Most Interesting Cases*, 2 vols (London: Chapman and Hall, 1888)

Foreman, Amanda, *Georgiana, Duchess of Devonshire* (New York: Modern Library, 2001)

Francis, Basil, *Fanny Kelly of Drury Lane* (London: Rockcliff, 1950)

Freud, Sigmund, 'Humour', in *The Standard Edition of the Complete Psychological Works of Sigmund Freud*, ed. and trans. James Strachey, vol. 21, pp. 161–6

Frow, Gerald, *'Oh Yes It Is!': A History of Pantomime* (London: BBC, 1985)

Gatrell, Vic, *City of Laughter: Sex and Satire in Eighteenth-Century London* (New York: Walker, 2006)

Geijer, Erik Gustaf, *Impressions of England, 1809–1810*, trans. Elizabeth Sprigge and Claude Napier (London: Cape, 1932)

Genest, John, *Some Account of the English Stage from the Restoration in 1660 to 1830*, 10 vols (Bath: Carrington, 1832)

Goodwin, Cliff, *When the Wind Changed: The Life and Death of Tony Hancock* (London: Century, 1999)

Goodwin, Thomas, *Sketches and Impressions: Musical, Theatrical, and Social, 1799–1885* (New York and London: Putnam, 1887)

Groede, C. A. G., *A Stranger in England; or, Travels in Great Britain* (London, 1807)

Gross, Dalton and Mary, 'Joseph Grimaldi: An Influence on *Frankenstein*', *Notes and Queries*, 28:226, no. 5 (1981), 402–4

Halliday, Andrew, *Comical Fellows; or, the History and Mystery of the Pantomime* (London: Thomson, 1863)

Hamilton, Nigel, *Biography: A Brief History* (Cambridge, Massachusetts: Harvard University Press, 2007)

Hartnoll, Phyllis (ed.), *The Oxford Companion to the Theatre*, 4th edn (Oxford: Oxford University Press, 1983)

Harvey, Robert, *The War of Wars: The Great European Conflict, 1793–1815* (New York: Carroll and Graf, 2006)

Hazlitt, William, *The Complete Works of William Hazlitt*, ed. P. P. Howe, 21 vols (London: Dent, 1930)

—, *A View of the English Stage* (London: Robert Stodart, 1818)

—, *Hazlitt on Theatre*, ed. William Archer and Robert Lowe (New York: Hill and Wang, 1957)

Hibbert, Christopher, *George IV: Regent and King, 1811–1830* (London: Allen Lane, 1973)

— (ed.), *Captain Gronow: His Reminiscences of Regency and Victorian Life, 1810–60* (London: Kyle Cathie, 1991)

Highfill, Philip, Kalman A. Burnim, and Edward A. Langhans, *A Biographical Dictionary of Actors, Actresses, Musicians, Dancers, Managers & Other Stage Personnel in London, 1660–1800*, 16 vols (Carbondale: Southern Illinois University Press, c.1973–93)

Hobbs, Sandy, and David Cornwall, 'Killer Clowns and Vampires: Children's Panics in Contemporary Scotland', in *Supernatural Enemies*, ed. Hilda Ellis Davidson and Anna Chaudhri (Durham, North Carolina: Carolina Academic Press, 2001), pp. 203–17

Hogan, Charles Beecher, *The London Stage, 1776–1800: A Critical Introduction* (Carbondale *et al.*: Southern Illinois University Press, 1968)

Holcroft, Thomas, *The Life of Thomas Holcroft*, ed. Elbridge Colby, 2 vols (New York: Blom, 1968)

Holmes, M. R., *Stage Costume and Accessories* (London: London Museum, 1968)

Hood, Thomas, *Hood's Own; or, Laughter From Year to Year* (London: Bailey, 1839)

Hume, Robert D. (ed.), *The London Theatre World, 1660–1800* (Carbondale and Edwardsville: Southern Illinois University Press, 1980)

Hunt, Leigh, *The Autobiography of Leigh Hunt, with Reminiscences of His Friends and Contemporaries*, 2 vols (New York: AMS, 1965)

—, *Leigh Hunt's Dramatic Criticism, 1808–1831*, ed. Lawrence Hutson Houtchens and Carolyn Washburn Houtchens (New York: Columbia University Press, 1949)

Hutcheson, Francis, *Reflections on Laughter and Remarks Upon the Fable of the Bees* (Glasgow, 1750)

Isherwood, Robert M., *Farce and Fantasy: Popular Entertainment in Eighteenth-Century Paris* (Oxford and New York: Oxford University Press, 1986)

Janus, Samuel, 'The Great Comedians: Personality and Other Factors', *American Journal of Psychoanalysis*, 35:2 (1975), 169–74

Jerrold, Blanchard, *Life of George Cruikshank in Two Epochs* (London: Chatto and Windus, 1883)

Kavanagh, Julie, *Nureyev: The Life* (New York: Pantheon, 2007)

Kelly, Ian, *Beau Brummell: The Ultimate Man of Style* (New York et al.: Free Press, 2006)

Kelly, Linda, *The Kemble Era: John Philip Kemble, Sarah Siddons and the London Stage* (London et al.: Bodley Head, 1980)

—, *Richard Brinsley Sheridan: A Life* (London: Sinclair-Stevenson, 1997)

Kelly, Michael, *Reminiscences*, ed. Roger Fiske (London: Oxford University Press, 1975)

Kemble, John Philip, *Lodoiska: An Opera in Three Acts* (London: n.d. [1794])

Kendall, Alan, *David Garrick: A Biography* (London: Harrap, 1985)

Khan, Mirza Abul Hassan, *A Persian at the Court of King George, 1809–10: The Journal of Mirza Abul Hassan Khan*, ed. Margaret Morris Cloake (London: Barrie and Jenkins, 1988)

Lennep, William Van, Emmett L. Avery, Arthur H. Scouten, George Winchester Stone, and Charles Beecher Hogan (eds), *The English Stage, 1660–1800: A Calendar of Plays, Entertainments and Afterpieces Together With Casts, Box-Receipts and Contemporary Comment*, 11 vols (Carbondale and Edwardsville: Southern Illinois University Press, 1960–79)

Lister, Martin, *A Journey to Paris in the Year 1698* (London: 1699)

Lombroso, Cesare, *The Man of Genius* (London: Walter Scott, 1891)

Low, Donald A., *The Regency Underworld* (Stroud: Sutton, 2005)

MacCarthy, Fiona, *Byron: Life and Legend* (New York: Farrar, Straus and Giroux, 2003)

Macdonald, D. L., *Monk Lewis: A Critical Biography* (Toronto: University of Toronto Press, 2000)

Mackintosh, Iain, *The Georgian Playhouse: Actors, Artists, Audiences and Architecture, 1730–1830*, Hayward Gallery Exhibition Catalogue (London: Arts Council of Great Britain, 1975)

Mackoull, John, *Abuses of Justice*, 2nd edn (London: M. Jones, 1812)

Malcolm, James Peller, *London Redivium*, 4 vols (London, 1803–7)

Marcham, Frank, 'Joseph Grimaldi and Finchley', reprinted from *Transactions of the London and Middlesex Archaeological Society* (London, 1939)

Marshall, Thomas, 'Ellar, the Harlequin', in *Lives of the Most Celebrated Actors and Actresses*, ed. Thomas Marshall (London, 1848)

Mathews, Anne, *Memoirs of Charles Mathews*, 4 vols (London: Richard Bentley, 1838–9)

Mayer III, David, *Harlequin in His Element: The English Pantomime, 1806–1836* (Cambridge, Massachusetts: Harvard University Press, 1969)

Mayes, Stanley, *The Great Belzoni: The Circus Strongman Who Discovered Egypt's Treasures* [1959] (London: Tauris Parke, 2003)

Miles, Henry Downes, *The Life of Joseph Grimaldi, with Anecdotes of His Contemporaries* (London: Christopher Harris, 1838)

Milhous, Judith, 'The Economics of Theatrical Dance in Eighteenth-Century London', *Theatre Journal*, 55:3 (2003), 481–508

Mole, Tom, *Byron's Romantic Celebrity: Industrial Culture and the Hermeneutic of Intimacy* (Basingstoke: Palgrave, 2007)

Moody, Jane, *Illegitimate Theatre in London, 1770–1840* (Cambridge: Cambridge University Press, 2000)

— and Mary Luckhurst (eds), *Theatre and Celebrity in Britain, 1660–2000* (Basingstoke: Palgrave, 2005)

Munden, Thomas Shepherd, *Memoirs of Joseph Shepherd Munden, Comedian. By His Son* (London: Richard Bentley, 1844)

Murray, D. L., *Candles and Crinolines* (London: J. Cape, 1926)

Nicholson, Watson, *The Struggle for a Free Stage in London* (New York: Blom, 1966)

Nicoll, Allardyce, *A History of Early Nineteenth Century Drama, 1800–1850*, 2 vols (Cambridge: Cambridge University Press, 1930)

Niklaus, Thelma, *Harlequin; or, the Rise and Fall of a Bergamask Rogue* (New York: George Braziller, 1956)

O'Brien, John, *Harlequin Britain: Pantomime and Entertainment, 1690–1760* (Baltimore and London: Johns Hopkins University Press, 2004)

O'Toole, Fintan, *A Traitor's Kiss: The Life of Richard Brinsley Sheridan* (London: Granta, 1997)

Oxberry, Catherine and William (eds), 'Memoir of Joseph Grimaldi', in *Oxberry's Dramatic Biography and Histrionic Anecdotes*, 5 vols (London, 1825–6), vol. 2, pp. 109–22

Parissien, Steven, *George IV: The Grand Entertainment* (London: John Murray, 2001)

Pasquin, Anthony, *The Children of Thespis. A Poem*, 3 parts (London, 1786–8)

Pickering, David, *Encyclopaedia of Pantomime* (Andover: Gale Research International, 1993)

Planché, James Robinson, *The Recollections and Reflections of J. R. Planché*, 2 vols (London: Tinsley Bros., 1872)

Playfair, Giles, *The Prodigy: A Study of the Strange Life of Master Betty* (London: Secker and Warburg, 1967)

Porter, Roy, and Marie Mulvey Roberts (eds), *Pleasure in the Eighteenth Century* (Basingstoke: Macmillan, 1996)

Press, Anita Louise, 'Sadler's Wells Theatre Under Charles Dibdin the Younger from 1800–1819: When Britannia Ruled the Stage', unpublished doctoral dissertation (University of Toronto, 1994)

Ranger, Paul, *'Terror and Pity Reign in Every Breast': Gothic Drama in the London Patent Theatres, 1750–1820* (London: Society for Theatre Research, 1991)

Ravel, Jeffrey S., *The Contested Parterre: Public Theatre and French Political Culture, 1680–1791* (Ithaca and London: Cornell University Press, 1999)

Raymond, George, *The Life and Enterprises of Robert William Elliston, Comedian* (London: Routledge, 1857)

Reynolds, Frederick, *The Life and Times of Frederick Reynolds*, 2 vols (New York: Blom, 1969)

Robson, William, *The Old Play-goer* (Fontwell: Centaur, 1969)

Rowell, George, *The Old Vic Theatre: A History* (Cambridge: Cambridge University Press, 1993)

Rudé, George, *Hanoverian London, 1714–1808* (Berkeley and Los Angeles: University of California Press, 1971)

Russell, Gillian, *The Theatres of War: Performance, Politics, and Society, 1793–1815* (Oxford: Clarendon, 1995)

Ryan, Richard, *Dramatic Table Talk; or, Scenes, Situations and Adventures, Serious and Comic, in Theatrical History and Biography*, 2 vols (London, 1835)

Sadlak, Antoni, 'Harlequin Comes to England: The Early Evidence of the *Commedia dell'arte* in England and the Formation of the English Harlequinades and Pantomimes', unpublished doctoral dissertation (Tufts University, 1999)

Saxon, A. H., *The Life and Art of Andrew Ducrow, and the Romantic Age of the English Circus* (Hamden, Connecticut: Archon, 1978)

Schlicke, Paul, *Dickens and Popular Entertainment* (London: Allen and Unwin, 1985)

Scott, Sir Walter, *Familiar Letters of Sir Walter Scott*, ed. David Douglas (Edinburgh: Douglas, 1894)

—, 'Essay on the Drama', in *The Miscellaneous Prose Works of Sir Walter Scott, Bart.*, 3 vols (Edinburgh: Robert Cadell, 1850)

Semmel, Stuart, *Napoleon and the British* (New Haven and London: Yale University Press, 2004)

Senelick, Laurence, *The Age and Stage of George L. Fox, 1825–1877* (Hanover and New England: University Press of New England, 1988)

Sheppard, F. H. W. (gen. ed.), *The Theatre Royal, Drury Lane and The Royal Opera House, Covent Garden*, in *Survey of London*, vol. XXXV (London: Athlone, 1972)

Simond, Louis, *An American in Regency England: The Journal of a Tour in 1810–1811*, ed. Christopher Hibbert (London: Robert Maxwell, 1968)

Smith, Charles Brintiffe, *Original Letters of Dramatic Performers, Collected and Arranged by Charles Brintiffe Smith*, Library of the Garrick Club, *c.* 1850, 9 vols

Smith, E. A., *George IV* (New Haven and London: Yale University Press, 1999)

Smollett, Tobias, *The Expedition of Humphry Clinker*, ed. Lewis M. Knapp (Oxford: Oxford University Press, 1992)

Southey, Robert, *The Life of Nelson*, 2nd edn, 2 vols (London: John Murray, 1814)

Stoddard, Richard Henry (ed), *Personal Reminiscences by Chorley, Planché, and Young* (New York: Scribner, Armstrong, 1876)

Stone, Lawrence, *The Family, Sex and Marriage in England, 1500–1800* (Harmondsworth: Penguin, 1979)

Straub, Kristina, *Sexual Subjects: Eighteenth-Century Players and Sexual Ideology* (Princeton, New Jersey: Princeton University Press, 1992)

Taylor, George, *The French Revolution and the London Stage, 1789–1805* (Cambridge: Cambridge University Press, 2000)

Thackeray, William Makepeace, *The Four Georges*, in *The Works of William Makepeace Thackeray*, vol. xviii (New York: P. F. Collier, n.d.)

Thornbury, Walter, and Edward Walford, *Old and New London: A Narrative of Its History, Its People and Its Places*, 6 vols (London: Cassell, 1873)

Tomalin, Clare, *Mrs. Jordan's Profession* (London: Penguin, 1995)

Wilson, Ben, *The Making of Victorian Values: Decency and Dissent in Britain, 1789–1837* (New York: Penguin, 2007)

Winslow, Jacques-Bénigne, *The Uncertainty of the Signs of Death, and the Danger of Precipitate Interments and Dissections, Demonstrated* (Dublin, 1746)

Winston, James, *Drury Lane Journal: Selections From James Winston's Diaries, 1819–1827*, ed. Alfred L. Nelson and Gilbert G. Cross (London: Society for Theatre Research, 1974)

Woods, Leigh, 'The Curse of Performance: Inscripting the *Memoirs of Joseph Grimaldi* into the Life of Charles Dickens', *Biography*, 14:2 (Spring 1991), 138–52

Worrall, David, *Theatric Revolution: Drama, Censorship and Romantic Period Subcultures, 1773–1832* (Oxford: Oxford University Press, 2006)

—, *Harlequin Empire: Race, Ethnicity, and the Drama of the Popular Enlightenment* (London: Pickering and Chatto, 2007)

INDEX